THE WORLD'S GREAT PAINTINGS

Translated from the French by Judith Hayward in association
with First Edition Translations Ltd, Cambridge, UK

Production: Jean-Paul Paireault

Typesetting: Mary Wray

Iconography: Monique Le Pelley Fonteny

Illustrations: Agence Giraudon

CLB 3238
© 1994 CLB Publishing

All rights reserved. No part of this publication may be reproduced,
stored in a retrieval system or transmittted in any form or by any
means electronic, mechanical, photocopying or otherwise without
first obtaining written permission of the copyright owner.

This edition published in 1994 by SMITHMARK Publishers, Inc.,
16 East 32nd Street, New York, NY 10016

SMITHMARK books are available for bulk purchase for sales promotion
and premium use. For details write or call the manager of special sales,
SMITHMARK Publishers, Inc.,
16 East 32nd Street, New York, NY 10016; (212) 532-6600.

Produced by Copyright Studios, Paris for CLB Publishing,
Godalming Business Centre, Woolsack Way,
Godalming, Surrey GU7 1XW

ISBN 0-8317-5155-X

Printed in Italy
by Milanostampa S.p.A. - Farigliano (CN)
10 9 8 7 6 5 4 3 2 1

The World's Great Paintings

Jean-François Guillou

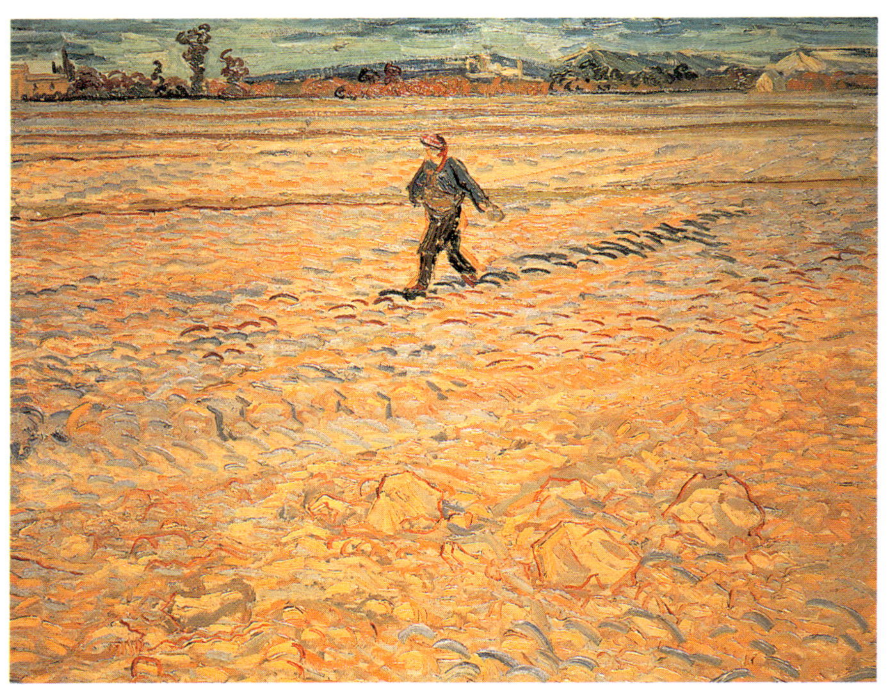

Van Gogh (Vincent) 1853-1890
The Sower
Private collection

CONTENTS

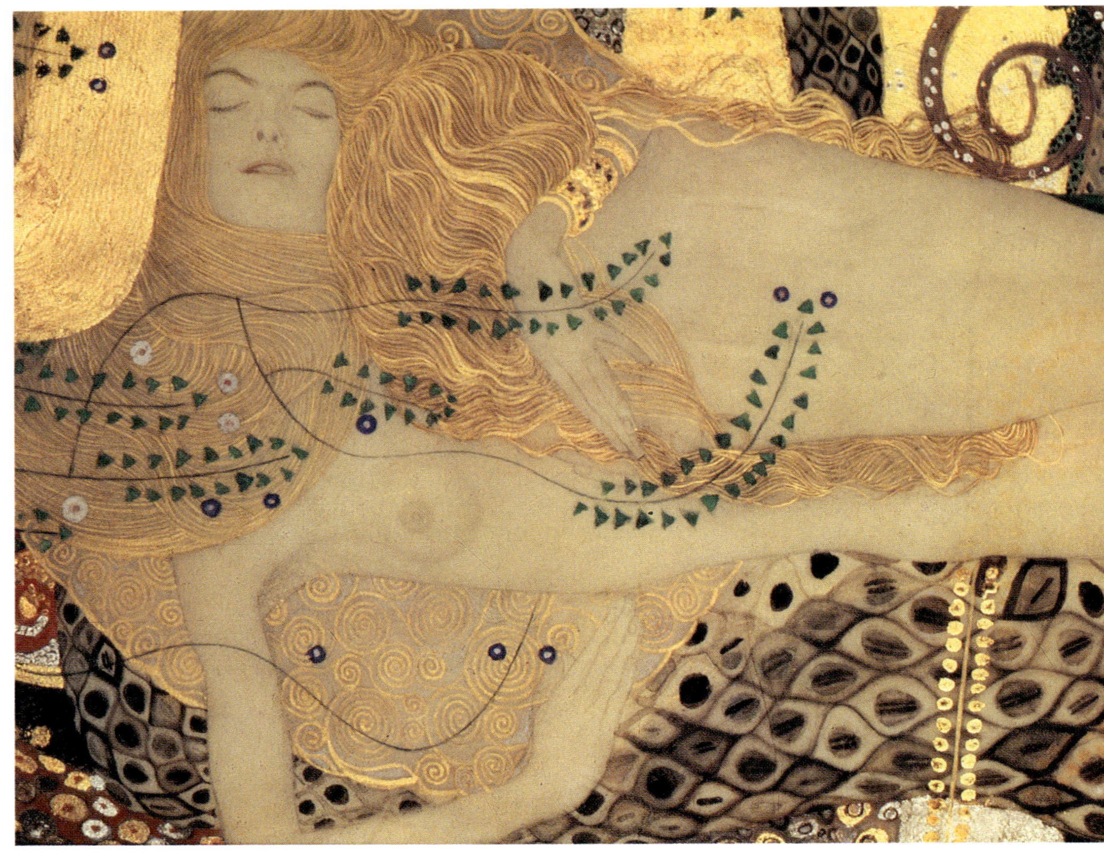

The world of the imagination in the West

From the time of Giotto in the trecento until the early decades of the 20th century Western painting was figurative. The problem we would like to address is the actual meaning of this use of the figurative. What do we represent when we paint? What is the meaning, sometimes concealed, sometimes multiple, of these images?

Art history tends to concentrate on the developments and breaks punctuating the succession of artistic movements, and likes emphasizing what distinguishes one painter or school from another. However, going beyond these divisions, the unity of Western art is derived from the permanence of the subjects treated. There is tacit agreement concerning the nature of what should be depicted, even if there is no agreement as to how it should be depicted.

The common basis constituted by subject matter throughout the history of Western painting, from pre-Renaissance times up until the explosion characterizing contemporary art, represents an extraordinary cohesive force. An historical and artistic phenomenon worthy of study in its own right, it might be resumed in these terms: total unanimity regarding the status of the image and representation, and objective agreement regarding subject matter.

This continuity enables us to read the long period that corresponds with the humanist age of our civilization as a single block, providing the key, so to speak, to the world of the imagination in the West between 1300 and 1900.

A diachronic interpretation of the history of painting leads us to concentrate on the development of form – something we have already attempted in another book. A synchronic interpretation, on the other hand, enables us to focus our attention on fundamentals. This type of approach is relevant only in the context of figurative painting, which is why this book ends with Malevich's Suprematism.

We have started from the premise that an image cannot be reduced to a simple formal code; it also conveys meaning, just as words do (the echo of *ut pictura poesis* persists far beyond Lessing's criticism, to the point when the 19th century gives way to the 20th). The question of the meaning of an image leads on to connecting the object painted with its intellectual environment, i.e. history and philosophy. We have made an arbitrary distinction between several thematic areas (religion, nature, humankind, history, the imaginary), chosen for convenience, but also because they correspond with easily identifiable points of reference. However, the problem areas often overlap from one theme to another and all circle round the central question of representation: what should one depict, why depict it, how should it be depicted?

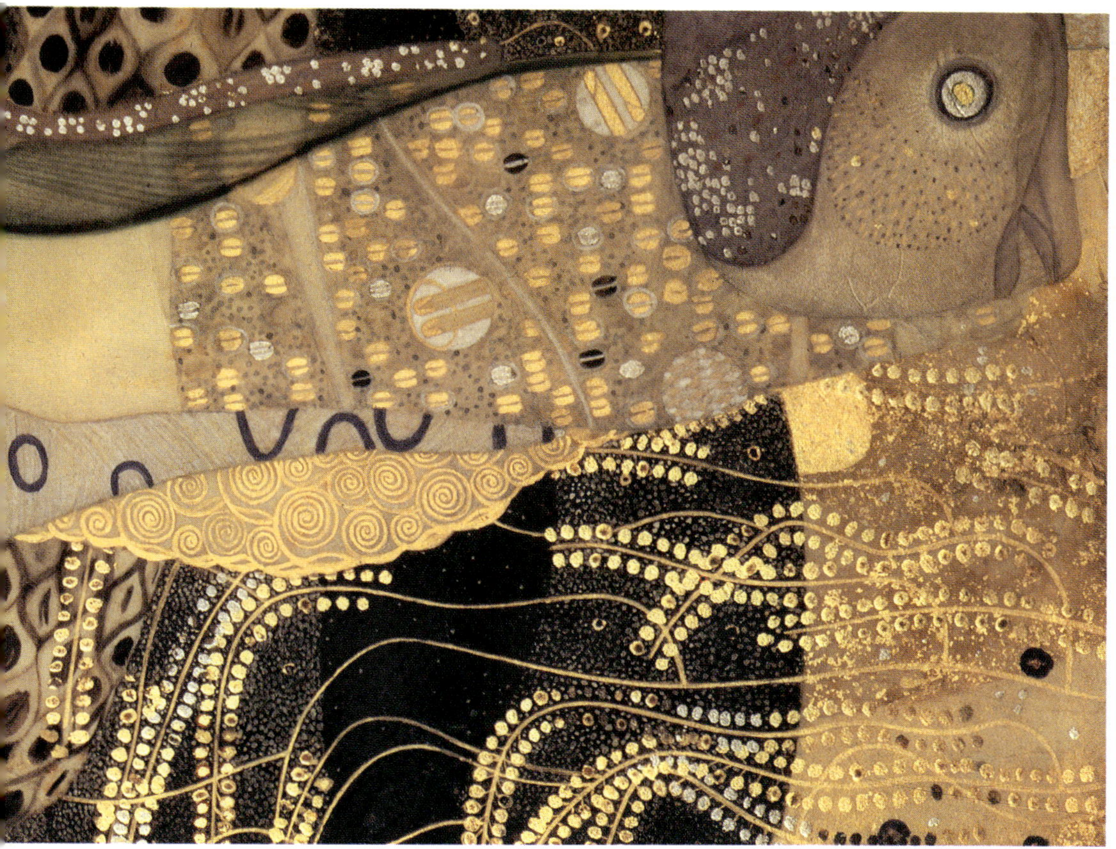

Obviously we again come up against the antinomies of the real and the ideal, reason and feeling, nature and fantasy, but they all rest on a profound belief in some power that the image has to convey a certain state of man in the world and his connection with the divine. The invention of form considered in this light is seen as an act of grace.

Finally, the idea that representation might become an impediment or obstacle did not gain currency until very recently in the long history of art, which began with cave painting. Painting has slowly dragged itself away from the religious sphere to conquer the temporal world. It has become secular (Flemish painters of course come to mind). But the price paid for achieving this autonomy has been a renunciation of the transcendent function of representation. In drawing closer to life painting has lost something of its magic: a development which culminated at the beginning of the 20th century in a profound crisis over the function of art. It is in this light that the desire for nonsense (non-sense) characterizing Dadaism and Surrealism and – more radical still – the questioning of representation associated with Suprematism should be understood. Malevich defined Suprematism as an ultimate representation, or to be more precise as a non-representation which could not be surpassed. But we may wonder whether in condemning representation his "non-objective world," coming as it did at the close of 600 years during which the representation of the world of the gods had moved towards that of the world of objects, does not in fact reveal a desperate wish to recover the sacred dimension in painting. For this is unquestionably what is at stake when we try to get to the bottom of the image. Just like a political system or a philosophical theory, an image is the reflection of a period. Without minimizing the value of the technical discourse which the plastic artist may be prompted to give on the image, we feel that it is legitimate and possible to approach it from a different perspective.

It has become commonplace to assert that we live in an image culture. Images are everywhere. But we more frequently submit to them rather than control them. Yet every image is a world, and every world generates meaning. Learning to see also involves learning to understand.

Our sole objective in this short summary is to show that looking for meaning in a work, rather than draining it and reducing it to just that meaning, in fact widens its perspective. The recognition of meaning does not affect looking adversely. Meaning accompanies looking, and carries it, as if revealing the true power of our eyes, for the richness of painting also lives in the mind.

Klimt (Gustav) 1862-1918
Water snakes I, 1904
Vienna, Österreichische Galerie

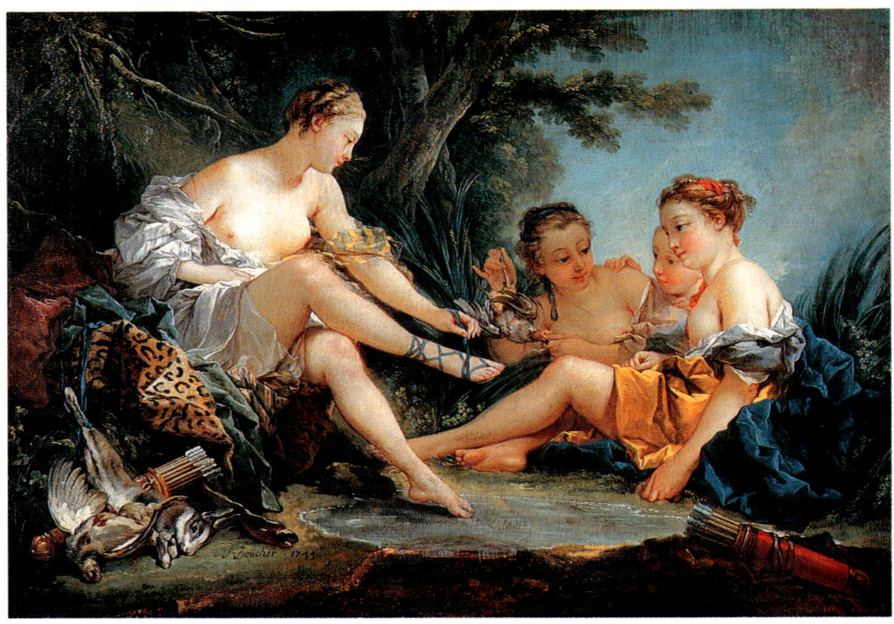

Boucher (François) 1703-1770
Diana after the hunt
Paris, Musée Cognacq-Jay

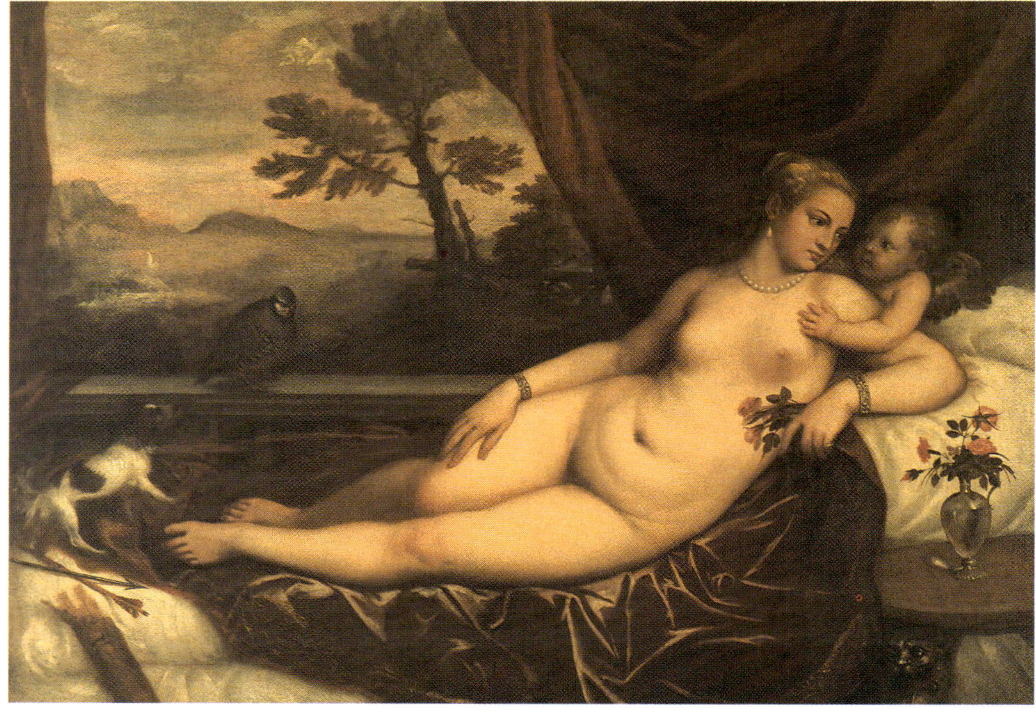

The two faces of love

Diana and Venus are the two faces of femininity, complementing one another and yet antagonistic. Diana is a figure of virtue, Venus the incarnation of desire. Diana is chaste, Venus voluptuous. Whereas Diana aims to subdue nature, Venus abandons herself to her instinctive sensuality and the selfish pleasures of the flesh.

As both a virgin and a mother Diana is the guardian of family values, protecting women during pregnancy, insuring that the family group will continue and watching over the line of descent. But her hieratic, inflexible love rejects the individual. There is no place for fantasy or whimsy in her art of love, nothing that deviates from the protective rule. Diana's love is synonymous with order and justice, i.e. first and foremost with submission to the norm and the collective will. It would be Venus who lured the prodigal son away from his native land and Diana who took him back to his father's house. There were thus these two categories, and when reinterpreted by Christianity they culminated in the quarrel between sacred and profane love.

With Diana and Venus love is seen as the founding principle of the whole human race. While it is the principle underlying all action, it is nonetheless capable of giving rise to two incompatible interpretations. Seen in a very schematic way, the first interpretation comes under the heading of social order. Diana's love integrates the individual into the group. It is a cohesive force, effecting the transition from the natural towards the cultural, for Diana's wildness only comes to the surface to punish impurity. Her fierceness operates towards establishing the ideal. In her the affirmation of femininity, which means acceptance of nature, and the refusal of masculine desire, insofar as it impedes the arrival of the ideal by drawing human beings back to their primitive urges, co-exist. Diana is a sister, or a daughter as viewed by her mother: a creature whose duty it is, by definition, to escape from desire. Diana is an Amazon, the product of a matriarchal view of woman.

Venus, on the other hand, embodies abandon to the pleasures of the senses. Her love, which is a destructuring force, represents a threat to the group, compromising its balance and smooth working. Venus asserts the absolute primacy of the rights of the individual over those of the group. She challenges laws and flouts prohibitions. Her love is blind, unconditional and carnal. While Diana seems to prefigure the Virgin, we might be tempted to see Venus as a luminous version of Eve, the sinner.

To sum up, Diana plays the role of the prudish older sister, a watered-down version of the castrating mother, while Venus is the lover, the eternal temptress, the source of pleasure and scandal. But painters were increasingly to merge these two figures, just as they have tended to set the figure of Mary beside that of Mary Magdalene: the mother and the prostitute, symbols of the fundamental ambivalence of the female figure.

Titian (Tiziano Vecellio, known as) c. 1488/1489-1576
Venus and Cupid
Florence, Uffizi Gallery

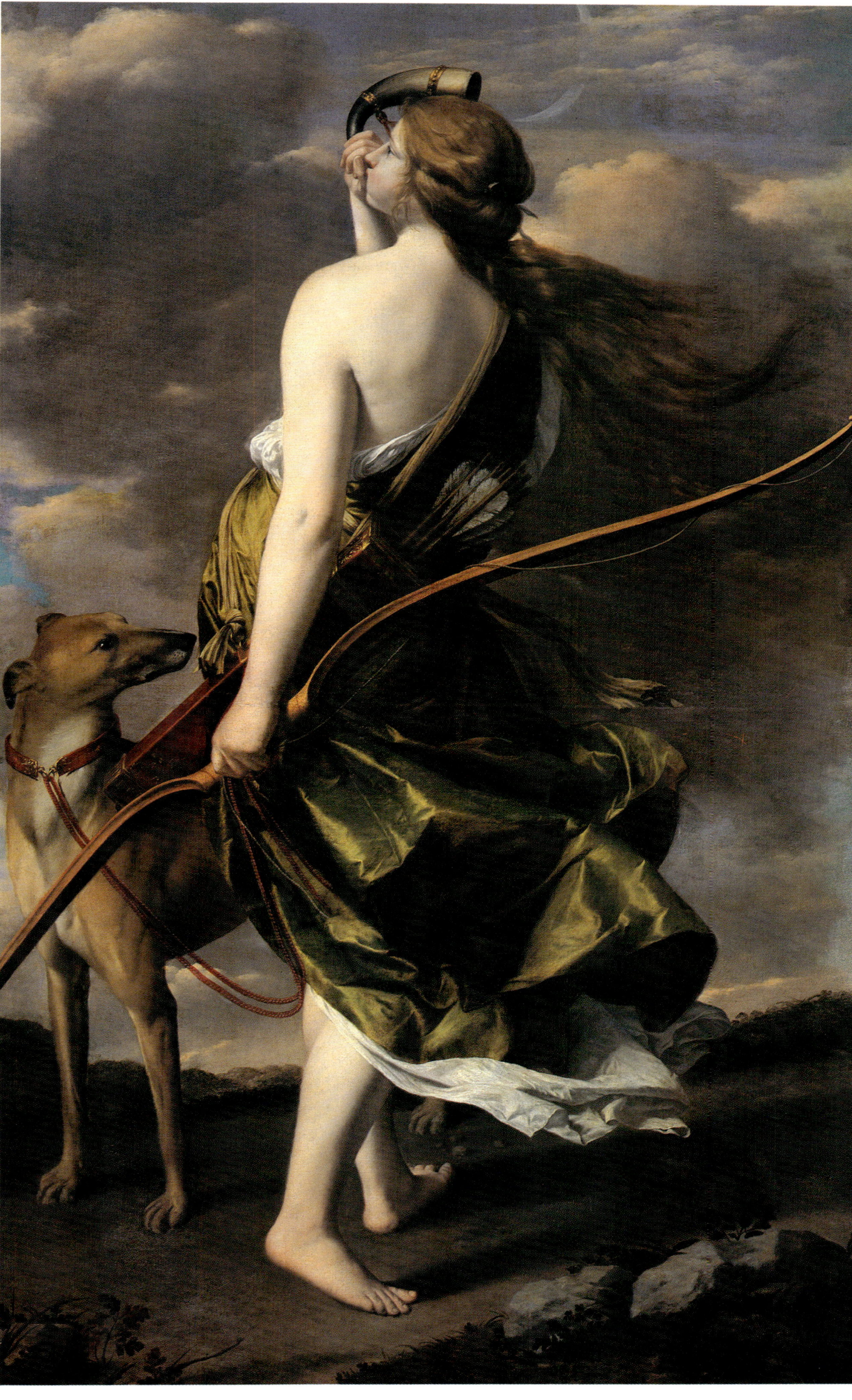

Diana or Artemis, the sister of Apollo, punished the curiosity of Acteon when he surprised her bathing by turning him into a stag who was immediately devoured by his own hounds. But she gave Hippolytus immortality after he had rejected the advances of his stepmother Phaedra and paid for his determined chastity with his life.

Gentileschi (Orazio) 1563-1639
Diana the huntress
Nantes, Musée des Beaux-Arts

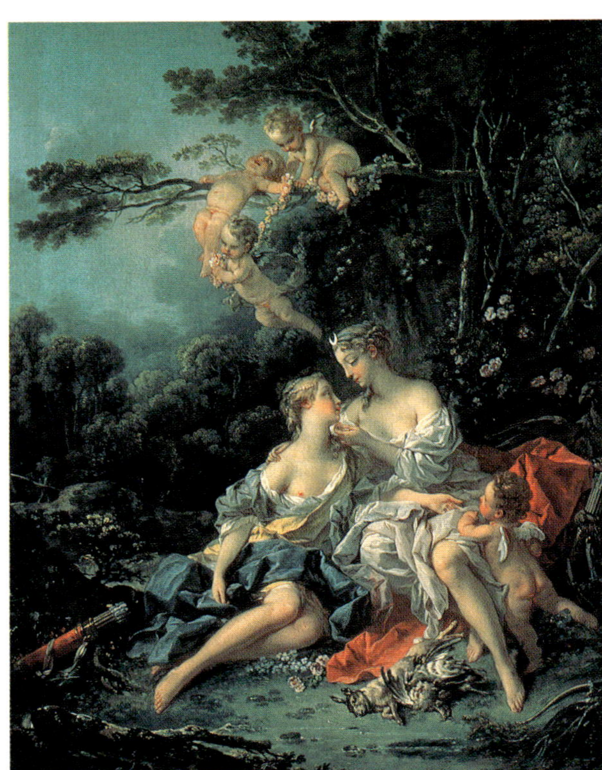

The subversion of the real

The gods are cheats. They become barefaced liars as soon as they fall in love and are willing to betray anyone or anything to satisfy their desires, as if it was only in the field of public order that reason were involved, while the private sphere remained in the grip of passion and stratagem, in other words the manipulation of appearances.

Jupiter took on the guise of a swan to woo and possess Leda, or that of a white bull with golden horns to ravish Europa. On another occasion he transformed Callisto, a nymph in Diana's retinue (and the daughter of Lycaon, king of Arcadia, whom the same Jupiter had turned into a wolf), into a she-bear to save her from the legitimate anger of Hera – first having seduced her disguised as Apollo. Then there was Daphne, who turned into a laurel tree to escape the attentions of the real Apollo. The list of deceptions practiced on Mount Olympus is endless, providing painters with an inexhaustible supply of themes and images, so rather than enumerating them it is more relevant to try and define their shared characteristics.

By its very nature the love of the gods is subversive, because it cuts across the established order and shatters the skillful hierarchy of the categories of existence. Seen in this light, reality is reduced to pure appearance subject to the law of desire. Living creatures – animal, vegetable or human – are not necessarily what they appear to be since desire has overturned natural law. So is it a swan that I see in this picture? Or Jupiter? Or, to be more precise, the representation of a swan conceived as the symbolic designation of Jupiter? The only elements of reality in the painting are neither Leda nor the swan, but the existence of a gaze trained on a form. No doubt I am like Leda, submitting to the seductive illusion of being fondled by a swan. No doubt I am "naturally" inclined to think that what I see must depict reality because in the final analysis, just like Leda, it suits me to do so. The relationship between the painter who nurtures the ambition of kindling illusion and the viewer who longs to believe in the veracity of his images is not so much a bargain between dupes as the happy coincidence of two desires.

This conjunction reveals the true essence of art, namely to produce illusions. The only certainty that can arise from contemplating a picture is that of the existence of a gaze taking cognizance of a form, a form which represents reality only in appearance since reality is not *in* the form. It *is* the presence of the gaze.

Just like Jupiter, the artist works out a trick. Everything is false in this representation of the world except for the representation itself. But the lie is fruitful since it produces reality. And even if what it represents is illusion, the image which forms in my consciousness is in fact very real, just as Helen and Pollux were in terms of mythology, born of an unusual union between beauty and a bird. To sum up, art is a true lie.

Boucher (François) 1703-1770
Jupiter and Callisto, 1744
Moscow, Pushkin Museum

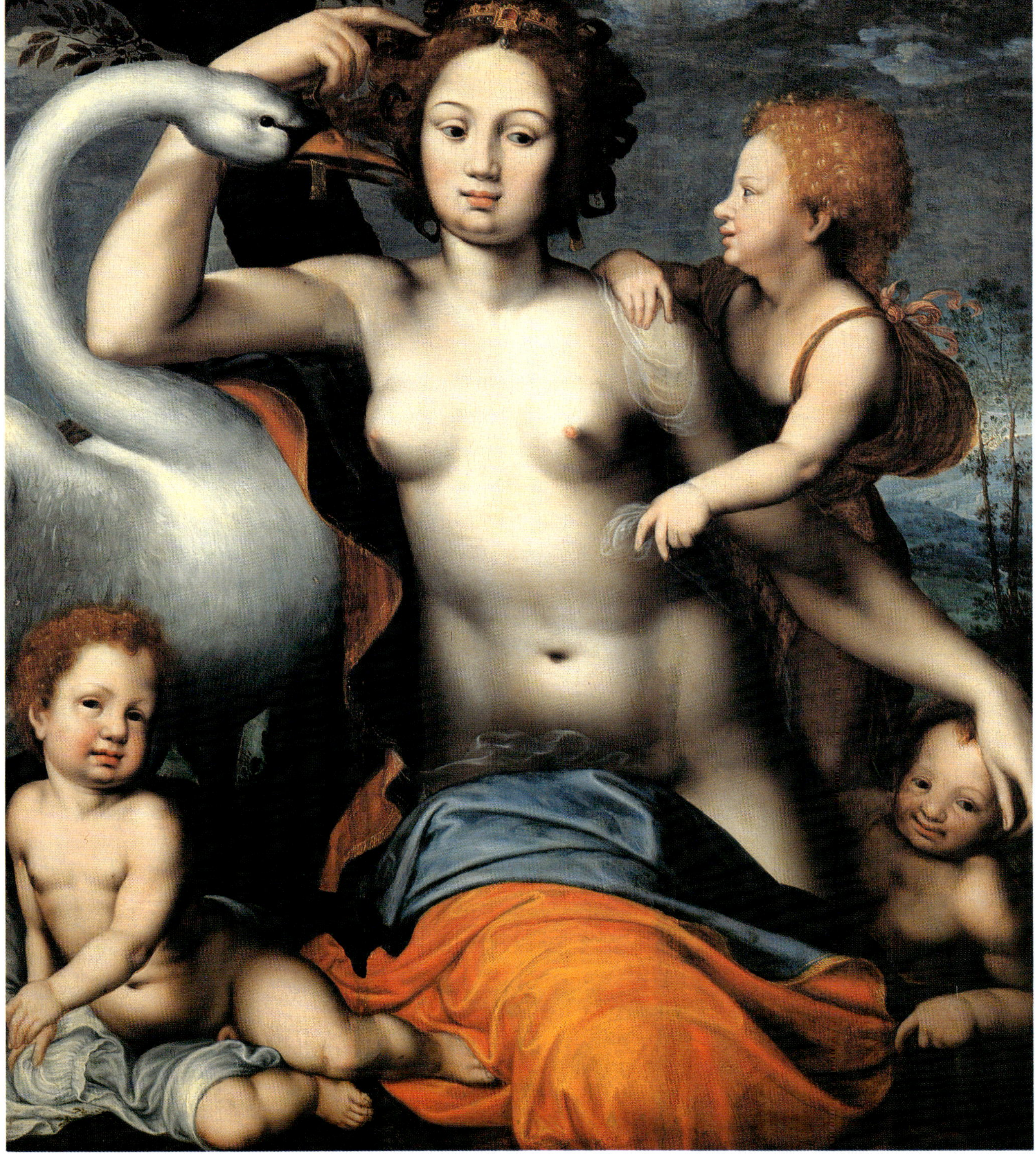

Leda married Tyndareus, the exiled king of Sparta. Tricked by Zeus, who had approached her disguised as a swan, she gave birth to four children: Helen and Pollux, fathered by Zeus, and Clytemnestra and Castor, fathered by Tyndareus. After his brother had been killed in battle Pollux persuaded his father Zeus to allow him to share his immortality with Castor.

Sellaer (Vincent) c. 1500-1589
Leda and the swan
Valenciennes, Musée des Beaux-Arts

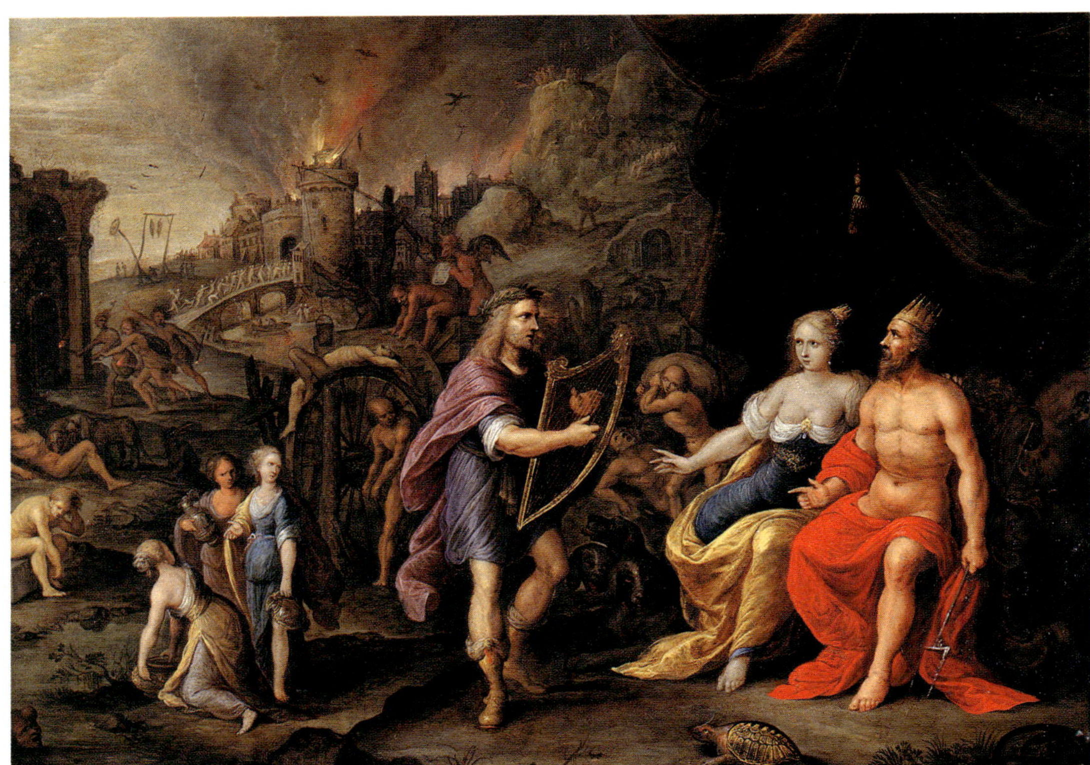

The curtain of appearances

What does in fact exist behind the world of forms? What are the final truths concealed beneath the veil of appearances? The answer given by mythology is that there is nothing, at least nothing of worth to man. Icarus burnt his wings trying to find out. Prometheus endured torture on Mount Caucasus because he had given the gods' fire to mankind. And Orpheus underwent the cruel experience of losing Eurydice for a second time because he could not resist the temptation of looking round when he was on the path leading them towards the light.

The manipulation of reality is the prerogative of the gods, and man, enchained in Plato's cave, is not yet ready to gaze on a truth that would blind him. Therefore he sees shadows, or forms, which he mistakenly takes for the things themselves.

As for the artist, he is like the hero in mythology, sometimes a demigod, the prisoner of two orders which contradict or fight one another: half man, half god, he is hybrid by nature. Does he show, or does he demonstrate? Does he enable us to see, or does he lift the veil? Is he a magus and a prophet, as Victor Hugo asserted? Or a spectator among other spectators, cleverer perhaps and more lucid, but imprisoned like the rest of us by the rule of appearances? Is he a peeping Tom or a visionary?

Such a debate will never reach a conclusion. What is more important to grasp and remember is the fundamental tearing process by means of which the artist defines himself. Creation is a process of tearing. We have to tear free from ourselves in order to become. We have to renounce in order to move forward. All creation is uncertainty since it wells up from what has never been, or to put it another way it is a radical novelty to which nothing is allied in a way that would make comparisons possible. Genius cannot be measured, but for the same reasons it is capable of error. God himself, after creating the world and human beings, regretted what he had done and found himself forced to drown his work beneath a flood.

Art is both uncertain and ambiguous: uncertain because it is a leap into the unknown, and ambiguous because it cannot entirely free itself of appearances – without their support it would lose all its intelligibility. The artist needs a viewer to exist just as God required the eyes of Adam to admire his handiwork. And Adam was accorded the privilege of naming everything in creation: "The man gave names to all cattle, and to the birds of the air, and to every beast of the field," we are told in Genesis. And yet can we see without knowing? Can we experience the beauty of a thing without making reference to some other thing? Can we appreciate without making comparisons? Is esthetic enjoyment possible without prior knowledge? We are inclined to reply that it is not.

Once we have made that admission we have to recognize that God placed Adam in an impossible position. Error was inevitable, and this means that man should not be held totally and solely responsible for it.

Francken (Ambrosius the Elder) 1544-1618
Orpheus in the underworld
Nîmes, Musée des Beaux-Arts

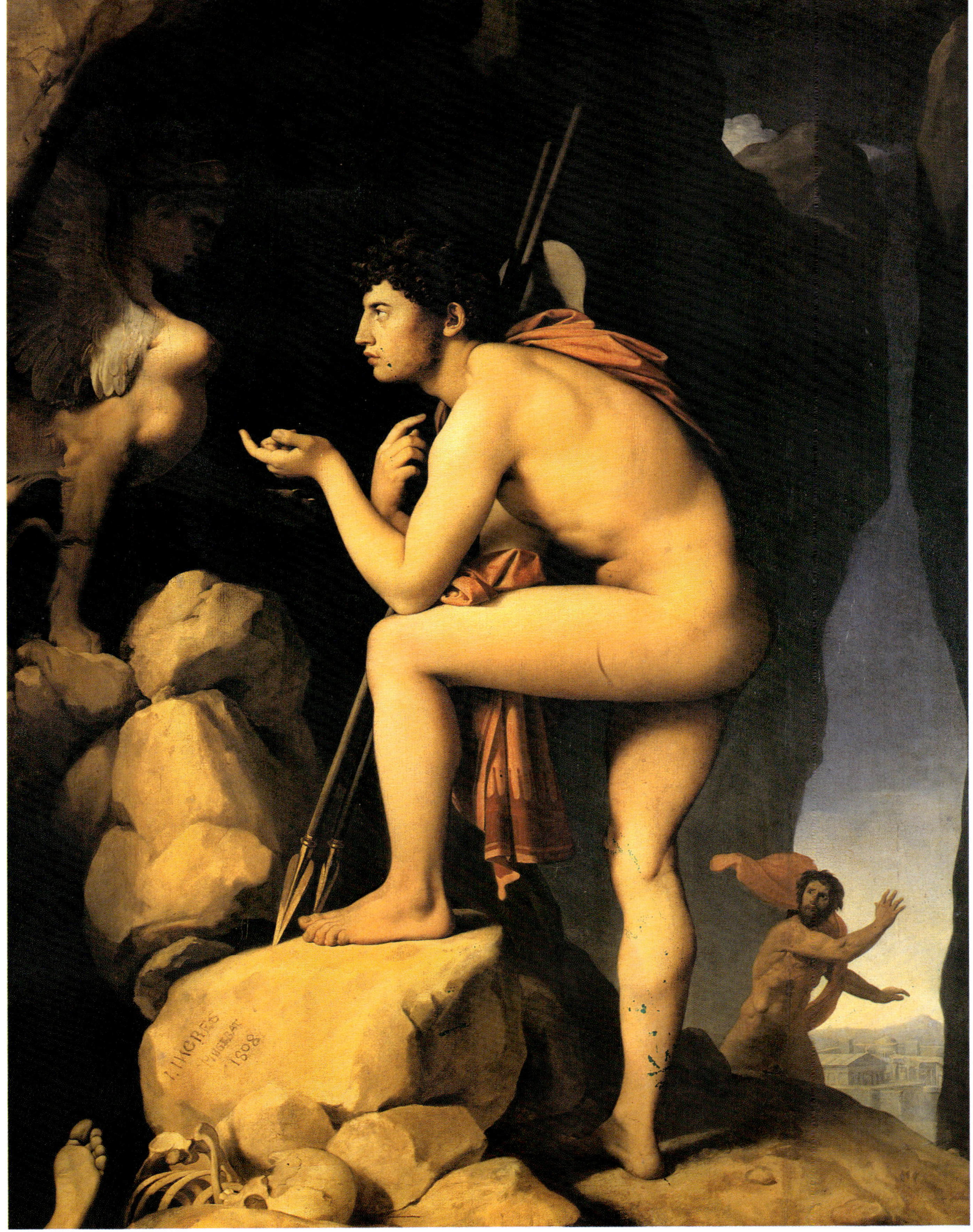

After killing his father Laius as the Delphic Oracle had predicted, Oedipus had to face the Sphinx which was barring the way into Thebes. After getting the better of it by answering the riddle it set, Oedipus was appointed king of Thebes and became Jocasta's husband, unaware that she was his own mother.
In this myth we find the close bond associating love with the problem of knowledge.

Ingres (Jean-Auguste Dominique) 1780-1867
Oedipus and the Sphinx, 1808
Paris, Louvre

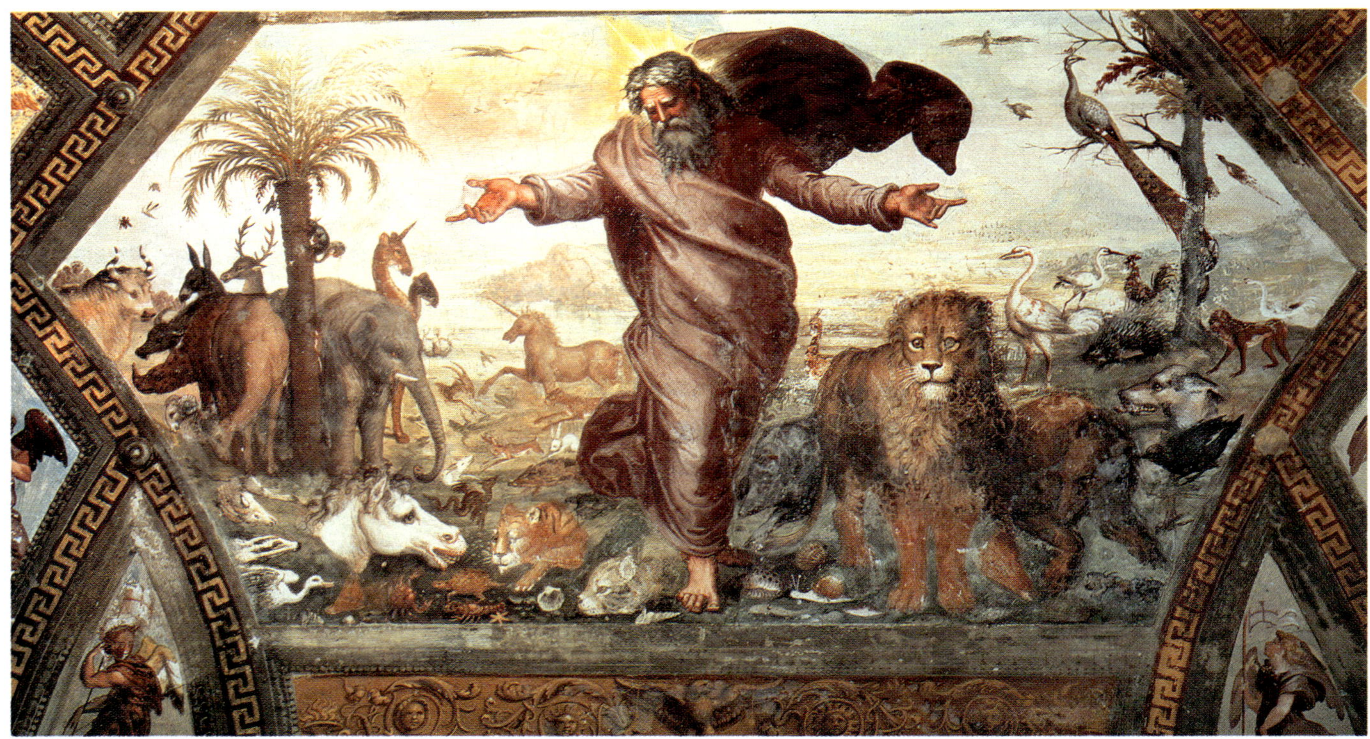

Earthly paradise

If we accept the Sumerian etymology Eden was a desert. God planted a garden there, the garden of Eden, i.e. the garden of the desert, which by way of a Greek translation then a French transcription became Paradise (park planted with trees and populated with animals). But since *eden* also means "delight" in Hebrew, purely as a result of phonetic proximity the oasis has become a place of pleasure – an extremely inappropriate name for such a monotonous abode. For Adam was terribly bored in Paradise. God took pity on him and created a female companion for him while he was asleep whom Adam on awakening recognized as "flesh of his flesh." The couple were given just one task: to till and keep the garden. They had complete freedom except for one prohibition encapsulating divine law in its entirety: they were not to eat any of the fruit of the tree of the knowledge of good and evil in the middle of the garden.

Thus from the very beginning knowledge was linked with evil and death. All learning is presented as essentially murky. God told Adam and Eve, " ... of the tree of the knowledge of good and evil you shall not eat, for in the day that you eat of it you shall die." But the serpent and tempter answered Eve by telling her: "You will not die. For God knows that when you eat of it your eyes will be opened, and you will be like God, knowing good and evil." Their eyes were indeed opened and their first realization was that they were naked, or perhaps that it was not good to be naked. What is new is not the nakedness, but the shame arising from it. Thus knowledge appeared in the form of a deep uneasiness, a feeling of inadequacy, as if mankind, through a kind of reflective gaze directed at his own finite nature, had suddenly become aware of the void. Thus, as Descartes so clearly saw, the path of knowledge started with the experience of doubt.

Because it is impossible to exercise free will without being able to judge the world, and because we cannot judge something without first comprehending the concepts of good and evil and so transgressing the prohibition laid down by God, the fact that I am human inevitably defines me as a sinner. To try out my freedom I have to break divine law. To move forward in my incarnation as the image of God, I have to start by denying the very god who made me free, thus denying the being that I wish to become.

One last thing: understanding starts by seeing. The awakening of awareness is first of all related to the eyes. The Decalogue forbids images of God because representing a thing means recreating it, nurturing the human ambition to equal God. The image is a reflection of the soul, and capturing an image means stealing part of the soul. God alone is entitled to capture souls, and he alone has the power to create creatures in his image: that is his main attribute. To see is to judge. But as only a vision inspired by God can lead to true knowledge, there will be good and bad images.

Raphael (Raffaello Santi or Sanzio, known as) 1483-1520
Creation of the animals, c. 1515-1520
Rome, Vatican, Loggie

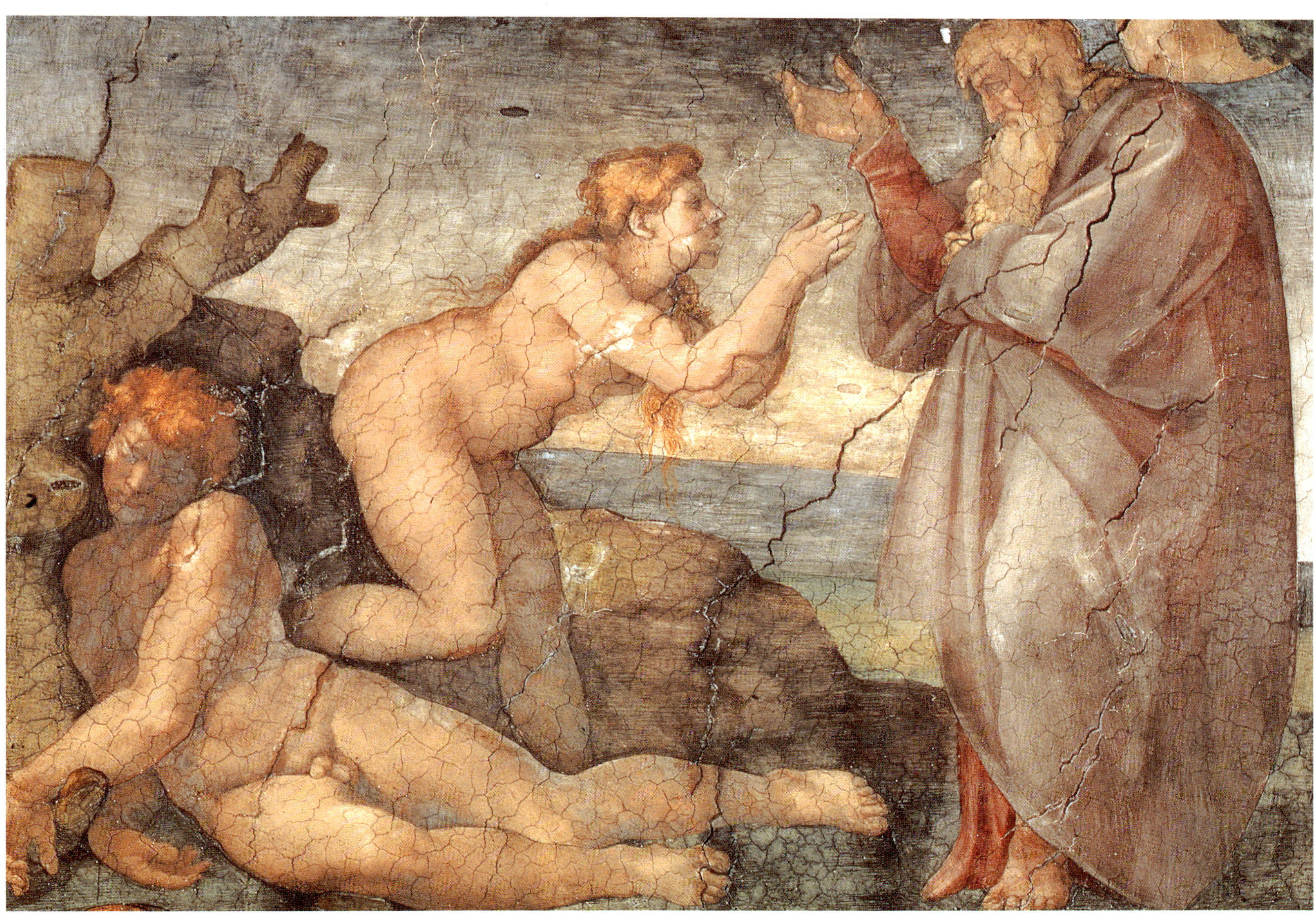

The name Eve, which is derived from the Hebrew Hawwa (she who gives life) is not mentioned in Genesis, where she is only the female counterpart of man, the other face or other side of humankind. This is undoubtedly the source of the persistent tradition according to which she sprang forth from one of Adam's ribs (Adam in Hebrew means the dust of the earth).

Michelangelo (Michelangelo Buonarroti, known as) 1475-1564
Genesis. Creation of Eve, 1508-1512
Rome, Vatican, Sistine Chapel

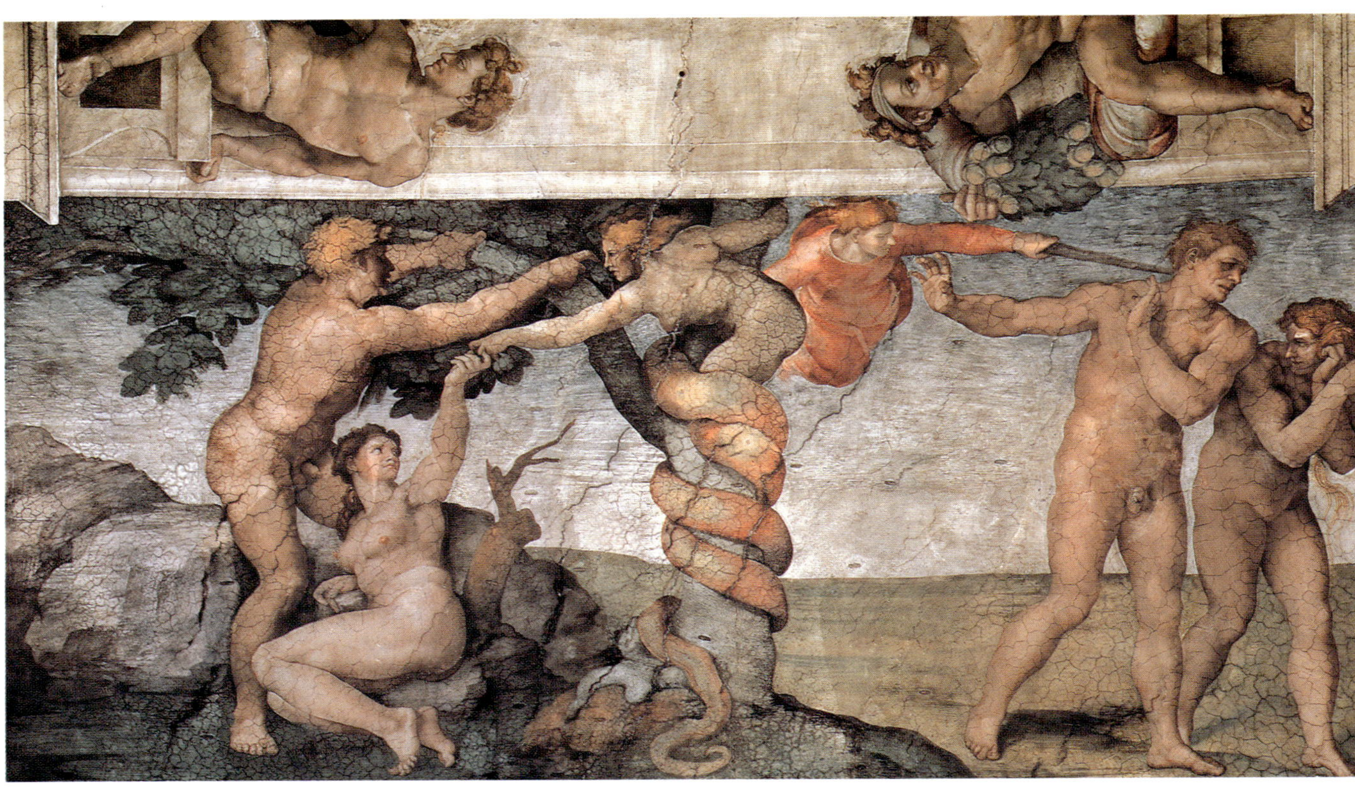

The mark of sin

Everything starts with this: history is the outcome of wrongdoing. And time, like a sign of our fall, is the mark of sin. Our finiteness has been uncovered. Between a past that is wasting away and a future that cannot be grasped the very substance of our being is escaping. I cannot know who I am because I am constantly in the process of becoming: this is both my freedom and my misfortune. I am free because I am imperfect, because my future has not been charted in advance. Wrongdoing has brought about my freedom, a freedom from which I expect happiness but which I am today experiencing in suffering. Becoming means serving an apprenticeship of sacrifice in the name of future generations – or in more egotistical terms in the name of that image of myself which I project into the future.

Sin was the first free act, the first act that took place outside the divine plan. It marks the beginning of time, or the end of eternity, the end of the eternal present. I have to sacrifice the present, so constructing a morality of renunciation – not renunciation of the present which overflows with the substance of paradisiacal eternity, but rather of that sort of developing vacuum constituted by the unceasing movement of my consciousness.

What is painting if it does not in fact entail capturing the instant and recreating a space according to the norms of the world of the imagination? Painting has in it something of the divine in that what the painter fixes on his canvas is a suspended instant, i.e. in the true meaning of the words an image of eternity. He acts as if his work could be seen as an instrument of redemption.

This is precisely what God does when he intervenes in history. The manifestation of the divine is characterized by a suspension of the passage of time. When Joshua requested help from the Lord to enable him to triumph over the peoples occupying the land of Canaan, Jehovah indicated his support in a very symbolic way by stopping the progress of the sun, just as He had plunged Abraham into a deep sleep before revealing the future of his descendants to him. The first step in turning back to God is amnesia.

Conversely the first sign signalling wrongdoing is awareness of the world. Because I am damned, I am free. Hell is the opposite of being deprived of freedom. It is absolute freedom which exhausts me: I cannot cope with it. Hell is the requirement that I be free, it is the obligation it places on me to make sense of the world in order to atone for my wrongdoing.

Everything proceeds as if humankind in turn was to try its hand at creation. But whereas God creates supremely, the majority of mortals can do no more than reproduce, replicate and duplicate. Considered in this light, we are better able to assess what art is about. For other than science art is the only true affirmation by humankind of a wish to break out of its creative impotence and disrupt the inevitability of suffering.

Michelangelo (Michelangelo Buonarroti, known as) 1475-1564
Genesis. Original sin and
Expulsion from Paradise, 1508-1512
Rome, Vatican, Sistine Chapel

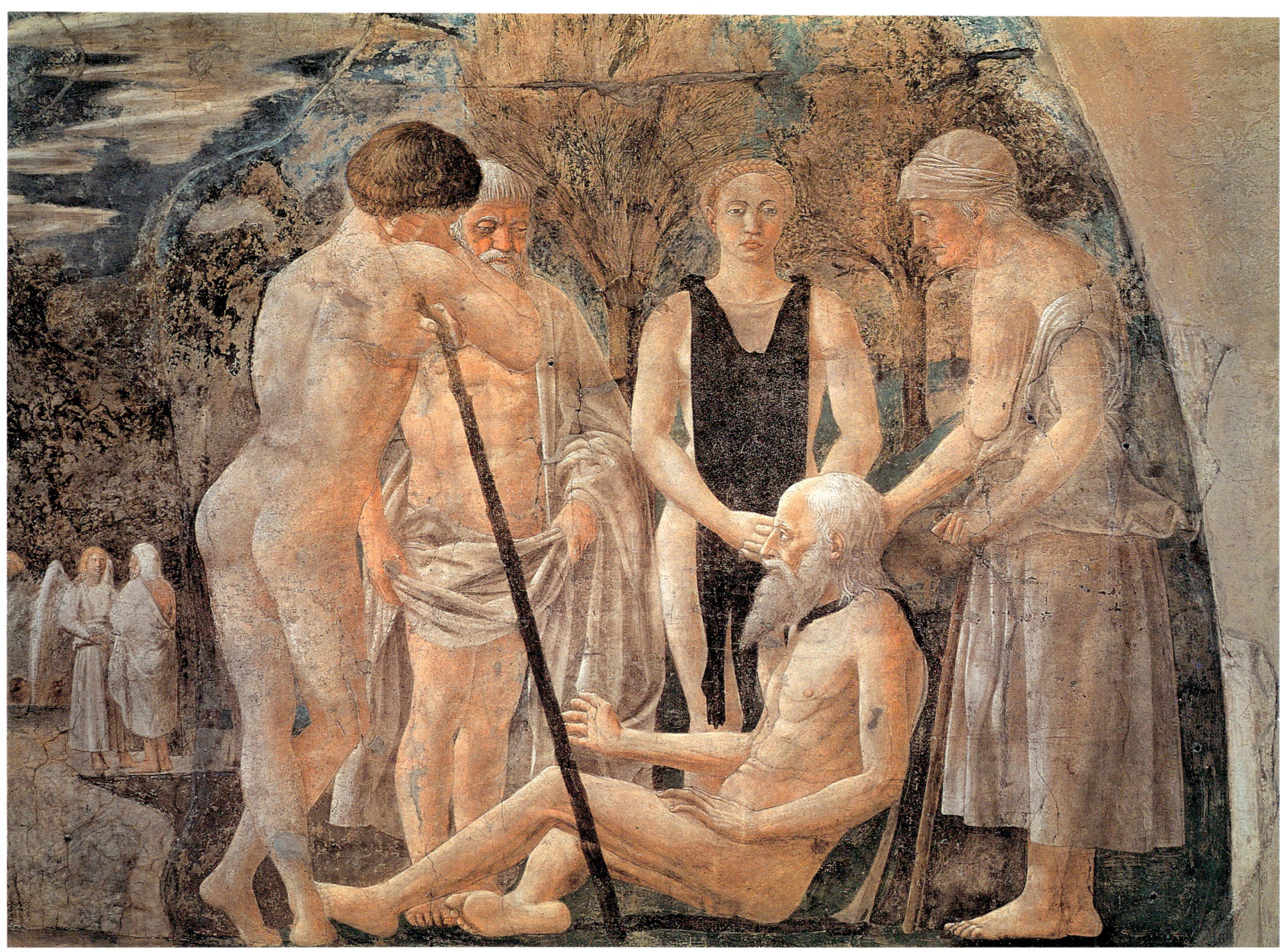

The Bible, adopting ancient Mesopotamian myths, makes a clear distinction between the tree of life which should be understood in a spiritual sense and the tree of knowledge in which evil finds its origin. Thus wisdom is opposed to knowledge: the true sage is an ignorant man, "poor in spirit," so science or learning could not possibly be the path leading to God.

Piero della Francesca (Piero di Benedetto or Piero dal Borgo known as) c. 1416-1492
Legend of the True Cross. Death of Adam, 1452-1459
Arezzo, Church of San Francesco

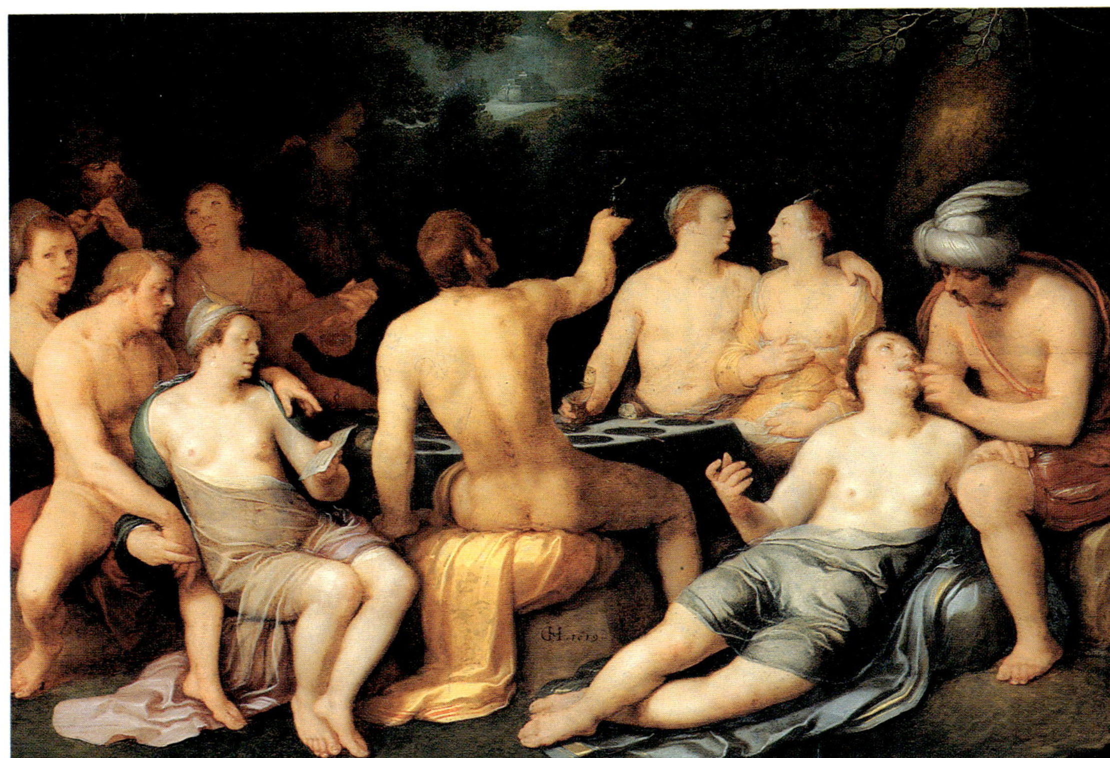

Divine anger

The Flood is a mutilation. Painting the Flood means painting the image of disaster, and at the same time painting disaster befalling the image. After shutting human beings out of the earthly paradise, for the second time in the history of burgeoning humankind Jehovah had to resolve to cut himself off from his own image.

Painting the Flood implies representing a temporary suspension of representation: a challenge which artists very often wriggle out of by performing a pirouette, like the lost airman in Saint-Exupéry's *Le Petit Prince* drawing the sheep in a box, with just an opening for air. The Flood could be summed up as a walnut shell with a few ventilation holes.

The image was diluted in the water cascading from the sky, with mud returning to mud. The clay collapsed, but the mold had not been lost. Jehovah destroyed the image, but retained the right to produce others. For the bone of contention was not representation as such, but the fact that the image was now setting itself up as the object of representation. The scandal, from God's point of view, was the realisation that the image itself had become a producer of images. The Book of Genesis tells us that "the sons of God saw that the daughters of men were fair; and they took to wife such of them as they chose." The created being seemed to have achieved autonomy and with autonomy the power to reproduce itself ad infinitum.

It was as if the proliferation of living beings – because the image was only the image of the image (the daughters of men) and no longer the image of the Creator (the sons of God) – was to be interpreted as a waste of substance, at the same time setting the earthly universe of deceptive appearances against the higher, transcendent reality of the divine.

Carried on ad infinitum, the duplication of the Divine Being would ineluctably blur the content of the message. The divine plan was going off the track and threatening to get lost. Ever since man had opened his eyes to the world, since the original sin, the image had in fact become increasingly diabolic. From being the image of the Divine Being, it had become a deceptive mirage by the time it was wiped out by divine decree in the catastrophe of the Flood.

In this connection three things are worth noting. Firstly, the concept of the image would be fully expressed in the iconoclastic movements associated with monotheism – the Catholic faith is in fact just an exception to the rule. Secondly, the idea that the image is the mirror of the soul can be found in almost every practice of religion, from the animist religions of Africa by way of voodoo to the Christian mystery of the Eucharist, which asserts the actual presence of the body and blood of Christ in the Communion bread and wine. Thirdly, the idea of the Flood is in fact borrowed by the writers of the Bible from a text that is 3,500 years old recounting the epic of Gilgamesh, a Mesopotamian hero who set off in search of immortality only to learn that the brevity of existence was the penalty imposed on men by the gods, who could no longer endure their dreadful disorder.

Cornelisz van Haarlem (Cornelis, known as) 1562-1638
Corruption of the world before the Flood, 1619
Douai, Musée de la Chartreuse

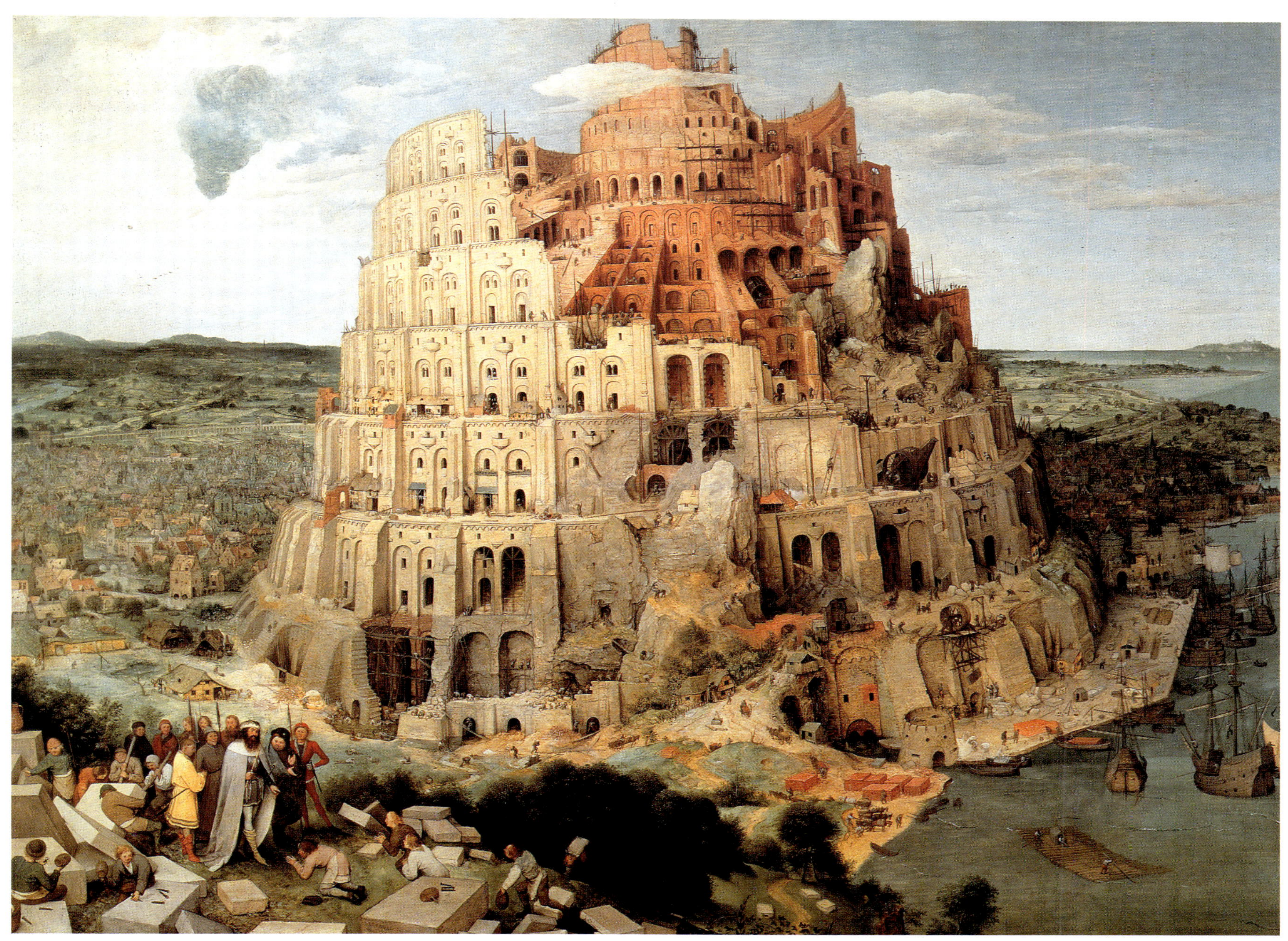

"On that day all the fountains of the great deep burst forth, and the windows of the heavens were opened. And rain fell upon the earth forty days and forty nights."

(Genesis 7:11-12).

Brueghel (Pieter the Elder) c. 1528/1530-1569
Tower of Babel, c. 1562-1567
Vienna, Kunsthistorisches Museum

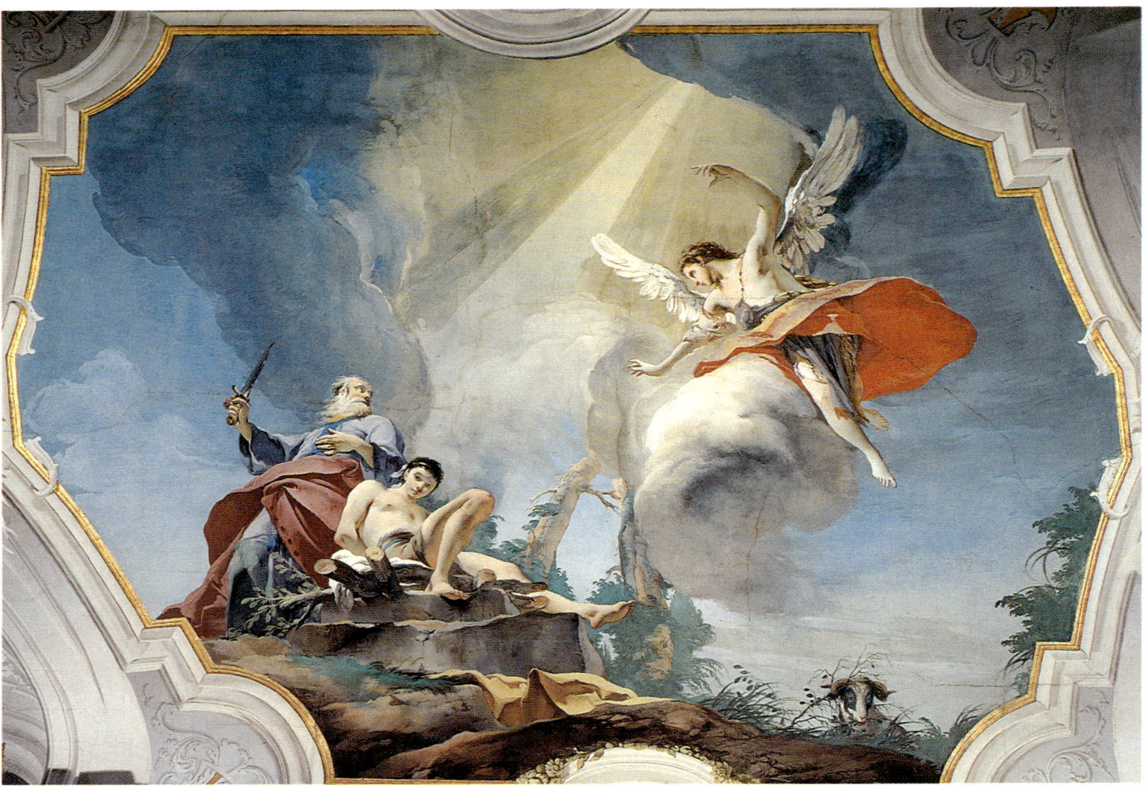

The birth of Israel

Jehovah tested Abraham's faith by asking him to sacrifice his only son Isaac. He then tested Jacob (he who is protected by God), the son of Isaac, by fighting all night with him in the form of an angel. That is how Jacob became Israel (he who fights with God): "Your name shall no more be called Jacob, but Israel, for you have striven with God and with men, and have prevailed" (Genesis 32:39). And the twelve sons of Jacob founded twelve tribes which were collectively known thereafter as the tribes of Israel. The two episodes share the idea of a test. Jehovah uses the first to insure Abraham's total submission. By means of the second, on the other hand, He appears to salute Jacob's rebellious strength: Israel, "strong *against* God." The second episode is certainly the more disturbing of the two. Since Jacob had been strong against God, he would be even stronger against men. The race of Israel then became God's representative on earth, the only group authorized to speak in his name. Israel became the chosen race. The agreement was sealed in the eyes of all by Jacob's limp, the visible outcome of his fight.

Here we have the sign placed on the image, like a signature proving the authenticity of a painting. Jacob is recognized as the true image of God because he recognized God when he saw him face to face: "for I have seen God face to face, and yet my life is preserved" (Genesis 32:30), Jacob says before he leaves the scene of the fight. Through the blow he inflicted on Jacob's thigh, God showed that He recognized his true image in him. And He recognizes it because He knows that Jacob has recognized him as his Creator.

The bond had already been written in the flesh of the chosen race through the introduction of circumcision in Abraham's time; circumcision that was deliberate and defined as the imprint of the finger of God on the flesh of man: "You shall be circumcised in the flesh of your foreskins, and it shall be a sign of the covenant between me and you" (Genesis 17:11).

With Jacob God completed his work by signing it and giving it a name, as if everything had inevitably to begin and end with the Word. From then on things became clearer on earth, with a true image, authenticated by Jehovah himself on the one hand, and an inferior brand of humanity on the other, what might be described as daughters of men of doubtful origins. Inflation had lived and the image had been restored to its original dignity. The image in return had to recognize Him in whom it had its origin as authentic. When Jacob was forced to leave the Shechem area after his children had slaughtered all the male inhabitants of the city, he gathered together everyone in his household and told them: "Put away the foreign gods that are among you, and purify yourselves, and change your garments" (Genesis 35:2). Thus the choosing of Israel was as much a contract as a supreme decision made by the Creator.

Tiepolo (Giovanni Battista) 1696-1770
Sacrifice of Isaac
Udine, Palazzo Arcivescovile

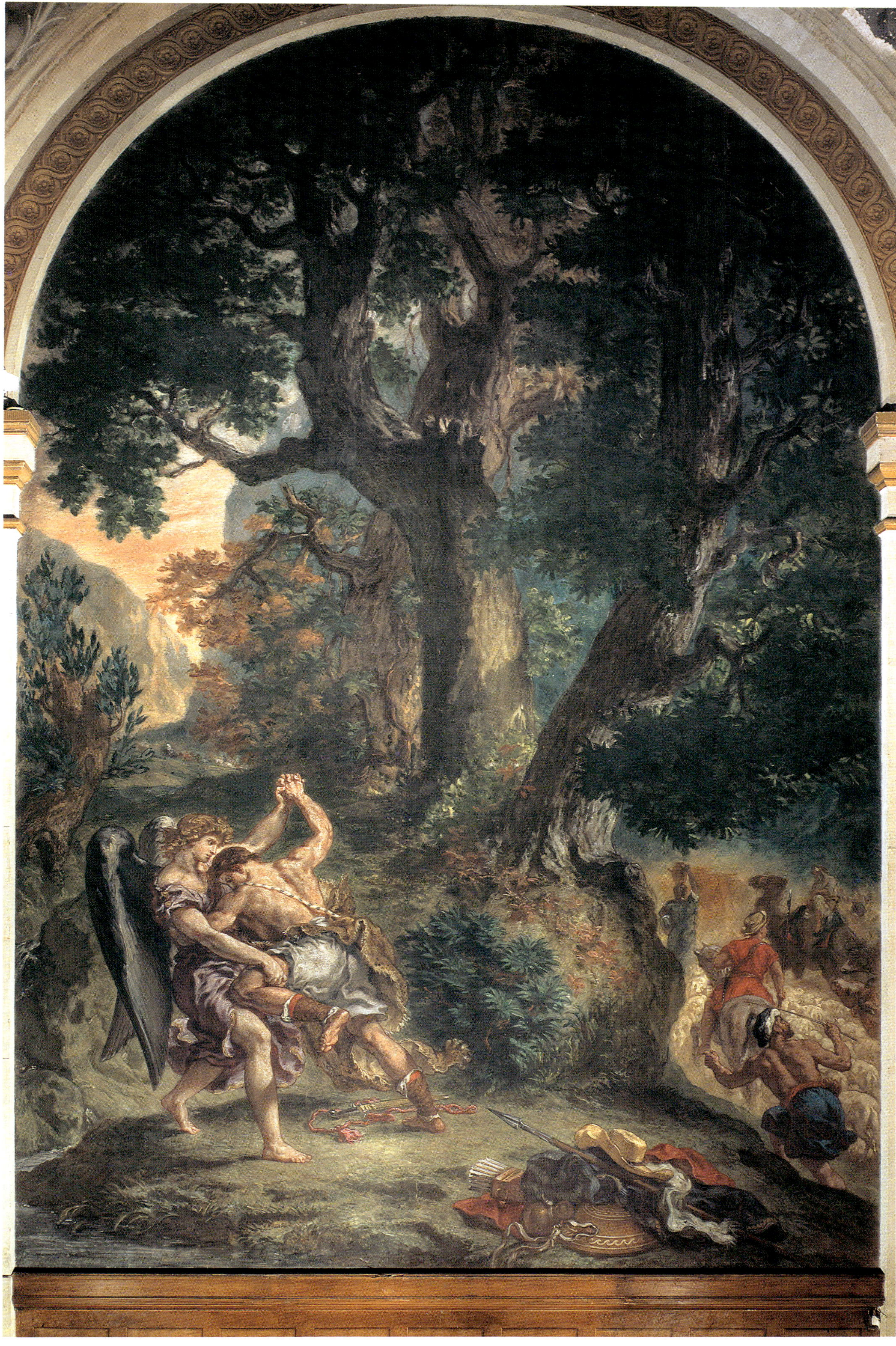

Jacob, the son of Isaac, grandson of Abraham, and (younger) twin brother of Esau, was his mother Rebekah's favorite. After obtaining his father's blessing making him heir to God's Promises by a trick, he had to flee to escape his brother's wrath. After spending twenty years in Laban's house Jacob was preparing to meet his brother again and ask his forgiveness when he met the One who would not say his name on the bank of a stream.

Delacroix (Eugène) 1798-1863
Jacob wrestling with the angel, 1853-1863
Paris, Saint-Sulpice church

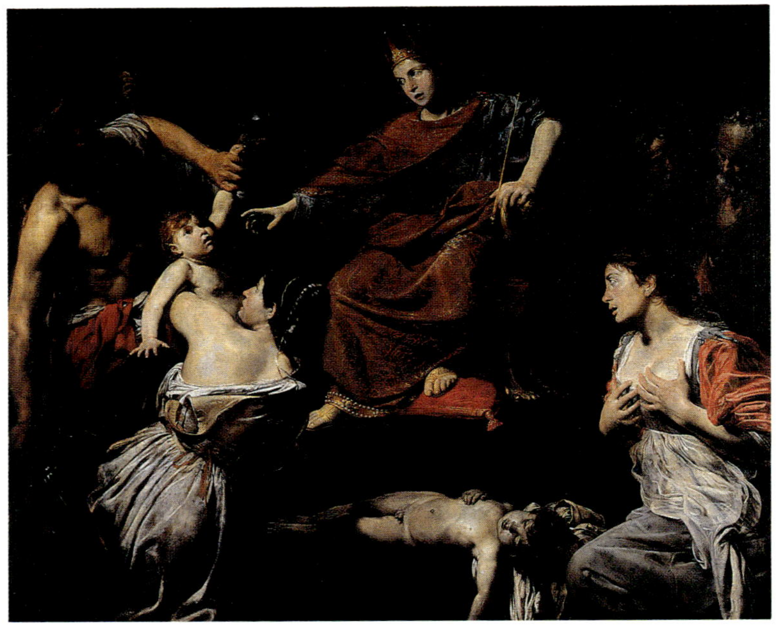

The kingdom of Israel

The kingdom of Israel was short-lived. Political unity lasted for less than a century, from about 1024 BC when Saul brought together the twelve tribes to form a single state until 926 BC, the year of the death of Solomon, David's son and successor.

If it is considered from the symbolic point of view, this part of the Bible story is an account of the recurring, obsessive theme of the complementary yet contradictory desire to equal and supplant one's father. David, the friend of Saul's son, was rejected by Saul who saw him as a rival even before David was finally anointed king by Samuel after Saul's death. Then there was Absalom, David's son, who rebelled against his father; after driving David to flight and taking possession of his concubines Absalom was put to death – admittedly against David's wishes.

Even the great Solomon, foremost among the just, could not withstand the influence of his many concubines, who urged him to adopt the cult of Astarte, a Canaanite fertility goddess. In spite of all this, faced with such denials, the jealous and terrible God of the Old Testament seemed strangely patient and inclined to forgive.

In our images which are influenced by Renaissance paintings, David personifies youth and Solomon wisdom. But both these images are false, as the Bible reveals. David, who committed adultery with Bathsheba, was culpably indulgent towards his sons and they repaid him very badly by rebelling against him several times. As for Solomon, a great lover of women, he turned to the worship of Moloch to please some of them, a cult that included the sacrifice of children among its practices.

In both cases the image does not tie in with the facts, but the only truth worthy of being passed down to posterity is the truth of representation, not that of reality. As long as all the representations in existence were equally valid because no hierarchy had been established among them, there was no problem. But immediately the Creator made some distinction between the amorphous crowd, He brought into being the rule of a single truth. The one and only God knows nothing of plurality. It is quite unimportant for the representation of the world to be in accordance with reality. The value of a truth does not reside in the fact that these two terms are identical, but in the exclusive right granted to one people to speak the truth: since there is only one truth, it must inevitably be true.

So here we have the creature rebelling against his Creator; almost as soon as he has been recognized by the Creator, the being created is already hastening to deny him, while the Father, at a loss, is reluctant to punish, holding his hand as if to avoid disowning his creation. It is as if the artist had become became the slave of his work after he had signed it. The Almighty is a prisoner of this externalized vision of himself, constrained by his own given word and almost astonished to hear himself murmuring, "So that is my own image." The image projected by a human race which has some difficulty in convincing itself that it has just invented monotheism is one of unsophisticated violence and childish greed.

Valentin de Boulogne (Valentin, Jean known as) 1591-1632
The Judgment of Solomon
Paris, Louvre

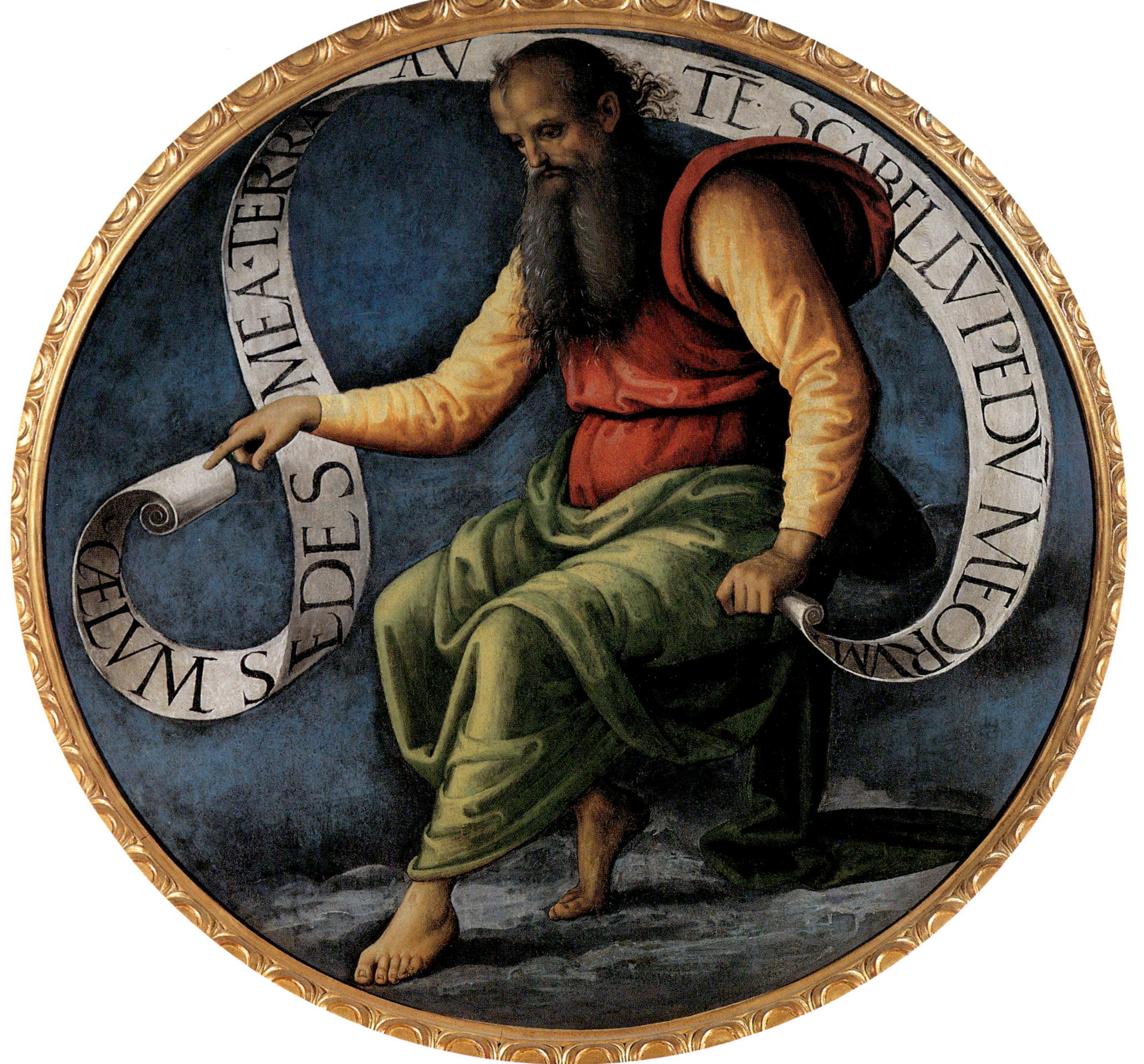

"Therefore the Lord said to Solomon, 'Since this has been your mind and you have not kept my covenant and my statutes which I have commanded you, I will surely tear the kingdom from you and will give it.... Yet for the sake of David your father I will not do it in your days, but I will tear it out of the hand of your son.'"

(1 Kings 11:11-12).

Perugino (Pietro Vannucci, known as) 1445-1523
King David (tondo)
Nantes, Musée des Beaux-Arts

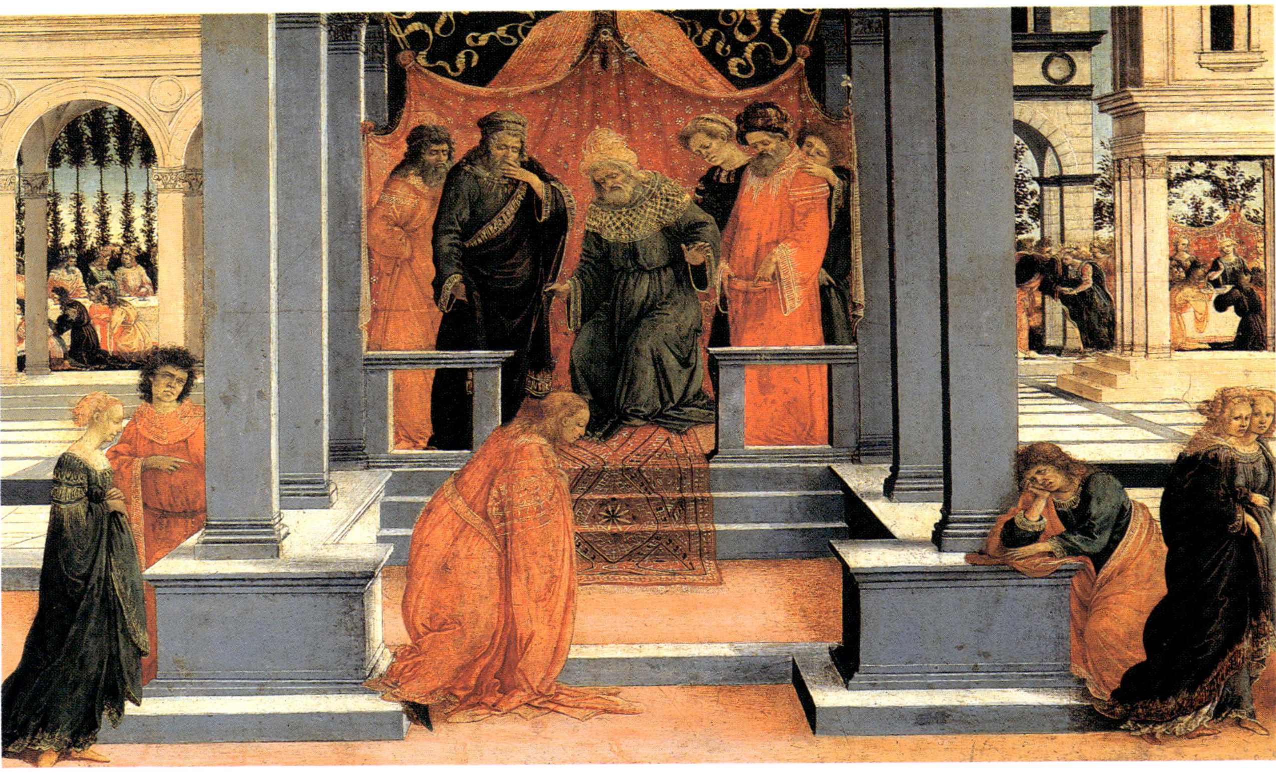

Captivity in Babylon

The relationship between God and his people as it is described in the Old Testament follows this pattern: betrayal, punishment, forgiveness. The internal quarrels dividing the kingdom until it was annihilated by Nebuchadnezzar in 586 BC come under the first heading. Thus the deportation of the people of Israel to Babylon after their defeat appears in the light of a merited punishment, as a trial imposed by God rather than by the actual Babylonians. Then comes the moment of pardon, the time when Jehovah announces that Israel has been restored to his favor: this is illustrated in the Book of Esther by the famous episode involving Esther and Ahasuerus.

There is a second lesson shadowing this first schema: the small but righteous man will triumph over the great, just as David overcomes Goliath. The nomads and vagrants who make up the children of Israel will survive every persecution and oppression provided they do not forget the word of God and abide by his Law. For strength does not come from numbers, it resides in trust, i.e. faith in Jehovah. An army may well win a battle, but only faith can move mountains.

A third point, the novelty of which is crucial to the future of monotheism, is this: faith will be effected through love. David triumphed through cunning and skill. What happens to Esther serves to complement the revelations of Moses: love is the key to redemption. We are a long way removed from the vengeful God of Abraham and Israel. In the Book of Esther, which describes events that took place in the 5th century BC, though it was probably written between 160 and 150 BC, the distant memory of pastoral times is fading and the narrator's style and images suggest a people that has become sedentary.

Esther, Mordecai's ward and a member of the tribe of Benjamin, lived at the time when King Ahasuerus, an imaginary ruler of Persia, held court at Susa. After she had dazzled the king who had recently set aside his wife, the royal crown was set upon her head. But this favor aroused the jealousy of the grand vizier, Haman, who decided to have all the Jews living in the Empire wiped out. However, the love uniting Esther and Ahasuerus was more powerful than all his plotting. After Haman had failed to conceal his anger towards his sovereign when Ahasuerus revoked the decree annihilating the Jews, he himself was finally hanged on the gallows he had intended for Mordecai. As may be guessed, Mordecai was then appointed grand vizier in place of Haman.

However, pride at getting the better of a more powerful people could not wipe out the bitterness of exile. Esther and her people were still the children of Israel. The success gained by Esther and Mordecai reinforced the feeling of frustration resulting from the Diaspora. Love (and here there can be no doubt that the book was written by someone who was sedentary) cannot be separated from attachment to one's land. The whole history of Israel is that of a painful renunciation of the nomadic way of life, and the slow acceptance of the bonds imposed by the mystic marriage of the people of Israel with their Lord.

Lippi (Filipo, known as Filippino) 1457-1504
Esther and Asahuerus, c. 1475-1480
Chantilly, Musée Condé

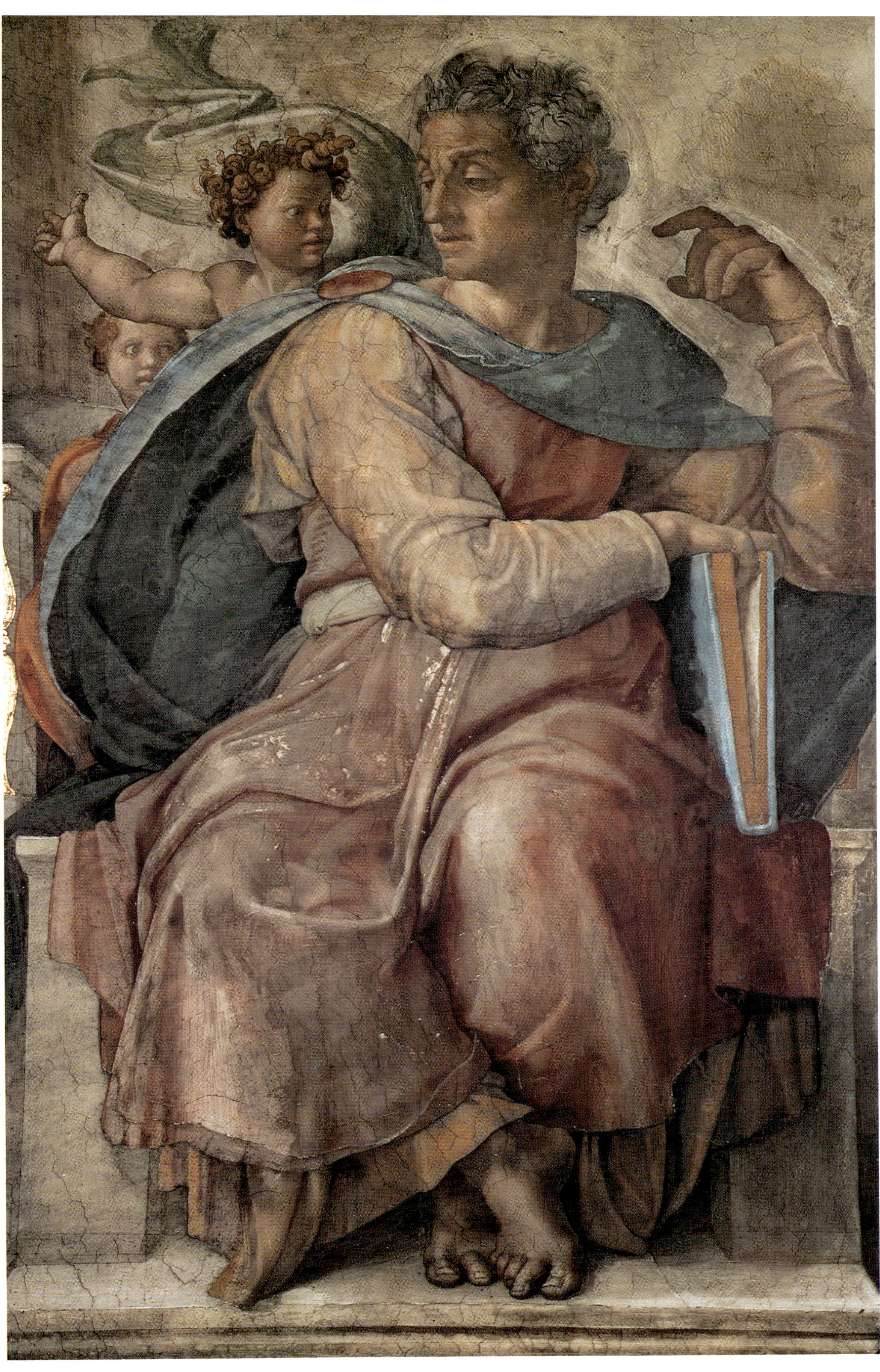

After witnessing the decadence of the kingdom of Israel the prophet Isaiah exhorted his people to return to the path of humility, while at the same time stressing the possible existence of a personal relationship between man and God, clearly foretelling the coming of a Messiah: "and as one from whom men hide their faces he was despised, and we esteemed him not. Surely he has borne our griefs and carried our sorrows."

(Isaiah 53:3-4).

Michelangelo (Michelangelo Buonarroti, known as) c. 1475-1564
The Prophet Isaiah
Rome, Vatican, Sistine chapel

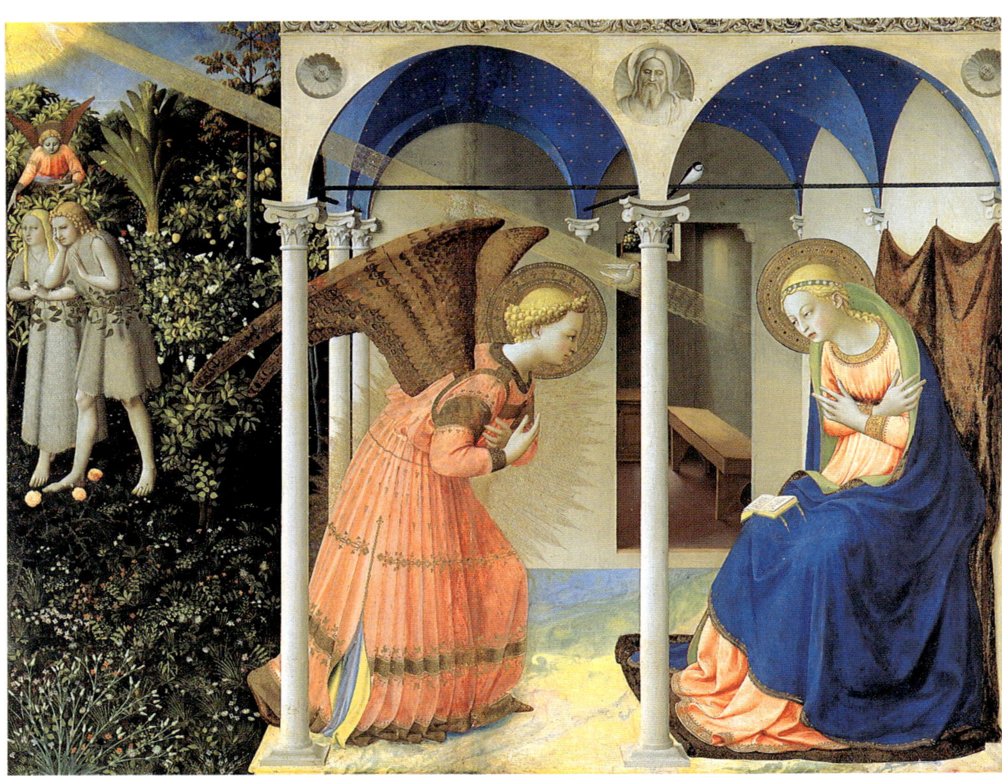

The Annunciation

"... the angel Gabriel was sent from God to a city of Galilee named Nazareth, to a virgin betrothed to a man whose name was Joseph, of the house of David; and the virgin's name was Mary. And he came to her and said, 'Hail, O favored one, the Lord is with you .... Do not be afraid, Mary, for you have found favor with God. And behold, you will conceive in your womb and bear a son, and you shall call his name Jesus. He will be great, and will be called the Son of the Most High; and the Lord God will give to him the throne of his father David, and he will reign over the house of Jacob for ever; and of his kingdom there will be no end.'"

That is how Luke's account of the Annunciation made to Mary begins. It covers barely ten verses in all, and throughout the New Testament Mary is mentioned by name just twenty times, which may seem very little for an event and a person that have achieved such a central place in Christianity.

The Messiah, the Lord's "anointed," was the person Israel had been awaiting for nearly a thousand years; his coming had been foretold even to David by the prophet Nathan. But there is still ambiguity in the wording of the Annunciation: will this *Mesiha*, known in the Greek language as Christ, really be "David's successor," i.e. king of Israel, or will he be merely a prophet, come to proclaim that it is time to turn back to God? For Israel, living under Roman domination after having endured that of the Greeks and the Persians, was expecting more than a simple promise of eternal salvation. A little further on, still in Luke, these words are put in the mouth of Zechariah, the father of John the Baptist: "Blessed be the Lord God of Israel, for he has visited and redeemed his people, and has raised up a horn of salvation for us in the house of his servant David, as he spoke by the mouth of his prophets from of old, that we should be saved from our enemies, and from the hand of all who hate us."

Mary for her part consents, without immediately realizing the implications of what she is doing. The Covenant made between Jehovah and the people of Abraham seventeen centuries earlier was about to be renewed through her. However, the word brought by Gabriel differs from the earlier apparitions or manifestations in that on this occasion it is explicitly stated that the Word will be made flesh in the flesh of the creature. Christ "will be born of woman": he will thus be the Son of man. A strange inversion, deeply laden with meaning, that burdens Mary with the heavy responsibility of guaranteeing the link between humanity and divinity.

Philippe de Champaigne gives us a version of this event which combines a liking for smooth surfaces and bright colors inherited from Rubens with the austere monumentality of French Classicism. Influenced by the Jansenist circles associated with Port-Royal, Champaigne chose a simple, clear setting which leaves hardly any room for emotion. Fra Angelico, on the other hand, with his subtle mysticism, betrays his training as an illuminator and a miniaturist. What lies between the two is what separates the heart from the head.

Fra Angelico (Fra Giovanni da Fiesole, secular name Guido di Pietro, known as) c. 1395/1400-1455
Annunciation, c. 1430-1432
Madrid, Prado

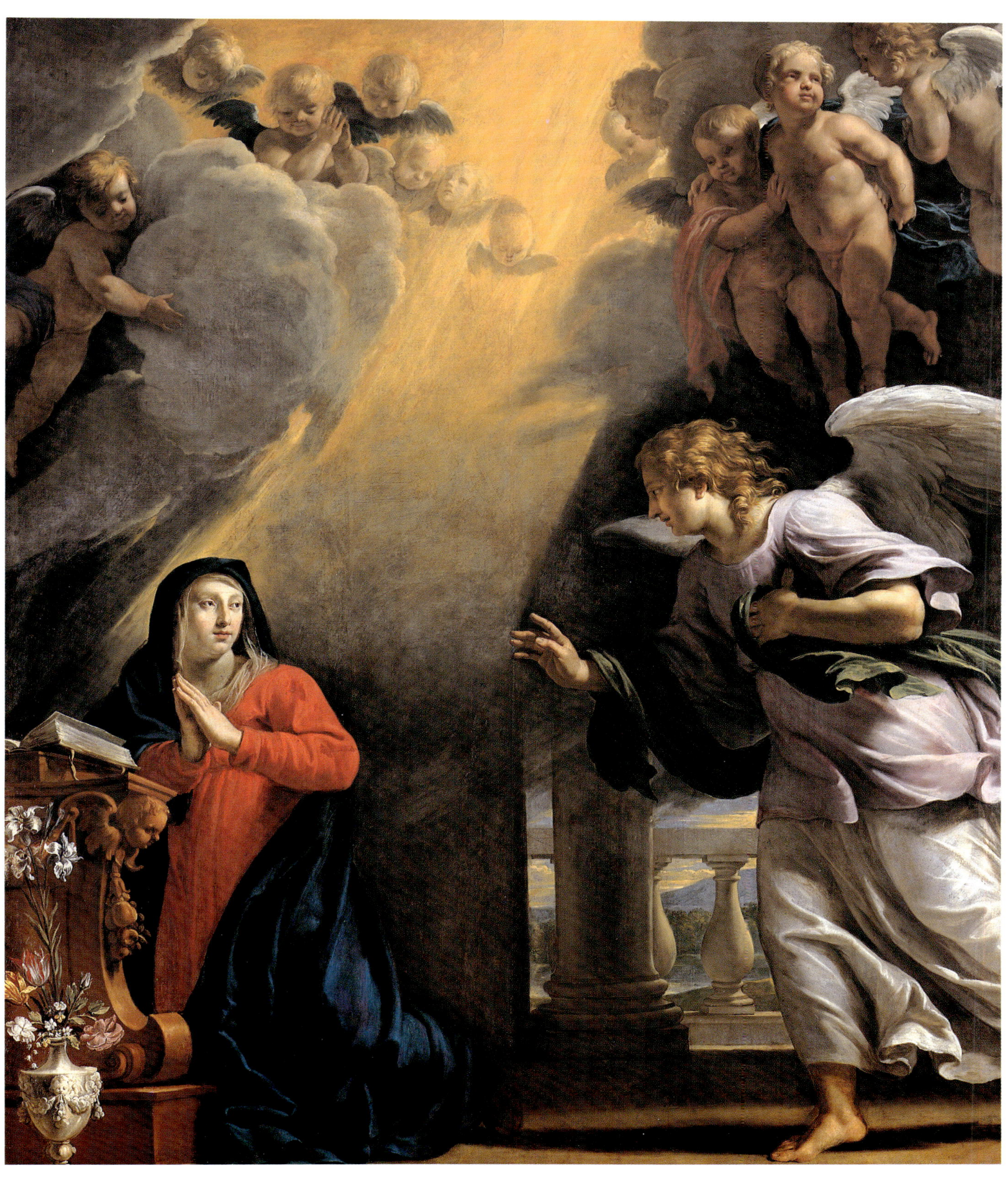

"And Mary said to the angel, 'How can this be, since I have no husband?' And the angel said to her, 'The Holy Spirit will come upon you, and the power of the Most High will overshadow you; therefore the child to be born will be called holy, the Son of God.'"

(The Gospel according to Luke 1:34-5).

Champaigne (Philippe de) 1602-1674
Annunciation
Caen, Musée des Beaux-Arts

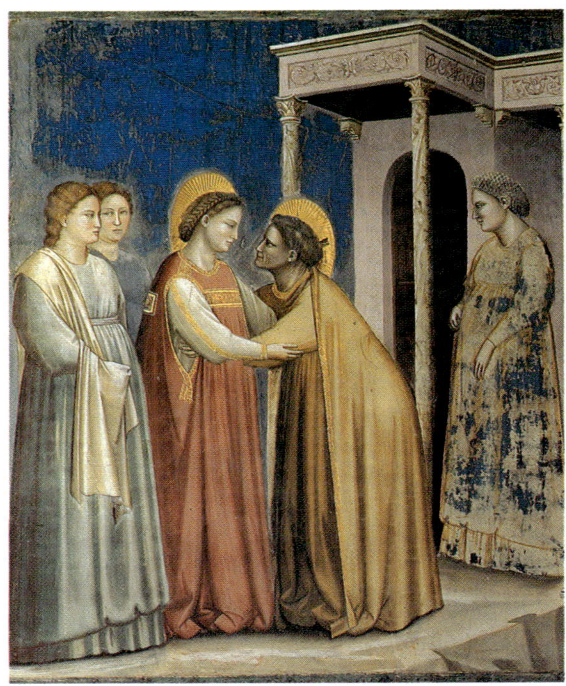

The Visitation

The incarnation is unquestionably the profoundest and most interesting of the Christian mysteries. Greco-Roman paganism loved divine metamorphoses, but the form taken on by one or other of the gods of Olympus was only the visible transcription of his stratagem, or rather his *duplicity*, and did not in any way alter his divine essence. Being, as the Greeks saw it, was not linked with appearances.

Here we are dealing with something entirely different. The Holy Spirit is not satisfied with making the womb of Mary fertile as He had done for her cousin Elizabeth, who then gave birth to John the Baptist. When Elizabeth on seeing Mary exclaims, "Blessed are you among women, and blessed is the fruit of your womb!" (Luke 1:42), she is not merely expressing her certainty that special grace has been assigned to the fruit of Mary's womb, she is proclaiming the divine nature of the child that will be born. And it is again Elizabeth who calls Mary "the mother of my Lord"; she is the first, prompted by the movement in her womb of her own son John the Baptist, to recognize Jesus as being both the Son and the Father of man, a creature to come and an uncreated Being. Thus Jesus will simultaneously and contradictorily be fully a man and fully God.

One of Giotto's achievements is that he managed to depict that contradiction. In the words of Lionello Venturi, "the divine image is presented, the human life is represented [...]. So Giotto's images are both abstract and concrete; they are the images of men caught up in the universal, classless and timeless [...]. The divine which becomes human speaks of sympathy and love; and the human which becomes divine is revealed in the dignity and moral stature."

Narratively speaking, the Visitation prefigures the meeting between Jesus and John the Baptist on the banks of the Jordan. John the Baptist had already recognized Jesus in his mother's womb: "And when Elizabeth heard the greeting of Mary, the babe leaped in her womb; and Elizabeth was filled with the Holy Spirit" (Luke 1:41). And it would be John again who said after baptising him, "Behold, the Lamb of God" (John 1:36), indicating to his disciples that this was the true Christ. John the Baptist is the mark of God placed upon Jesus.

The incarnation, made possible by Mary's open acceptance and the total self-renunciation to which the divine Being committed himself, is an act of love and suffering without which the redemption could not have taken place. God in his absolute perfection is incapable of taking upon himself all the sins of the world. Only a man can do this. The return of the being created to the Creator presupposes that the Spirit must first come among men: as in the stages of inversion typical of the rites of passage in primitive societies, the Creator becomes the fruit of the being he has created. And he who is All gives himself to mankind in the appearance of the most extreme deprivation. Thus when he came into the world his parents were at Bethlehem. Far away from her home and family, turned away by the only inn in the town, Mary gave birth in a cowshed and the newborn babe was laid in a manger.

Giotto (Giotto di Bondone, known as) c. 1266/1267-1337
Visitation, 1303-1305
Padua, Scrovegni chapel

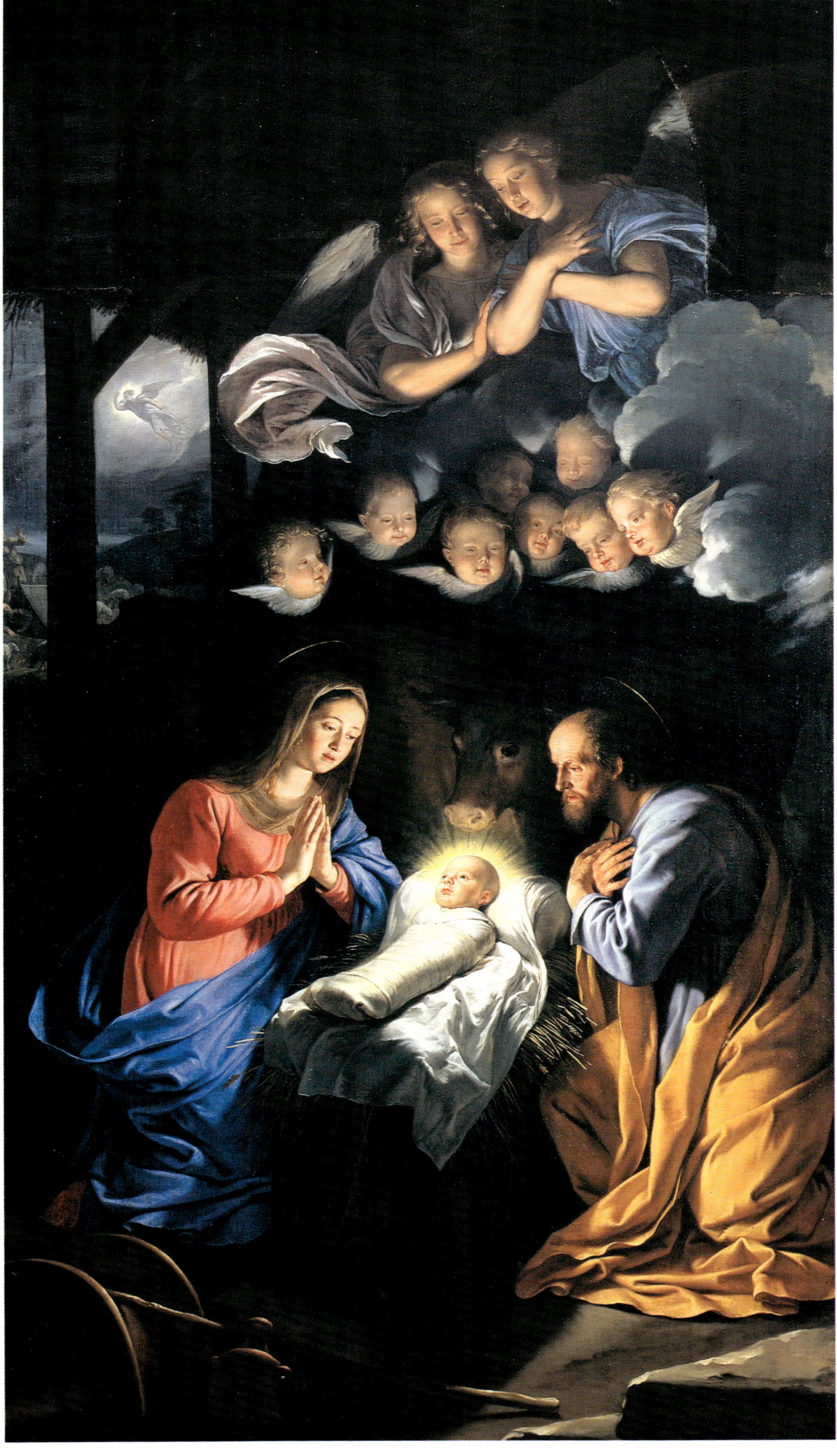

"And the Word became flesh and dwelt among us, full of grace and truth; we have beheld his glory, glory as of the only Son from the Father."

(The Gospel according to John 1:14).

Champaigne (Philippe de) 1602-1674
Nativity
Lille, Musée des Beaux-Arts

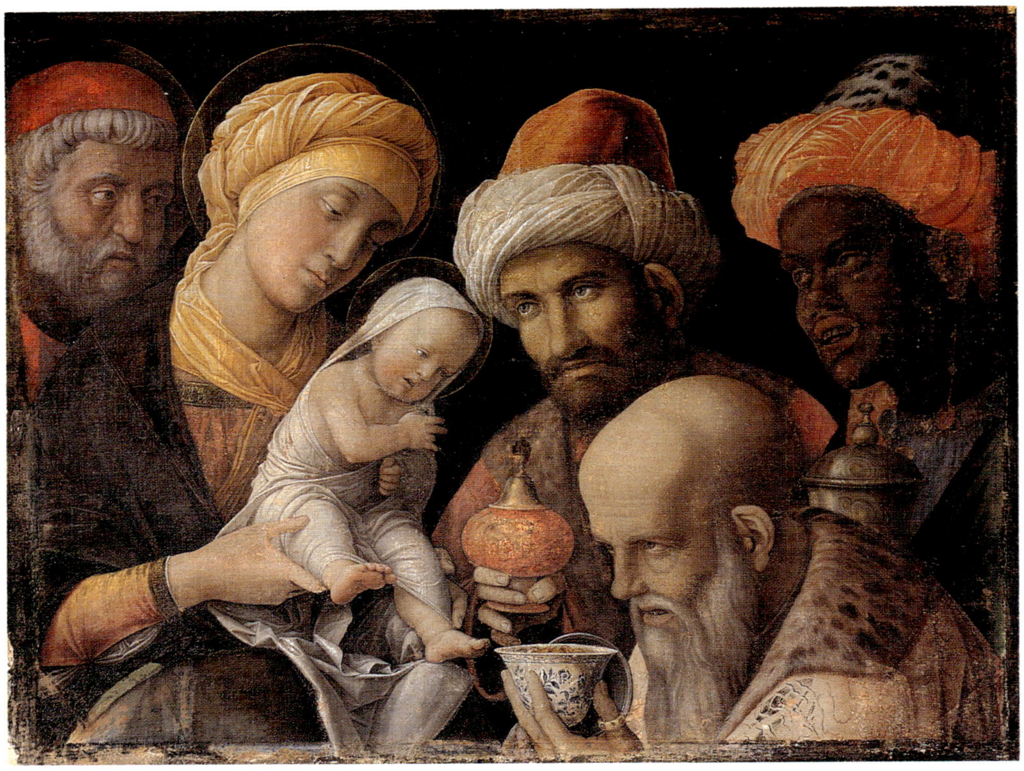

The Adoration

When the Child appears, he must be recognized, and this is done first by the shepherds and then by the Wise Men. If we accept that the shepherds represent the people of Israel at their most humble level, but also at the level closest to the pastoral origins of the children of Abraham, then the role of the Magi is to represent foreign nations and their arrival prefigures the universal dimension of the Christian message.

The Magi say they have been guided by a mysterious star – obviously a sign of divine will. The star is the light of the sky, which can be interpreted with equal validity in a literal or a metaphorical sense. The light of the star is divine guidance. Whether the star was a comet or the result of the conjunction of the planets Venus, Saturn and Jupiter or not is virtually irrelevant. The main point is that men, and important men at that, who did not belong to the race of Israel, came and prostrated themselves before the "king of the Jews," bringing him gold, frankincense and myrrh. Because of the number of presents, it was inferred at a later stage that there were three Wise Men. This number recalls the three sons of Noah (Shem, Ham and Japheth). The descendants of these three, populating each of the three continents known at that period (Africa to the south, Asia to the east and Europe to the north), together made up mankind. The figure three is also a reference to the trinity of the One God which is the basis of the first mystery of Christianity. The gold, frankincense and myrrh thus refer both to the three components of mankind, represented by the three Magi, and the three members of the Holy Family, the symbolic arrangement of whom may be read as a terrestrial echo of the trinitary composition of the single God. The 4th-century poet Juvencus read the three gifts as three symbols of the true nature of Christ: Christ the king through the gold on which kingdoms are built; Christ the atoner through the myrrh, an aromatic substance associated with the dead; and Christ as God through the incense which is used in worship: three items designating the One and Only.

Mantegna's version of the Adoration is in line with the symbolic reading of the event, both in its substance and its form. Unlike Rubens at a later date who became sentimental about the anecdotal aspects of the meeting, or El Greco who gave a visionary interpretation of it, Mantegna conceived the Adoration with the rigor of a geometrician: three Magi, three dimensions, a single God. This *manner of seeing*, often regarded as cold and hard, abjures any psychological drift and any sentimentality. It is not a child that is being worshiped, but a God. Using the medium of the plastic arts Mantegna transcribes the austere elegance of the concept rather than an emotion. The rigidity of the figures and even their positioning reveal the carefully considered intentions of a theatrical director. Unfortunately, the excessive theatricality is ultimately inhibiting, and we might have wished for the characters in this painting to express more love and life.

Mantegna (Andrea) 1431-1506
Adoration of the Magi
London, Christie's

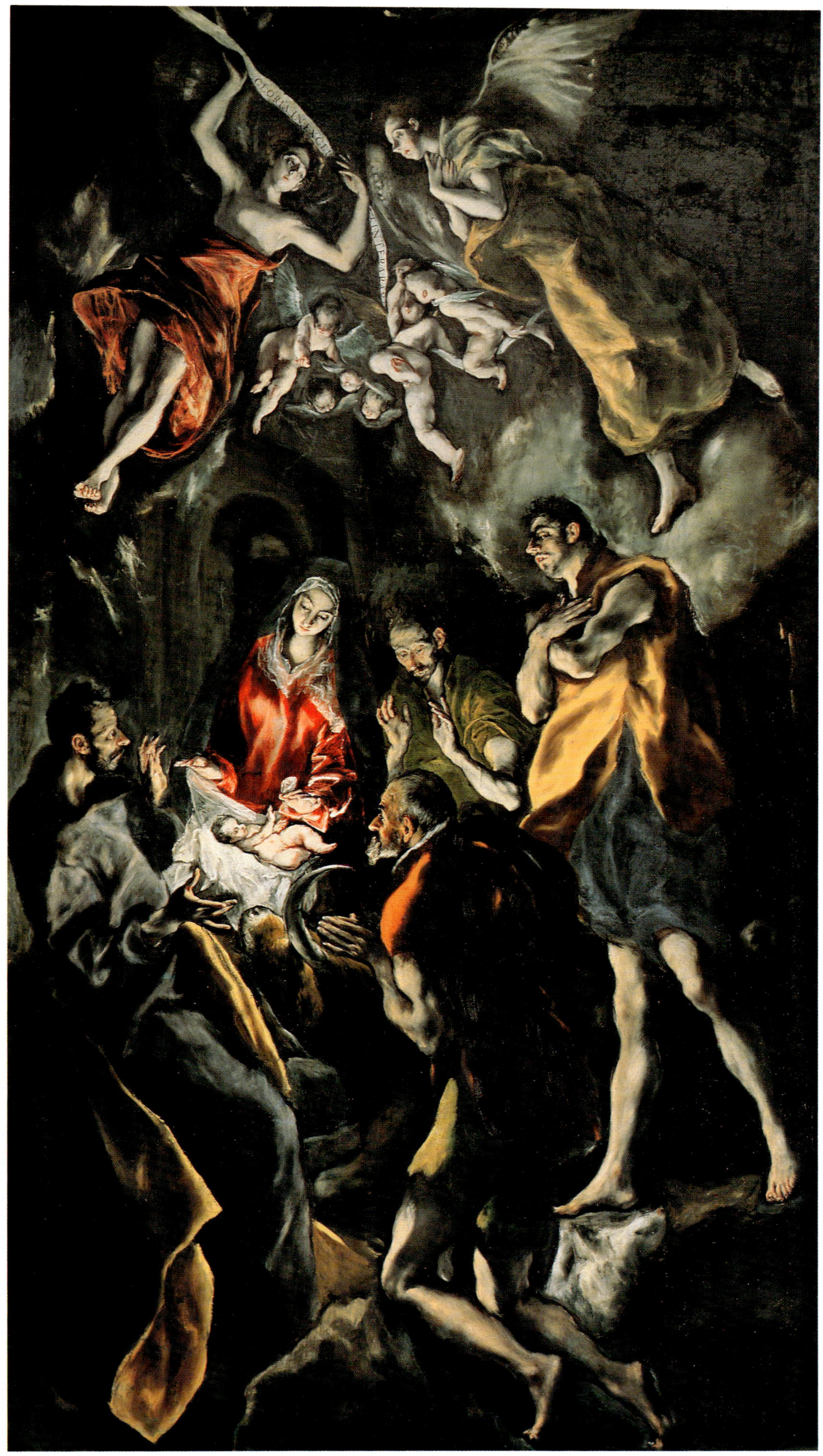

"When they saw the star, they rejoiced exceedingly with great joy; and going into the house they saw the child and Mary his mother, and they fell down and worshiped him. Then, opening their treasures, they offered him gifts, gold and frankincense and myrrh."

(The Gospel according to Matthew 2:10-11).

El Greco (Domenikos Theotokopoulos, known as) c. 1541-1614
Adoration of the shepherds
Madrid, Prado

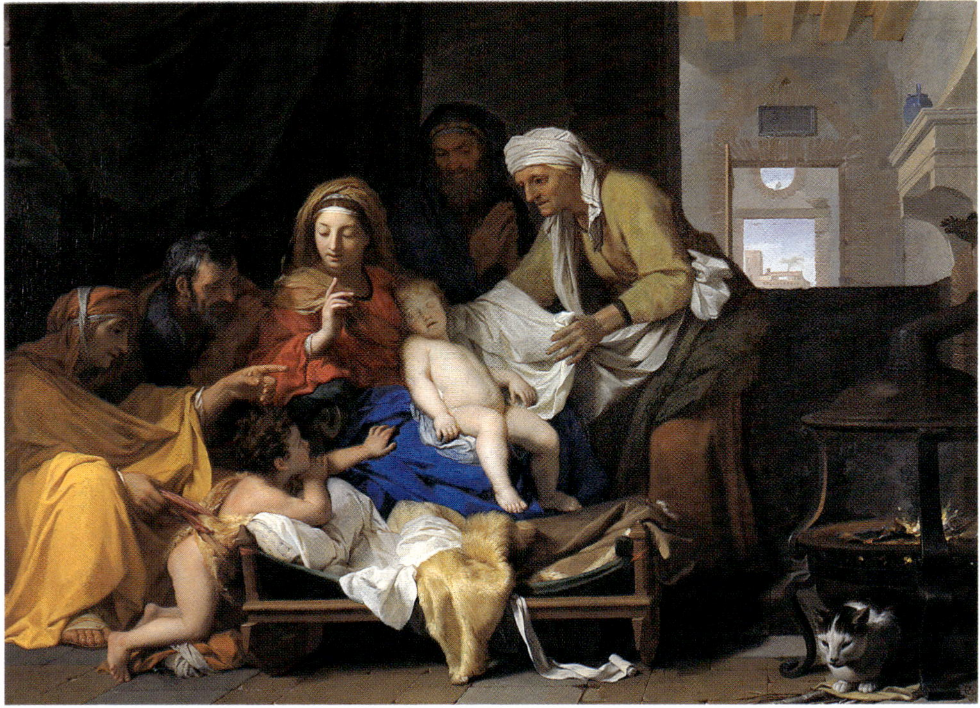

The childhood of Christ

Virtually nothing is known about the childhood of Christ. Matthew briefly mentions the flight to Egypt and the slaughter of the innocents at Bethlehem: "Then Herod, when he saw that he had been tricked by the wise men, was in a furious rage, and he sent and killed all the male children in Bethlehem and in all that region who were two years old or under." Then Christ appears as an adult, after spending his childhood in Nazareth.

Luke on the other hand emphasizes the circumcision which took place eight days after the birth of Christ, stating that it was then that he was given the name Jesus, and the presentation in the Temple where the child is recognized by Simeon and the prophetess Anna as the Savior foretold in the Scriptures. Luke adds another episode, very much appreciated by painters, describing Jesus among the teachers in the Temple; theologically it is very important because for the first time we see Christ publicly proclaiming his divinity.

Thus the childhood of Christ was a period of silence and apprenticeship. Ernest Renan writes that "His family does not seem to have loved him, and at times he appears hard on them. Like all men who are exclusively preoccupied by an idea, Jesus sometimes paid scant attention to family ties. Attachment to an idea is the only tie which people with such natures recognize."

In the absence of detailed information, painters have been able to allow their imaginations a free rein. Thus Le Brun depicts a quite delightful *Infant Jesus sleeping*. Le Brun, a great director of the Académie royale and a pupil of Poussin, was the advocate of Classicism in France. Loyal to the teaching of Raphael, he maintained that it was the artist's main task to correct the "imperfections" of nature according to the criteria of beauty as defined in antiquity. It may be this very lack of "imperfections" which makes the scene so unconvincing in spite of the skillful placing of the figures and the expert mixing of the colors.

The approach of Piero della Francesca, mixing Flemish realism with Italian idealism in his *Madonna of Senigallia*, is far more interesting: earth and sky, body and spirit, line and light are harmoniously conjugated to provide us with an image of perfection, taken from everyday life, in which the architecture suggests God the Creator, the light the Holy Spirit, and the Child the God of love.

With the advent of the Child God ceased to be Other, a radically different absolute, He was no longer that remote enigma which only the word of the prophets could attempt to approach. Quite the opposite: through the presence of Jesus he now stood shoulder to shoulder with the human beings he had created, accepting responsibility for their destiny, just as a father might for the acts of his son. He was no longer united to man through expectation of man's submission and obedience but through absolute, unconditional love, since Christ would go so far as to sacrifice himself for the salvation of mankind. Through this love He had also ceased to be the God of one race, but was universally present in each and every person: through the Son he had become the God of men.

Le Brun (Charles) 1619-1690
Infant Jesus sleeping, 1655
Paris, Louvre

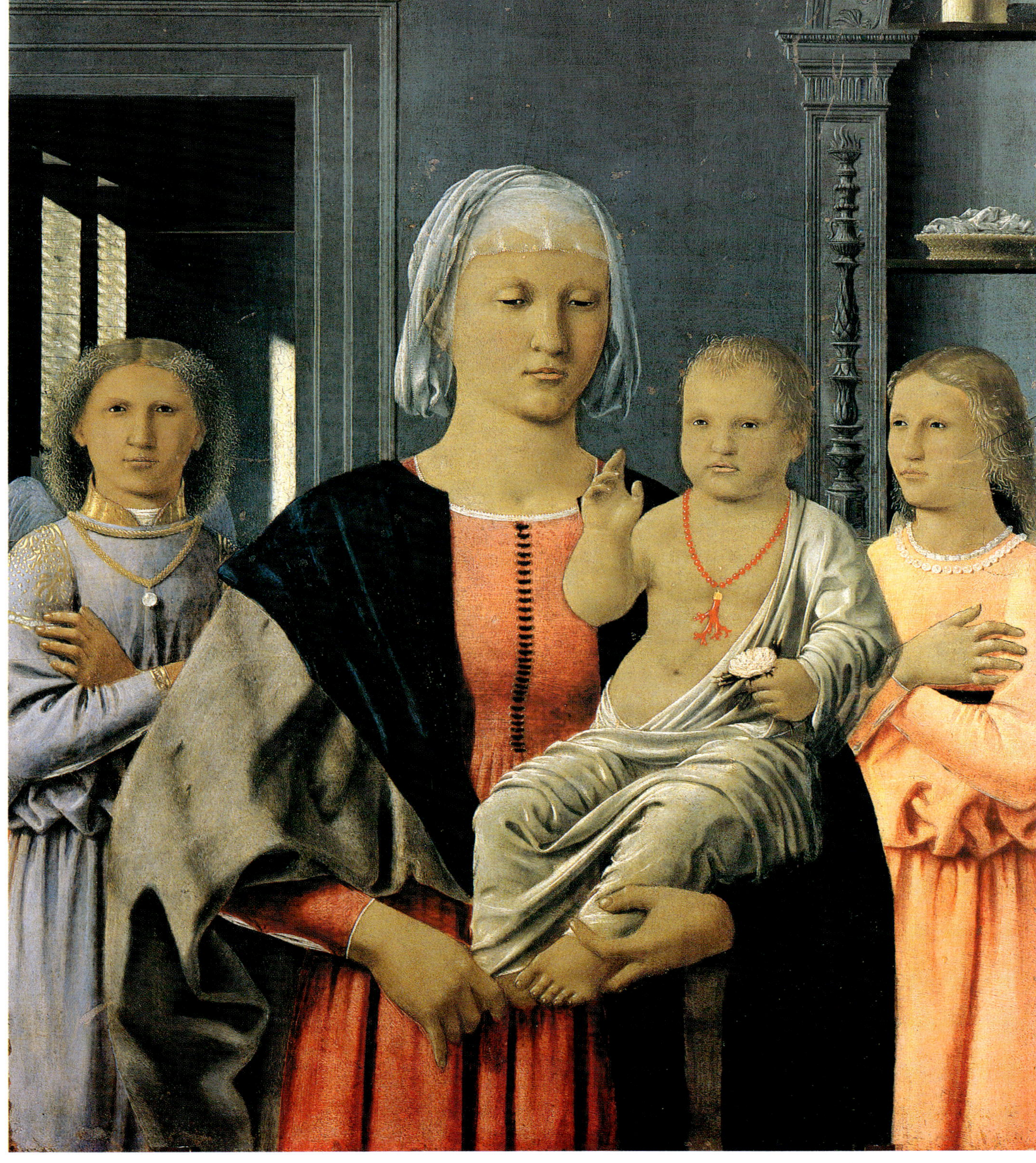

The Madonna of Senigallia, painted in the latter part of Piero della Francesca's life, is a successful synthesis of the "monumental and the intimate" in which space is indicated in equal proportions by light and line.

Piero della Francesca (Piero di Benedetto or Piero dal Borgo, known as) c. 1416-1492
Virgin and Child with two angels, known as the Madonna of Senigallia, c. 1472
Urbino, Galleria Nazionale delle Marche

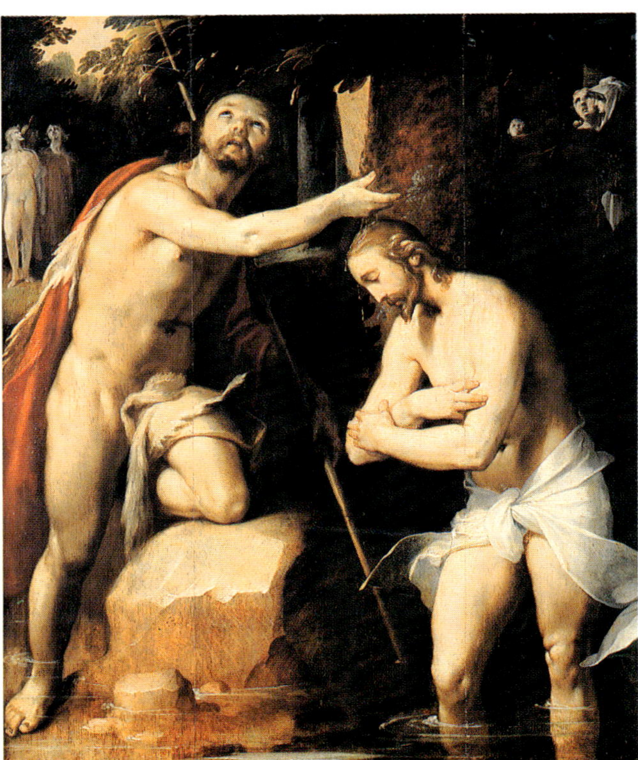

The baptism of Christ

The baptism of Christ by John the Baptist marked the end of the era of the prophets. The baptism, through the gift of the Holy Spirit, offers remission of sins and opens up the way to the kingdom of God. Paul wrote to the Corinthians that through the baptism man "is a new creation; the old has passed away, behold, the new has come" (2 Corinthians 5:17). We are dealing at the same time with a rite of passage and a return towards God, for "God was in Christ reconciling the world to himself" (2 Corinthians 5:19). First and foremost, this baptism means reconciliation and regeneration through communion in love.

Historians know very little about John the Baptist, the central character in this initiatory event. He would certainly have been influenced by the Essenes, and may possibly have been familiar with some Buddhist rites which were then being disseminated to the Mediterranean shores via Babylon. John carried out baptisms in the waters of the Jordan not far from the Dead Sea. "Within a few months he thus became one of the most influential men in Judea," Renan wrote, "and everyone had to reckon with him. The people regarded him as a prophet, several believing that he was Elijah risen from the dead. [...] It does not appear that he had the faintest inkling of the great idea which led Jesus to triumph, the idea of a pure religion; but he did valuable service to that idea by substituting a private rite for legal ceremonies requiring priests, rather like the flagellants in the Middle Ages who acted as the precursors of the Reformation in depriving the official clergy of their monopoly over the sacraments and absolution."

Baptism, which opened up the possibility of a personal relationship between man and his God, gave the crowds that rushed to see John a premonitory glimpse of the end of the humiliations of the Jewish people. In doing so he still left some uncertainties unanswered: only Jesus would be able to resolve these. John the Baptist did not make it clear whether the act of baptism had a political significance or not, since he was challenging both the occupying Roman forces and the upper classes of Israel. Disappointing the expectations of the crowd surrounding him, made up of the poor and wretched, men and women of the people, tradesmen, people in modest circumstances who were certainly not impervious to his attacks on the Pharisees, the learned elite, John the Baptist refused to make a clear statement.

Possibly to the chagrin of some of his followers, Jesus cleared up any ambiguity when the time came: "Render therefore unto Caesar the things that are Caesar's" (Matthew 22:21), he declared to the Pharisees who were trying to put him in the wrong. Jesus had come to preach love, not rebellion. And baptism was the manifestation of this: baptism washes the world clean of its wrongdoing and is the basis of the New Covenant. What the Flood had ravaged with water was now restored by water, but in a new way which gave the relationship with God a personal, individual, therefore universal character. This struck at the very roots of the idea of a chosen race which had been the basis of Judaism, so constituting the most serious threat that Israel had ever had to face.

Cornelisz van Haarlem (Cornelis, known as) 1562-1638
Baptism of Christ
Douai, Musée de la Chartreuse

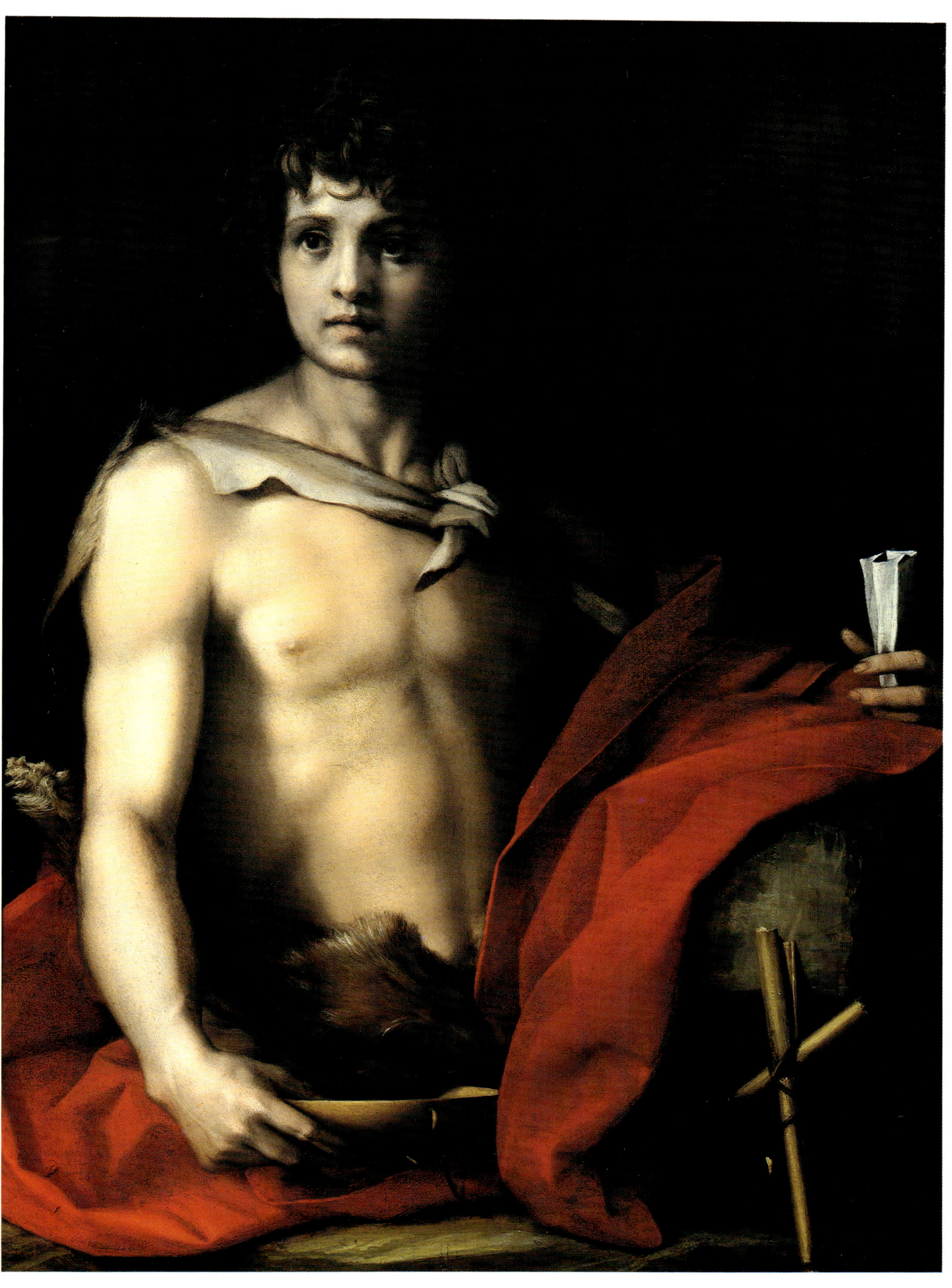

For all peoples surrounded by desert water takes on a sacred dimension. A gift from God, it is the transparent symbol of life and balance; and balance is the key word in the esthetics of Andrea del Sarto, a follower of Raphael.

Andrea del Sarto (Andrea d'Agnolo, known as) 1486-1530
St. John the Baptist, c. 1520
Florence, Pitti Palace

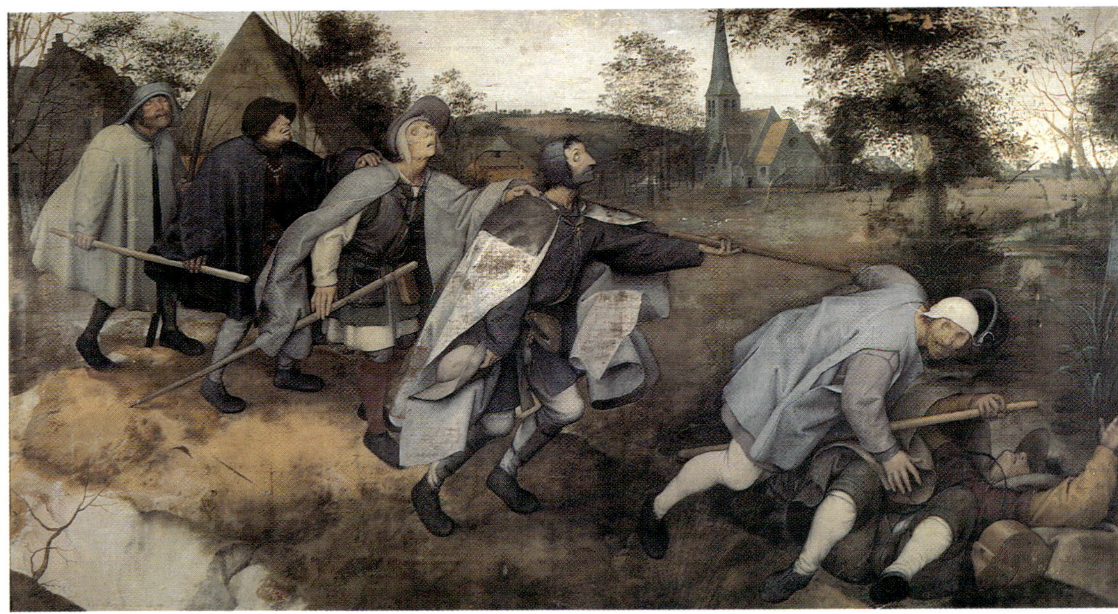

The Word of God

Christianity turned monotheism into an idealistic faith. The most striking affirmation of this is in the first chapter of the Gospel according to John. "In the beginning was the Word, and the Word was with God, and the Word was God. [...] In him was life, and the life was the light of men."

However, this idealism which theologians subsequently made sterile and offputting was originally a sensual theology deeply rooted in the material activities of this world. Thus Matthew, talking of John the Baptist, describes him as a poor hermit clad only in "a garment of camel's hair, and a leather girdle round his waist; and his food was locusts and wild honey" (Matthew 3:4). So the purest asceticism retained the imprint of material poetry.

Jesus was ignorant of Greek and Hellenist civilization. He had a simplistic image of the Roman Empire, made up of power, ostentation and arbitrariness. His frequent use of parables reflects this state of mind, a pictorial approach to the mystery of religion, for a parable is also a riddle. It has two opposing objectives: to make a lesson that is by nature abstract accessible to the people by illustrating it with a concrete example – an elementary principle of teaching; but at the same time, conversely, to speak to them only in riddles so that "hearing they do not hear, nor do they understand" (Matthew 13:13), in order to make people aware of the gulf separating the perceptible world from the kingdom of God. It is as if the aim were to show that an intellectual approach to the mystery is impossible, and to point to a mystic approach based on love conceived as a *priori* certainty of the existence of the Other as the only approach possible: love experienced through faith, an act of belief and trust – abandonment to God. This is the meaning of Christ's visit to Lazarus's sisters, Martha and Mary; the simple realism of the episode is perfectly rendered by Vermeer. Martha, "distracted with much serving," annoyed at the sight of her sister sitting at the feet of Jesus, says, "Lord, do you not care that my sister has left me to serve alone? Tell her then to help me." But Jesus' answer is: "Martha, Martha, you are anxious and troubled about many things; one thing is needful. Mary has chosen the good portion, which shall not be taken away from her." Martha looks down, as if she had been caught doing something wrong. She seems almost to want to obliterate her awareness of the bread she is placing on the white tablecloth: true nourishment – spiritual nourishment – is to be found elsewhere. It is the Word of God.

Finally miracles too, with the resurrection of Lazarus as the most moving example, operate in the same way as parables. They are a metaphor which, in the case of Lazarus, points forward to the resurrection of the last day. Both miracles and parables are messages with a double meaning. The Word of God is cryptic: it is not a question of understanding, but of believing. It is in this that Christianity reveals itself as a truly Oriental cult which in almost every respect is at the opposite end of the spectrum from Greek rationality.

Brueghel (Pieter the Elder) c. 1528/1530-1569
The parable of the blind, 1568
Naples, Museo di Capodimonte

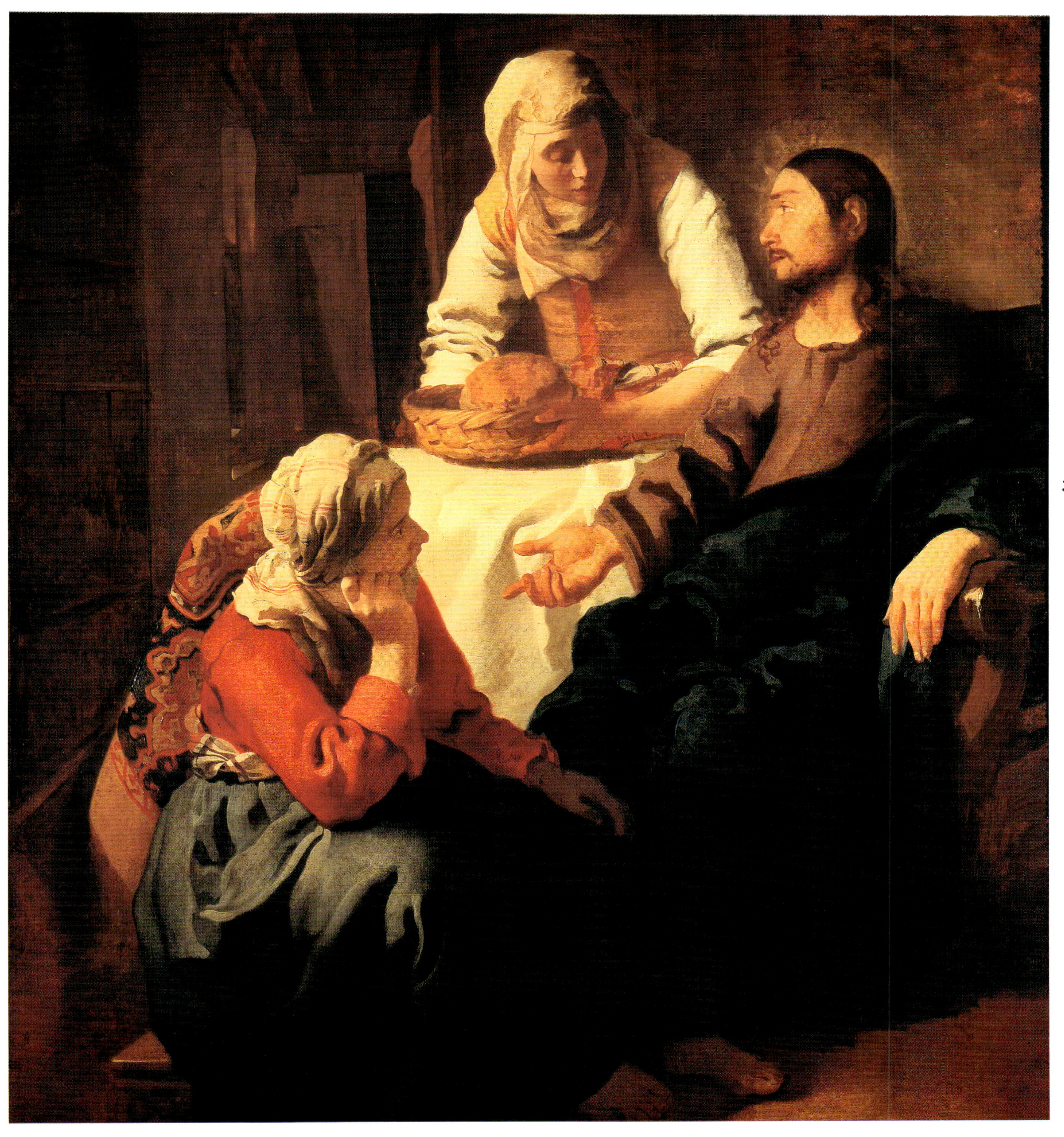

"His speech is most sweet, and he is altogether desirable. This is my beloved."

(Song of Solomon 5:16)

Vermeer van Delft (Jan Vermeer, known as) 1633-1675
Christ in the house of Martha and Mary, 1654-1656
Edinburgh, National Gallery of Scotland

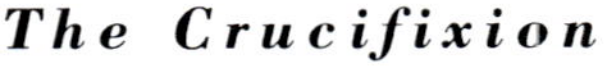

The Crucifixion

Jesus introduced the Eucharist at the Last Supper. It proclaims the real presence of Christ under the guise of bread and wine. Communion renews his sacrifice for the salvation of mankind. Because we love, we kill. And because we love, we eat. Christianity is a strange religion which gives its believers the opportunity to eat God every week: eating God so as to be permeated with his substance, as in any form of cannibalism, though here we are talking of theophagy in its strictest sense. God is in the Host (the victim), but he may no longer be with Christ on the Cross. Christ is then purely man, and he doubts his Father: "And about the ninth hour Jesus cried with a loud voice, 'Eli, Eli, la'ma sabach-tha'-ni?' that is, "My God, my God, why hast thou forsaken me?" (Matthew 27:46).

All representations of the Last Supper, the trial or the Crucifixion of Jesus play on the irreducible ambiguity concerning the exact nature of what is being shown. Who is being scourged in this picture by Piero della Francesca? The scene has been heightened to extreme theatricality, and the protagonists are symbols (except for those in the foreground, who are certainly the Duke of Urbino's half-brother and two of his advisers, all three implicated in the Serafini conspiracy). Christ in his chalky whiteness seems to be the central element of an idealized architecture, a mineral, supernatural being, accepting the scourging purely as a humiliation but not as a source of pain. He is God made visible rather than the martyred Son. Grünewald in the *Crucifixion* on his Issenheim retable, on the other hand, elects to show a man in all the wretchedness of his tortured body. Only a few decades separate these two works as the 15th century made way for the 16th, separating the end of the Middle Ages from the Renaissance, still groping to find its way.

But looking at them side by side is sufficient to enable us to understand what separates one from the other: "abstract idealism," J. Nordström writes, "is giving way to a new art which sees its true objective as the exact reproduction of the real world in all its individual, changing forms." This is true up to a point, for Grünewald in his way is still painting an idea, a symbol. Grünewald is not painting Christ, but the humanity he embodies: this is where the true break between the Middle Ages and the Renaissance lies. It is not so much a question of exchanging an idealistic interpretation for a realistic vision of the world as of moving from a theological concept to an anthropological concept of the universe: this means seeing the nature of Jesus more as a symbolic representation of suffering humankind than as a figure of the embodiment of the Word.

Through this splendid mystery we represent the Father by the Son, and the Creator by the creature he has made, so that the Cross becomes the supreme focus of the inversion of the order of things, the place where values are turned upside down, the point of intersection between human destiny and the divine plan. God becomes man to show the way that will bring man back towards Him, and an era is ended so that the Word can be implemented.

Piero della Francesca
(Piero di Benedetto or Piero dal Borgo, known as) c. 1416-1492
Flagellation, c. 1445
Urbino, Galleria Nazionale delle Marche

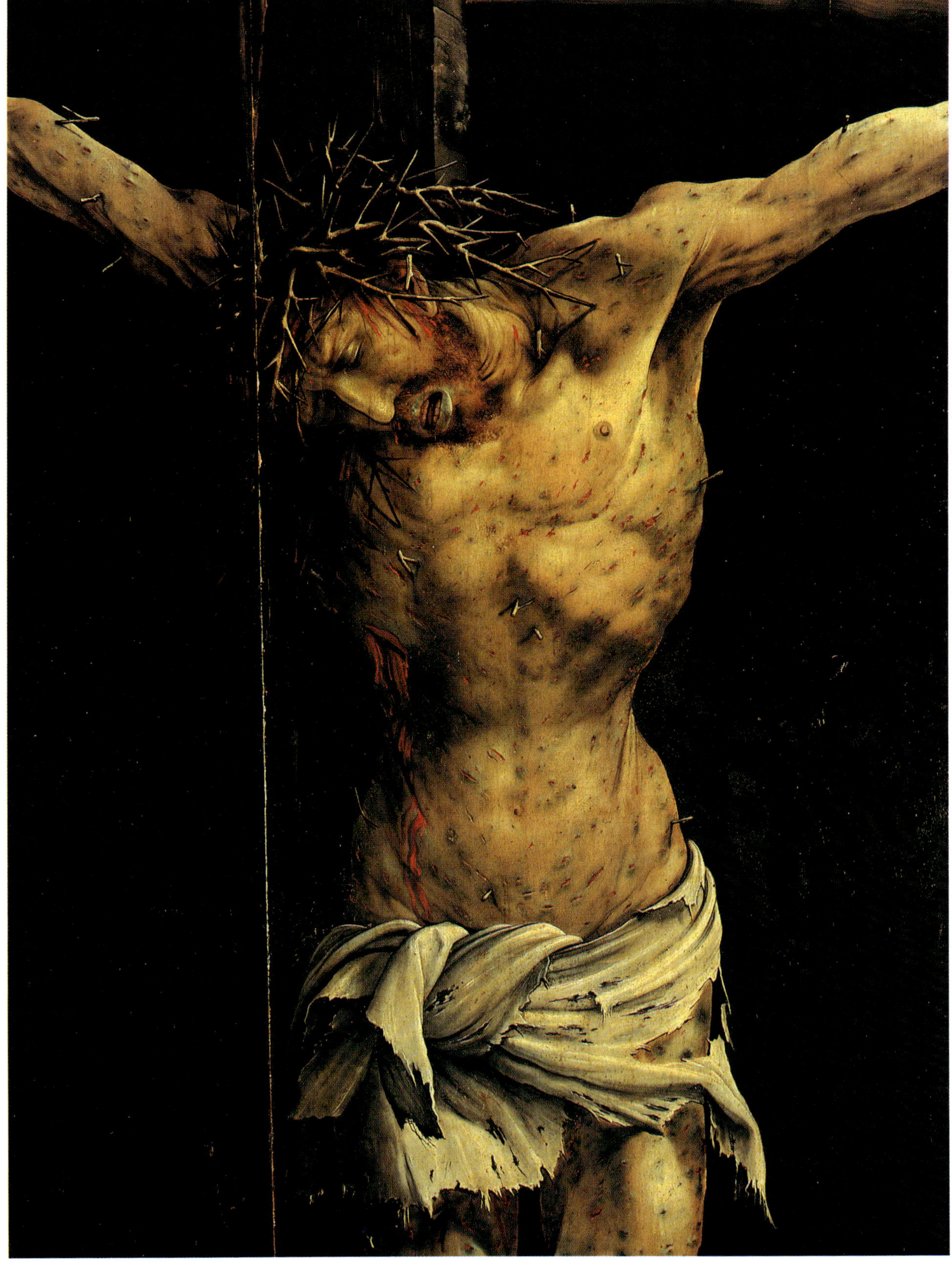

"To climb is to immolate oneself. / All summits are harsh. / Olympus slowly turns into Calvary; / martyrdom is written everywhere; / a huge cross lies in our deep night; / and we see bleeding in the four corners of the world / the four nails of the Cross."

Victor Hugo
Les Contemplations

Grünewald (Mathis Gothart Nithart, know as) c. 1475/1480-1528
Issenheim retable. The Crucifixion
Detail: Christ on the Cross, c. 1512-1516
Colmer, Musée d'Unterlinden

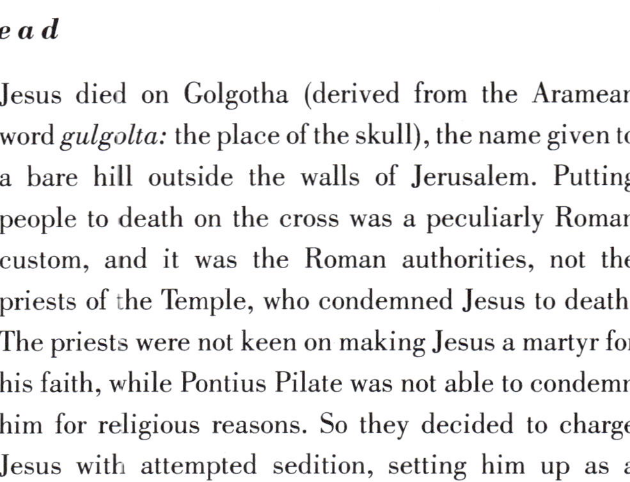

Christ dead

Jesus died on Golgotha (derived from the Aramean word *gulgolta:* the place of the skull), the name given to a bare hill outside the walls of Jerusalem. Putting people to death on the cross was a peculiarly Roman custom, and it was the Roman authorities, not the priests of the Temple, who condemned Jesus to death. The priests were not keen on making Jesus a martyr for his faith, while Pontius Pilate was not able to condemn him for religious reasons. So they decided to charge Jesus with attempted sedition, setting him up as a political agitator.

The sentence reserved for this kind of misdemeanor was hanging or beheading. In this case crucifixion, regarded as more ignominious, was preferred. Usually it was reserved for slaves or thieves, and it was carried out only by the Romans, unlike stoning, which was used only for religious offenses and could be ordered by Jewish dignitaries. So Jesus was crucified; however, a quick death spared him the frightful suffering intended for him.

Then came the deposition from the Cross: an essential, yet paradoxical scene relating to the *presence* of Christ. Is it a God that is being depicted, or the lifeless body of a martyr? Botticelli chose to look forward. In spite of the grief of the "women of Galilee," we can already see light radiating out of the youthful body. Death is only a passage leading to eternal life. Grünewald's approach, on the other hand, is much more ambiguous. It is hard to detect the promise of resurrection in the gray flesh already bearing the mark of death. Rather than grief, Grünewald depicts the moment of doubt. The macabre realism with which he dwells on the signs of the ordeal, the uncompromising cruelty of the portrayal, ring out like a warning addressed to Christianity, then torn between the Reformation and the Counter-Reformation. "Let us not commit the supreme sin a second time," seems to be the essential message the painter is addressing to the spectator.

Although Mary is almost always depicted at Jesus' side in this scene, her presence is not mentioned in any of the three synoptic Gospels (Matthew, Mark and Luke). In fact the central person is not the mother of Christ, but Mary Magdalene. It was she who was present at the foot of the Cross during her master's dying hours, and she again who was present when he was laid in the tomb. Finally, it was again Mary Magdalene, coming back on the day following the Sabbath to embalm the body, who found the tomb open and empty. "Let us suppose," wrote Ernest Renan, "that Mary Magdalene's powerful imagination played a crucial role in this episode. The divine power of love! A sacred moment in time when the passion of a woman suffering from hallucinations gave the world a resuscitated God!"

The news of the death of this one Jew among many did not spread beyond the borders of the land of Canaan. Jesus was unknown or virtually unknown to the historians of the 1st century, surviving only in the memory of a narrow circle of disciples. While the Romans were scattering the Jews to the four corners of the earth, the Christians, reduced to a semi-clandestine state, preserved their unity, learning how to communicate within the cult of a pure religion which was (for the time being) free of any political ambitions.

Botticelli (Sandro di Mariano Filipepi, known as) 1445-1510
Lamentation, c. 1490
Munich, Alte Pinakothek

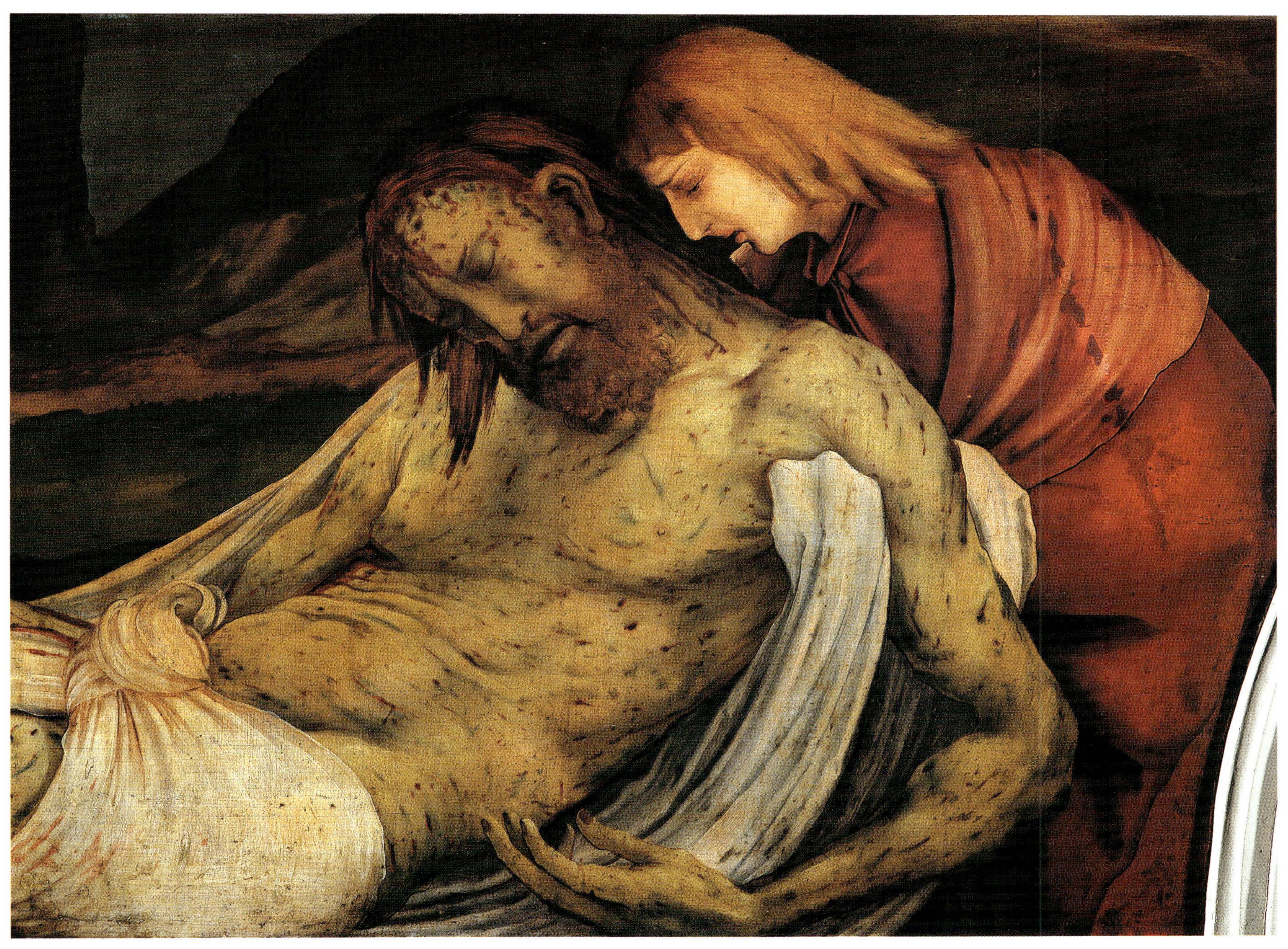

"When the recognition of a single person by a great number becomes quite shameless, this marks the beginning of glory."

F. Nietzsche
Die Fröhliche Wissenschaft
(The Joyous Science)

Grünewald (Mathis Gothart Nithart, known as) c. 1475/1480-1528
Issenheim retable. The entombment.
Detail: John supporting Christ, c. 1512-1516
Colmar, Musée d'Unterlinden

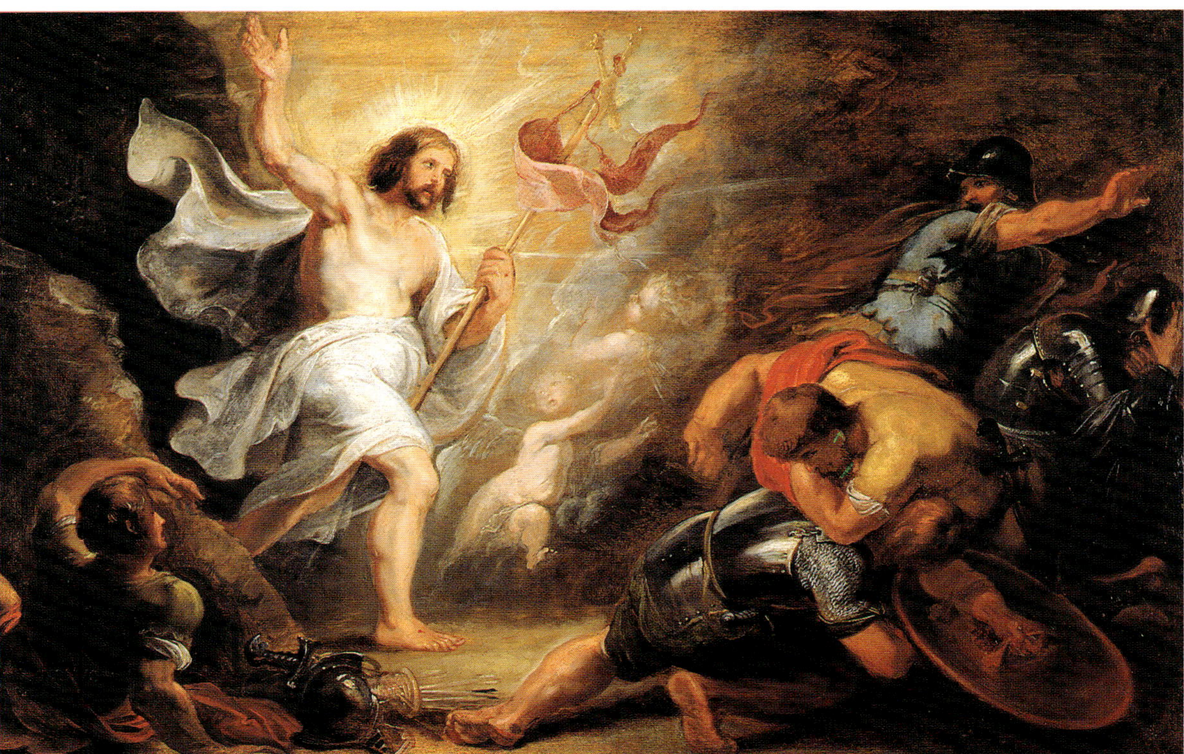

The image of the invisible

Painting the resurrection means making the invisible visible, depicting the unthinkable and trying to give form to the infinite. It is not Christ the man who rises from the dead, but the living image of the Father. The body that is taken down from the Cross is just a corpse, a dead form, whereas the One walking towards Emmaus is the perceptible form of the Creator. He is a transfigured body. But what is a transfigured body? Paul's reply in his First Epistle to the Corinthians, Chapter 15, is that it is a "spiritual body. If there is a physical body, there is also a spiritual body," meaning a body in the spirit, a mental body which is attuned to the idea of a body of light, taken up again in the episode of the transfiguration. This is not matter of some sort reflecting light, but a body that is itself light and the source of that light, an energy *causa sui*, giving origin to itself, which is one of the attributes of the Creator.

What is being represented here is a play of light, just as the deposition in contrast is playing with matter. A sinister, onlooking light bathes the deposition, whereas light emanates from the very body of Christ once the resurrection has taken place, opening up the way to the idea of a shape that is nothing but light.

Considered from this point of view, the resurrection might be regarded as the emblematic theme of the painting. It may also be regarded as such insofar as a painting is just a painted instant, suspended between what has come before and what will come after, marking the break between the two. Unlike writing, which deploys its narrative web in duration, the picture is obliged to condense a whole plot into a single act, a single gesture. That instant which Roland Barthes calls a *numen* "is like the silent gesture of a god who brings a destiny into being by a simple inflection of his will without even making any comment or explanation regarding that destiny. [...] The pictorial *numen* is a kind of absolute event which in some way *checkmates* interpretation."

The resurrection is the *numen* of the history of mankind. Everything refers back to it and everything flows from it: as the end of the earthly kingdom and the promise of the heavenly kingdom, the instant of the resurrection is the crucial moment when the human and the divine, the finite and the infinite, the before and the after interpenetrate one another: "For as in Adam all die, so also in Christ shall all be made alive" (1 Corinthians 15:22), Paul wrote to the Corinthians. It is a crossing of the ways, the instant when a choice is made and salvation for humankind becomes possible – though this does not mean that sin has been abolished ("For some have no knowledge of God" {Paul, 1 Corinthians 15:34}), but that it has ceased to be the inevitable fate of men. This might also be interpreted symbolically as an act of exorcism and a rehabilitation of the image.

Rubens (Peter Paul) 1577-1640
Resurrection of Christ
Marseilles, Musée des Beaux-Arts

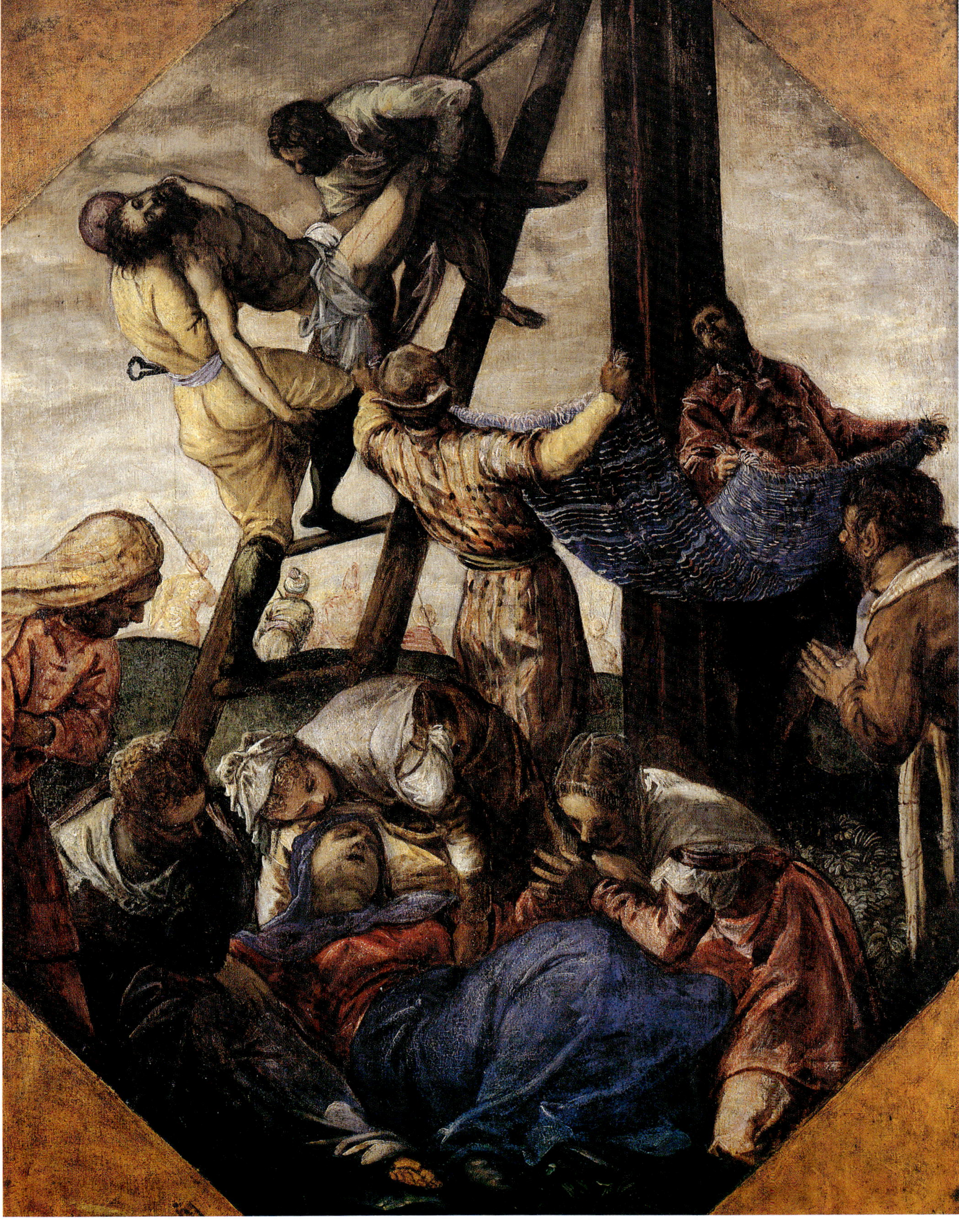

While a bleeding body is being brought down and people believe they are lamenting the death of a man, the spirit rises and departs. What in fact gives the scene its meaning is elsewhere, in the before and the after. The true subject of this painting, beyond the actual episode, is invisible.

Tintoretto (Jacopo Robusti, known as) 1518-1594
Deposition, c. 1560-1565
Caen, Musée des Beaux-Arts

The road to Damascus

The word apostle comes from the Greek *apostolos,* meaning "envoy." They were sent by Christ "to the ends of the earth" to bear witness to the Gospel preached by their master. The witnesses were apostles and martyrs, with the two concepts being closely linked. They suffered martyrdom in their bodies to bear witness to the coming of the kingdom of the spirit, the Holy Spirit, who inspired and guided them, conferring on them some of the "supernatural" powers that had been Jesus' prerogative.

When he chose them, Jesus had already warned them of the dangers of their mission. "I send you out as sheep in the midst of wolves; so be wise as serpents and innocent as doves. Beware of men; for they will deliver you up to councils, and flog you in their synagogues, and you will be dragged before governors and kings for my sake, to bear testimony before them and the Gentiles. When they deliver you up, do not be anxious how you are to speak or what you are to say; for what you are to say will be given to you in that hour; for it is not you who speak, but the Spirit of your Father speaking through you" (Matthew 10:16-20).

In the years following the death of Jesus the word apostle was applied by extension to Christian missionaries such as Paul and Barnabas, who had never in fact associated with Jesus. Paul, whose Jewish first name was Saul, belonged to the tribe of Benjamin. He was a Pharisee, and very active in hounding down the members of the first Christian community in Jerusalem. After being granted permission by the high priests to go to Damascus to carry out the same task there, he was struck blind on the way and did not recover his sight until three days and three nights had passed, through the grace of the Holy Spirit. The conversion of this sworn enemy of the Christians created a great stir among them and among the Jews in Damascus and Jerusalem. Pursued by his former friends, the Pharisees, Paul was arrested after making three great journeys in Asia Minor, Cyprus and Greece. He was taken to Rome c. 60 AD to be tried there as his status as a Roman citizen required, and condemned and executed in the reign of Nero four or seven years later.

Paul had chosen to take his message to the Gentiles (non-Jews) and he was their greatest apostle. When an apostolic council was held in Jerusalem in 48 AD to decide whether newly converted heathens had to be circumcised in accordance with the law of Moses, the apostles accepted Paul's view that observance of the law of Moses was irrelevant to the Gentiles: a very important decision for the Christian church as it opened the way to universality. But at the same time it meant a break with the Old Covenant, of which circumcision was a reminder and a mark, thereafter replaced by the New Covenant, celebrated in the rite of the Eucharist in the material form of bread (the body of Christ) and wine (the blood of Christ). This was an exemplary piece of intuition, arising from the substitution of the concept of love for that of being chosen; it brought about the change from early Christianity to Catholicism, which in its etymological sense means a universal religion.

Cuyp (Kiup Aelbert, known as) 1620-1691
Conversion of St. Paul or The road to Damascus
Amiens, Musée de Picardie

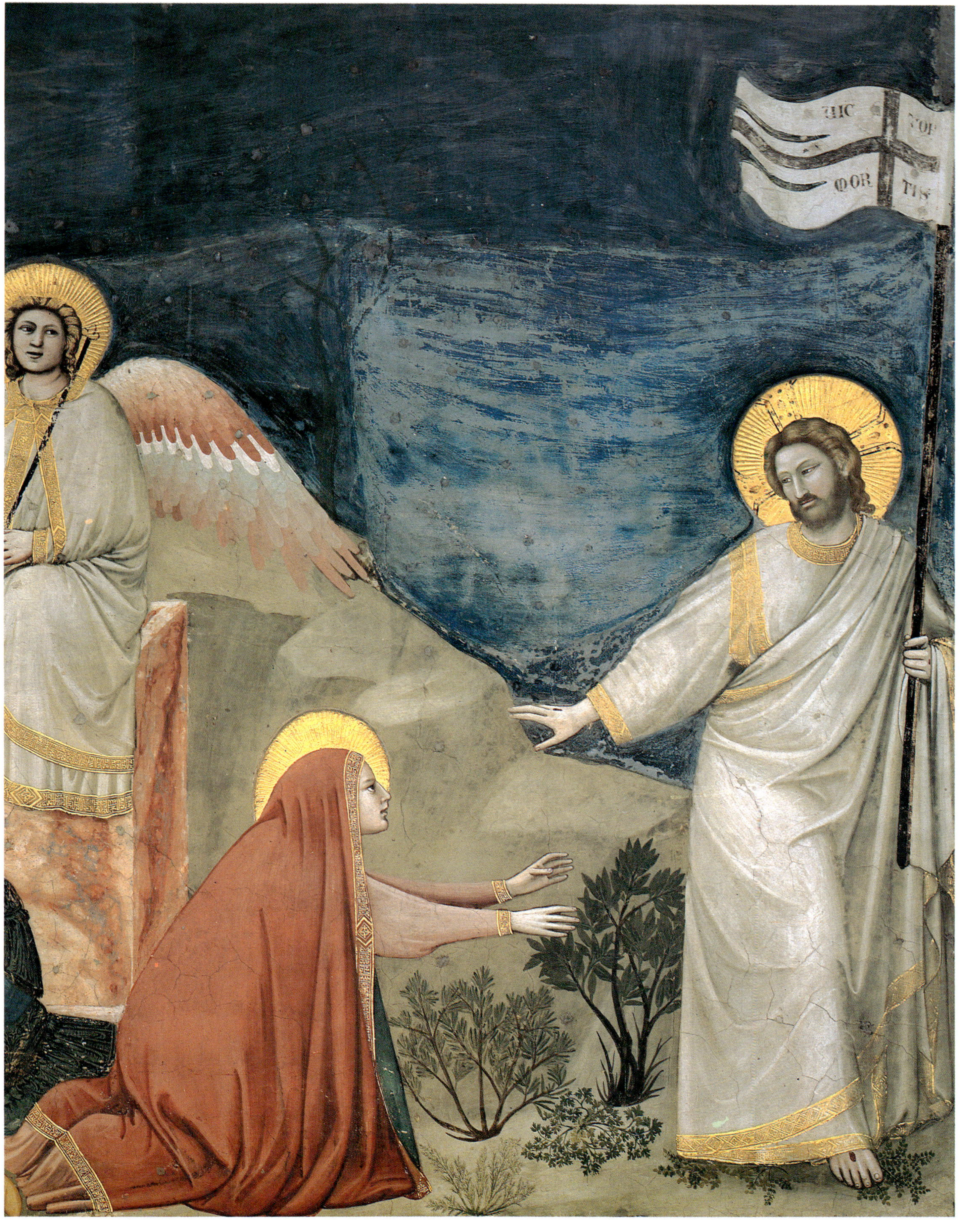

"Jesus said to her [Mary Magdalene], 'Do not hold me, for I have not yet ascended to the Father; but go to my brethren and say to them, I am ascending to my Father and your Father, to my God and your God.' Mary Magdalene went and said to the disciples, 'I have seen the Lord'; and she told them that he had said these things to her."

(Gospel according to John 20:17-18).

Giotto (Giotto di Bondone, known as) c. 1266/1267-1337
Noli me tangere or Christ appearing to Mary Magdalene (after restoration)
Detail: Christ and Mary Magdalene, 1303-1305
Padua, Scrovegni chapel

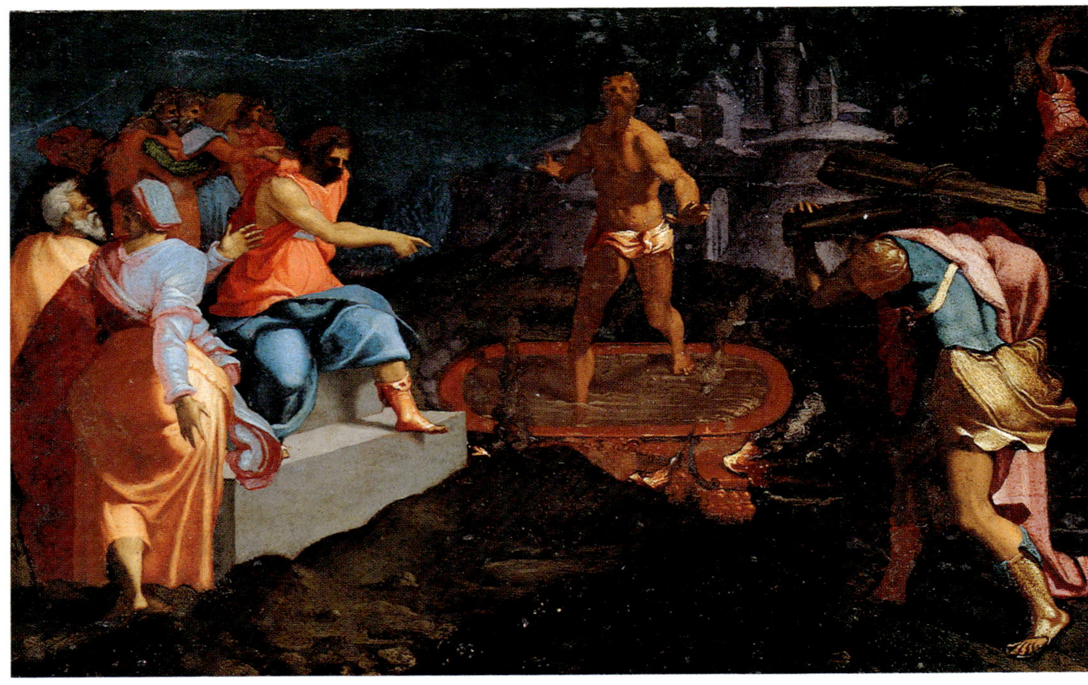

Blissful death

The idea of martyrdom is in itself quite simple: it is a matter of proving the existence of God the Redeemer through total indifference to suffering and death. The martyr must be the image of living faith, a person who renounces the uncertainties of the moment in exchange for eternal salvation, who quite literally forgets him or herself to offer himself to his God.

Martyrdom as an example also foreshadows the dualism of soul and body which was a structuring factor in Christian thought in the Middle Ages: "I abandon my body to save my soul." In his Second Letter to the Corinthians, Paul was already underlining the problem raised by the body that is subjected to martyrdom and by the idea of a resurrection of our bodies on the day of the Last Judgment. If the body is only a perishable envelope, then its martyrdom has little value. But since it is made in the image of God, it is also part of the divine spark that survives within us. This raises a difficulty, a mystery, which Paul resolves by making a subtle distinction between the visible earthly body and the invisible celestial body. In other words, all earthly images are imperfect. All that can be perceived by the eye is a sign of the finite nature of our earthly existence ("For we know that if the earthly tent [body] we live in is destroyed, we have a building from God, a house not made with hands, eternal in the heavens" 2 Corinthians 5:1). And this culminates quite strangely in the paradox of martyrdom as one of the richest sources of inspiration of Christian iconography (here that of St. John the Evangelist, painted by Daniele da Volterra). But this may be only an unfortunate, late effect of the example provided by martyrdom, as the first Christians made no distinction between the body and the soul: this was something invented by Church theologians. In the eyes of the early Christians man was still an image of God, a unitary being. It was only with the coming of the concept of Purgatory and the development of fundamentally dualist theories such as Catharism that the idea of martyrdom became associated with contempt for the body and hatred of the flesh. The medieval fondness for infernal iconography was the result of this development. Nonetheless, when Giotto painted his *Last Judgment* at a time when the Pope was no longer based in Rome and the Franciscans were virtually suspected of heresy, when Christianity was at a very low ebb, his message rang out like a call to return to the simplicity of the first centuries of the faith. With its simple realism his *Hell* seems to remind us of our duty to respect the body while at the same time not using it as an instrument of lasciviousness: a body which has sought only enjoyment on earth will atone for its fleeting pleasures through everlasting martyrdom.

To sum up, the martyr does not abandon his body because he despises it; on the contrary, he makes this abandonment a gift to the God he loves – a gift which associates love and suffering, where the pain of the ordeal can hardly be distinguished from the joy arising from the unconditional surrender of oneself. Martyrdom is an act of faith through which the victim chooses to imitate Christ to the very point of death: communion with Jesus in the form of the sacrifice of the body.

Daniele da Volterra (Ricciarelli Daniele, known as) 1509-1566
Martyrdom of St. John the Evangelist
Douai, Musée de la Chartreuse

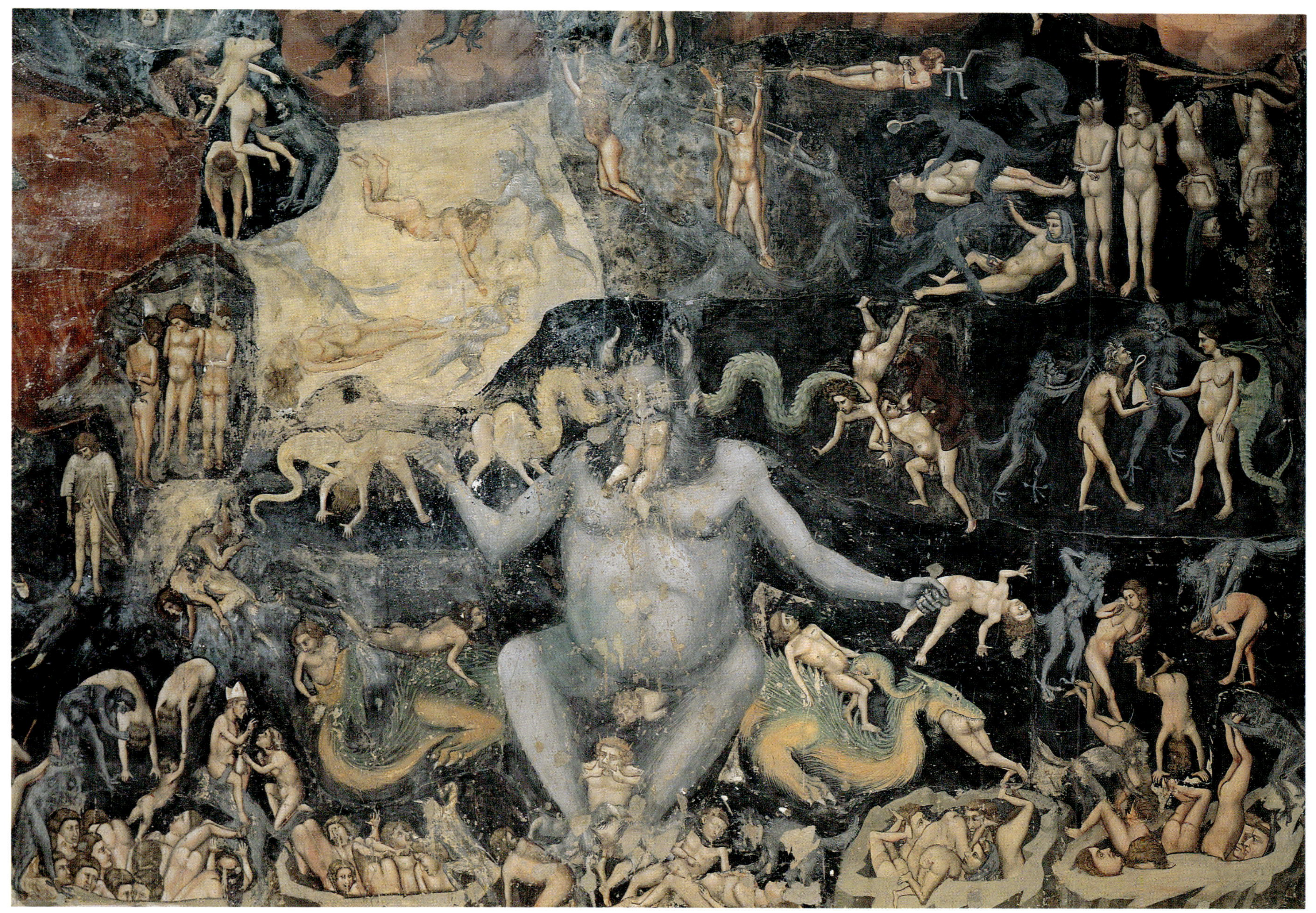

"But as for the cowardly, the faithless, the polluted, as for murderers, fornicators, sorcerers, idolaters, and all liars, their lot shall be in the lake that burns with fire and brimstone, which is the second death."

(Revelations 21:8).

Giotto (Giotto di Bondone, known as) c. 1266/1267-1337
Last Judgment. Hell (after restoration)
Detail: Satan among the damned, c. 1303-1305
Padua, Scrovegni chapel

50

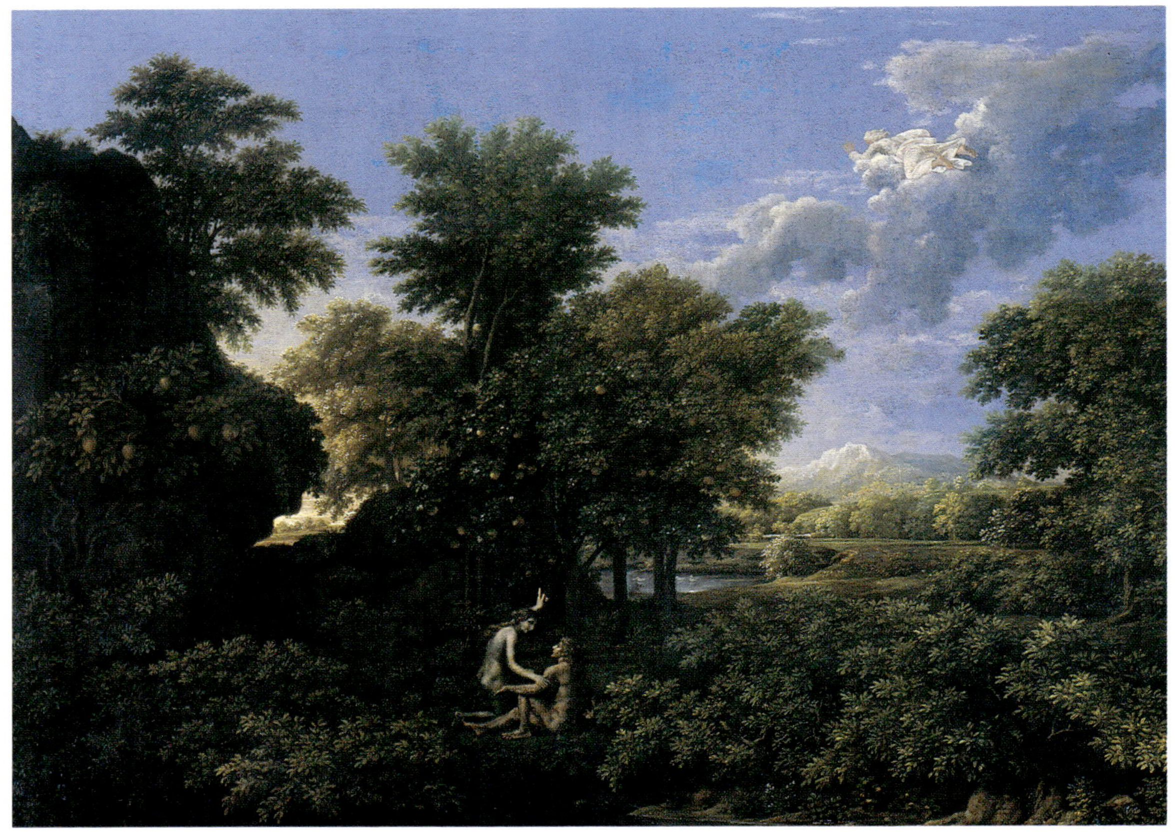

Poussin (Nicolas) 1594-1665
Spring or Earthly paradise
Paris, Louvre

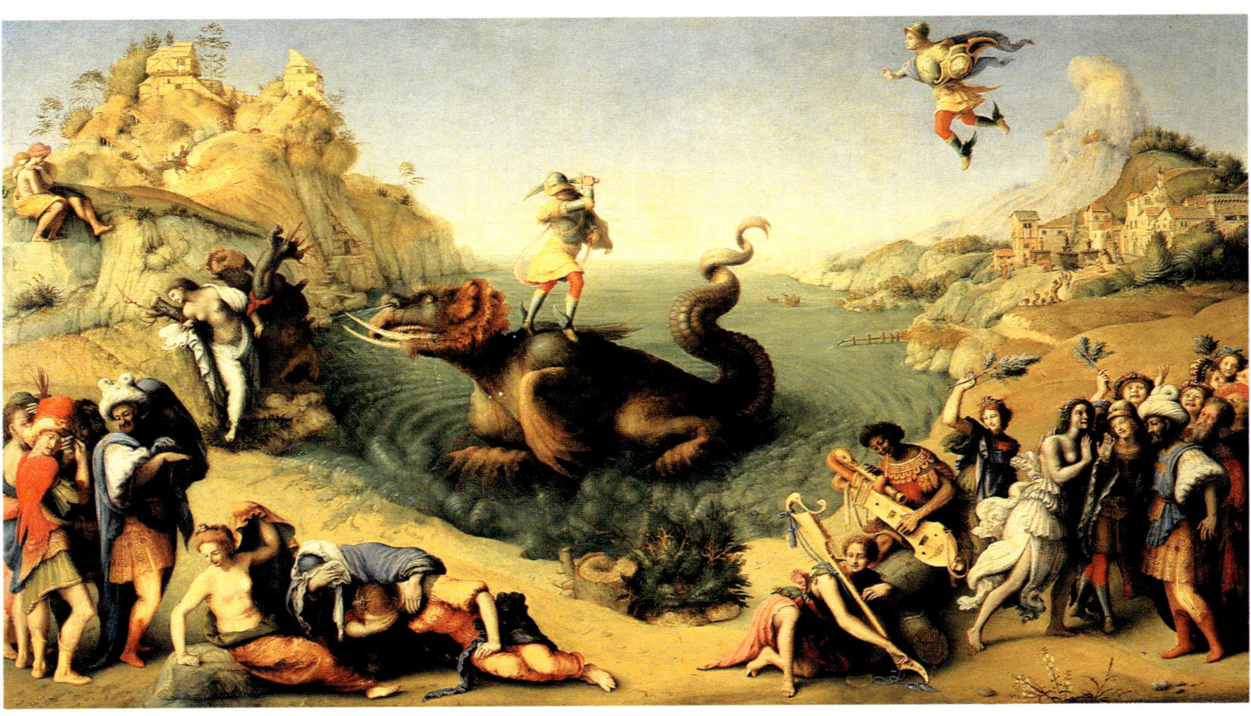

Monsters as a mirror

Monsters come from the dark and mysterious depths of the sea or the earth. They are themselves a mystery and also the guardians of mystery. They embody the transgression of an order, the overthrow of a state. The monster is a mutant, and any transformation or development implies going through a monstrous phase preceding and preparing for rebirth. It was by this kind of logic that Robespierre justified the Reign of Terror. The day of the monster is a period of chaos and confusion. Representing disorder, monsters herald the death of the old order and the coming of the new. As guardians of mystery, they are an obstacle that cannot be bypassed, indicating the presence of some other place symbolized by a treasure to which they guard the entrance. That is why overcoming a monster also implies conquering oneself. The man who confronts it will surely die, either to disappear for ever, or to be reborn as a hero. Thus there is an ambivalence between good and evil in the monster, which is both a symbol of material powers and something that must be traversed to reach the realm of the Spirit, without our ever knowing exactly who has sent it or why.

Monsters are tests imposed on men to try them. This is true of the Leviathan, "king over all the sons of pride" (Job 41.34). "His sneezings flash forth light, and his eyes are like the eyelids of the dawn. Out of his mouth go flaming torches; sparks of fire leap forth" (Job 41:18-19). A creature of water and fire, the Leviathan is a metaphor for ambition, sleeping at the bottom of the sea as temptation slumbers deep in our consciousness.

If we accept that monsters are the form taken by our phantasms, we will also accept that every monster, and possibly even more the way in which the hero overcomes it, reveal something about the civilization that produces them.

Piero di Cosimo, who appreciated the ease with which antiquity combined realism and fantasy, chose Perseus as a subject for his painting. As always in Greek legends, myth and reality coexist side by side: Andromeda, a young virgin offered as a sacrifice to Poseidon to assuage his anger, is about to be devoured by a horrible sea monster. Perseus turns up and offers to rescue her. The values glorified by his exploit are valor and cunning, combined with a sound business sense: "If [Andromeda] is mine once she has been rescued thanks to my courage, I will undertake to do it," is the offer the hero makes to her terrified parents as the monster draws near to her. "Her parents accept the conditions – who would have hesitated? – beg him to act, and promise him a kingdom as a dowry into the bargain" (Ovid, *Metamorphoses*, IV). As it is a good deal, Perseus honors it immediately, slaying the beast and taking possession of the young girl.

It is a different story where Job is concerned: he triumphs in the test by refusing to confront the Leviathan and humbling himself before God. What we learn is this: monsters are mirrors and the truth they contain depends on the nature of their opponent.

Piero di Cosimo (Piero di Lorenzo, known as) 1461/62-1521
Perseus and Andromeda
Florence, Uffizi

"This garden does not represent Adam and Eve fulfilling God's command; on the contrary it shows how they transgressed. Man [...] has turned his back on the fountain of life to drink at the fountain of the senses which like the fountain in the 'Rose' is intoxicating, but fatal."

Walter Bosing
Hieronymus Bosch

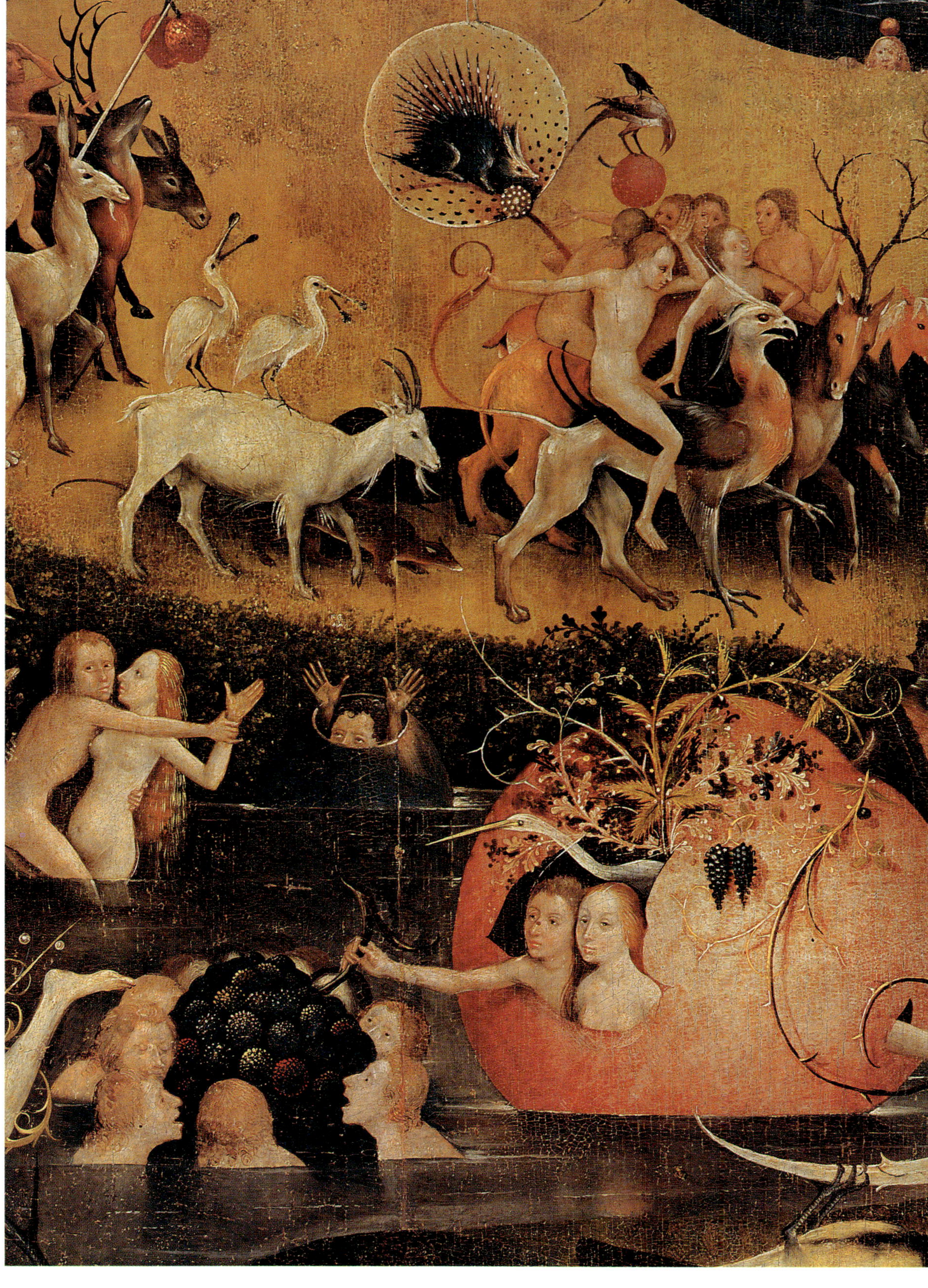

Bosch (Hieronymus Van Aecken, known as) c. 1453-1516
The garden of delights
Details from the central panel: fantastic animals, c. 1500-1516
Madrid, Prado

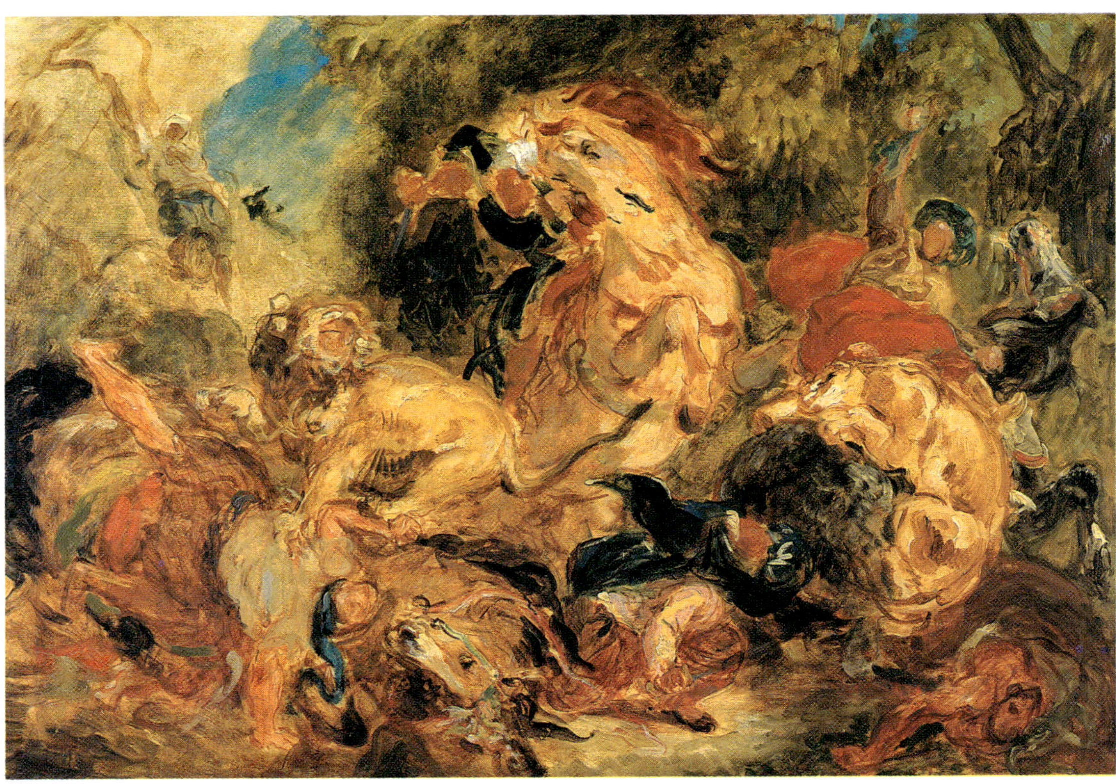

The hunter and his prey

Compared with demonological iconography, the portrayal of large wild animals such as lions and tigers strikes us as almost serene. While they offer an image of potential violence, it is nonetheless within the context of natural order. Monsters remind us of our secret terrors, whereas wild animals are indisputably external to us. Studied, listed, cataloged, they provide a useful touch of exoticism without threatening our sense of security. Images domesticate and tame them, making their wildness familiar to us. And in spite of everything we feel we do in fact belong to this animal kingdom, as scientists since Darwin have told us. Monsters endanger the order of things, while large wild animals confirm it. After man, they represent the next highest link in the great chain of life. Therefore it is only fair that after hunting the gazelle, the lion should in turn be hunted by man. That is how things should be and how they are, beautiful and reassuring like a lovely harmony. The combat between man and beast has the beauty of a classical tragedy because it restores man to his proper place in the universe: even Hemingway's old man in *The Old Man and the Sea* emerges victorious from his struggle, even though his catch is eaten by sharks. He has won because the combat has given him back his place at the heart of creation. Hunting is a hymn to nature: that is the hunter's mythology. No matter if not everyone agrees. The hunter exists and demands to be painted, alongside his victim.

When Troy painted a hunting scene, he was not painting nature, but the society of his day. While Rousseau in the mid-18th century was outlining the fundamentals of a social contract based on the natural equality of all men, the aristocracy took refuge in their own principles, reaffirming the values of the only natural right in which they believed: the right of the strongest, the right of might, the right of blood. In a society defined as being naturally unequal and hierarchical, one with different social orders such as the *ancien régime* in France, hunting was the prerogative of the nobility. The common people labored, the clergy prayed and the nobility carried arms, at war or while hunting.

With the coming of the Romantic movement things changed to some extent, but essentially they remained the same. Influenced by Byron and his chimeras, Delacroix exalts a different kind of nobility, the nobility of the heart and of adventure, but elitism is still present, tinged with a rather knowing condescension towards these strange, picturesque lands. The Romantic artist, basically in agreement with the nobility of the *ancien régime* though for different reasons, rejected the middle-class rationalism which was becoming the norm in the 19th century, just as he rejected its corollary, the Industrial Revolution.

The Romantic was attracted by the elegance of inequality, by natural violence, chaos and tumult, imagining upheavals that only wild nature – or revolution – could provide: nature which ultimately combines excess and harmony.

Delacroix (Eugène) 1798-1863
Lion hunt
Paris, Musée d'Orsay

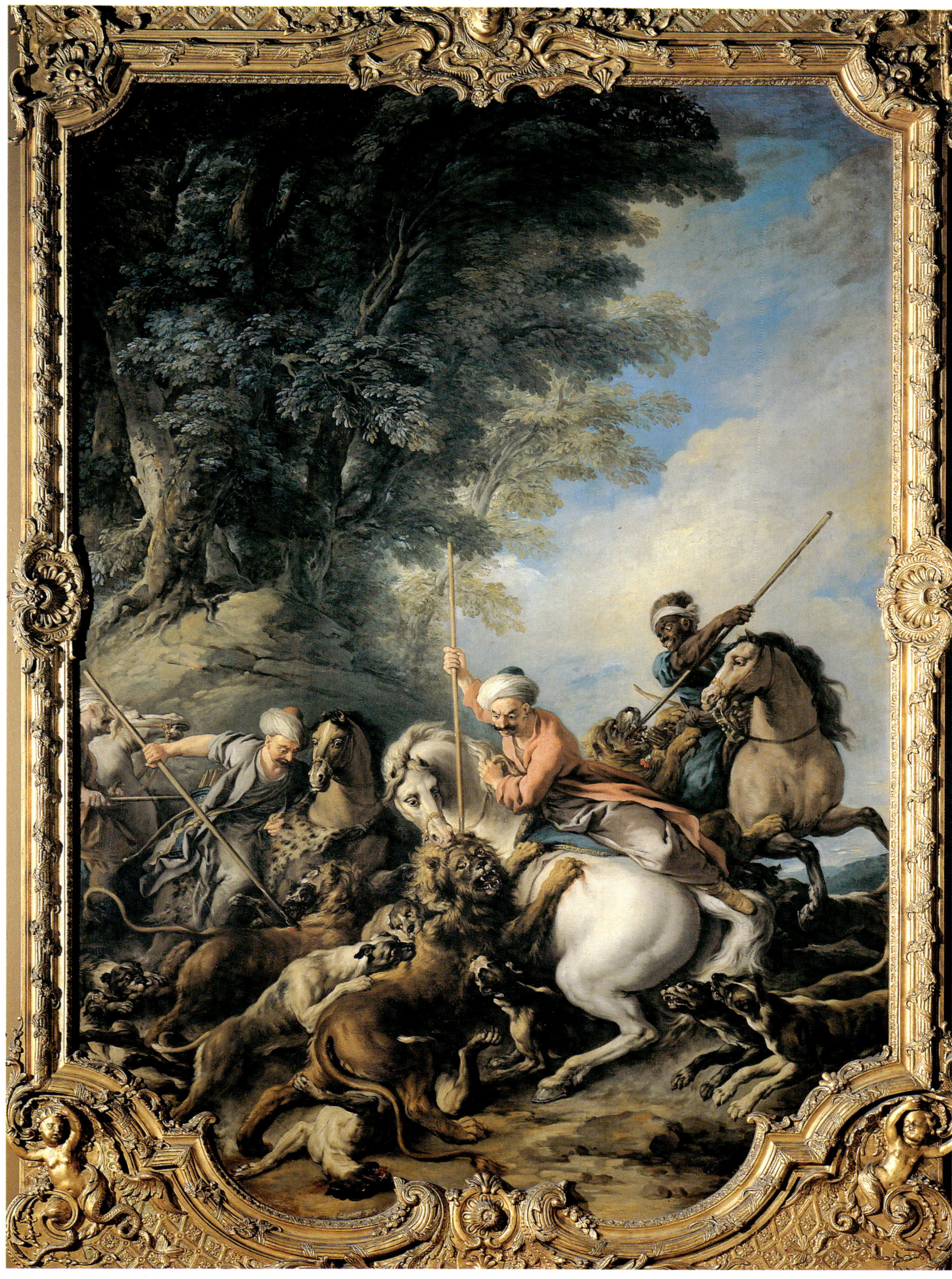

Troy made a specialty of hunting scenes, which were a reminder, amid the ostentatious luxury of Versailles, of the "natural" origins of the nobility now committed to a life of idleness.

Troy (Jean-François de) 1679-1752
Lion hunt by the Turks
Amiens, Musée de Picardie

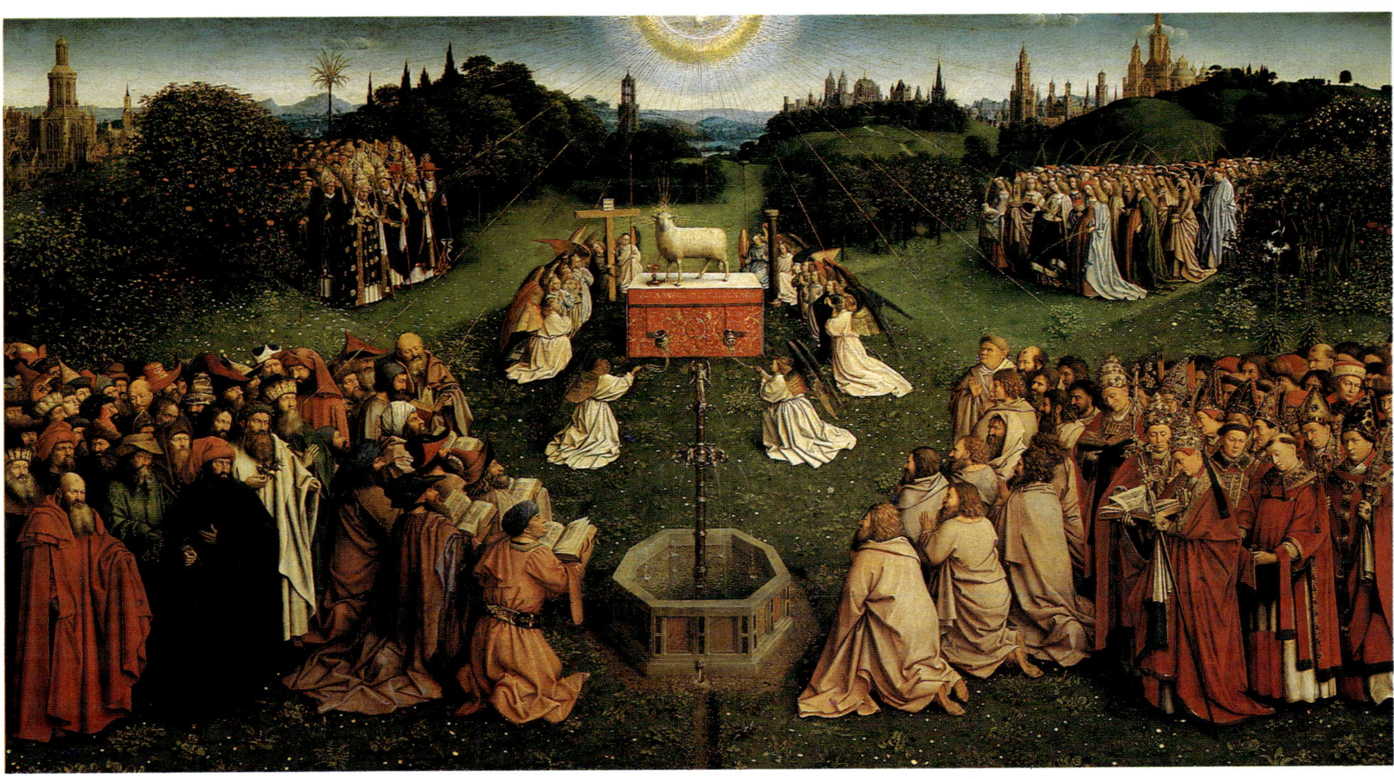

The beast and the symbol

Animals – the bronze serpent or the mystic Lamb – can also becomes signs, signifying something other than their own existence and becoming a mystic symbol. The episode relating to the bronze serpent recounted in Numbers and depicted by Vouet describes how the Jews who had followed Moses out of Egypt began to tire of their sojourn in the desert and spoke against their God: "Then the Lord sent fiery serpents among the people, and they bit the people, so that many people of Israel died. And the people came to Moses, and said, 'We have sinned, for we have spoken against the Lord and against you; pray to the Lord, that he take away the serpents from us.' So Moses prayed for the people. And the Lord said to Moses, 'Make a fiery serpent, and set it on a pole, and everyone who is bitten, when he sees it, shall live.'" (Numbers 21:6-8).

Jesus referred back to this story, comparing himself to the bronze serpent (John 3:14-15), allowing Jean Borella to comment that "the serpent is not necessarily a symbol of evil, for Moses, Christ or Christian exegesis." Thus, bearing in mind that monsters belong to the world of the imagination and wild animals to the world of nature, we can accept that symbolic animals belong to the world of the intellect. The first is a vector for phantasms, the second for reality, and the third for meaning. The serpent or Christ on the Cross – since symbols become confused – indicates that it is possible for destiny to have a meaning, in this case salvation. Those who look at the sign will be saved. This symbol is redemptive: the image saves man from chaos and every plastic artist in the world, be he painter, sculptor or architect, anyone and everyone who strives to give form to what is formless, snatches some share of Being from chaos. Considered in this way, the symbolic animal is the luminous version of the monster which operates only at the heart of the chaos, incarnating its impossible form.

The Mystic Lamb, another symbol of Christ, assumes all the sins of the world. The sacrificial Lamb is there to cleanse the world of evil: its sacrifice is the necessary prerequisite for the collective salvation of mankind. In this we recognize the exact definition of the role of the Messiah. The Lamb is the symbol of Christ, and Christ the symbol of God. There again we find a sign, i.e. a perceptible form intended to convey a meaning. But the sign is not God, just as the image is not reality, merely the idea I have of it. The idolater believes that the divinity is present in the image, confusing the sign and its objective referent, i.e. God. This was the mistake made by the Israelites in the desert when they tired of waiting for Moses to come back and decided to worship the golden calf. In their mind the golden calf was not a symbol; it was not the image of a god, but the god himself.

Considered in this light, the great polyptych of the *Adoration of the Mystic Lamb* by Hubert and Jan Van Eyck, for the very reason that it is a mystic painting, might be described as an abstract painting.

Van Eyck (Hubert and Jan) c. 1366?-1426 and c. 1390/1400-1441
Polyptych of the Mystic Lamb
Central panel: Adoration of the Lamb, 1432
Ghent, St. Bavo's Cathedral

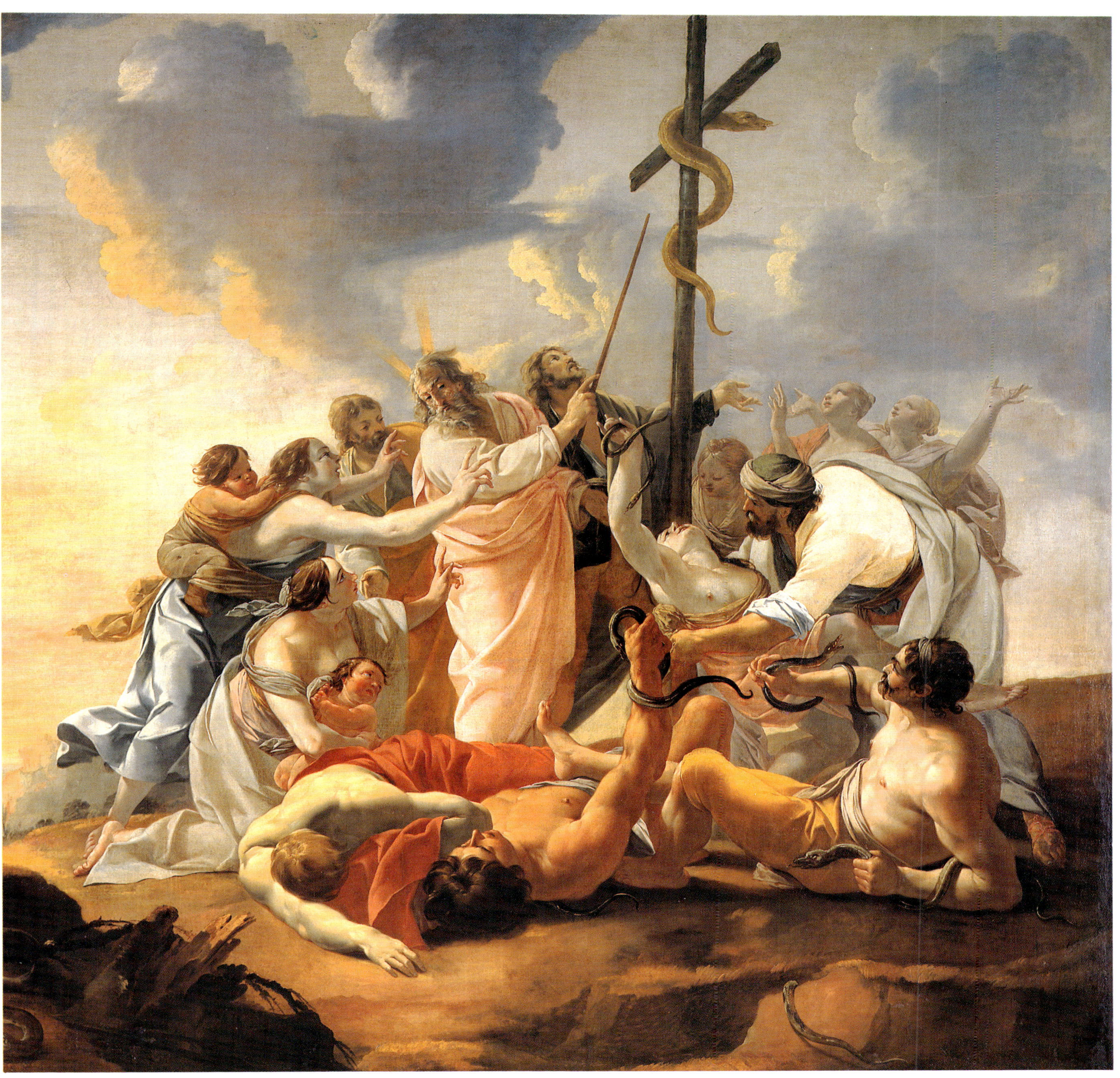

Hardly threatened by Poussin's stay in Paris (1640-1642), Vouet reigned supreme over French painting and taste between 1630 and 1649, the year of his death, establishing a style inherited from Correggio and Parmigianino and tempered by the lessons of Bolognese "Classicism."

Vouet (Simon) 1590-1649
The bronze serpent (detail)
Toulouse, Musée des Augustins

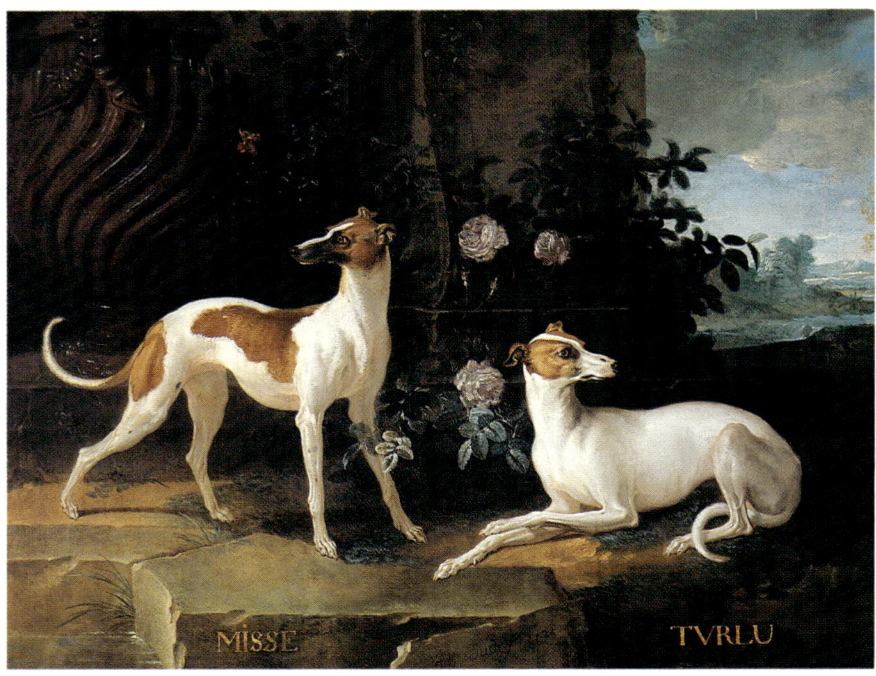

Of dogs and goldfish

Finally we come to the last form of animal representation, the domestic pet, a kind of animate object, a decorative motif of varying shape, a pictorial counterpoint to the main subject and in extreme cases no more than a touch of color. This brings us back to the original question: what are we painting when we paint a king's dog, what are we painting when we paint a goldfish? The realism with which Van Eyck depicted the Arnolfinis' dog has been praised. It may be the first "true" dog in the history of painting. But what is it doing in this domestic scene? It is certainly not a symbol in the sense that the Mystic Lamb and the bronze serpent are. We might be more inclined to say that it serves as an indicator of reality. As a pet it indicates the domestic indoor world where the wife reigns supreme. It is a fairly small dog with a bright, resolute look in its eye, reminding us of the social position of Signor Arnolfini, an Italian merchant living in Bruges in 1420. Thus it is an emblem rather than a symbol, insofar as the emblem has both a social and an ornamental connotation. The animal has not been included just because it "looks nice," but more specifically as an indicator of its master's esthetic sense. In looking at the dog, you are looking at the master. This also applies to Oudry's painting of Louis XV's bitches. They have natural elegance, come from a superior breed, and are thoroughbreds – everything testifies to the characteristics "naturally" appertaining to the aristocracy, even the touch of controlled fierceness implied by one animal's standing position: behind the elegance there is still strength and the instinct of the pack, the clan spirit, breeding.

Having read this far, the reader may well be wondering, "But what about the goldfish, which social class does it represent?" If someone other than Matisse had painted it, it might have been the emblem of the middle classes: no longer the ambitious townspeople of the 15th century, dissatisfied and expectant, but a social class that has "arrived," which has long since established its authority; like the goldfish, it has not enough to do, is bored, observes itself and turns in circles. It is a tempting analogy, but unfortunately wrong in the case of this picture: because Matisse's goldfish is not a goldfish. All it has retained of the goldfish is the oblong shape and the red-gold color. But the shape and color no longer refer to reality: abstraction is taking over from formalism. Writing in 1951 Henri Matisse said, "With more absolutism, more abstraction I achieved a form retaining only the essential, and of the object which I once used to present in the complexity of its space I kept only the sign; this is enough, and is essential to make it exist in its own form and for the setting in which I conceived it."

Everything that exists is reduced to its form and the form to its color. The painter is no longer a sociologist or historian, or even a metaphysician; he has become a pure plastic artist rejecting the opposition between the living and the mineral, the animal and the human: his only reality is that of color, i.e. light.

Oudry (Jean-Baptiste) 1686-1756
Misse and Turlu, two of Louis XV's greyhounds
Fontainebleau, Musée du Château

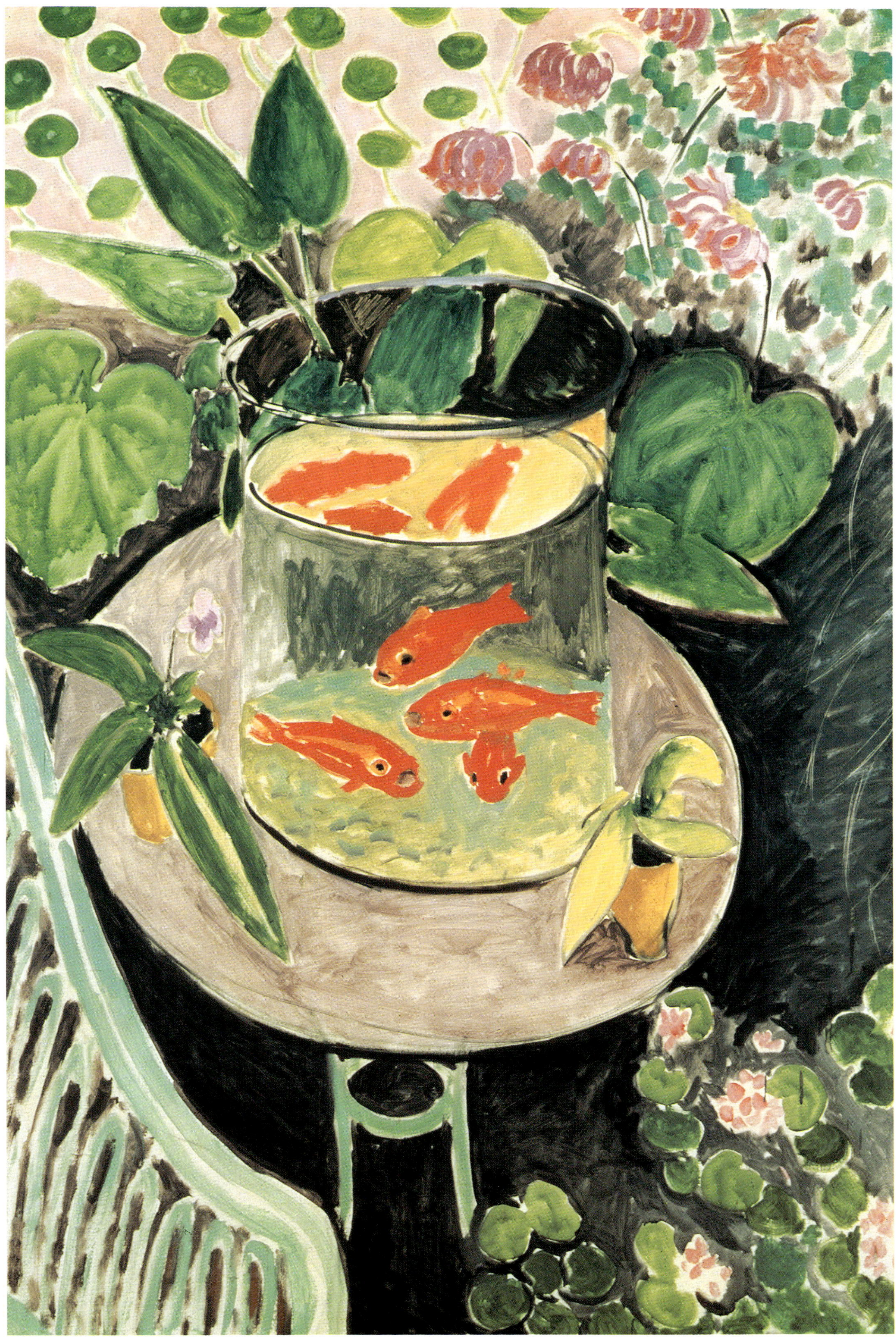

"I was not interested in copying a picture [...]. What point was there in copying an object which nature provides in countless numbers and which we can always imagine more beautiful? What is important is the relationship between the object and the artist [...] Only the plastic form has true value."

Henri Matisse

Matisse (Henri) 1869-1954
Goldfish, 1911
Moscow, Pushkin Museum

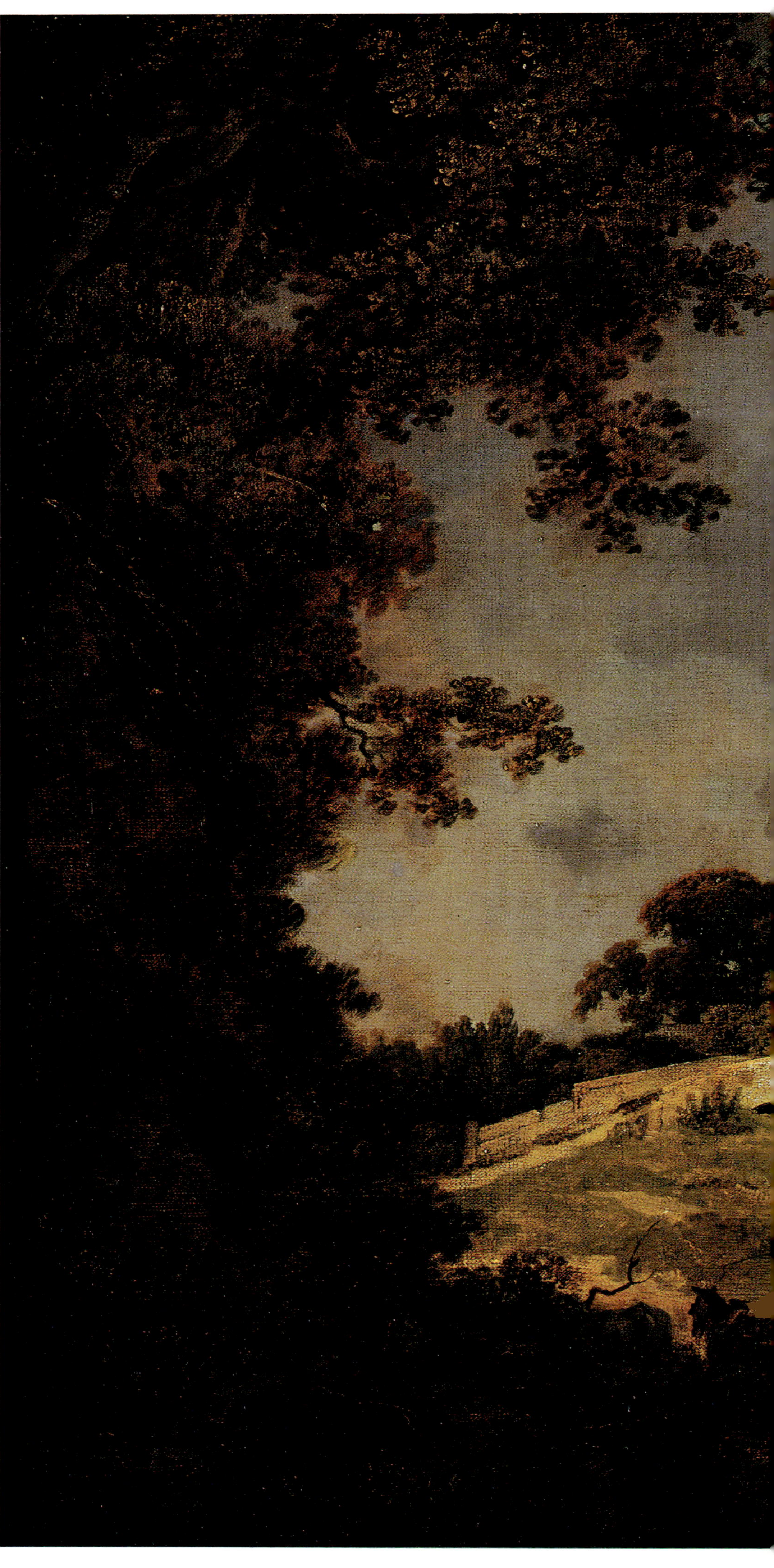

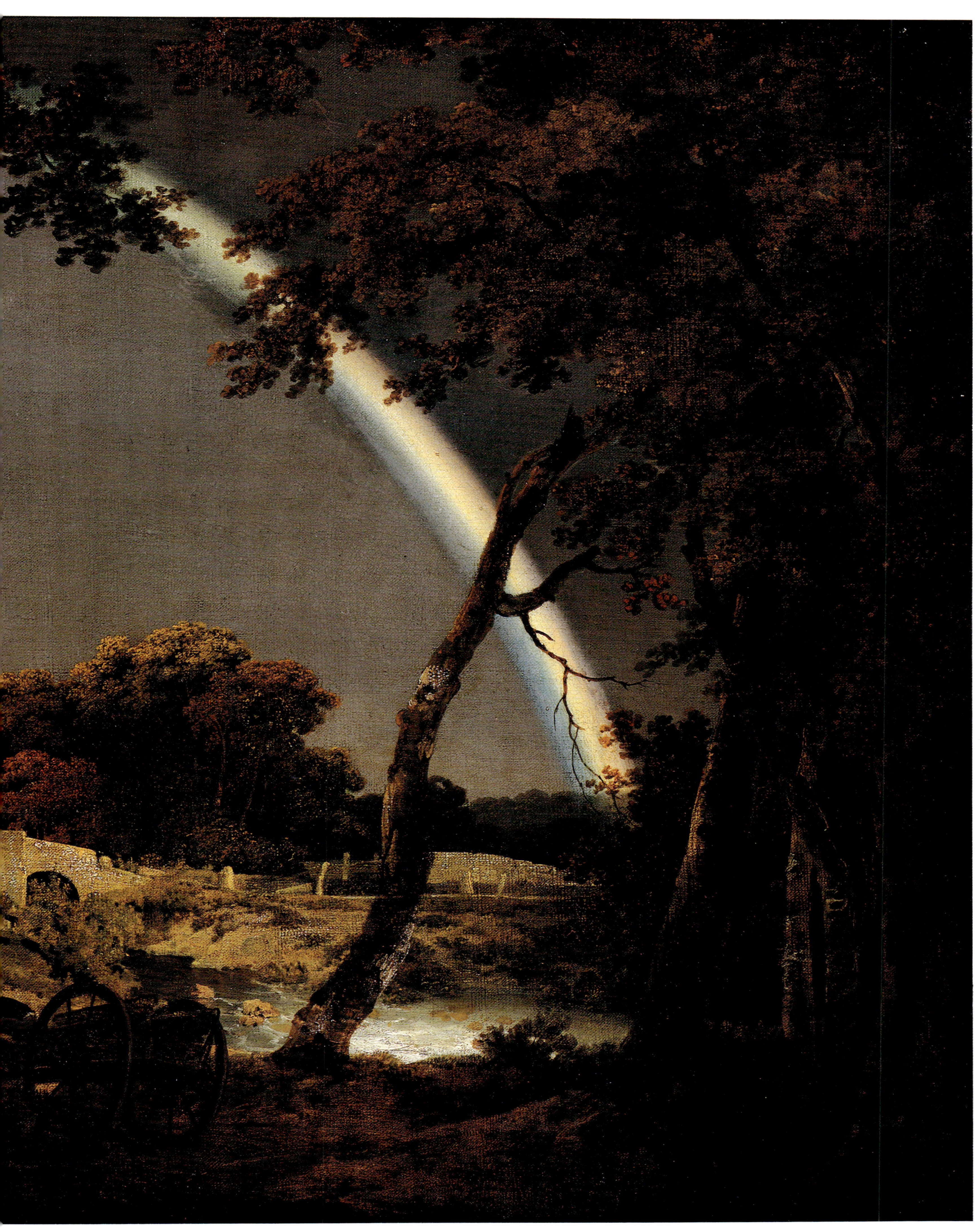

Wright of Derby (Joseph, known as) 1734-1797
Landscape with a rainbow, 1794
Derby, Museum and Art Gallery

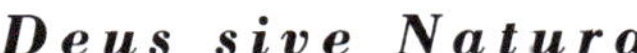

Deus sive Natura

Contrary to what people often think, in the Middle Ages people in the west regarded nature with the greatest suspicion. It was a theological period and could not get away from the idea of the earth as being marked by original sin. Those who worked the land, the peasants, were at the lowest rung on the human ladder. We have to wait for the first stirrings of the Renaissance at the beginning of the 15th century to see artists such as Altdorfer or the Limbourg brothers showing a true interest in landscape.

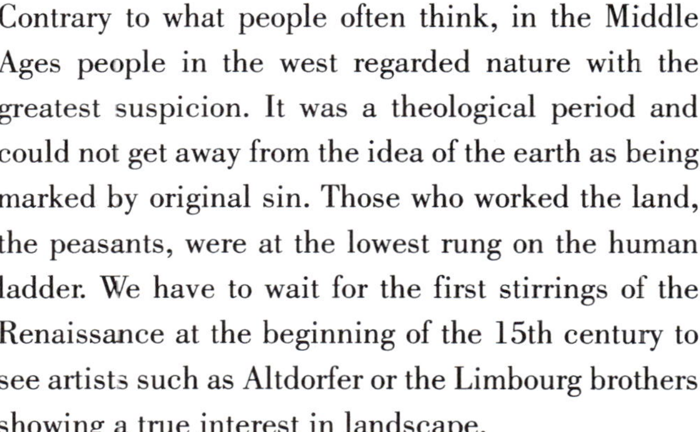

In the 17th century landscape was virtually accepted as a genre in its own right: a change of taste, probably, in an environment that was itself altering and becoming more "human," but also at a deeper level the return to the forefront of certain ideas of the world which had been dormant for more than 1000 years since the fall of the Roman Empire. In this connection we talk of a rediscovery of nature, but it is still necessary to state clearly what such a rediscovery presupposed.

The coherence of the Middle Ages was based on ideas of violence and the right of the strongest, and all social, cultural and religious relationships were structured round these. The Renaissance actually broke this state of affairs by substituting an ideal of balance and harmony for an ideal of power. Leonardo da Vinci sought this harmony in the proportions of the human body, and others after him looked for it in nature itself.

Therefore it seems safe to assume that the blossoming of landscape painting in the 17th century was linked with the rediscovery of the pantheistic doctrines which had dominated Hellenistic culture, and more particularly with the rediscovery of Stoicism. Seeking harmony in the spectacle afforded by nature implies a belief in the immanent presence of God in the world. Looked at like this, painting nature comes down to painting the image of the presence of the divine: not God himself, since this philosophy rejects the idea of a personal God, but the representation of his omnipresence, i.e. his omnipotence. Nature is not God (we are not dealing with animism), but God, as he is everything, is totally present in his creation as he is totally present in everything. Or, to put it another way, since God is nothing other than an absolute and universal presence, nature should be seen not as a product of creation, but as a perceptible form of God and so, like Him, as an eternal and infinite form that has not been created.

Poussin's and Claude Lorraine's painting is contemporary with (or earlier than) the pantheist ideas of Giordano Bruno and Spinoza. The feeling of harmony derived from studying a picture by Poussin cannot be reduced to a simple material harmony, any more than it points to a transcendent harmony belonging to the spirit: in Poussin's work matter and spirit merge in substance at the very point where our eye perceives what we call harmony. An image of the world, an image of God – these landscapes are much more than exercises in style: they are acts of faith.

Rubens (Peter Paul) 1577-1640
Landscape or Ruins from the Palatine Hill in Rome, c. 1600-1608
Paris, Louvre

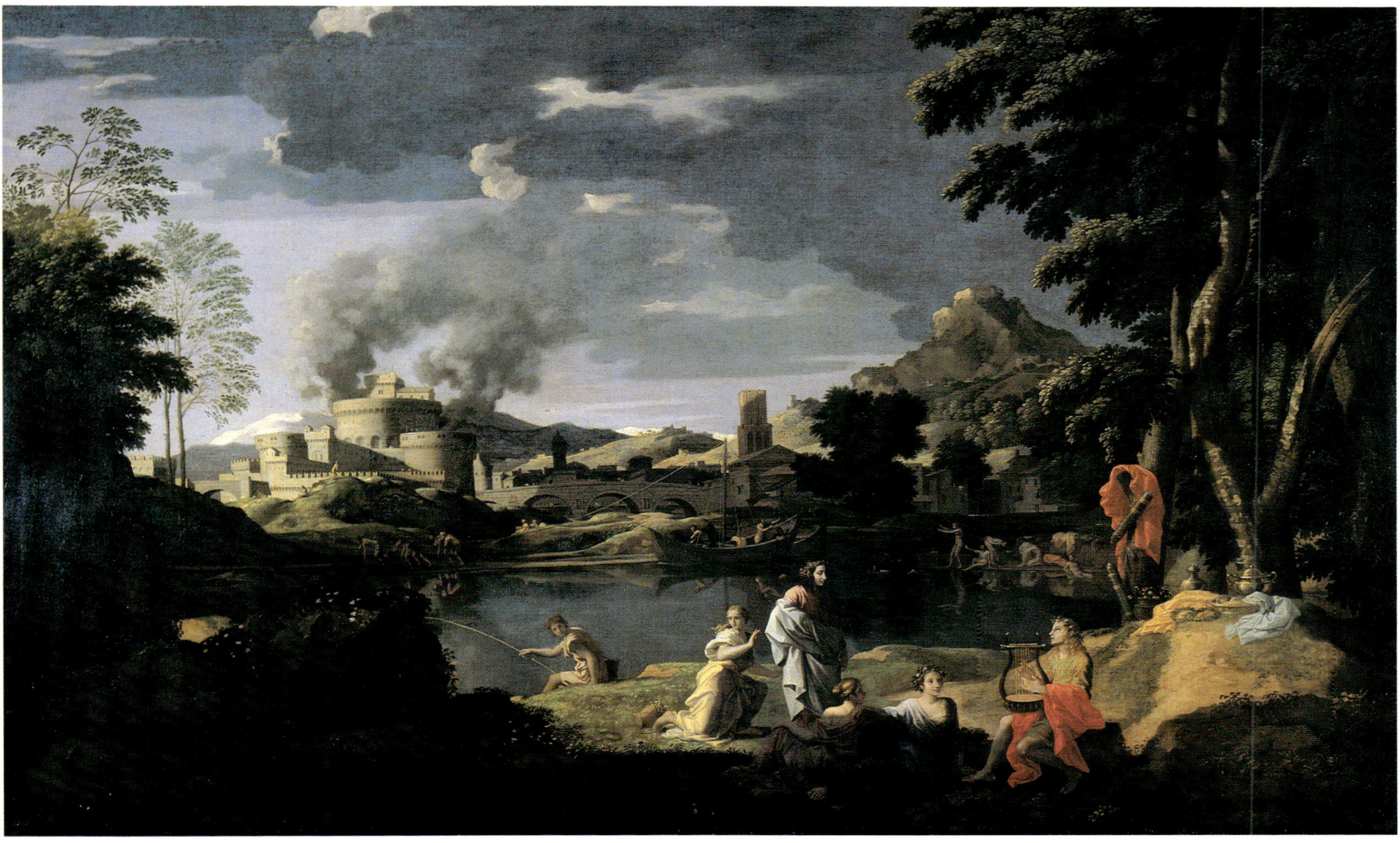

"In 17th-century landscapes [...] human action is no longer represented as a drama [...]. That is why the people are small and what they are doing is anecdotal even when the theme has been borrowed from antique history."

G.C. Argon

Poussin (Nicolas) 1594-1665
Orpheus and Eurydice
Paris, Louvre

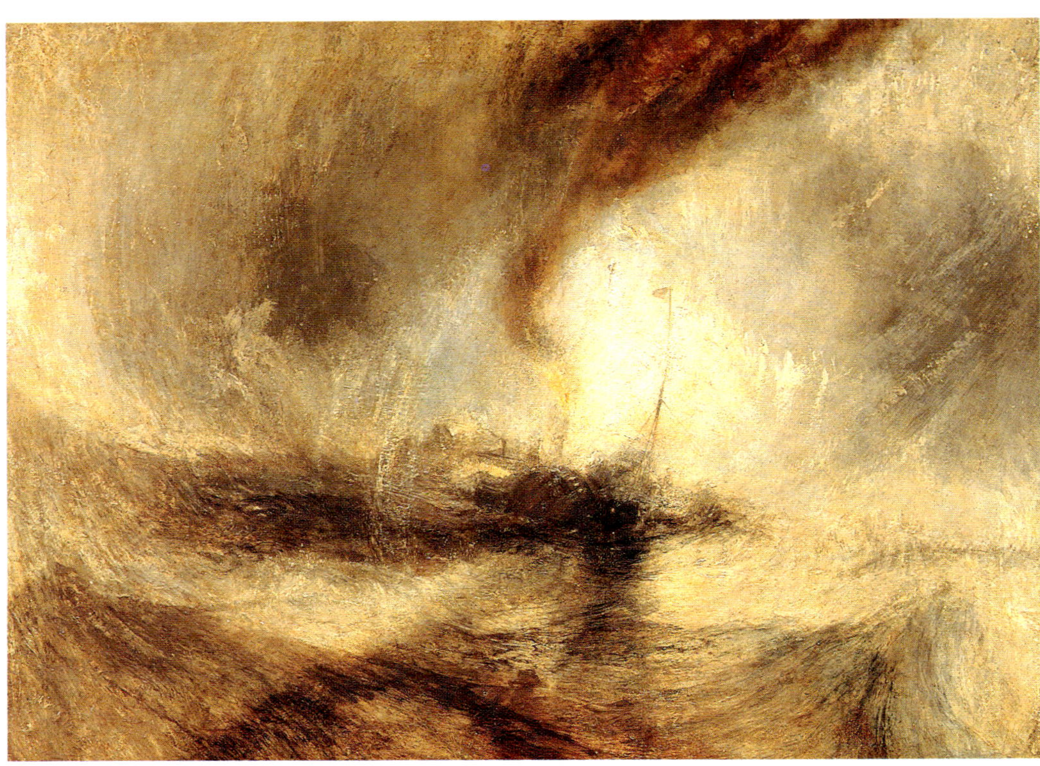

The fury of the elements

Without making it explicit, the concept of natural harmony implies the idea that nature is stable, with harmony and plenty as its attributes: eternal nature knowing nothing of time except the regular rhythm of the seasons. As the concrete form of the divine, this nature knows nothing of the void and can be composed only of a single matter. "I find it repugnant," Descartes wrote, "that a void or a place where absolutely nothing exists should be." Void is unthinkable in a universe entirely permeated with the presence of God; the matter constituting it, since it can come only from the Creator who is single and infinite, is like him limitless and uniform in substance.

By the end of the 17th century, however, the theory of universal gravity propounded by Newton had deeply shaken such certainties. His theory was warmly endorsed in France by Voltaire and obtained final acceptance in the 18th century. Van Leeuwenhoek perfecting the microscope in Delft carried out the first observations of protozoa, spermatozoids and microbes. Stretched to incredible limits in the direction of the infinitely large and the infinitely small by such discoveries, nature lost its reassuringly human dimension. In the field of biology, John Ray and then Linnaeus and Jussieu after him undertook the classification of the species, leading to a realization of their marvelous diversity. Their work was taken up and furthered by Buffon, leading in the mid-18th century to his monumental *Histoire naturelle.* The dream of immutable nature had collapsed. The dogma of creation out of nothing was swept aside, and the way opened to evolutionary theories. From then on, as Michel Le Bris put it, "nature has a history, but its history is not ours, man is not the measure of the world, but a wisp of straw tossed into a huge roaring river with no source and no end, cast into deep blackness. Then consciousness loses its bearings and doubts its powers: in this maelstrom bearing along eras, civilizations, continents, man appears negligible, moved by forces that are infinitely superior to him ...."

In ceasing to be ideal, nature becomes sublime. In Kant's words, "We call things that are great in absolute terms sublime," meaning things the limits of which we cannot apprehend. "The sublime [lies] in a formless object insofar as the unlimited [is] represented in it or thanks to it, and the notion of totality is nonetheless [added] to it by thought."

The sea is the supreme figure of the sublime. Boundless, infinitely mobile and unfathomable, it is the prime element through which we experience our finiteness. In the height of a storm, the unleashing of the elements, abolishing any stable form which the mind can fix on to, leads to a suspension of thought. Turner was the first to capture the ways nature in its sublimeness could be extended in plastic terms. His depiction of movement with no reference whatsoever to form translated the scientific upheavals of the century of the Enlightenment into pictural form.

Turner (Joseph Mallord William) 1775-1851
Snowstorm: steamboat off a harbor's mouth, c. 1840-1842
London, Tate Gallery

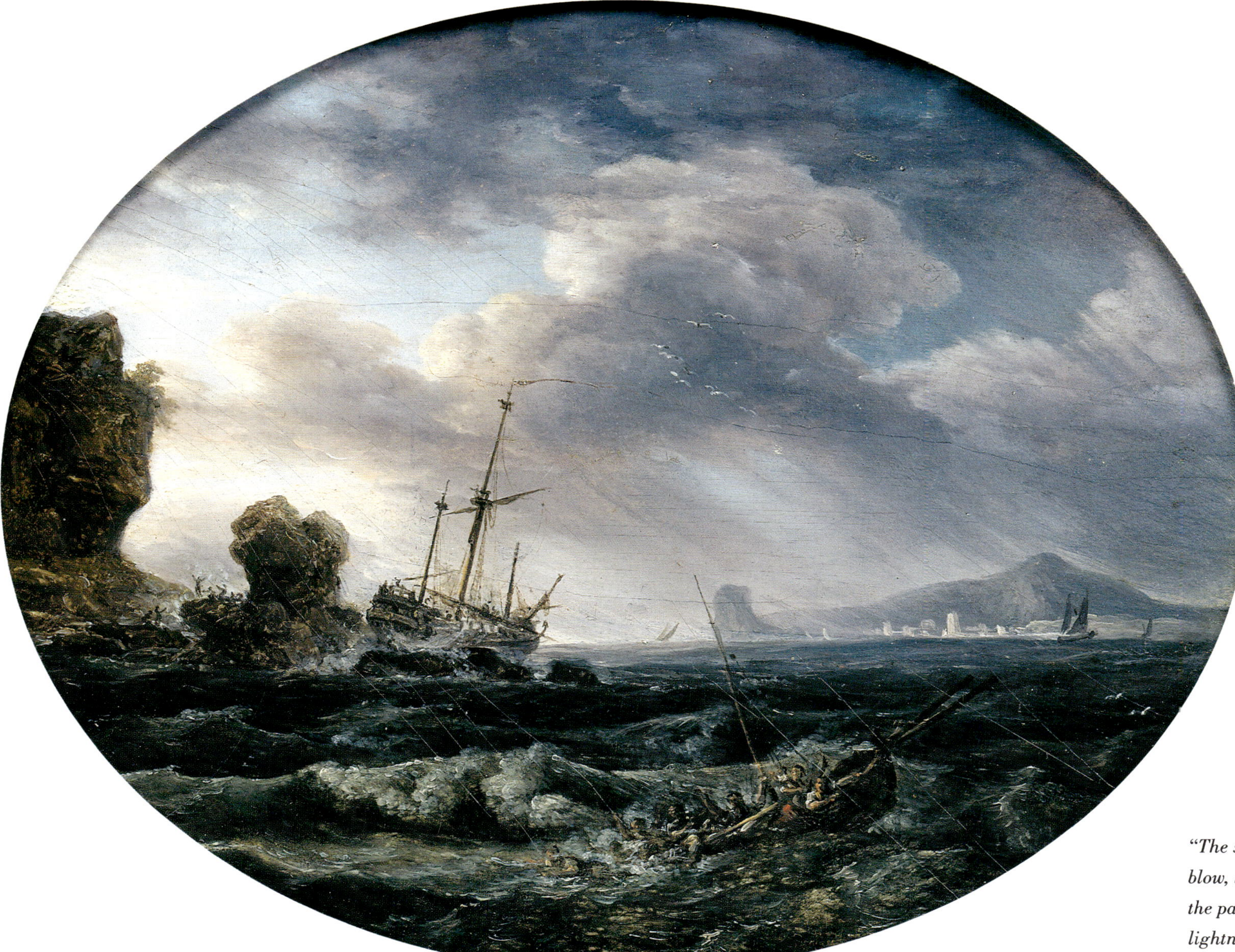

"The sea roars, the winds blow, the thunder rumbles: the pale somber gleam of lightning flashes through the clouds [...]. We can hear the noise of the ship's sides cracking open; its masts are bent, its sails torn. On the deck some men stand with their arms raised to heaven; others have cast themselves into the waters. The waves dash them against the nearby rocks where their blood mingles with the white spume breaking over them."

Denis Diderot
Les Salons

Vernet (Joseph) 1714-1789
Shipwreck
Dunkirk, Musée des Beaux-Arts

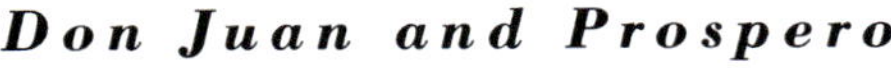

Don Juan and Prospero

The drama of human consciousness is identified with the mysterious gestation of the universe. Human awareness is its considered and unconsidered reflection. It may also be the blurred memory of original chaos.

The way everything happens is as if a sudden distortion of the field of consciousness had in a sort of rebound shock snapped the unity of the psyche; as if acquiring a deeper knowledge of the world entailed as a corollary a painful apprenticeship in doubt.

What place is there for thought and feelings in a world solely composed of matter and void? And more serious still, what place is there for morality? Can there be any morality other than that of the laws of physics? If not, man is left faced with two equally unacceptable options: barbarism or scientism.

Romantic painters rebelled against any such claims and sought their standard-bearers among the poets. Don Juan, a figure symbolizing refusal who appealed to Delacroix, illustrates the denunciation of the gulf opened up by the rejection of transcendence. His cynicism sounds like despair: "Hypocrisy is a fashionable vice," he says, "and all fashionable vices pass for virtues." Don Juan pretends to believe only in mathematical truths: "I believe that two and two make four, Sganarelle, and four and four make eight." – a sad piece of knowledge when it comes down to it, which cannot compensate for the loss of Heaven and Hell. The arrogance and provocative impiety of Sganarelle's master in Molière's *Don Juan* are a cry to the Father. They are a search for a boundary, a norm, an interdiction: in other words, the quest for a morality which would restore some meaning to this infinite matter which science was revealing. The Commander's vengeance is less of a punishment to Don Juan than a real deliverance.

Faust, Justine, Valmont and perhaps even Frankenstein are the new mythic figures invented by the modern age to express its disarray. The coming of science and the death of God seem to open up the way to the shipwreck of morality, with the work of Sade amidst the cataclysm of the French Revolution being its splendid, lugubrious funeral oration. "All Sade's work," Pierre Klossowski wrote, "seems to be just one desperate cry directed at the image of inaccessible virginity, a cry enveloped and almost set in a canticle of blasphemy." The Romantics grieved over the remains of an ideal nature in which people could no longer believe.

Between the barbarism of the world's origins and the terrors of reason, salvation comes yet again through asceticism: "We are such stuff as dreams are made on," Prospero says in *The Tempest*, "and our little life is rounded with a sleep." So we have to turn back to God, not knowing him but believing in him. Prospero concludes: "Now I want Spirits to enforce, art to enchant: / And my ending is despair / Unless I be relieved by prayer; / Which pierces so, that it assaults / Mercy itself, and frees all faults."

Wright of Derby (Joseph, known as) 1734-1797
Shakespeare: "A winter's tale." The storm
London, Christie's

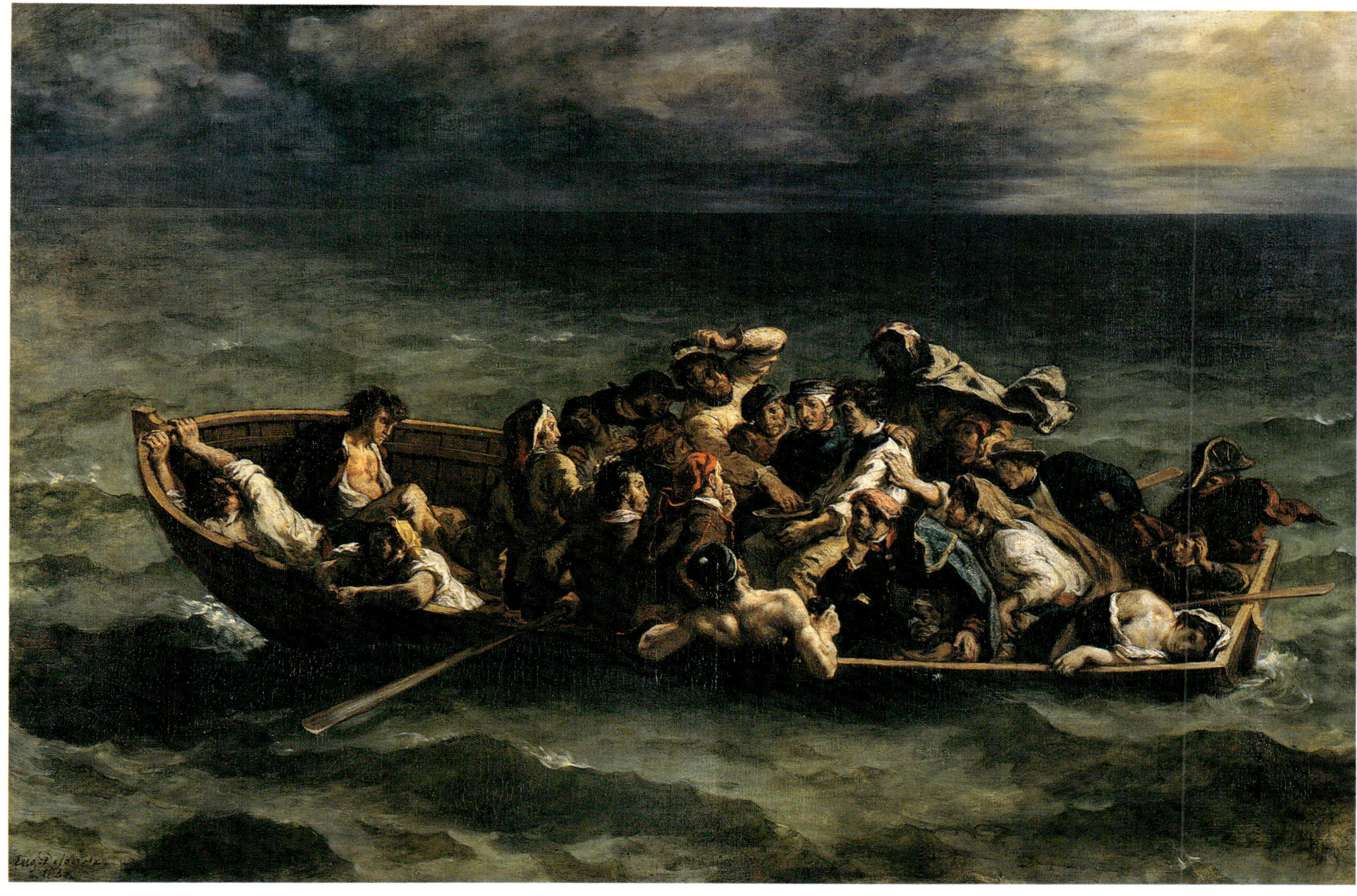

"Delacroix is the French expression of the drama that shook the artist's soul in the first half of the 19th century."

Théophile Gautier

Delacroix (Eugène) 1798-1863
The shipwreck of Don Juan, 1840
Paris, Louvre

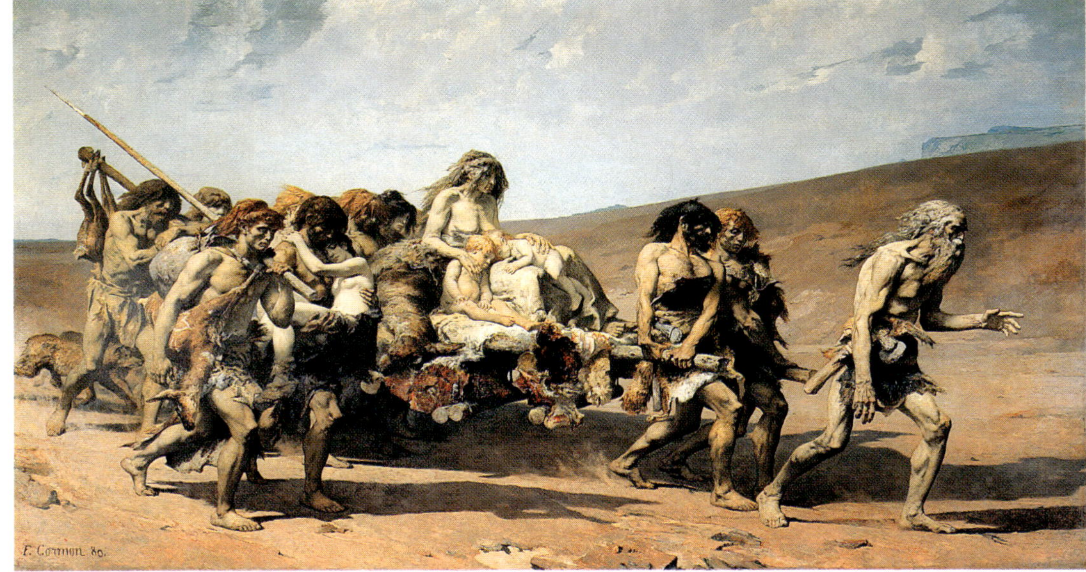

The mark of Cain

However, there is a middle way between the ideal landscape of Poussin and nature in turmoil as depicted by Wright of Derby. In painting the *Angelus* Millet tried to rediscover the path towards nature on a human scale: not seen as metaphysical and transcendent, but simply the image of earth telling the tale of the daily toil of the humble, those who do not think about the world, but fashion it with their imperfect hands with no thought beyond insuring their own survival.

For the peasant a moment of contemplation is just a short break in a daily round whose rhythm is dictated by the demands of the soil. This obvious submission to the great biological pulsation was in fact experienced by Millet himself, and he made it his purpose in life to bear witness to it. Reacting against the perversions of city life and the social and moral ravages resulting from industrialization, reacting too against a form of progress which reduced the majority to the new slavery of working-class life, Millet wanted to show that the only work worthy of man was work which would preserve the meaning of life: work which would allow man to retain his dignity as a man.

Poussin painted as a philosopher, Turner as a visionary, while Millet set out to paint as a peasant: to paint men and women whose faces were anonymous bent over the demanding soil which yielded nothing easily, and to express in a few simple, strongly constructed compositions all that was owed to them.

Millet did not dream of a golden age. He did not idealize what he painted, even if we cannot quite describe his work as realistic. Rejecting both of these terms, he chose a solution consisting entirely of half-tones; at the end of his life this evolved into a symbolism of moderation and balance.

Thus when he became a painter of the peasant world, he preferred a bondage that was at one with the great harmony of nature rather than the curse of wandering which appealed to the Romantics.

In Millet's mind industrialization and the start of the rural exodus, the huge hemorrhage of people from the countryside that resulted from mechanization, were identified with a new curse.

When Cain, the farmer, killed his brother Abel, God condemned him to eternal exile. Now the new exodus appeared in the light of an unjust punishment, with the roles reversed between a Cain-like figure who had redeemed his wrongdoing through toil and a threat from the town, assimilated with Hell.

A place of redemption, a necessary purgatory, the countryside was thus perceived as the refuge of the pure in heart escaping from the towns which had become a place of perdition.

Cormon (Fernand Anne Piestre, known as) 1845-1924
Cain (Victor Hugo: La Légende des siècles), 1880
Paris, Musée d'Orsay

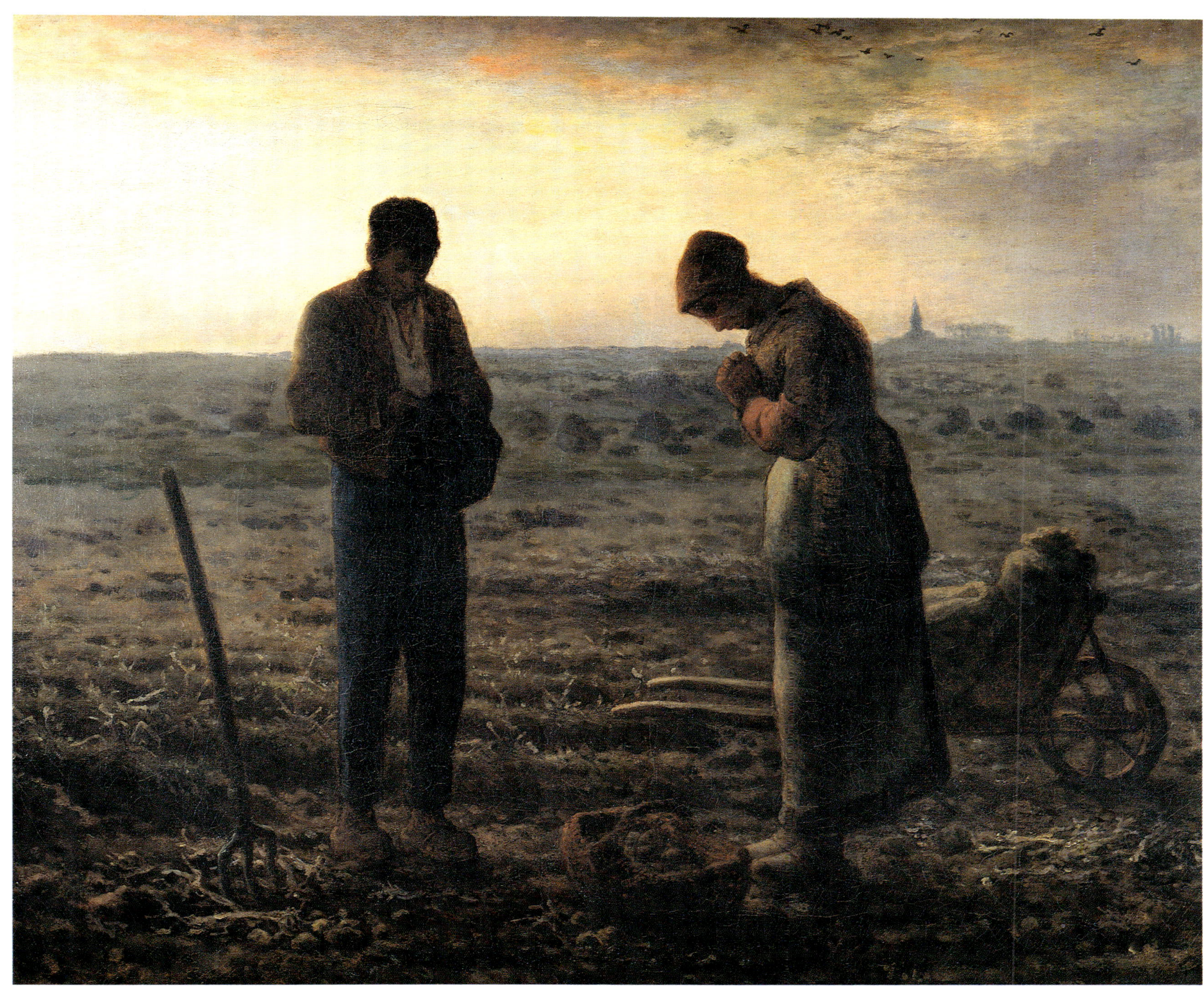

"I heard [...] the faint, barely discernible sound of a bell rising up to me through the dusk [...]. It was the angelus of some far distant village [...]."

Victor Hugo
Le Rhin

Millet (Jean-François) 1814-1875
The angelus, 1857-1859
Paris, Louvre

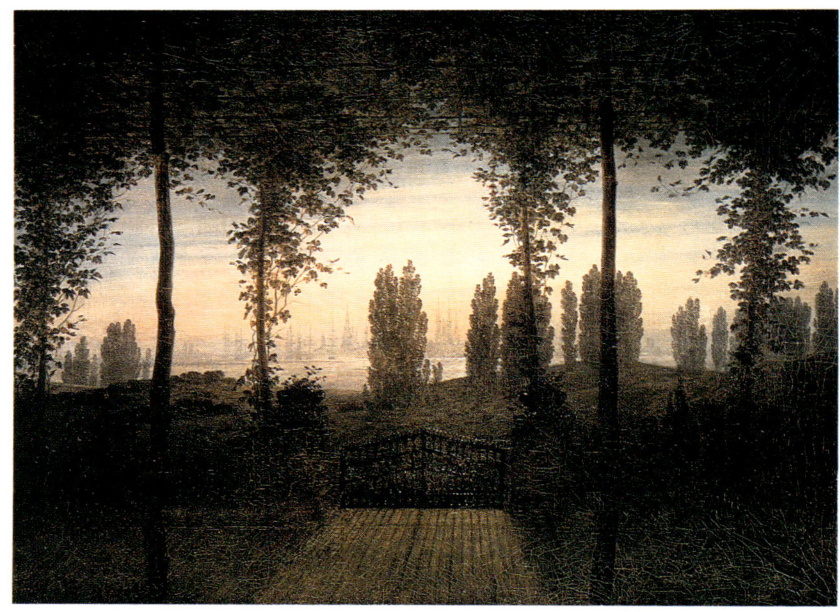

The bare waiting place

In Friedrich's landscapes everything expresses a sense of waiting, expectation. Neither harmony nor suffering is the major element in his work, but waiting. Men, trees, mountains seem to be suspended in a supernatural silence. Everything is looking towards the horizon. Everything, down to the very stones in the walls, seems to be directed towards some other place which we cannot see. In Poussin's work all nature was present on the canvas. With Friedrich you might almost believe that nature is no more than a line on the horizon. His nature does not spread out towards us like waves unleashed by a storm. There is no echo here of the Titanesque rumblings working within it. All we see on the canvas is the bare place where we await the divine.

The poverty and sparseness of what can be seen indicate the impossibility of another invisible world beyond it, beyond the horizon line: a world that is here today on this earth but inaccessible to man, as if this marked the boundary of 18th-century pantheism. According to Friedrich, the divine is not expressed, properly speaking, through landscape. On the contrary, it is through the simplification of landscape, by removing the picturesque and the anecdotal, that we can reach a higher understanding of the meaning of nature. Thus Friedrich renews the link with the Christian tradition which had always mistrusted landscape, fearful of seeing the old pagan myths reemerge under cover of the depiction of nature. In spite of its sense of balance and serene, serious austerity, Friedrich's landscape does not set out to be an image of harmony. Man is not communicating with nature here, but is waiting within it, at the heart of it, for a different reality to arrive. His landscapes, whether centered on a distant light (*Two men looking at the moon*, 1819 and *Moonrise over the Sea*, 1822) or on the monochrome expanse of the ocean (*Chalk Cliffs at Rügen*, 1818), or crossed by a blurred line separating light from shade (*Abbey in the Oakwood*, 1810), all refer back to the idea of a break between material reality and a truth of a different order which keeps all its mystery. Michel Le Bris considers that "It is probably [...] Adam Heinrich Müller [...] who came closest to Friedrich when he imagined the 'artist's eye' as the point of pure contemplation from which the idealness of the real and the reality of the ideal could be intuitively grasped."

Friedrich himself wrote, with the Tetschen retable in mind, that landscape "represents the necessary mediation between the two worlds, between the pure divine light whose source is hidden from us and the shadow in which we live." The space in the canvas then becomes the mystic place of initiation where the painter, following in the footsteps of poets who endeavor to say the unsayable, tries to show us the invisible.

Friedrich (Caspar David) 1774-1840
In remembrance of Johann Emanuel Bremer
Berlin, Charlottenburg

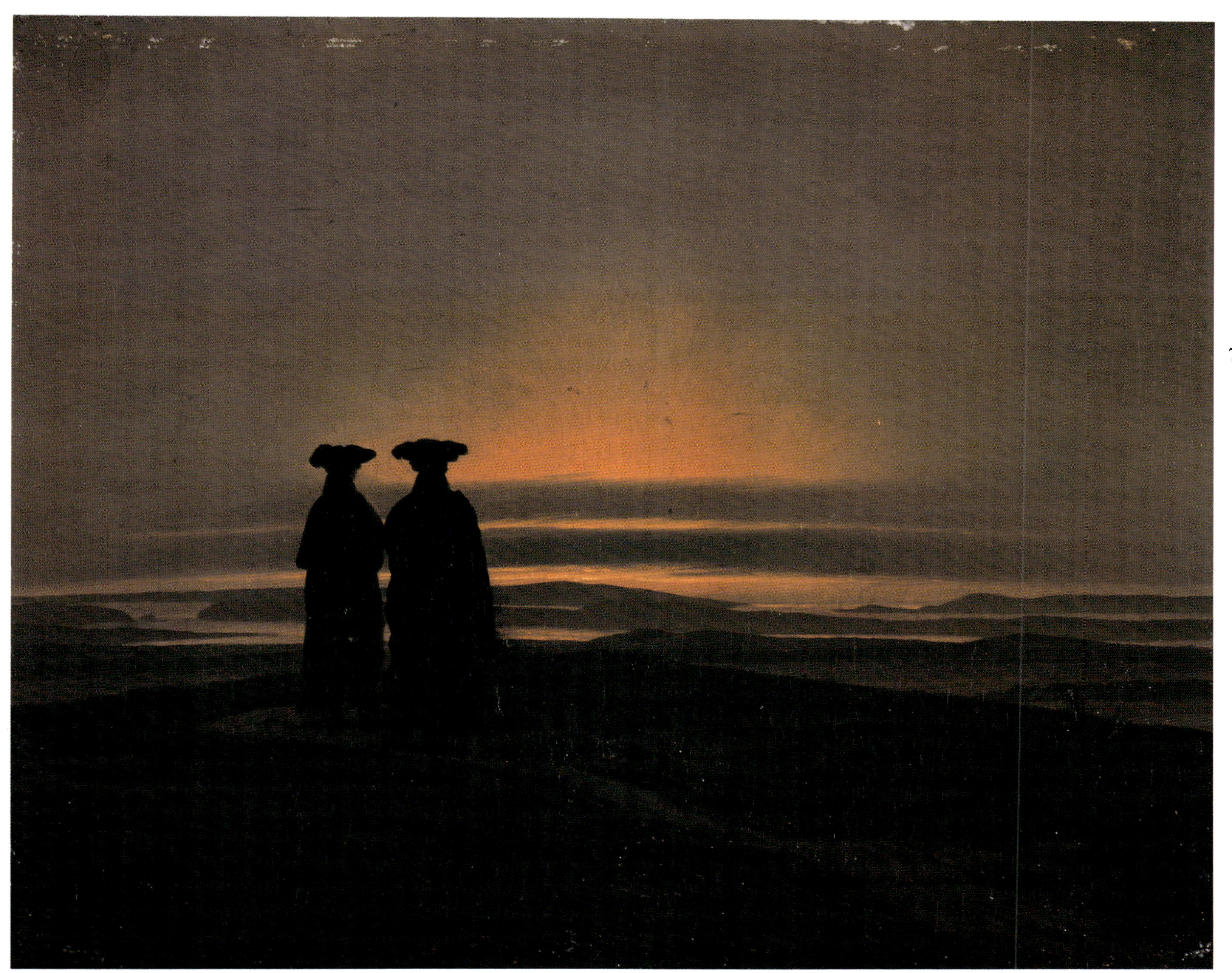

"Friedrich's painting is full of symbols and bathed in mist [...]. It is calm, somber and serious, as if agonized by the fate of the man who stands on the edge of this life scrutinizing the horizon of his own presence in the world."

H.-A. Baatsch

Friedrich (Caspar David) 1774-1840
Moonrise over the sea, 1822
St. Petersburg, Hermitage

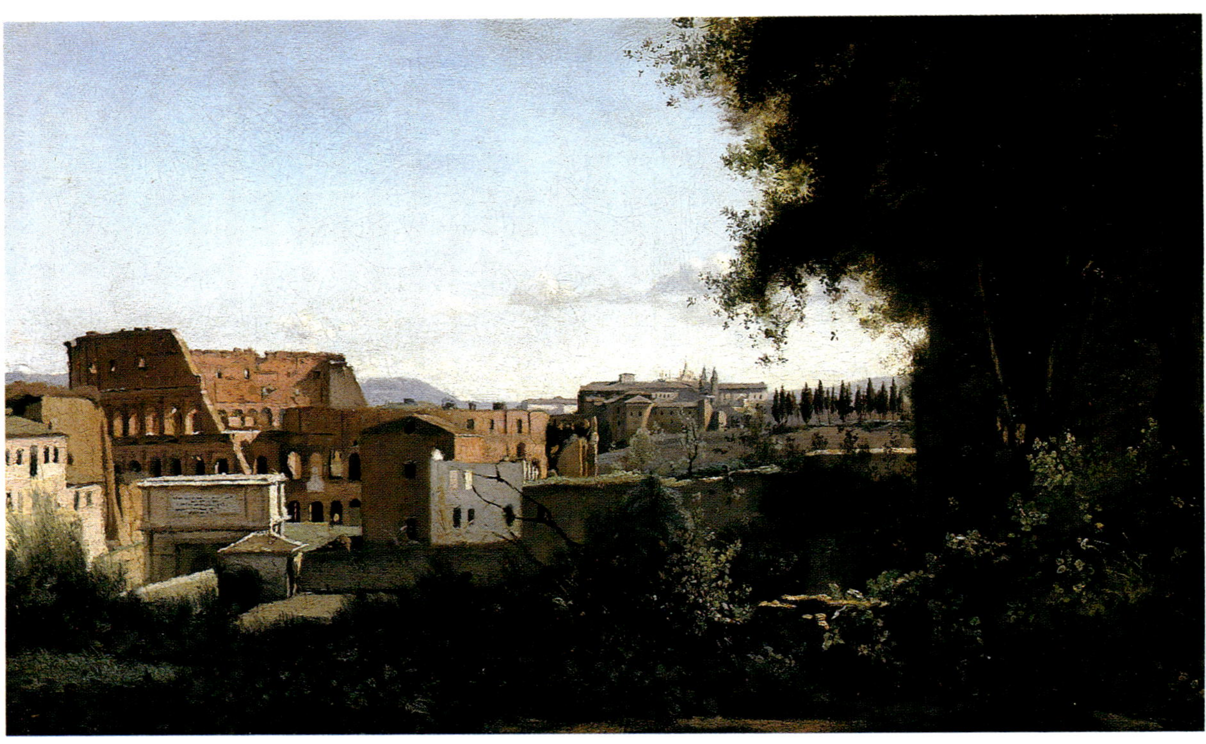

Metaphors of memory

The fashion for ruins dates from the Renaissance. The originality of views of ruins, and more generally of all architectural landscapes, in comparison with the treatments of landscape discussed so far lies in the way the work of man and that of nature are juxtaposed on canvas, introducing a temporal dimension.

On reading Joachim du Bellay's *Antiquités de Rome* we come across the following verses which must have been familiar to Corot:

You who gaze, marvelling at Rome,
On the ancient pride which threatened
the heavens,
Those old palaces, those bold hills,
Those walls, those arches, baths and temples,

Consider when you see such extensive ruins
What injurious time has eaten away,
Since these old fragments still
Serve to inspire the most industrious workers.

Gazing at ruins is linked with meditating on the past, to a *reflection* on the work of man, i.e. turning in on oneself, on one's own history. But it is also a way of highlighting (both literally and figuratively) the fleetingness of existence. The harmony between the ruin and nature is just an illusion. Nature is reborn from its own ashes every spring: ruins are not. There is no new spring, either for men or for civilizations which, like individuals, are mortal. There is no new spring, but there is perhaps the hope of passing on an example to others in the form of heritage ("*Since these old fragments still / Serve to inspire the most industrious workers,*" in du Bellay's words.) Nature when it reproduces itself is always the same, whereas man evolves: the ruin is the measure of that evolution – a measure both of what separates man from his past and what ties him to it. Faithfulness and change. Ruins, to the eyes of the painter, write a subjective history of past civilizations. They are the yardstick by which our present can be measured.

There is another tendency, illustrated by Claude Lorraine's *Architectural landscape:* to try and reconstruct the ruin, not just to resuscitate past grandeur but in a kind of way to undo the work of time through the recreating magic of the imagination. We are then dealing with something quite different: it is no longer a question of enhancing current experience through the experience of bygone centuries, but of turning our backs on reality and plunging into the phantasm of an ideal world where time, and so nature, no longer hold sway. But this is the very opposite of what Corot is expressing in his *Colosseum seen from the Farnese Gardens.*

Corot (Camille) 1796-1875
The Colosseum seen from the Farnese Gardens, 1826
Paris, Louvre

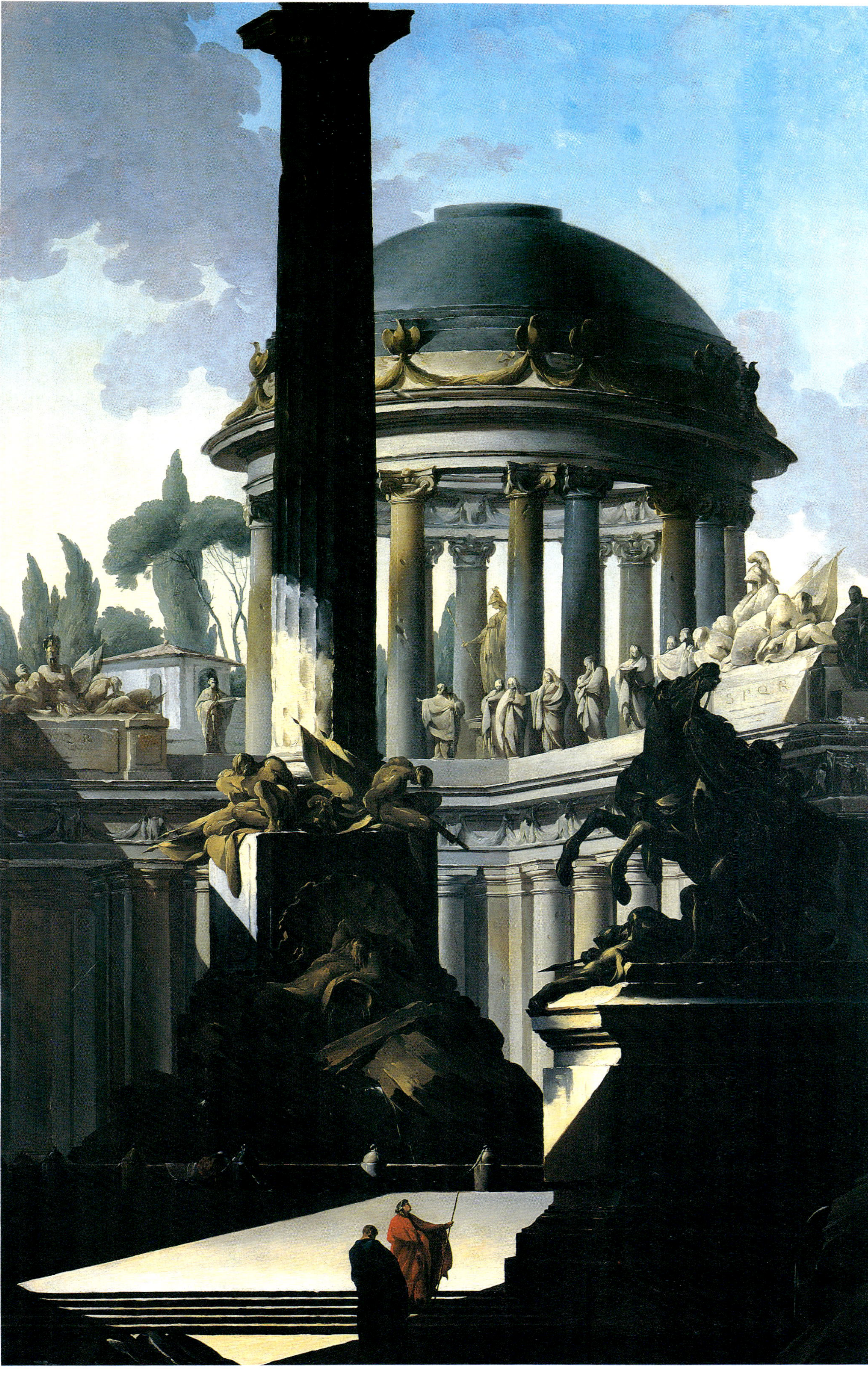

"[Claude Lorraine] is at the other end of the spectrum from people like Van Goyen and Ruysdael who will provide a portrait of a town or country. His essentially Roman vision becomes so broadly lyrical that we forget the motif and remember only universal harmonies."

Pierre Francastel

Lorraine (Claude Gellée, known as Claude) 1600-1682
Architectural landscape or Caprice with ruins of the Roman forum
Paris, Louvre

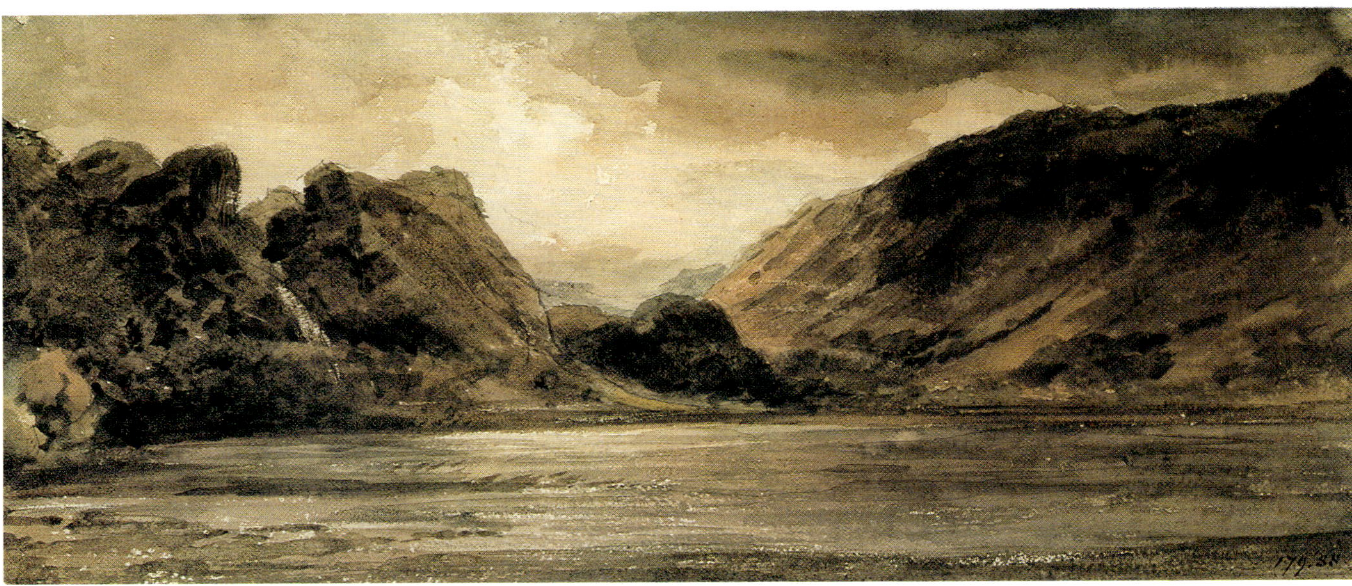

The finger of the painter

Since the 16th century so many experiences, ambitions and things had been invested in landscape painting that by the mid-19th century one might have thought, with the towns becoming the image of reality and industrialization seeming to promise everyone that nature would cease to exercise tyranny over man, that the genre had run its course. However, the very opposite happened.

For then came the English painter Constable, who suggested with false simplicity that artists should be content with painting what they saw; that they should agree once and for all to abandon all their Classical, Baroque, Neo-Classical or Romantic whims and fancies and just look around them and paint what they saw .... Look and paint, with no philosophical background, no religious pretensions, without anything that even claimed to be sublime. Look and paint what you see: in short, represent what our eyes observe.

This was the origin of Realism – for every trend must have its name. As an approach it is less simple than might first appear, for when it comes to representation painters have very rarely indeed represented reality for its own sake. Forgetting the formulae learnt in the studio and the laws of perspective laid down since the *quattrocento* means forgetting everything, or almost everything, of the pictorial traditions of the West. And you cannot make a clean sweep of four centuries of your trade without risking getting into very deep waters indeed.

So Constable was careful not to work out a program or proclaim unduly great ambitions: to paint with the eye, that was his *credo*, taken by the French painters of the Barbizon school. When Courbet inherited the same lesson, he liked its simplicity. To paint with the eye, he thought, and better still to paint with the body, hands, and everything that constitutes a man, with the heart and guts: Courbet painted with the frenzy and naivety of a man wanting to remake nature for a second time. Courbet does not paint the cliffs at Etretat, he reconstructs them. He paints in the same way that a builder constructs a house, without elegance, but with a complete knowledge of his trade. His knowledge is the fruit of experience. His cliffs are not a pure vibration of light, as Monet's were to be, but they carry within them the full weight of the centuries. In his work form does not come from the mind, it comes from the touch.

Anyone who is at all familiar with Etretat knows that before he painted its cliffs Courbet first went down onto the shingle when the tide was out, that he caressed the base of the cliffs, raised his eyes and then truly understood what matter was. Realism of that kind cannot be dissociated from experience: "I know my country," Courbet declared, "and I paint it." His knowledge is not comprehension, but apprehension. With him the painter gives up any attempt to remake the world, but really gets to grips with the world as it is.

Constable (John) 1776-1837
Derwentwater: stormy evening, 1808
London, Victoria and Albert Museum

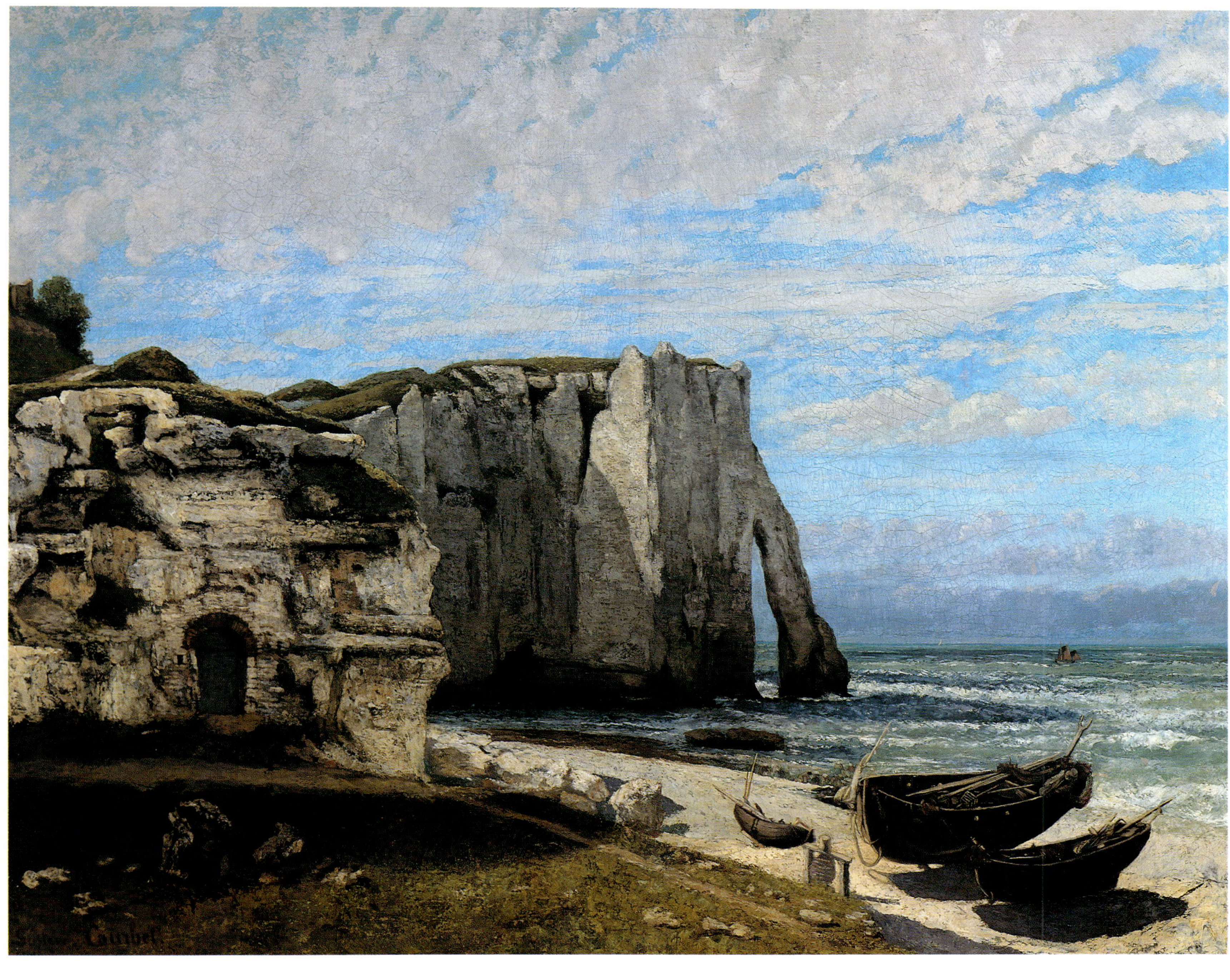

Courbet (Gustave) 1819-1877
Cliffs at Etretat after the storm, 1869
Paris, Louvre

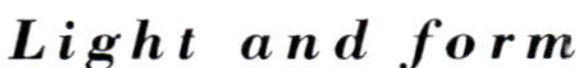

Light and form

We know that Impressionism is rooted in Realism. Perhaps it is less concerned with likeness, but like Realism it abjures transcendence. We have noted above that this concept went well beyond the context of religious or mythological painting. To give a short résumé of the situation, all painting since wall painting had had a religious dimension to a greater or lesser extent, including landscape. The Realists and the Impressionists broke with that tradition. Describing Cézanne's work, Schapiro wrote: "What [he] accomplished is uniquely important to our concept of art. His work is the living proof that a painter can attain profundity of expression in giving form to what he perceives of the world around him without resorting to inspiration derived from religion, myth or some well defined social movement."

When painting a landscape Courbet was still concerned with the need for objective resemblance: the undergrowth on the canvas, for example, was intended to reproduce in two dimensions the appearance of the actual three-dimensional undergrowth. The object represented dictated its form to the artist. The development introduced by painters like Monet, Cézanne or – a little later – Bonnard regarding the criteria of representation consisted mainly in tipping the scales down on the side of the painting subject – the artist – while at the same time respecting the characteristics peculiar to the object being represented. In other words, they caused Realism to evolve towards subjective formalism: landscape was conceived as a visual impression and therefore primarily as the outcome of the play of light on a form bereft of all cultural references. The analysis that could be made of this interaction (between form and light) varied of course from one individual to another. That is where the subjectivity which is the expression of the artist's creative talent inevitably lies, in spite of the almost scientific claims sometimes put forward by these artists.

As for Cézanne, who is glibly labeled a precursor of Cubism with a reference to the comment he made late in life about the cylinder, the sphere and the cone, people tend to forget too quickly that his work continued to be based on a study of color. He said that it was necessary "to introduce into our vibrations of light represented by reds and yellows enough blue tones to enable people to sense the air." Of course Cézanne did not totally renounce form, decomposing it in multiple planes and sometimes reducing it to a simple touch of color. But in the final analysis the gap between him and people like Monet or Bonnard is not as great as it might first appear. Where these painters are concerned, it is not so much an opposition of concept that separates them as a difference in style. When Bonnard writes that "the picture is a series of spots that combine and eventually form the object, the bit the eye can range over without being jolted" he is doing no more than stating what Cézanne spent his whole life striving for.

Bonnard (Pierre) 1867-1947
Landscape at Le Cannet, 1928
Private collection

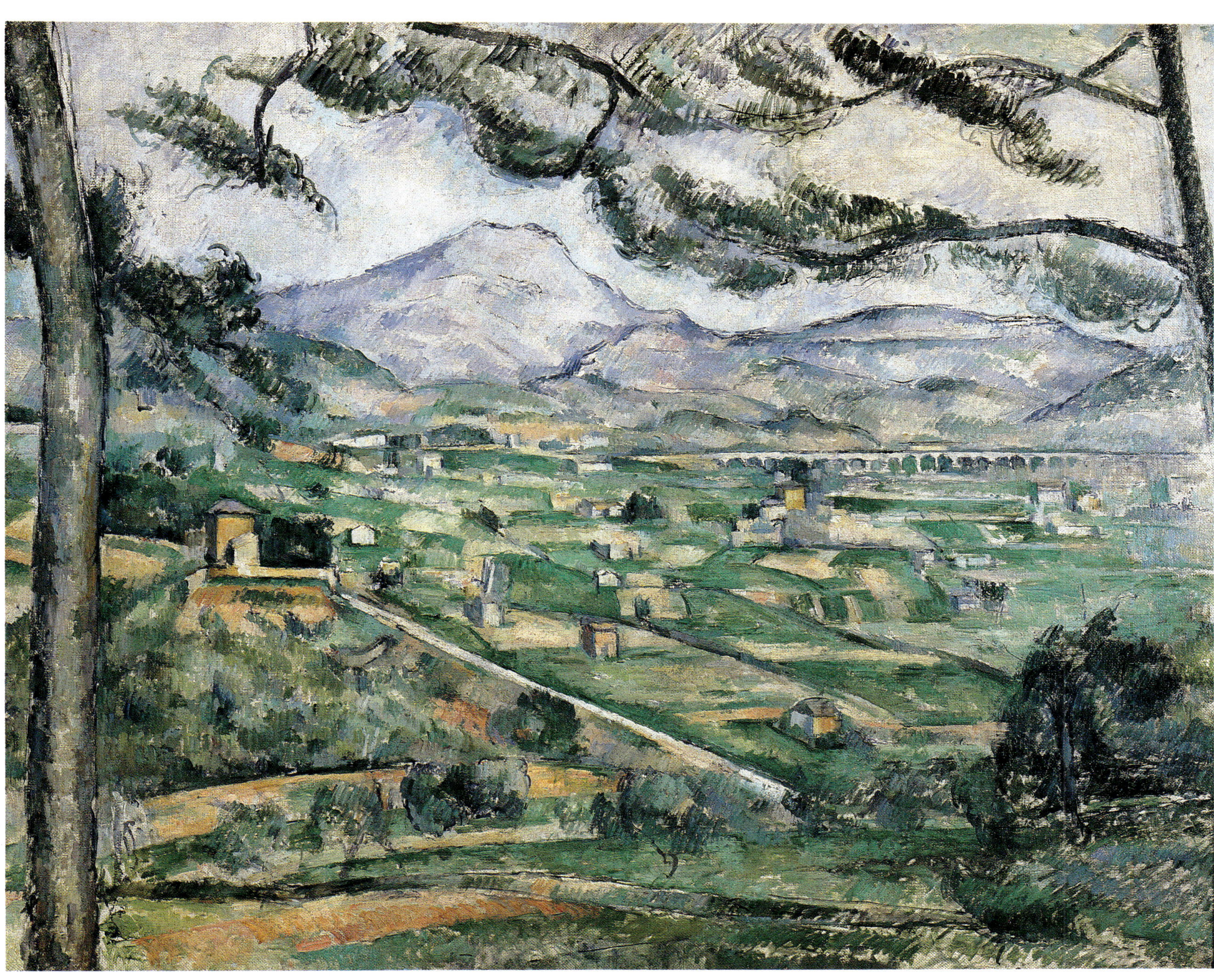

"The conquest of style by any great artist coincides with his conquest of liberty, being the only proof that he has achieved the latter and his only means of attaining it."

André Malraux
Les voix du silence

Cézanne (Paul) 1839-1906
Montagne Sainte-Victoire with the tall pine-tree, 1885-1837
Washington, Phillips Collection

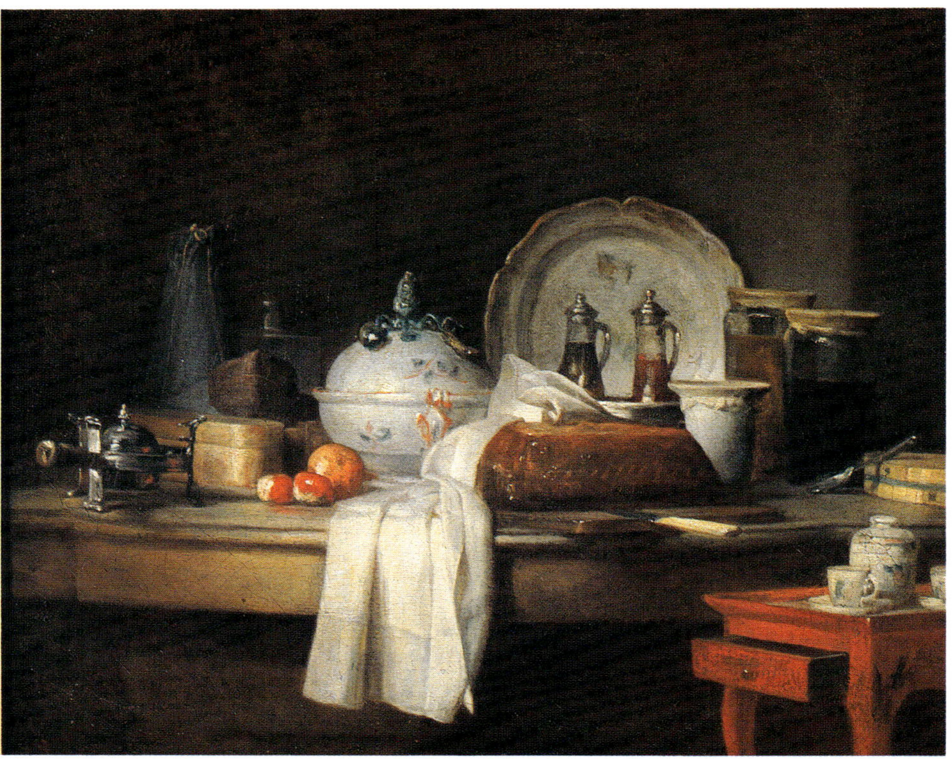

Still-lifes

Writing in the *Salon de 1765* Diderot observed: "Chardin's work is odd. He shares with the highly contrasted style the characteristic that when we look at his work closely we do not know what it is, but as we move farther away the object takes shape and eventually becomes as it is in nature." Up until Chardin's day still-lifes had in fact set out to imitate nature, but to imitate it in a rather special way. In a still-life (or to use the French term *nature morte*) the object has been taken out of its context and rearranged beside other objects in an arbitrary order that has nothing to do with life or nature. Hence the description "still" life or nature "morte." While landscape painting seeks to express a universal connection between man and nature, still-lifes express a special connection with the object, based on a concrete experience and reflecting Locke's empiricism – especially in the work of 18th-century English painters.

Thus it is perfectly natural for a study of this genre to close our rapid review of the spectacle of nature, for it clearly demonstrates that the representation of nature is not the same thing as a reproduction of nature. When he paints an apple or a bunch of grapes, the artist does not reproduce the object: he produces an image of it, a completely different thing. Because still-lifes are unencumbered by any historical or religious connotations, they enable us to formulate a minimalist redefinition of the role of the painter with regard to nature and the society in which he works. The painter is an artist who takes a given repertory of forms and creates other forms from them. No doubt this restricts his field of action, but paradoxically it also gives him complete freedom at the very heart of his art.

It can be stated categorically that the periods when painting has flourished (Flemish naturalism, Impressionism, Cubism) have corresponded with times when painting maintained the greatest independence in its attitude towards the other arts. And conversely, the times when Horace's principle of *ut pictura poesis* (Classicism, Neo-Classicism and Romanticism) has prevailed have been those when the genre was regarded with the greatest contempt.

In a letter to Emile Bernard on 12 May 1904, Cézanne wrote: "The artist must despise any opinion not based on intelligent observation of the character. He must be wary of the literary cast of mind which so often leads the painter to deviate from his true path – the concrete study of nature – and become lost for too long in intangible speculation."

Through still-lifes the painter can regain the lost identity of his art. From Chardin to Cézanne the only real difficulty ever to exist was this: their constant concern with the way light palpitated on a form; and it occupied their whole lives.

Chardin (Jean-Baptiste Siméon) 1699-1779
The sideboard or The remains of lunch
Paris, Louvre

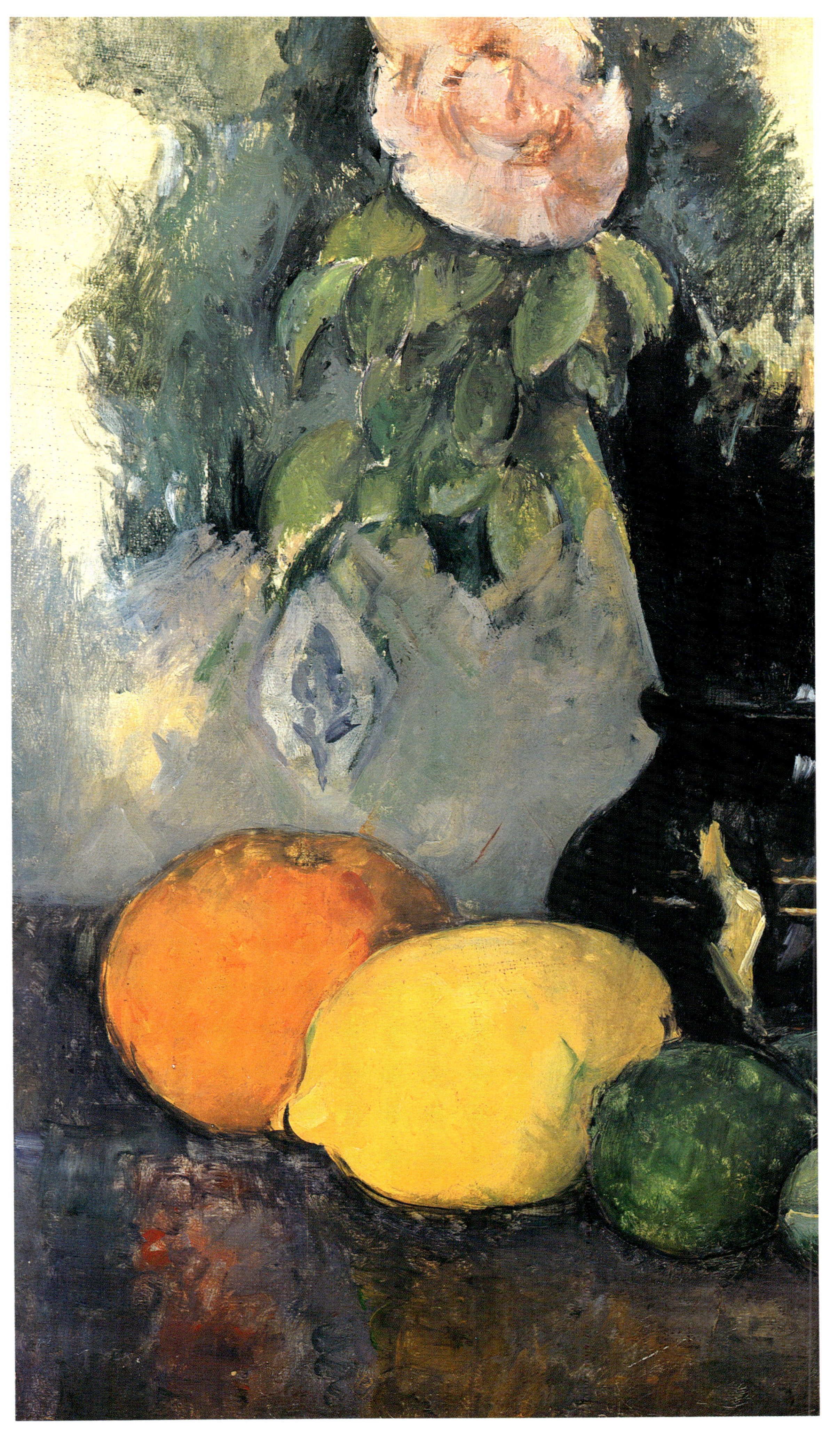

Cézanne (Paul) 1839-1906
Flowers and fruit, c. 1886
Paris, Musée de l'Orangerie

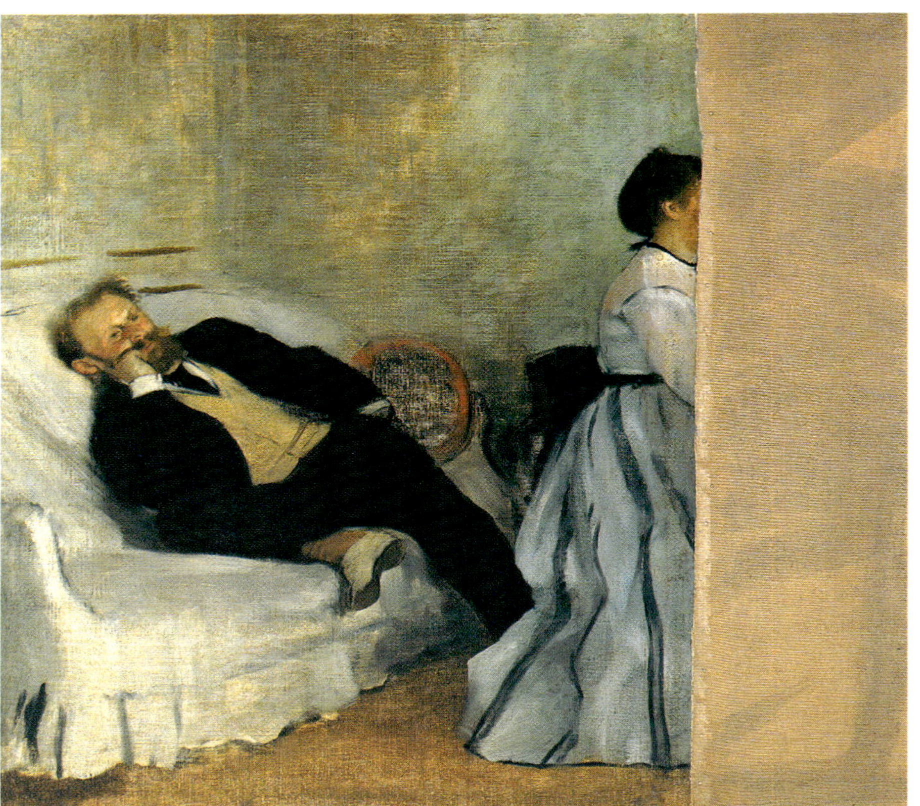

Degas (Hilaire Germain Edgar de Gas, known as) 1834-1917
Edouard Manet and his wife, 1868-1869
Kitakyushu, Municipal Museum of Art

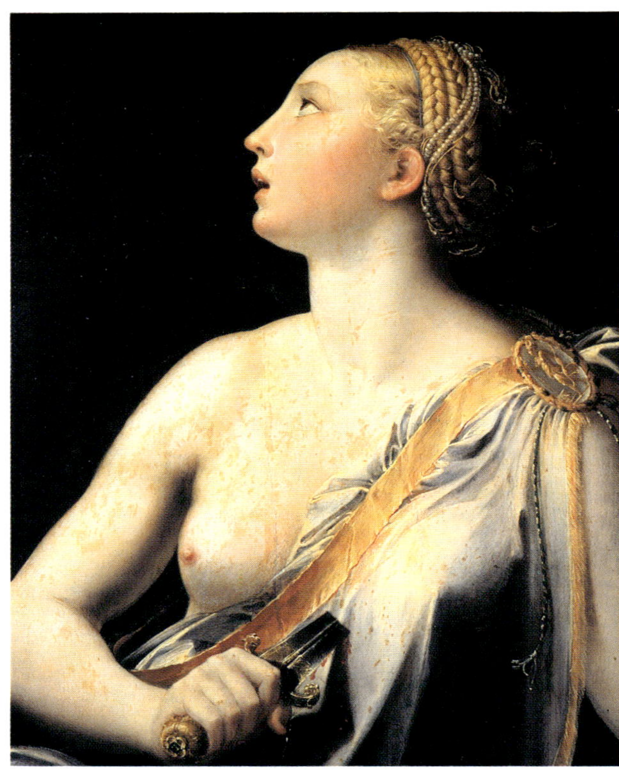

The ideal and its double

"The image of the body in the form of a portrait was reassuring," Marc Le Bot wrote. "The portrait bore witness to the stable identity of the body of its model: to the stable identity of any model. The portrait resembled the model because the model wanted his or her body to be like a normalized image of the body." That is why the body and the still-life are so different. If the object depicted in the still-life can be perceived as a form foreign to my own identity, the image of the body on the other hand, even the body of someone else, irrevocably refers me back to myself and my way of being in the world, my way of being in relation to the world. The image of the body is a metaphor of the universe and my place in the universe; it is both a measure of that and the measure of my desire. In the image of the body there is the conflicting representation of the irrational poetics of desire and of the expression of a normative formalism. The body is the contradictory figure of moderation and immoderation.

What is at stake here is in fact the very idea of beauty. What is beautiful? Is it what evokes the ideas of order and balance in me? Or is it what provokes the disordered emotion of desire in me? In Raphael's portrait of Maddalena Strozzi, painted about 1505, the beauty of the pregnant woman – which refers back to the image of the Virgin – celebrates the unitary character of the human and the divine. If the woman's face "bears witness to the stable identity of the body," as Marc Le Bot put it, it also goes beyond the body and bears witness to the stable identity of nature. The human figure is an extension of natural harmony and in a way its culmination, its supreme manifestation. It is the place where nature becomes super-nature, where the painter, while respecting the imperatives of mimetic realism, achieves the highest degree of idealization of the human figure. This is the source of the equivocal feeling we always have in front of a face painted by Raphael that we are looking simultaneously at the fleshly reality and the idealization of that reality.

Parmigianino's work extends Raphael's approach, but in it the form loses its appearance of serene harmony and becomes strained, revealing a tension not present in Raphael. No doubt it owes more to the example set by Michelangelo's frescoes which Parmigianino saw in Rome in 1534, and from which he borrowed the "serpentine figure."

However, it would be a mistake to interpret the elegance and almost precious grace of Parmigianino as betokening a superficial vision. The non-realist elongation of the bodies attests to a deep dissatisfaction, or to put it another way to his anguished fear that he could not manage to grasp all the complexity of natural harmony. In Parmigianino's style there is a wish to push the expression of perfection farther and farther until it has been taken beyond reality, beyond the norm. That is why Parmigianino's formal refinement is close to the elegance of despair.

Parmigianino (Francesco Mazzola, known as) 1503-1540
Lucretia, c. 1535-1540
Naples, Museo di Capodimonte

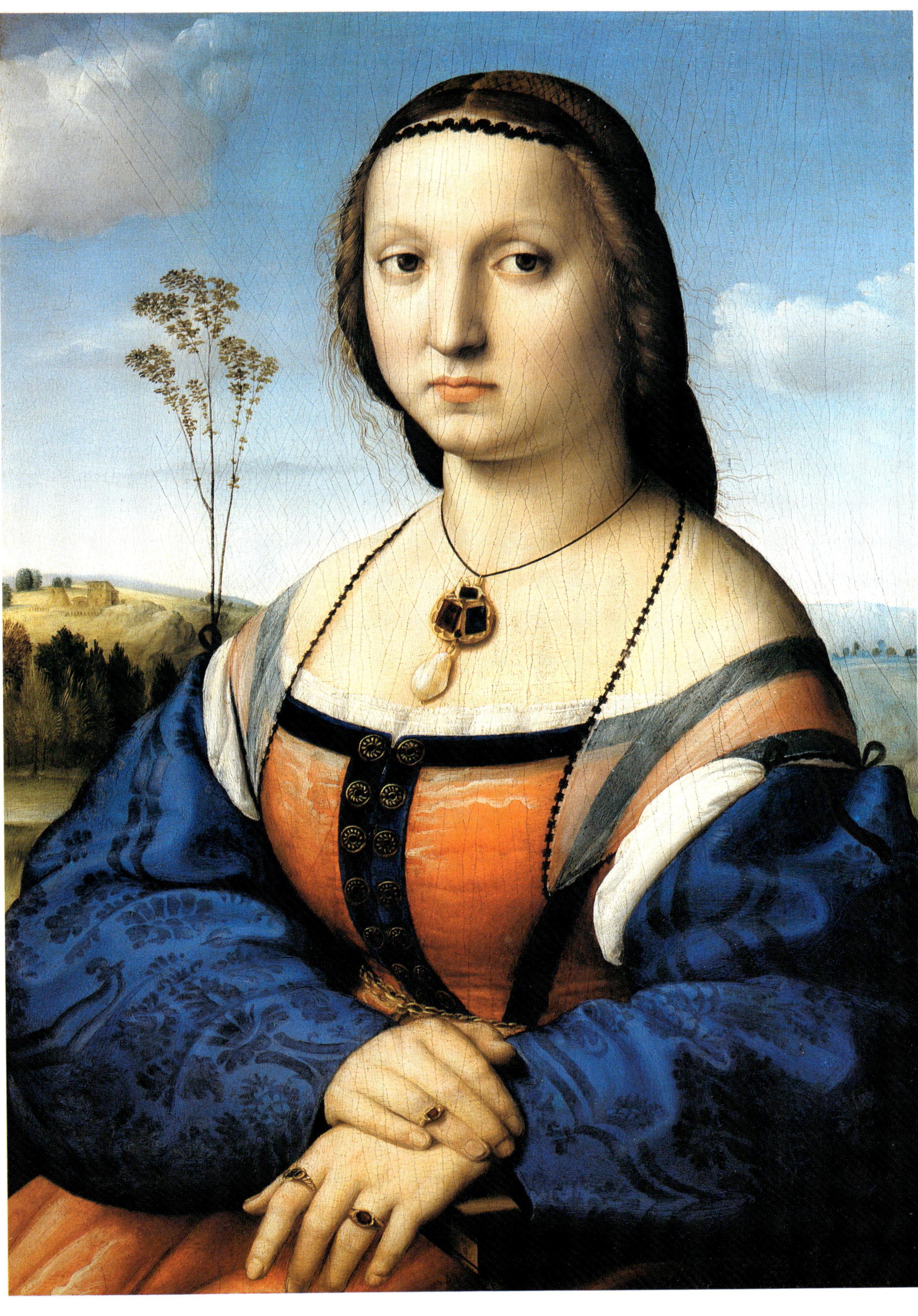

"Beauty is a rationally determined harmony of all the parts that make up a thing, so much so that it becomes highly improbable that anything can be added, taken away, or altered."

Leon Battista Alberti
De re aedificatoria

Raphael (Raffaello Santi or Sanzio, known as) 1483-1520
Portrait of Maddalena Strozzi Doni, c. 1505-1506
Florence, Pitti Palace

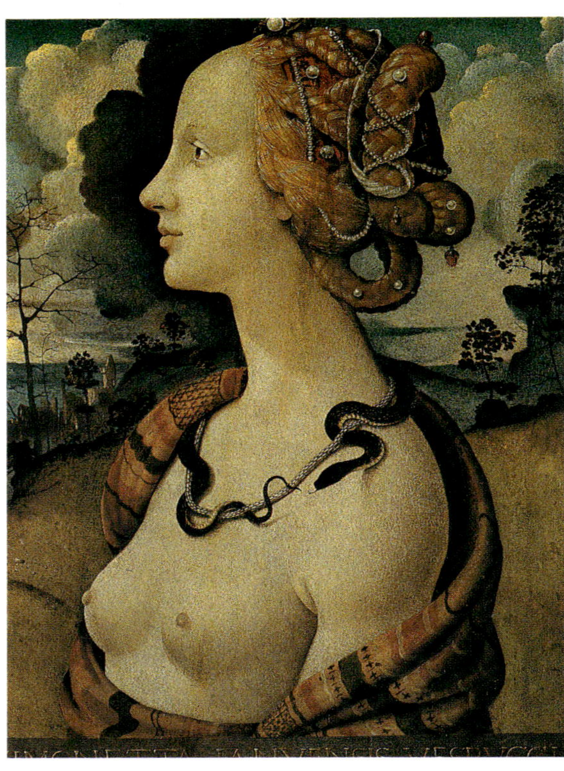

The painter and his model

Looking at the sensuous approach of Piero di Cosimo and the glacial treatment meted out to the figure by Ingres, we might almost see them as marking the beginning and the end of the rediscovery of antiquity. From what he had learnt from the Greeks Piero di Cosimo chose to retain the feeling of intimacy with nature expressed in their myths, while Ingres much later seems to reduce the antique heritage to a few intangible rules and procedures. In the words of Odilon Redon, the "scholastic idol will never awaken life in generous hearts." He also wrote: "Ingres is an honest, serving disciple of the masters of another age. As he lacks reality and true vital warmth, his only chance of enduring is in the temperate spheres of that banal, bored world which admires traditional beauty on the authority of others and in the spirit of conservation [...]. He is one of those people who do not animate others, so he is not alive; he is death itself." It is a harsh judgment, but his analysis is fruitful.

What is at stake here is not deciding whether the primary concern when representing the human figure should be drawing and whether only noble subjects should be sought – even if debates of this nature may have seemed crucial to the people of the time. The true question, the true problem, is that the value of a representation is tied up with the nature of the links between its creator and its period. In other words, the ideal of one period will not be the ideal of all periods. Raphael is great because he expresses the ideal of the Renaissance. Ingres is criticized because his esthetics are out of step with the aspirations of his time. Setting out to create ideal art is a dangerous chimera which can only lead to a dead end, to the cul-de-sac of official art.

Does this mean that once the Renaissance was over no further attempt should have been made to express the ideal? Yes, possibly, if the ideal set out to be comprehensive. No, if on the other hand the search for the ideal is centered on the meeting between the painter and his model. The ideal today can no longer claim to be universal. The modern ideal is the form which the artist gives to his or her relationship with the other person. Experience has now supplanted the norm. The truth of a face no longer depends on the esthetic canon, but on the authenticity of the relationship which the artist has with that face. And desire – we come back finally to Piero di Cosimo, who was praised for his ability to capture "from life" the whole truth of a person – might well be the structuring element of the confrontation between the painter and the model. If we accept that form can result from the sublimation of desire for the other, then it is possible that this may be the modern expression of our need for the ideal: possible, but not certain. For Barthes writing about the "Divine" Garbo said: "Garbo was the visible embodiment of a kind of Platonic idea of the human being, which explains why her face is sexless while at the same time being in no way questionable. [...] The description of her as 'divine' no doubt was designed less to convey superlative beauty than to suggest the essence of her physical person, come down from a heaven where things are formed and finished in the greatest light." With her the dynamics of desire reached their destination in contemplating the ideal.

Piero di Cosimo (Piero di Lorenzo, known as) 1461/62-1521
Portrait of a woman, known as Simonetta Vespucci
Chantilly, Musée Condé

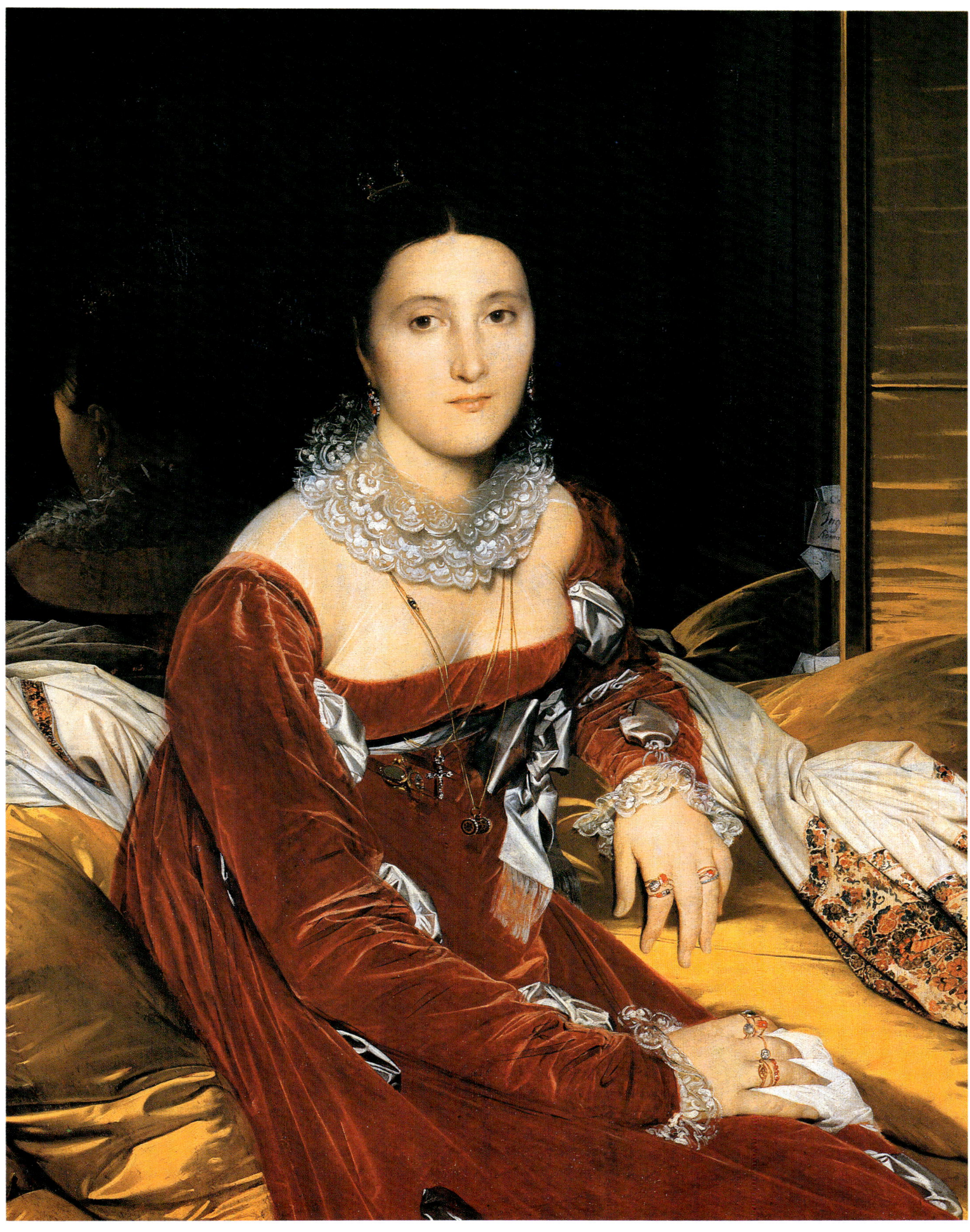

"Monsieur Ingres may be regarded as a man endowed with estimable qualities, as an eloquent lover of beauty, but he is devoid of that energetic temperament which is the essential requisite of genius."

Baudelaire
Exposition universelle, 1855, Beaux-arts

Ingres (Jean Auguste Dominique) 1780-1867
Madame de Senonnes, 1814
Nantes, Musée des Beaux-Arts

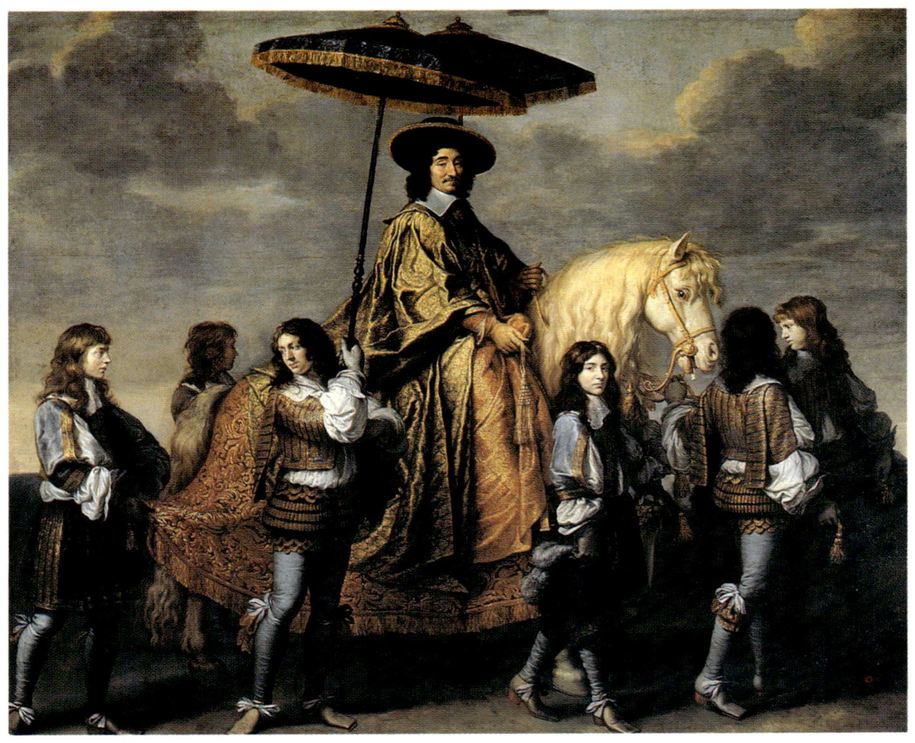

A means of making distinctions

Another approach to the architecture of a body is to envisage it not in its relationship with the absolute but as it connects with that other invisible body which it presumes to reflect and echo: the social body. Artists were asked to turn this shared possession into a means of making distinctions, and we have to admit that they were completely successful. The appearance of the bodies of the humble implied that it was in their nature to be dominated, and the bodies of the powerful demonstrated that it was in their nature to be dominant. The individual body thus became a living metaphor of the social body.

Le Brun, who ruled over the French Académie throughout the second half of the 17th century, was a great master of this genre. He put his art at the service of the celebration of the powerful. Pierre Francastel is fierce in his criticism: "The only thing that Le Brun really feels is the prestige of the self-made man. [...] Like everything else the portrait was to a large extent controlled after 1660 by the court painter and great patrons were happy to comply with him and have themselves depicted as virtual sovereigns. Vanity which was the mainspring underpinning Louis XIV's omnipotence inspired [this] ceremonial style."

Chancellor Séguier, painted on horseback in a three-quarter pose in all his sumptuous finery, dominates the two groups of three young men who form his escort. In a skillfully calculated composition, where drawing takes precedence over color, the light area formed by the horse's head – on the right – is balanced on the left by the darker area formed by the two sunshades. If the sectors covered by the gaze of each of the people are added together, it will be realized that they cover the entire scene. Thus nothing here is left to chance and plastic composition seems to take the place of psychological analysis. When it comes down to it, the portrait of the chancellor tells us nothing except that he is chancellor, and through the fact that he has painted it, it tells us that Le Brun is Court Painter to the king. Art here is not even celebrating itself, but is content to pay homage to a hierarchy which is deliberately reflected in the arrangement of the composition.

Velazquez, confronted with a similar subject, approaches it in an entirely different way. In his portrait of the queen of Spain, Maria Anna of Habsburg, the artist does not deny the aristocratic superiority of his model, but that superiority is not given pride of place: it is not presupposed, but is inferred from the queen's physical presence. In contrast to Chancellor Séguier, whose face is painted only because good taste demands that a face should sit on top of a body, the queen's face is the narrative heart of the composition. Her eyes express all the haughtiness and boredom of a woman born to reign.

When painting portraits of the powerful, Velazquez directs his attention not so much at their aristocratic essence as at the reality of their existence as aristocrats. Because he refocuses attention on the individual rather than the group to which he or she belongs, the painter opens up the way to a wider requestioning of values.

Le Brun (Charles) 1619-1690
Chancellor Séguier
Paris, Louvre

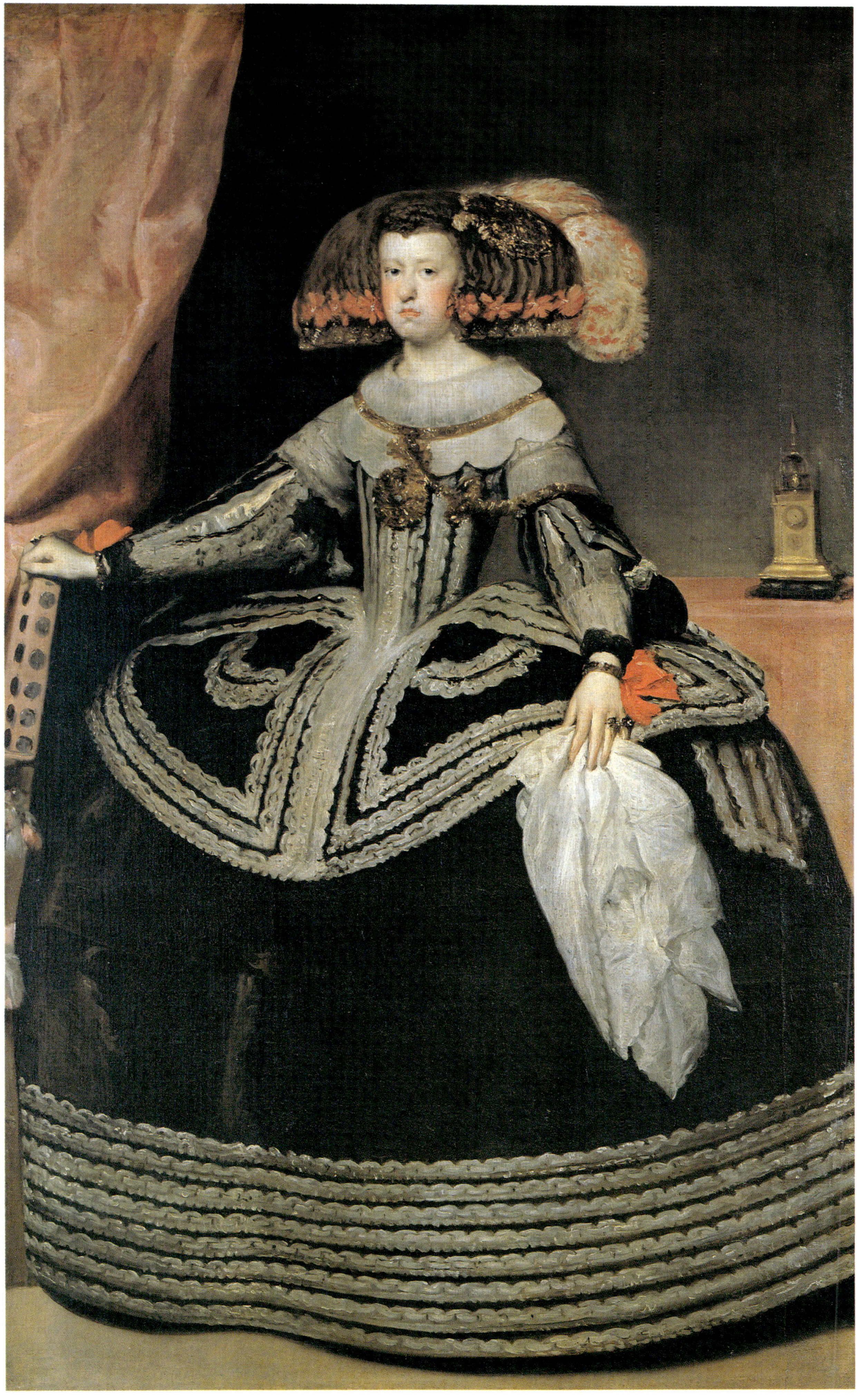

"It was not the intellectual aspect which dominated art [in Spain], and they were much more concerned with giving an immediate impression or truth or with the feeling to be conveyed than with fitting in with an ideal defined by scholars."

Victor-Lucien Tapié
La baroque

Velazquez (Diego Rodriguez de Silva y) 1599-1660
Queen Mariana of Austria
Paris, Louvre

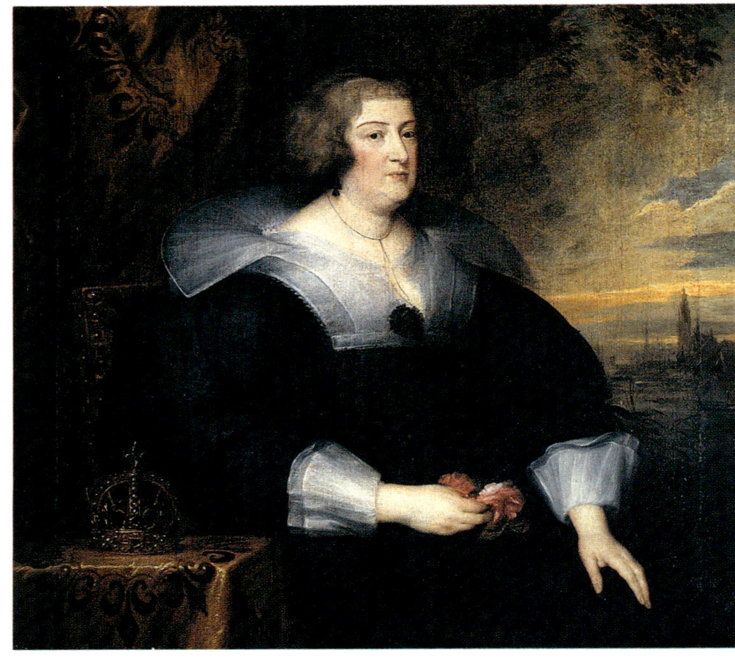

The painter and the monarch

Another way of approaching the interpenetration of the social order and the pictorial order might be to see if we can find the outline of a socio-political context in the way the artist treats the figure. If we consider Bronzino working in the mid-16th century and Van Dyck working in the first half of the 17th, we can find interesting parallels between these two fields.

Bronzino was one of the second generation of Mannerist artists. He was born in Florence in 1503 and grew up in a turbulent period. After the death of Lorenzo the Magnificent in 1492, his sons Pietro and Giuliano were driven out of Florence because they had become allies of the French king and also, mainly, because they wanted to break with the Medici family's populist tradition. The elder branch of the family returned to power in 1512, but were subject to the control of the sometimes rival authorities of the Pope and the emperor. In 1532 power finally fell into the hands of Alessandro, a Medici bastard of uncertain parentage and a protégé of Emperor Charles V. But the new duke's excesses and debauchery attracted general reproof, and five years later he was assassinated by his cousin Lorenzino (Musset's Lorenzaccio). The people of Florence then chose to entrust Cosimo I, a scion of a younger branch of the family, with ruling the duchy. He was much more astute, and established the power of the dynasty for the two succeeding centuries.

However, Cosimo I's power seemed doubly unlawful in the eyes of the other great families reigning in Europe, firstly because he came from the people, and secondly because the Italian nobility had its origins in trade and finance, a background that was too common to impress the military aristocracy of old states such as England or France.

Whereas monarchy had long since become hereditary in the great western kingdoms, in the Italian cities princes were still – at least in theory – elected to office. Cosimo I was well aware of the dangers of such a system and set about concentrating all real power in his hands and his hands alone.

This is where Bronzino came in. The flawless, refined style which he perfected for the court of the Medicis seemed to give *a posteriori* legitimation to the power which history had given to Cosimo. But its main function was to make people forget that history. To endure Cosimo's power had to convey the impression that it had always existed. That is the symbolic meaning of the formal purity of Bronzino's faces.

The work of Van Dyck reveals a different strategy. Making no attempt at idealization, Van Dyck tried to locate the aristocratic essence of his model through psychological exploration. It was a bold gamble because it meant that the artist had to choose between displeasing his patron or lying. But when he achieves his objective, he gives us a completely convincing picture of a nobility which dominates because it is "naturally" superior to the hoi polloi.

Van Dyck (Sir Anthony) 1599-1641
Marie de' Medici, 1631
Lille, Musée des Beaux-Arts

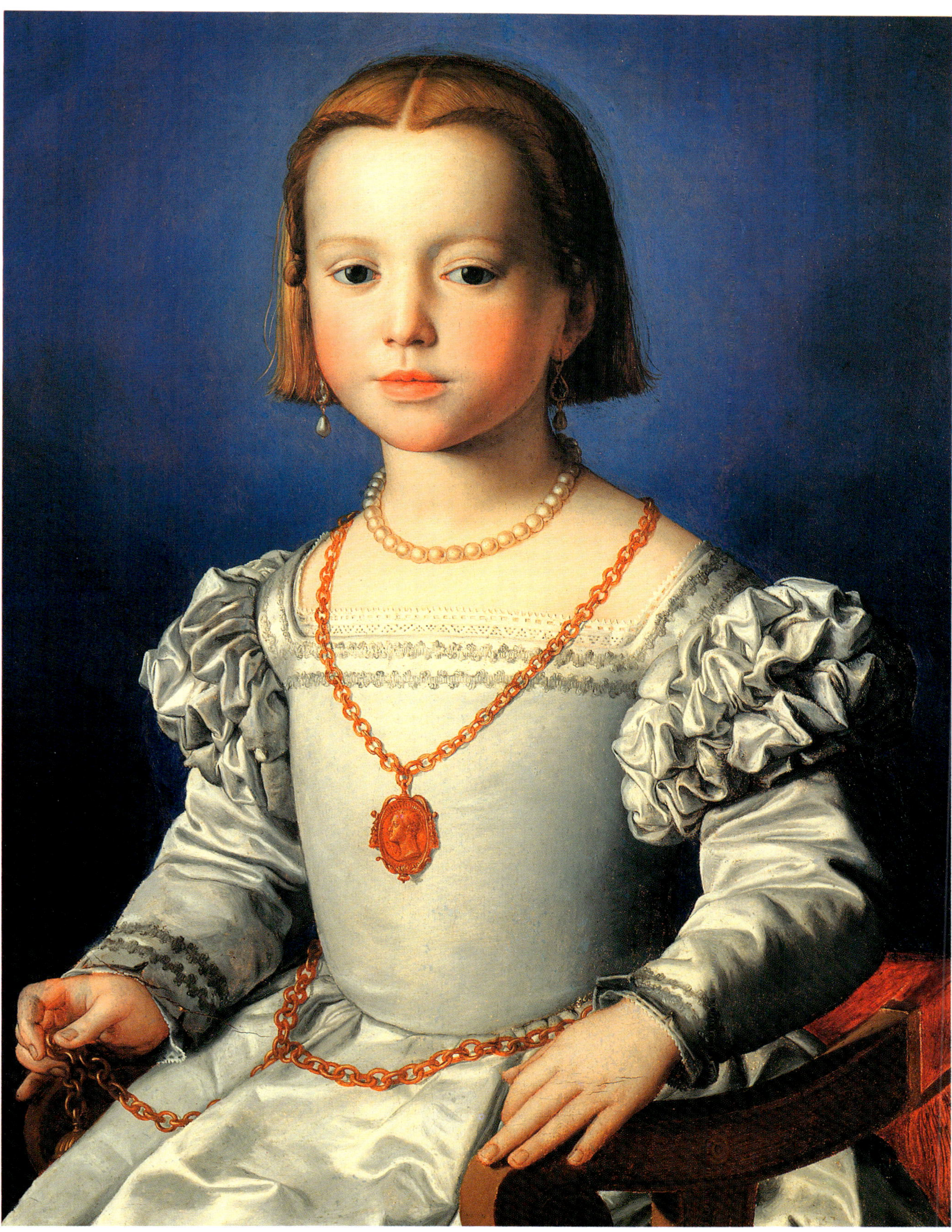

"In this strictly defined genre [portraiture] Bronzino stands head and shoulders above other court art in Europe; and his example is still a pattern to stylish portraitists, starting with Ingres who studied Bronzino a great deal."

André Chastel
Dictionnaire de la peinture italienne

Bronzino (Di Cosimo Allori Angelo, known as) 1503-1572
Isabella de' Medici
Florence, Uffizi

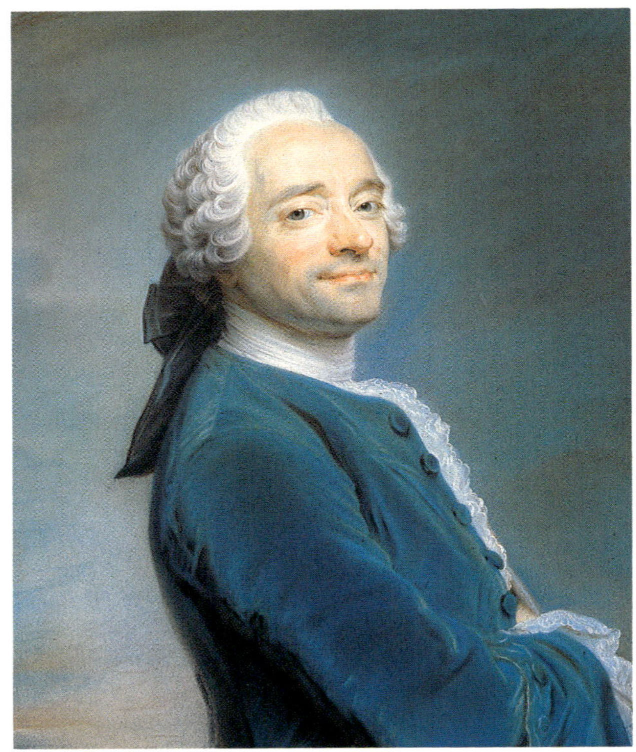

The biographical face

We read the future in the lines of the hand and the past on the lines on a face. When the artist does a self-portrait of himself as a young man, he is just skimming over a potential form, still only a surface. He is practicing his scales. The technique is more important than the subject. He paints himself because that choice spares him the necessity of confronting a strange model who would divert his attention away from himself. To sum up, the young man paints the portrait of an identity that is gestating. And without admitting it to himself he may also be painting a portrait of eternity, i.e. an image which has not yet given time a hold on it. The man who is still nothing gives his art the task of giving him form. It is through painting that he begins the exist, and the self-portrait is the visible outline of that occurrence: in the true as well as the figurative sense it is the birth certificate of the artist.

The self-portrait is also a confession. Even if it lies, it reveals the artist, not so much by what he shows us or hides from us, but by the way in which he sets about doing it. The object is less significant than the manner. The pastel by Maurice Quentin de La Tour skims elegantly over an affable face, but does not dwell on it. The care with which he treats himself is the expression of true politeness. As a work it is both brilliant and superficial, but it would be a mistake to dismiss it too quickly. La Tour is not Rousseau – though he did produce a portrait of him; he is not introspective. What he likes in a face are the aspects that are directed outwards, an alert, bright gaze, a knowing smile. The double on the canvas seems to be quizzing the artist as if to preempt any sudden lurch towards profundity. "Slide over the surface, oh ye mortals, do not go too deep," Sartre's grandmother used to say. By dint of trying too hard to understand, you may end up by forgetting what you are looking for. This humility is present in the self-portrait by de La Tour. As a result, in spite of the slightly glib nature of the work – for silence inevitably is hiding something – we feel an immediate liking for the man. "The style is the man," Buffon declared: words that are tailor-made for this generous artist.

Artists with a more tormented temperament choose a different path. In their youth they may have allowed their nascent style to dictate a form for their face – Rembrandt springs to mind, but Tintoretto too – but once they have reached maturity it is as if the process underwent a subtle change; it is no longer up to painting to give a form to the man, it is up to time to give a form to painting. What the biographical face then recounts is the story of a gradual forgetfulness of self. Any traces of narcissism in a youthful self-portrait disappear in self-portraits painted in maturity, and instead we find a progressive confusion of the artist with his art.

That is why a successful self-portrait is always more a portrait of painting than a portrait of the painter.

La Tour (Maurice Quentin de) 1704-1788
Self-portrait
Amiens, Musée de Picardie

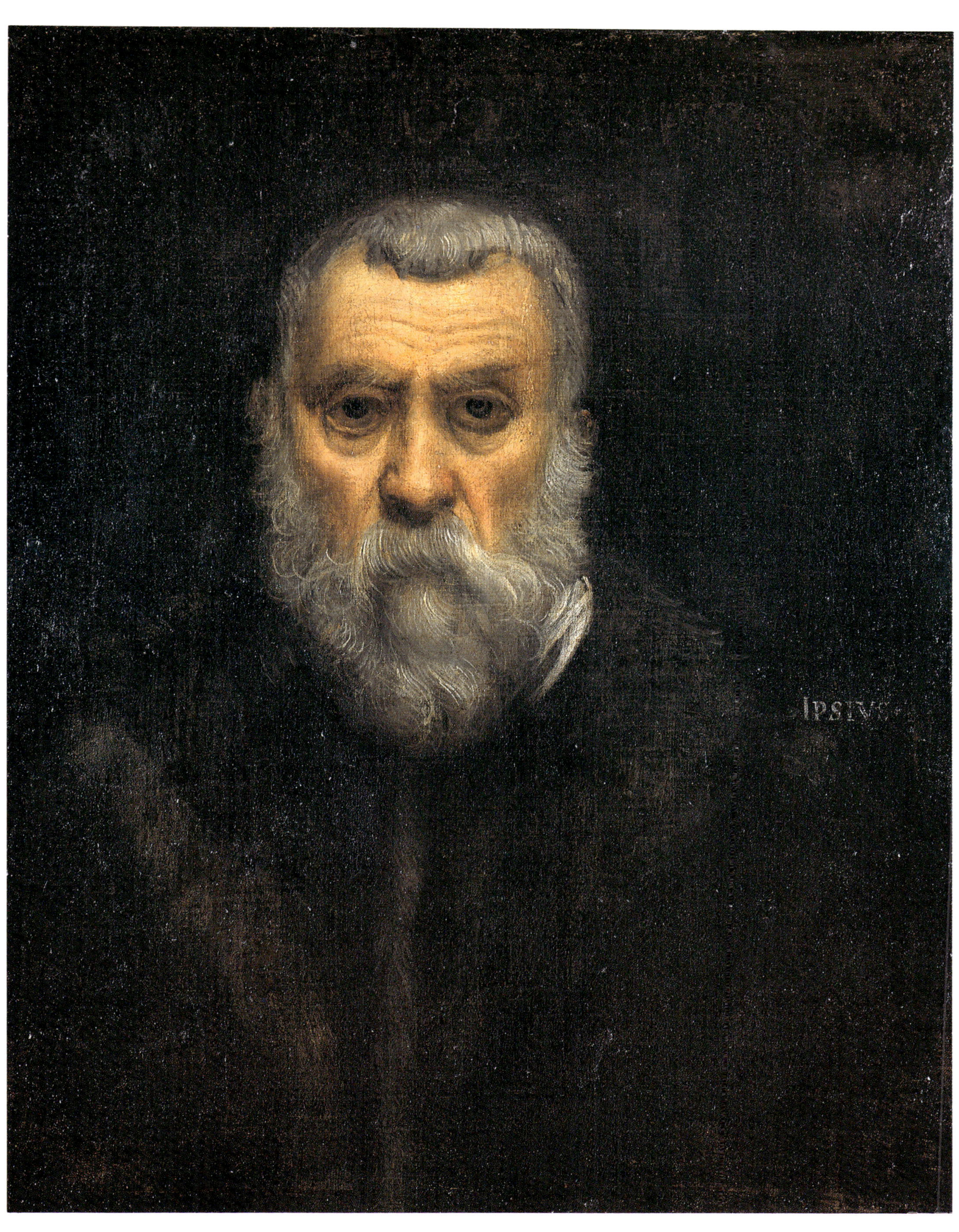

"Whatever the figure invented may be, it is Tintoretto himself depicting himself here in his earthly solitude, it is his own body that he molds from the clay."

Jean-Paul Sartre
Le séquestré de Venise

Tintoretto (Jacopo Robusti, known as) 1518-1594
Self-portrait
Paris, Louvre

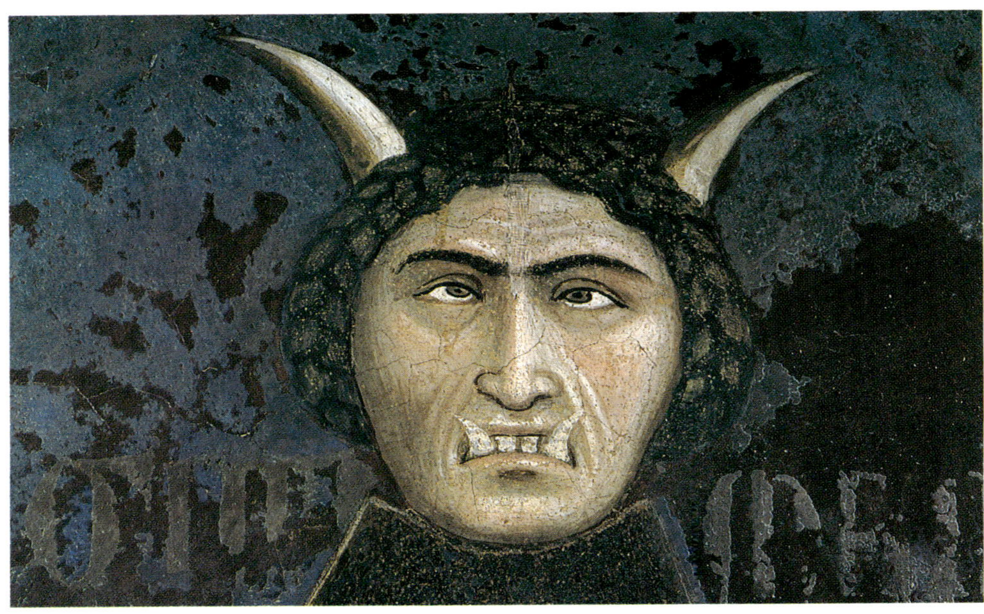

Portrait of an abstraction

In the etymological sense allegory is an image that speaks, or to be more precise a way of speaking through an image. It is a means of giving life to an abstraction, animating it. The allegory makes a complex truth explicit, makes an idea visible.

Greeks were not familiar with allegory and its use did not become widespread in Rome until the Lower Empire. In its pictorial form it seems to be incompatible with the Platonic theory of ideas which defines them as pure intellectual forms; Plato considered the painter incapable of satisfying the demands of reason because he was satisfied with the simple appearance of things, i.e. with the aspect of perceptible reality farthest removed from the idea.

We have to wait for the first stirrings of the Renaissance to see the painter taking up allegory; until then it had been the preserve of poetry (this is no doubt connected in some way with the rediscovery of Horace's program summed up in the famous formula: *ut pictura poesis*). The allegory personifies a vice or a virtue. It is a synthetical expression of the complexity of the activity of the intellect. But the "ideas" so represented are no longer Plato's transcendent entities: they are the form the intellect gives to the outcome of its confrontation with reality. St. Thomas wrote: "The idea is the internal form shaped by the understanding. And we imitate its effects through the will of the artist." Thus at the point where the Middle Ages and the Renaissance meet we are confronted by an inversion of Platonic theory: pictorial allegories are no longer obscuring the truth, as Plato would have maintained in the *Republic*, but revealing it at the very heart of the living being. And in this guise they represent the stepping-stone enabling us to pass from the world of the senses to realities of a spiritual order.

The purpose of allegorical representation is to separate out something coherent at the heart of the profusion of the perceptible world. It is a question of giving a form not only to what has been produced by reason, but also to the sphere of human passions. This is why the face imposes itself as the most appropriate form; it has the capacity to express both the rational and the irrational. The allegorical face is the material form given to the internal ideas that Thomas Aquinas mentioned. It is a true repertory, a language in fact, firstly because it externalizes a thought content, and also because each representation constitutes one element of this synthetical language. Just as some astrophysicists now believe that the Universe is the shape of God, the allegory might be defined as the human form of the divine order, and paradoxically as the possible form of disorder, as is illustrated in Siena by the *Allegory of Good Government* by the Lorenzetti brothers. Thus allegory defines reality as a new field for the reason to experiment with. In doing so it puts the painter in a role previously reserved for the philosopher, giving him the responsibility of making reality intelligible. But because allegory still retains the confusion between ethics and esthetics, it prohibits true emancipation. Until the 19th century painting would continue to conceive of beauty as the expression of truth.

Lorenzetti (Ambrogio) fl. 1319-1348
Allegory of good government.
Detail: The effects of bad government; Tyranny, bust, 1338
Siena, Palazzo Pubblico

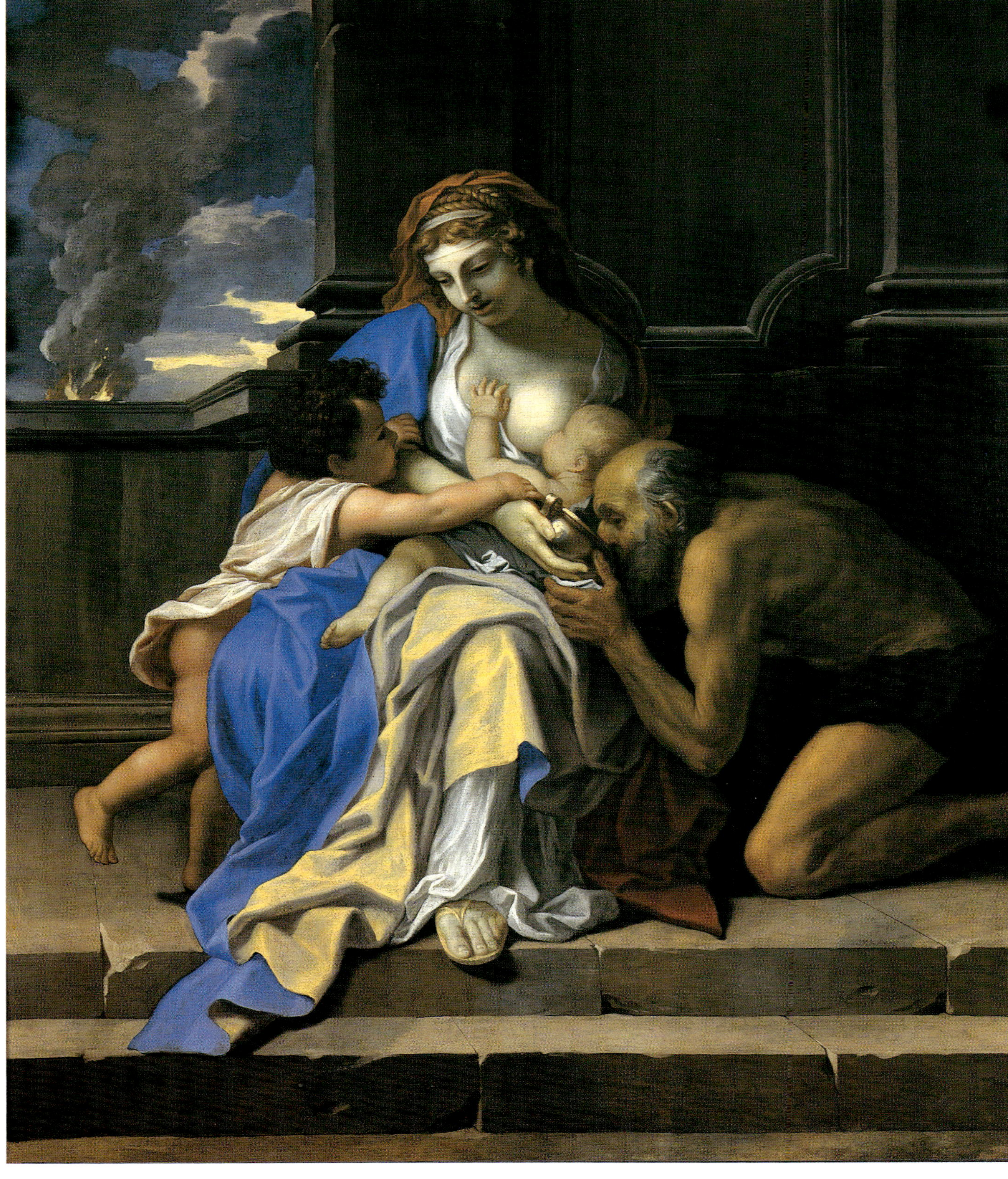

"No-one will deny that the 17th and 18th centuries produced masses of obscure, insipid and totally boring allegories."

Rensselaer W. Lee
Ut pictura poesis

Le Brun (Charles) 1619-1690
Charity
Caen, Musée des Beaux-Arts

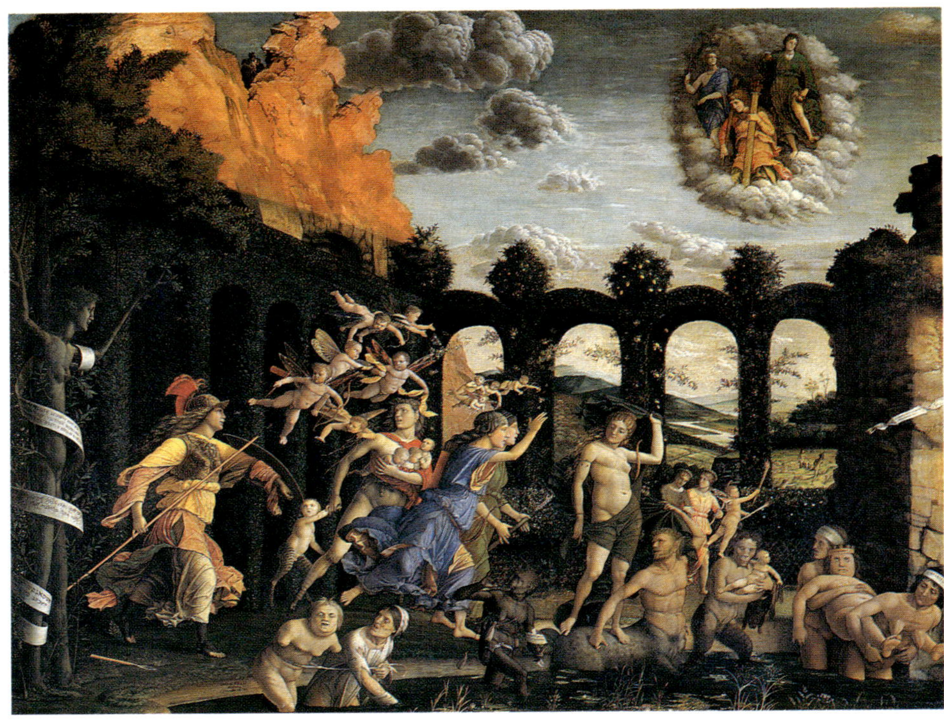

The body, space and the idea

"Ficino [...] characterizes [beauty], coming close to Christian Neo-Platonism , as a 'ray emitted by the face of God' which first passes through the angels then goes on to illuminate the human soul and finally the world of physical matter; Alberti on the other hand [...] countered that metaphysical interpretation of beauty with the purely phenomenal interpretation of classical Greece: 'Beauty consists in a harmony and accord of the parts with the whole.' [...] In turning away from a metaphysical interpretation of beauty, for the first time there was a severing of the links between the 'beautiful' and the 'good' which had been unbroken since Antiquity ...."

These are the words of Panofsky; though he went on to qualify this brilliant distinction, he unquestionably highlights the essential debate which was only partly resolved by the Romantics' affirmation three centuries later of the creative power of the imagination. Representing the human figure, and nature in more general terms, confronts the painter with the question of the origin of beauty. In the name of what principle or doctrine can a figure be said to be beautiful? Because it is the visible form of a transcendent truth, or because it is the appropriate expression of an immanent formal harmony? And even if it is the latter, where does the idea of harmony within me which makes me find it beautiful come from: from a confused memory from the sphere of ideas, or from my own earthly experience? Raphael wrote, "To paint a beautiful woman ... I avail myself of a certain idea which comes to my mind," but he does not tell us how that idea came to his mind. Thus the Renaissance, suspended between Platonic idealism and Locke's empiricism, appears more as a period of transition than a pure, simple rediscovery of Antiquity.

The placing of the body in perspective, which is a Renaissance phenomenon, can likewise serve both these theses. If we interpret monocular perspective, the theory of which was worked out by Brunelleschi, as the birth certificate of the dogma of the realism of vision, we can legitimately claim that the process snatched the body out of limbo and put it back down on the bedrock of concrete experience. But if, on the other hand, we remember that the use of perspective substitutes space that is understood by the intellect for space that is perceived by the senses, then we are taking from the artist the possibility of a subjective apprehension of reality. The forms which he recomposes on his canvas with the human figure at their center "constitute entities that have their own laws and essence." (P. Francastel). That is what happens in Mantegna's work; for him, putting the body in perspective has surely less to do with trying to achieve an effect of reality than with inscribing it in a formal setting the rigor of which removes it from the world of the senses, projecting it into the incorruptible sphere of the idea.

Mantegna (Andrea) 1431-1506
Wisdom triumphing over the vices
Paris, Louvre

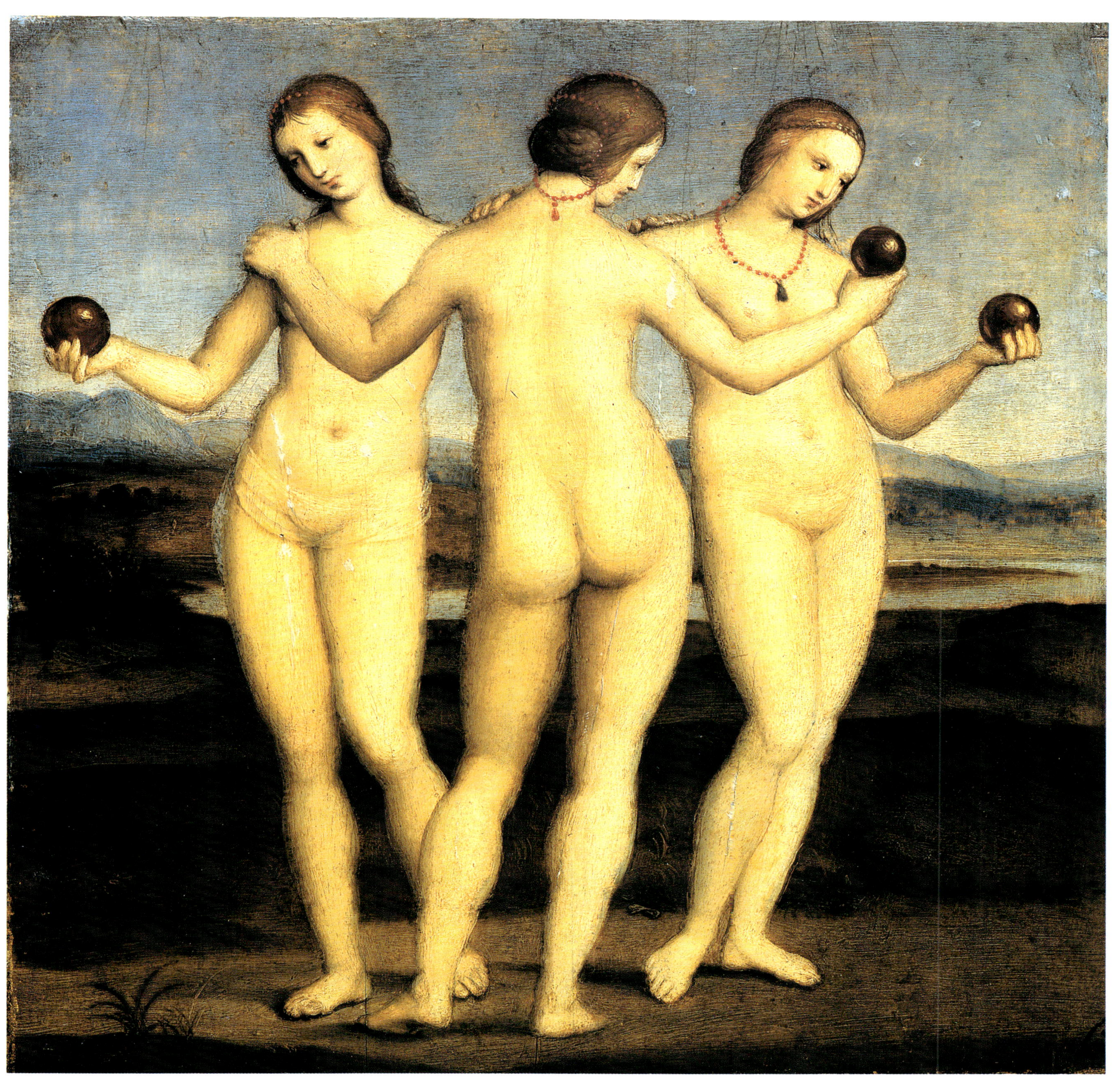

"The Renaissance demanded that its works of art should at the same time be true to nature and beautiful, not as yet perceiving the slightest contradiction in this."

Erwin Panofsky
Idea

Raphael (Raffaello Santi or Sanzio, known as) 1483-1520
The Three Graces, 1501
Chantilly, Musée Condé

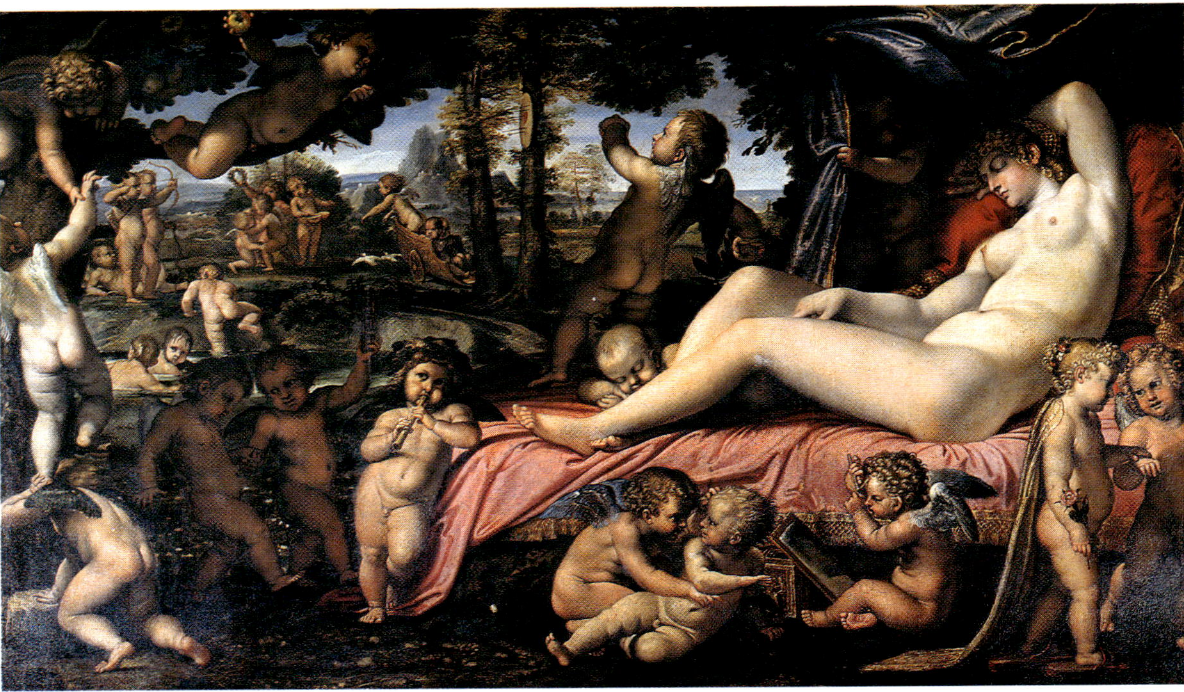

Fat and Thin

We know the distinction Levi-Strauss drew between the raw and the cooked. In a not dissimilar vein we can attempt to place the many representations of the body into the opposing categories of sensuous opulence and mystic asceticism: the body or the fight between fat and thin .... What it really comes down to is the fight between the body as it is and the ideal body; the body as it is experienced against the body as it is thought; a fight between the senses and meaning.

The emaciated body of Bicci di Lorenzo's Christ is a body that is denying its flesh. A body that is on the way to being disincarnated, it might be described in popular parlance as "just skin and bone." It is an empty envelope and we cannot imagine that it contains the organs that healthy nature ought to have put there. This man does not have a body in the ordinary sense: at best he has the idea of a body. It is something that has been borrowed, a temporary, transitory form with a purely utilitarian value. We understand straight away that such a body cannot enjoy existence: enjoy in the sense of deriving pleasure from its own functioning. That body is devoid of senses. Its wasted forms decree a rule that contains its own disappearance, its own negation. It is in fact an essence that has strayed into a living being, which has no role there, nothing to do with it; and we might almost say of the essence too that it can barely be seen. We are a long way away from the "alcoves of purple where the stretched out shapes seemed to place a block of fair light under Titian's eyes" (E. Faure). The body of Christ is bathed in a supernatural, metaphysical light which seems completely ignorant of the frailties of the flesh.

The form made woman is something else again, the epitome of natural harmony, with the register placed less on true light than on the interplay between shadow and light. The fact that the body of Christ shows nothing does not imply that it is hiding something. It is the eclipse preparing the way for a return to pure light; it will acquire meaning through its disappearance. Venus on the other hand allows us to see only so as to give shape to desire, i.e. to bring about the disordering of the senses: she is the stuff of concupiscence. The body offered is the breeding ground of desire. The more it displays itself, the more one wants to see it. And the more one sees it, the more one thinks it is hidden: seen in that light jealousy can be regarded as the final culmination of desire. We expect nothing substantial in the physical sense of the term from thinness, because in a way it is a metaphor of transparency. Fat on the other hand, because it is an opaque volume, will never entirely reveal itself to the unveiling ray of the light. Light on the fat body exists only in the dialog it sets in motion with shade. And the body takes shape only in the fundamental duplicity with which it is portrayed: the more the body is there, the less it is there, as the illusion allowing it to appear is greater. The more you think you see, the more you blind yourself. This gives rise to the distinction that can be made between two forms of representation: in one, expressing all the diversity of the appearance leads the senses astray; the other, because it sets out to represent the essence, shuts out the deceptive appearance of the perceptible world.

Carracci (Annibale) 1560-1609
Sleeping Venus, 1602
Chantilly, Musée Condé

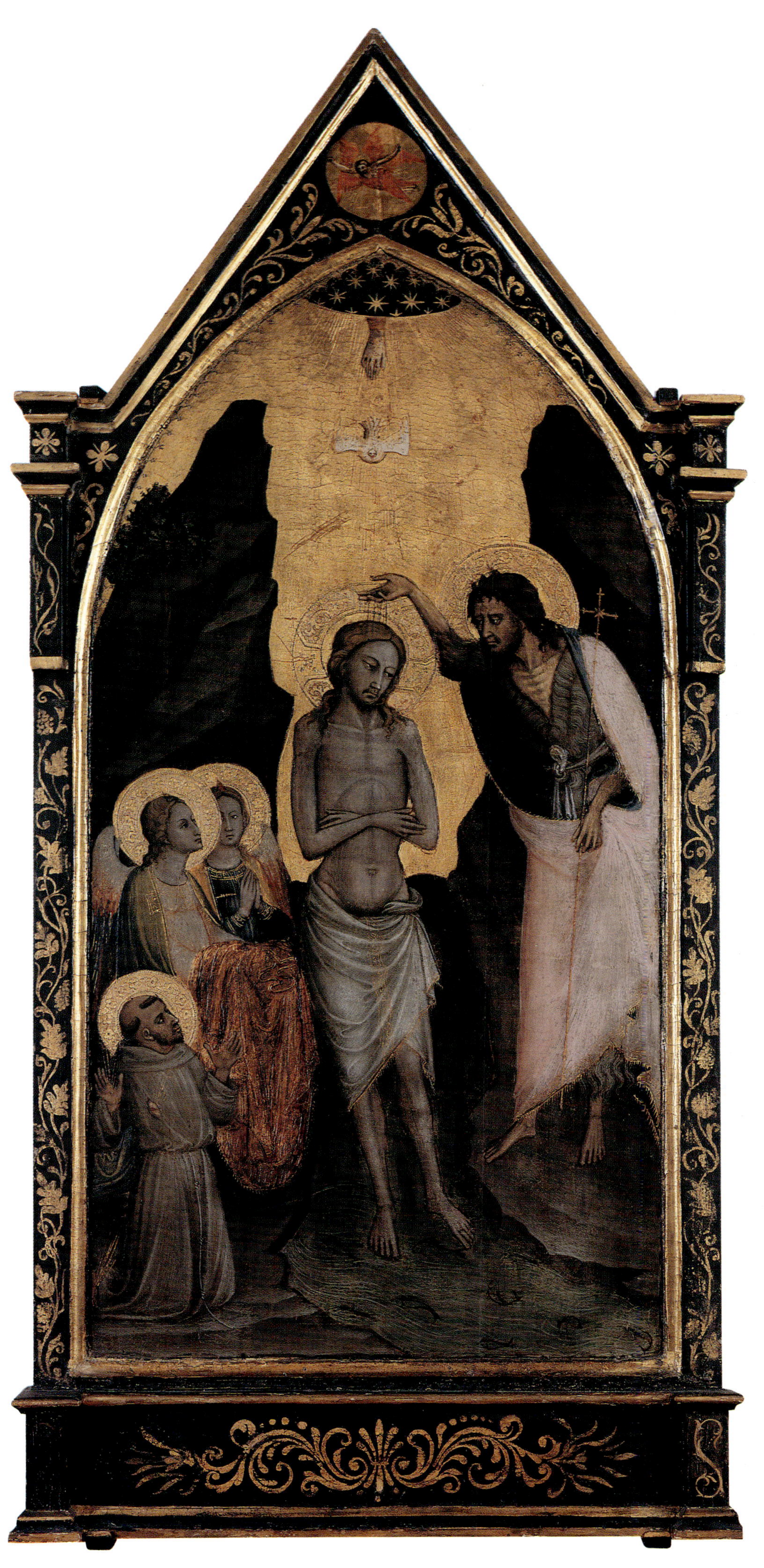

Bicci di Lorenzo 1373-1452
Baptism of Christ
Nantes, Musée des Beaux-Arts

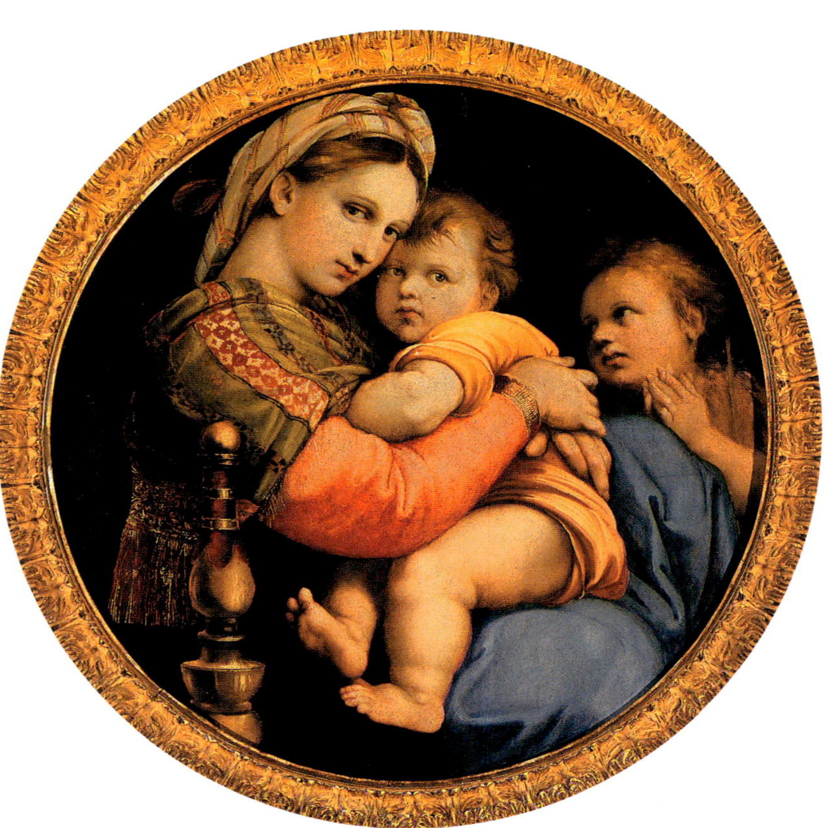

The veil and the unveiling

The classic distinction between the essential body and the body of the senses spelt out above can be regarded as relevant until the 18th century, until the start of publication of scientific treatises on the body. By the 19th century the body had become an object to be considered rationally, and since then the body has belonged to science. And since sexuality could at last be expressed acceptably, it might be claimed that the veil could be lifted from the female body without causing moral offense.

Michel Foucault, who questioned the prevailing belief that sexual repression had been instituted by the middle classes, claimed that there had never been as much discussion about sex as during the last two centuries. Bourgeois hypocrisy did not so much lie in suppressing sexuality as in transforming the way it was talked about: Foucault wrote, "And we have to ask ourselves whether *scientia sexualis* – in the guise of decent positivism – does not at least sometimes function as *ars erotica.*"

It would seem that from then on the body ceased to be the symbol of sin and became the symbol of knowledge. With the advent of Freud, unveiling the body and the language of the body became a necessary preliminary to establishing the truth, since psycho-analytic theory revealed that all knowledge is governed by an unconscious background structured by sexuality. In a strange reversal of values, the body which had been a symbol of negative knowledge since the time of Eve became the positive emblem of knowledge to be acquired. And the unveiling of its nakedness then came to be viewed as a moral as well as a scientific act.

Looked at in this light, the veiled body of the Virgin was irrelevant. The truth was no longer perceived as being beyond the body, it was no longer ineffable. Not only could it be expressed, it had to be. Nudity proclaimed itself as a conquest. The middle classes, armed with their positive knowledge and anxious to demonstrate their social maturity, clamoured for nudes, more nudes and yet more nudes, until the academy exhibitions were virtually overflowing with them. But since they all wanted to express the same objective norm, in the end they all looked similar, like this Venus by Amaury-Duval, only too obviously doing obeisance to Ingres's *La Source.*

It goes without saying that the artist would have dismissed the charge that the forms he displayed so unreservedly on the canvas were ambiguous. Scientific debate was there to guarantee the morality of the work. Because it had become a scientific object, the sexual body had likewise become a body with no history, a soft entity freed from its shaded areas and bereft of relief. *Scientia sexualis* turned the sexual body into an sexless body. The body of the young mother depicted as the Madonna, summed up in a breast extended to the child's lips, was asexual for different reasons: as a nursing body it was temporarily withdrawn from the mechanics of desire. She could no longer offer it because it no longer belonged to her. The barely pubescent Venuses of the 19th century, on the other hand, could not offer their bodies because they now belonged to the realm of science.

Raphael (Raffaello Santi or Sanzio, known as) 1483-1520
Madonna of the chair, c. 1515-1516
Florence, Pitti Palace

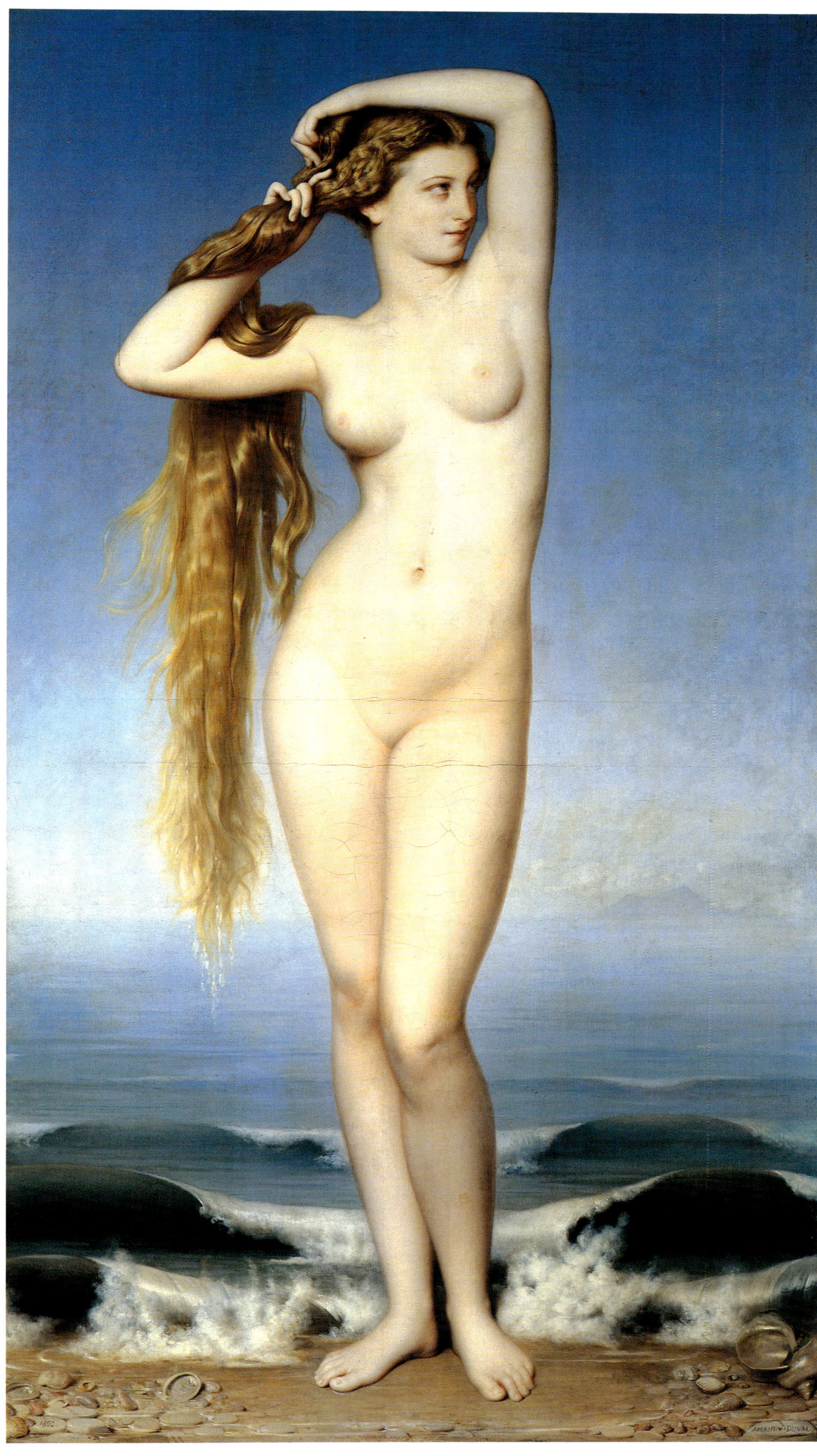

"The flesh tones after being kept in store have taken on transparent hues, becoming pinkish and yellowish, reminiscent of both Russia leather and the petals of a rose."

Emile Zola
Mon Salon

Amaury-Duval (Pineu-Duval Eugène, known as) 1808-1885
Birth of Venus
Lille, Musée des Beaux-Arts

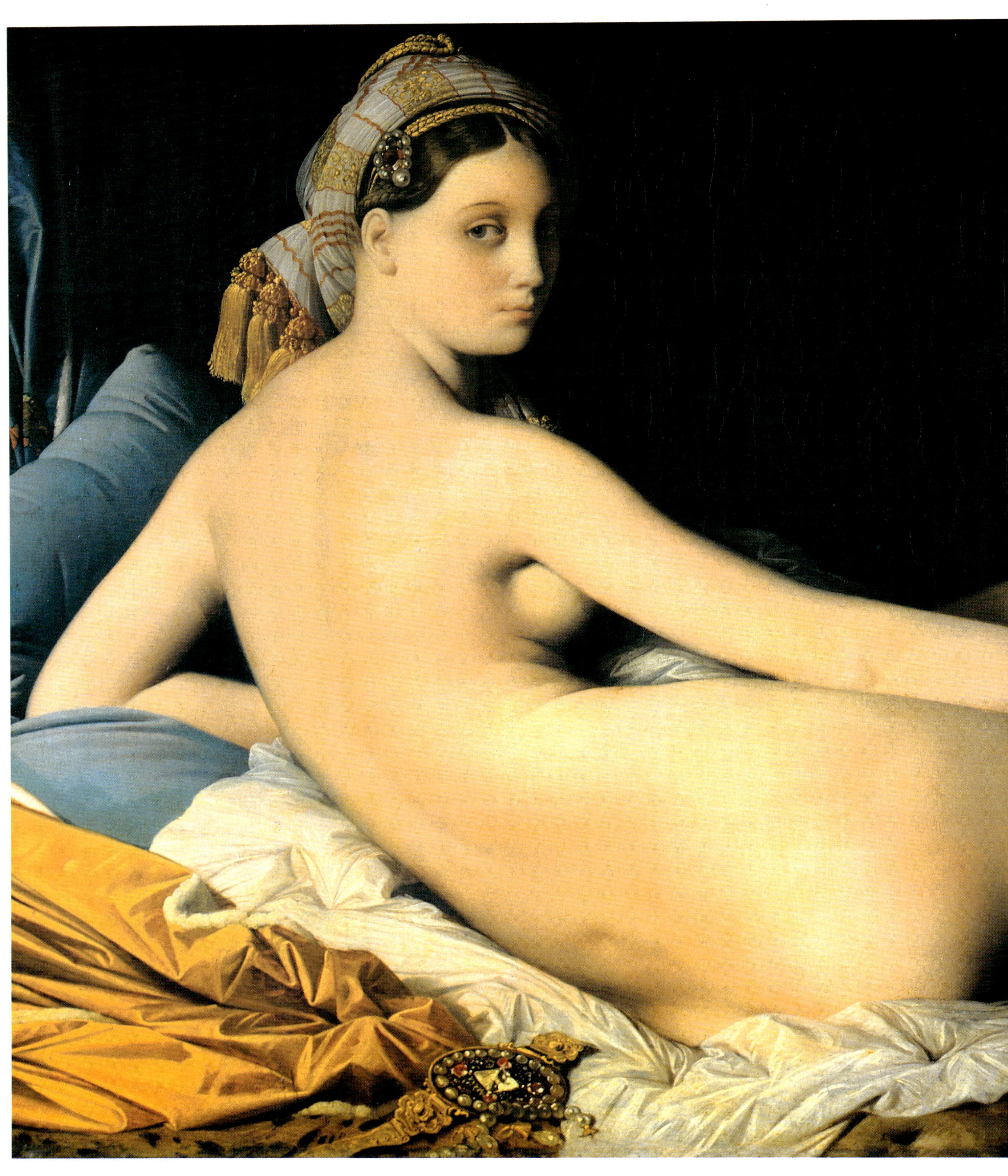

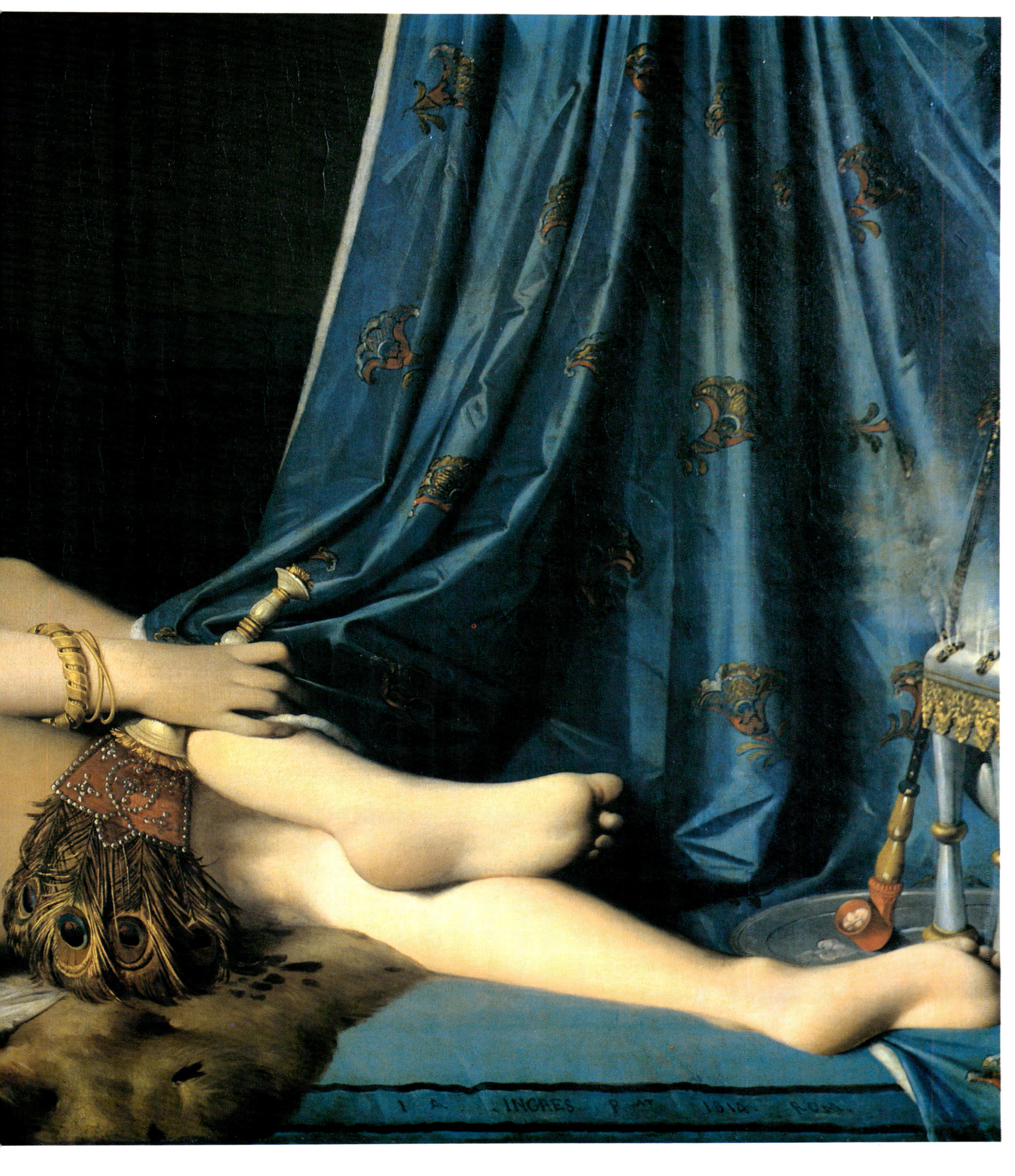

Ingres (Jean Auguste Dominique) 1780-1867
La Grande Odalisque, 1814
Paris, Louvre

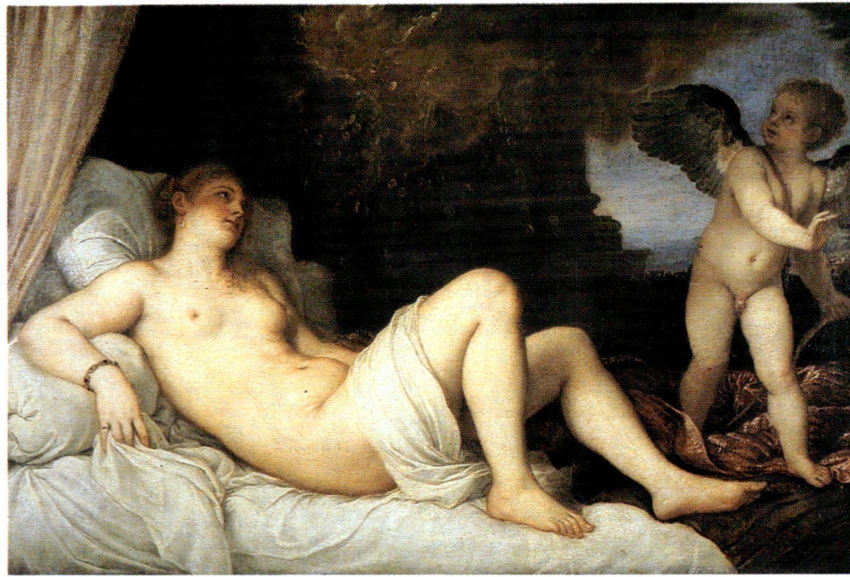

Subjective bodies

Kenneth Clark wrote that "the antique scheme had involved so complete a fusion of the sensual and the geometric as to provide a kind of armor [...]. Once this armor had grown unwearable, the nude [...] became a dead abstraction ...." This was how the official 19th-century painters failed, in trying to pursue, in Ingres's wake, an impossible objective norm the definition of which was rather over-hastily attributed to Raphael. We are reminded by R.W. Lee that "Alberti and Vasari – Raphael too in his famous letter to Castiglione – had associated with a direct experience of nature the Idea which raises art above the simple imitation of things. But rather than contributing to building up a theory of esthetics their thoughts on this subject remained naive or fragmentary."

The solution adopted by the succeeding generations, with the Impressionists first among them, seems to have consisted of giving primacy to a subjective expression of perception and paying less attention to the application of an objective norm. The expression of this new subjectivity was more concerned with color than with line. In very approximate terms, that was the way chosen to get the representation of the body away from Classical idealism on the one hand, and scientific positivism on the other: painting not what is or what ought to be, but what is perceived. And it just so happens that the eye perceives colored masses first before conceiving of the lines that organize them.

The great forerunner in this field was Titian, whose expressive use of color for the first time verified what has become an axiom of modern art: color is form. Undoubtedly this aspect of Titian's work does not receive enough attention. The antique body, hence the Renaissance body as well, constituted the ideal figure of harmony. Humanism had made it into a concrete idea, a form serving as a medium insuring the transition from the universe perceptible to the senses to the pure sphere of the Idea.

Seen in this context, ordaining the primacy of color in one's painting was more than a simple esthetic whim, it was a revolution. Saying that color came first meant rendering the transcendent ambitions of painting null and void. Color was no longer the outcome of the artist's dialog with the idea, but of a concrete, intimate confrontation with the model. The form was no longer outlined first: subjective chromatism against objective formalism, this was the game subtly played around the heritage of Raphael.

Painting three centuries after Titian, Renoir made a similar experiment and like Titian went through a period of doubt. "About 1883 there was a kind of break in my work," he wrote. "I had taken Impressionism as far as it would go and this had led me to the conclusion that I could neither paint nor draw." A sentence such as this is a measure of the power of tradition. In the work of even the boldest artists, until the dawn of the 20th century color continued to be a seed of anarchy: generally speaking, order was line.

Titian (Tiziano Vecellio, known as) c. 1488/1489-1576
Danaë and the shower of gold
Naples, Museo di Capodimonte

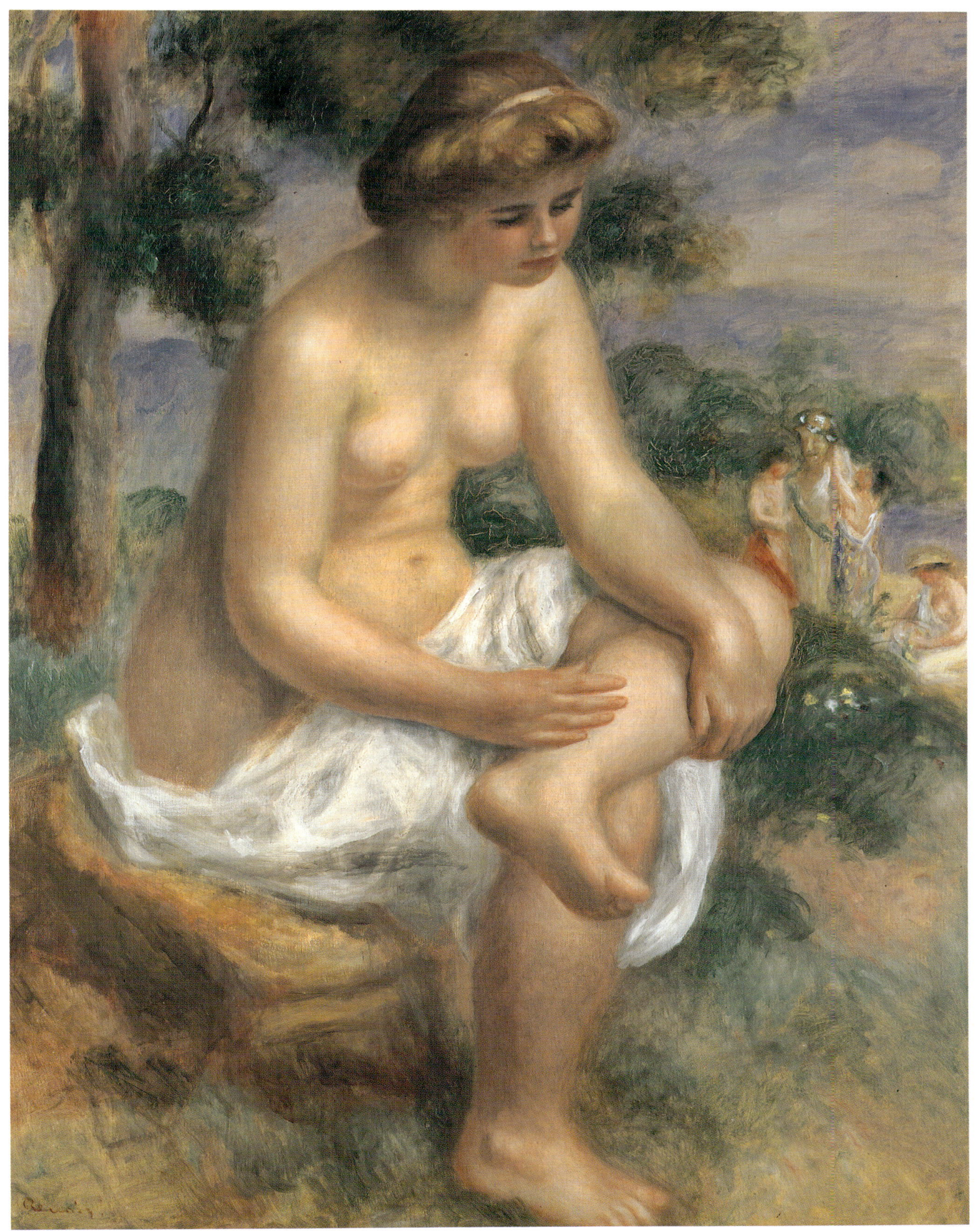

"The supreme vision of the greatest painters is that which can be found in Renoir's, Titian's or Hals's last paintings [...], the vision that kept vigil within them when they began to go blind."

André Malraux

Renoir (Pierre Auguste) 1841-1919
Woman bather sitting in a landscape, known as Eurydice, c. 1895-1900
Paris, Musée Picasso

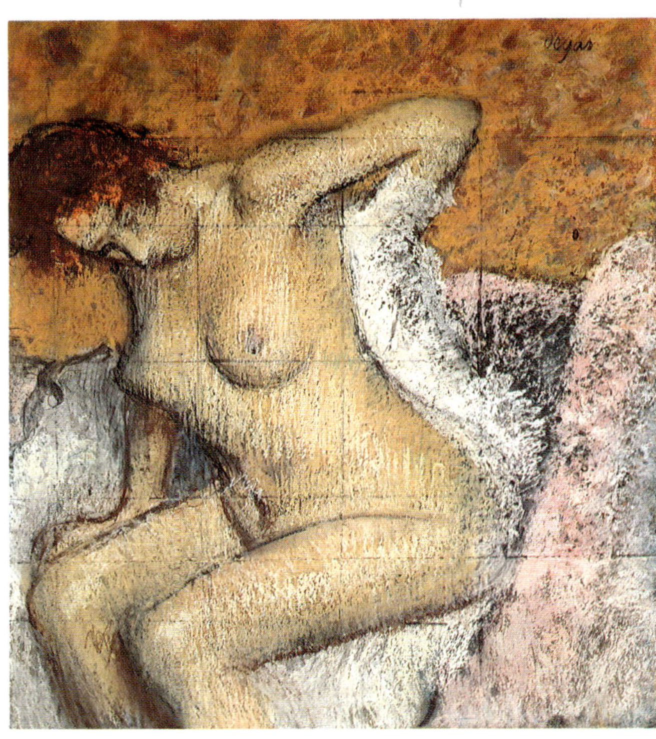

The body, the painter and style

When the representation of the body ceased to be the pursuit of an idea, it became the mirror of the representation that the artist has of it. When the line as norm gave way to color, the body became the mirror of the painter's subjectivity. It became the matter through which color, i.e. light, took form: it became the expression of a style. In the words of Gide, a style is the ability "to paint a specific subject with sufficient power for the generality of which it was part to be comprised in it."

Degas's women have that power. This is achieved firstly by the skill used in framing them, refusing to reduce the reality of the painted body to the narrow frame of the work, opening it up in a kind of way to a space that is not depicted, external to the frame, that is reconstructed mentally on the basis of indications provided by the work. In this sense his work is linked to Realism, but it also goes beyond Realism because it transcends the reality of the model in the advent of a style. Just as Flaubert could say, "Madame Bovary, c'est moi," Degas could have said, "That woman drying herself is me." These women are neither individual personalities, nor are they representatives of the universal: they exist only through Degas's style, they are the style, they are the shape of his internal world. Malraux wrote that modern art "is the annexation of forms by an internal schema which takes or does not take the form of figures or objects, but of which figures and objects are no more than the expression. The initial desire of the modern artist is to make everything subordinate to his style, starting with the most primary, naked object [...]. The conflict which had for such a long time set painters and objects against one another finally erupted."

What is going on here is nothing other than the end, the overstepping, of the conflict between idealism and realism. What is at stake is no longer knowing whether the body should be represented in accordance with pre-established esthetic canons (idealism) or in accordance with its objective appearance (realism): henceforth the truth of a representation would result from the artist's ability to express what Malraux called his "internal schema" through an objective form. In other words, with the birth of modern art of which Degas, like Cézanne and Gauguin, was a precursor, the idea of representation was turned completely on its head: whereas it used to be the artist's mission to express a form, it is now the form that expresses the artist. And this brings us both to the problems posed by Expressionism and those posed by phenomenology: the truth of this body I am painting resides neither in an ideal body of which it is just the imperfect image, nor in the body itself as an object, but in the way it appears to me. The truth of this body is not the body which is in itself unattainable, but this body insofar as I perceive it: the truth is the phenomenon, i.e. for the painter a certain state of light. This is unquestionably a radical reversal of which Bonnard was the direct heir, but Gauguin too was affected – though the conclusions he drew from it were completely different; shortly before his death he declared: "truth is pure, cerebral art."

Degas (Hilaire Germain Edgar de Gas, known as) 1834-1917
After the bath, c. 1900
St. Petersburg, Hermitage

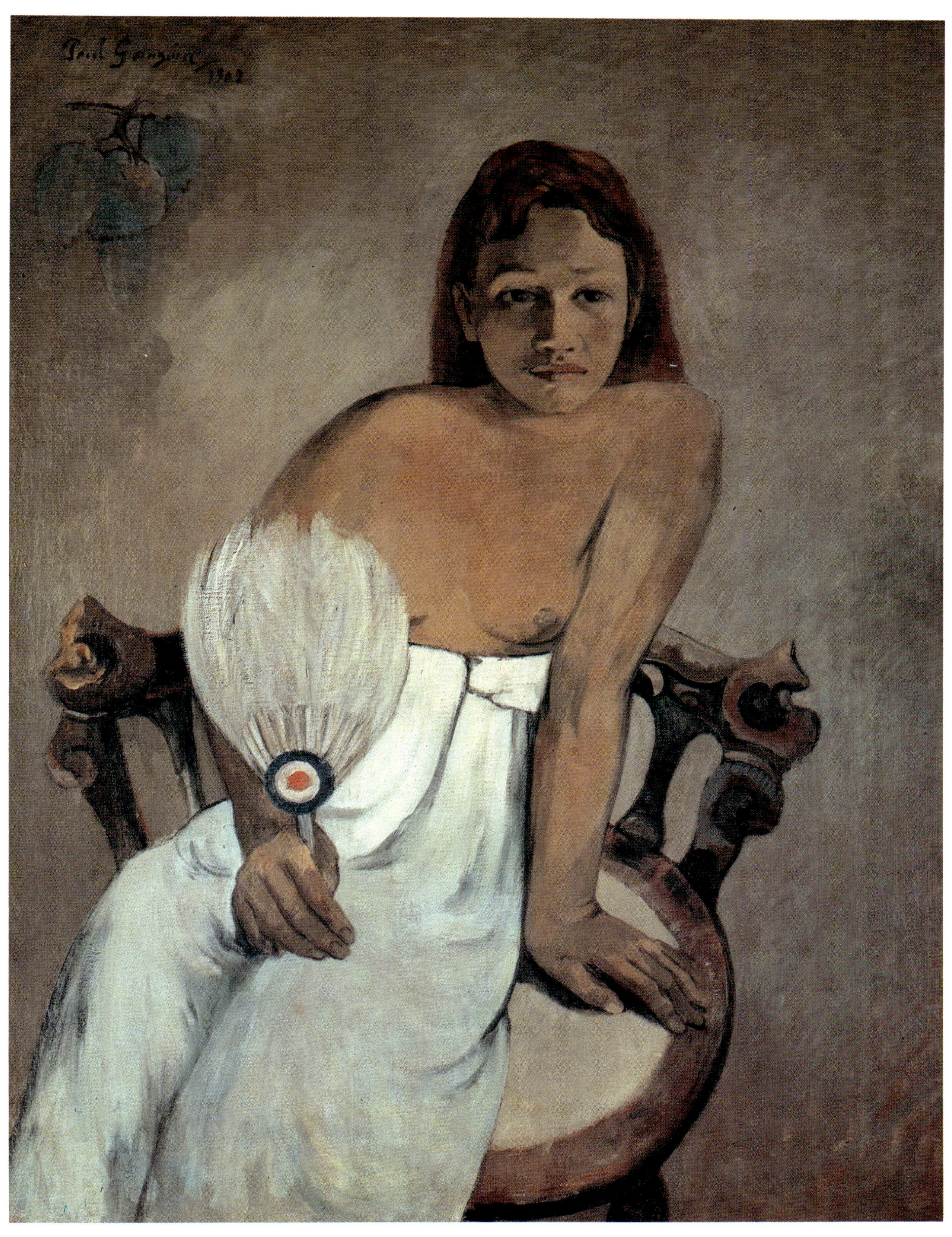

"Primitive art springs from the mind and uses nature."

Paul Gauguin

Gauguin (Paul) 1848-1903
Girl with a fan, 1902
Essen, Folkwang Museum

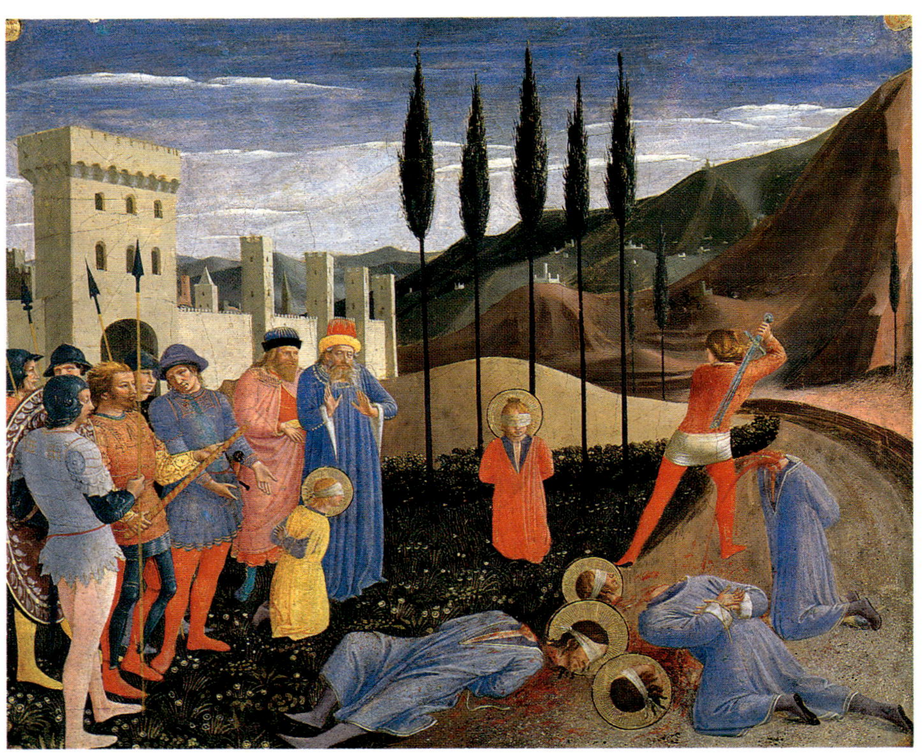

Sacrificial forms

Readers will perhaps be surprised at this stage of our study to find works by Fra Angelico, de La Tour or Van Dyck. It is in fact a strange detour and no doubt calls for an explanation. At the same time as the Renaissance and Classicism became keen to invent an ideal body, doubt persisted alongside the proclaimed certainties, as an underground working, invisible but always present, or as the wish to destroy the work for fear that it would turn out to be unworthy of the hopes vested in it. The temptation to destroy the body, to dislocate it – or at the very least to distend its forms – was always present for these obstinate builders of the human body.

In metaphorical terms the painting of martyrdom also involves painting the martyrdom of painting, of the fundamental, virtually inevitable, ineluctable dissatisfaction which results from any quest for perfection: and this was not only perfection of the body, but that of the work in its entirety. Seen in this light, the arrow piercing St. Sebastian's body is also the material sign of doubt: a symbolic laceration of the painted surface, an incision of the body. But it expresses more than doubt: it is also the indication of a curiosity and a will that will not accept defeat, always aiming to push back the frontiers of the visible. The arrow then functions as an interrogation of appearances, requestioning them at the very moment of their triumph; going beyond the flawless surface of the body, it claims the right to rummage in its entrails. And we may note that de La Tour characteristically paints a body which denies the shot that pierces it, so refusing to be examined. The body which refuses analysis is thus fixed in its perfection, and dies ....

The martyr, like the painter, wants to believe in the existence of a truth concealed behind the world of appearances. He makes a religion of his belief, the painter an art. The arrow that explores the body, the paintbrush traveling over the surface of the canvas, are motivated by this basic conviction. That does not mean that art, like religion, is a search for a reality concealed under the outer appearance of the world: it might perhaps be more accurately described as an attempt to give meaning to the phenomenon by the act of depicting it. Just as martyrdom came and gave meaning to the life of St. Sebastian, the work of art would like to set itself the mission of giving meaning to the meaninglessness of the world.

But giving a meaning to the world involves recreating it. Malraux wrote: "Art is in fact born [...] from the determination to snatch forms away from the world to which man is subjected and place them in the world he controls [...]. The great work of art is not quite truth as the artist believes: it is. It has arisen. It is not an end but a birth."

The martyr tears himself away from the world through sacrifice, and the artist through creation. For this is what it is really all about: not copying reality, but recreating it, reconstructing it. To quote Malraux again, "All great works strike us as demiurgism."

Fra Angelico (Fra Giovanni da Fiesole, secular name Guido di Pietro, known as)
c. 1395/1400-1455
Retable of the Virgin and Child.
Part of predella: martyrdom of St. Cosmo and St. Damian, c. 1435
Paris, Louvre

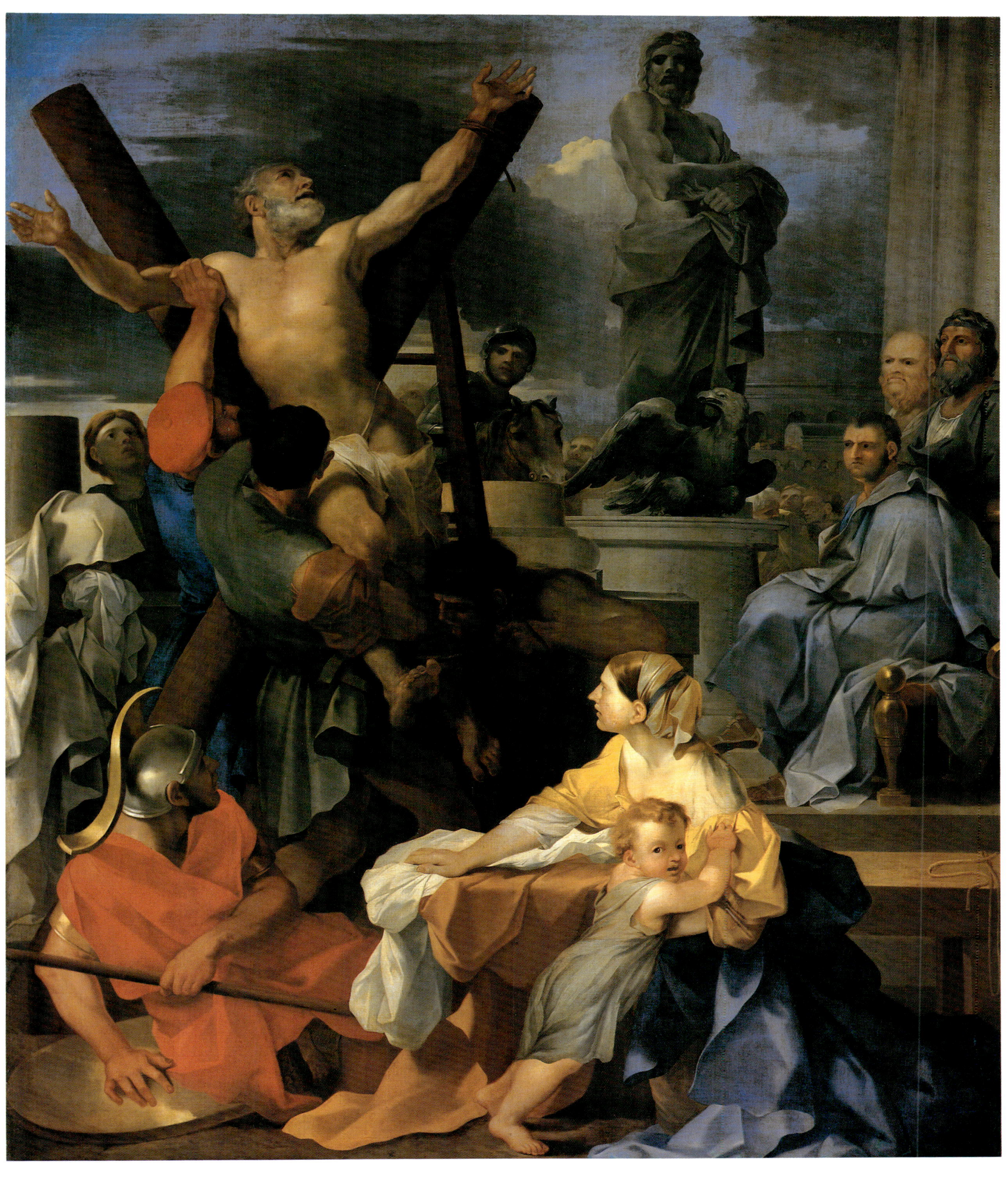

Bourdon (Sébastien) 1616-1671
Martyrdom of St. Andrew
Toulouse, Musée des Augustins

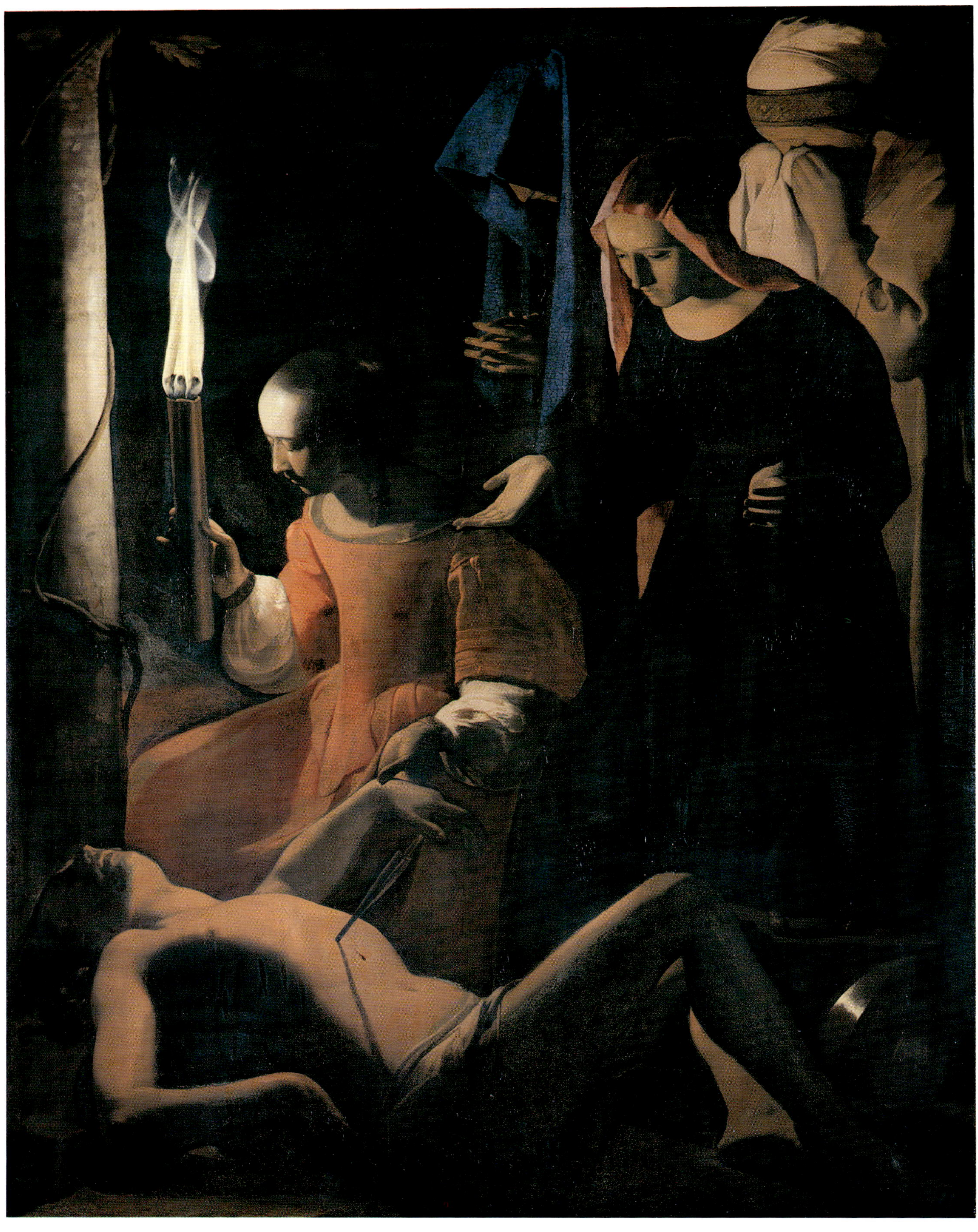

La Tour (Georges de) 1595-1652
St. Sebastian tended by St. Irene
Paris, Louvre

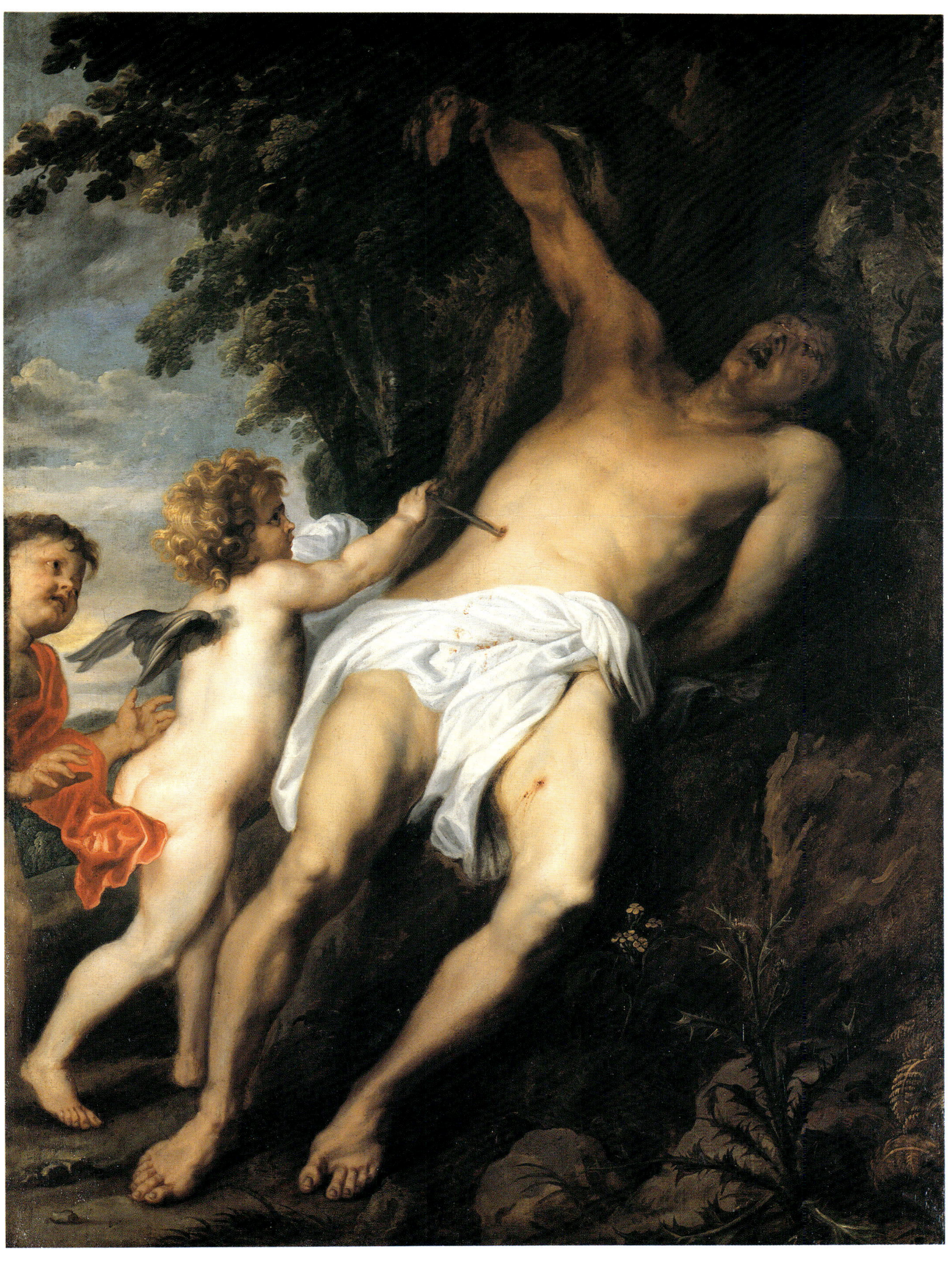

Van Dyck (Sir Anthony) 1599-1641
St. Sebastian succored by angels
Paris, Louvre

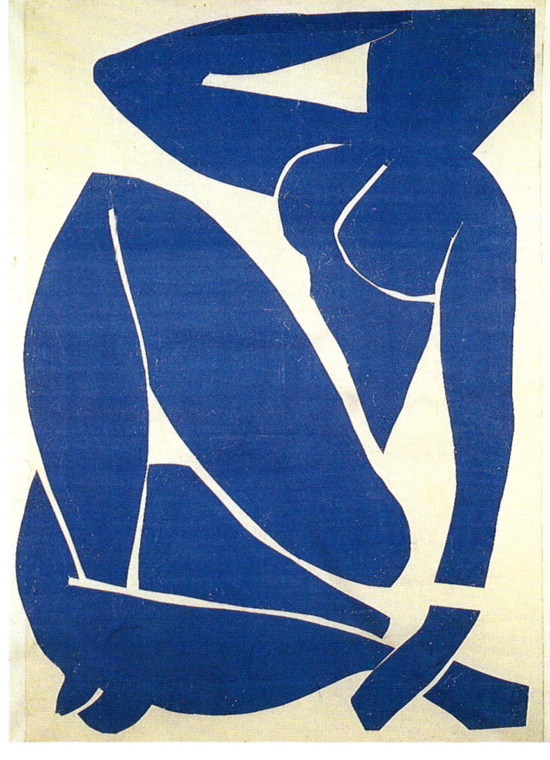

Reconstructing how we see

We are therefore talking about reconstructing in order to give meaning. The meaning will not be universal, valid for everyone and for always, but one which exists only in and through the work of art. "In the work of art or in theory, as in the perceptible thing, meaning is inseparable from the sign," wrote Merleau-Ponty. "Thus expression is never completed." If this is so, the meaning of the human being that emanates from the reconstruction of the body could not exist outside the work itself: the meaning exists only through the sign, i.e. the work.

Nonetheless, the reconstructed form is a free form: it is the form the artist has given to his freedom. But this freedom is also its boundary. It is a form born out of the creative imagination of the artist, not a form in itself, absolute and codified for eternity, but rather the concrete expression of a moment of vision. Picasso wrote that Cubism "expresses all that our reason and our eyes perceive within the bounds of what can be achieved by drawing and color." He is of course talking about the reason of the individual, for universality is out of place here. Picasso said more than once that Cubism does not need mathematics. It is neither an exact science nor an abstract science: it is first and foremost a living art. The search for a new meaning, a new truth, is not constructed in opposition to reality: quite the opposite. Reconstructing reality does not imply denying it, but trying to express a whole area of it that hitherto has not been properly known. In fact the artist is not so much reconstructing reality as our manner of seeing it. Cubism does not change the body – it simply looks at it in a different way. In the words of Michel Leiris, "I do not think we can regard Picasso as an *a priori* enemy of the world [...]. It seems to me that for him it is much less a question of recreating reality for the sake of recreating it than of tackling the incomparably more important task of expressing all its possibilities, all its conceivable ramifications, so as to get a slightly tighter hold on it, really to touch it. Instead of being a vague association, a remote panorama of phenomena, what is real is then illuminated through all its pores, we penetrate it, and for the first time it really becomes a REALITY."

Finally we have come to the very foundations of phenomenology: what makes reality exist is not the thing itself but the gaze the individual directs on it – a gaze which is never neutral. Each pair of eyes is like a world looking at the world. Each gaze reinvents the world because it is not content with seeing the world but, on seeing it, rethinks it: "I paint things as I think them, not as I see them," Picasso said. This thought would lead Matisse, his friend and his only true rival, to the unsurpassable syntheses of his cut-out gouaches, "forms decanted down to the essential" which preserve only "the adequate sign [of the object] which is necessary to make it exist in its true form."

In their work the body has thus once again become a sign, i.e. both a mental thing and an object of meaning.

Matisse (Henri) 1869-1954
Blue nude III, 1952
Private collection

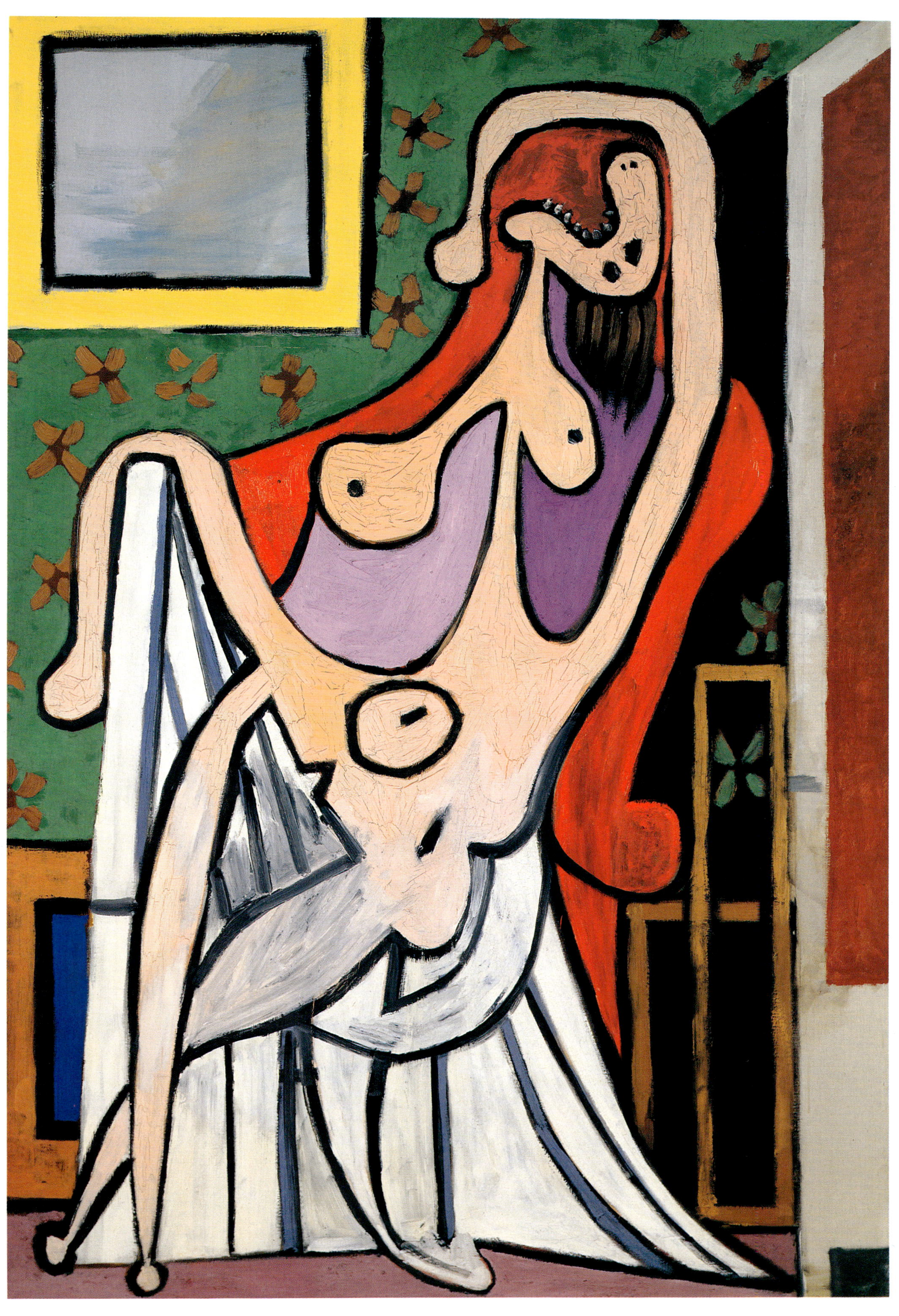

"Putting both eyes on the same profile, whatever 'common sense' may say, is a way of reestablishing the truth, it is the synthetical metaphor of the global, total nature of the object."

Benito Pelegrin
"Rhétorique de la Méditerranée"
Esprit, January 1982

Picasso (Pablo Ruiz) 1881-1973
Large nude with red armchair, 1929
Paris, Musée Picasso

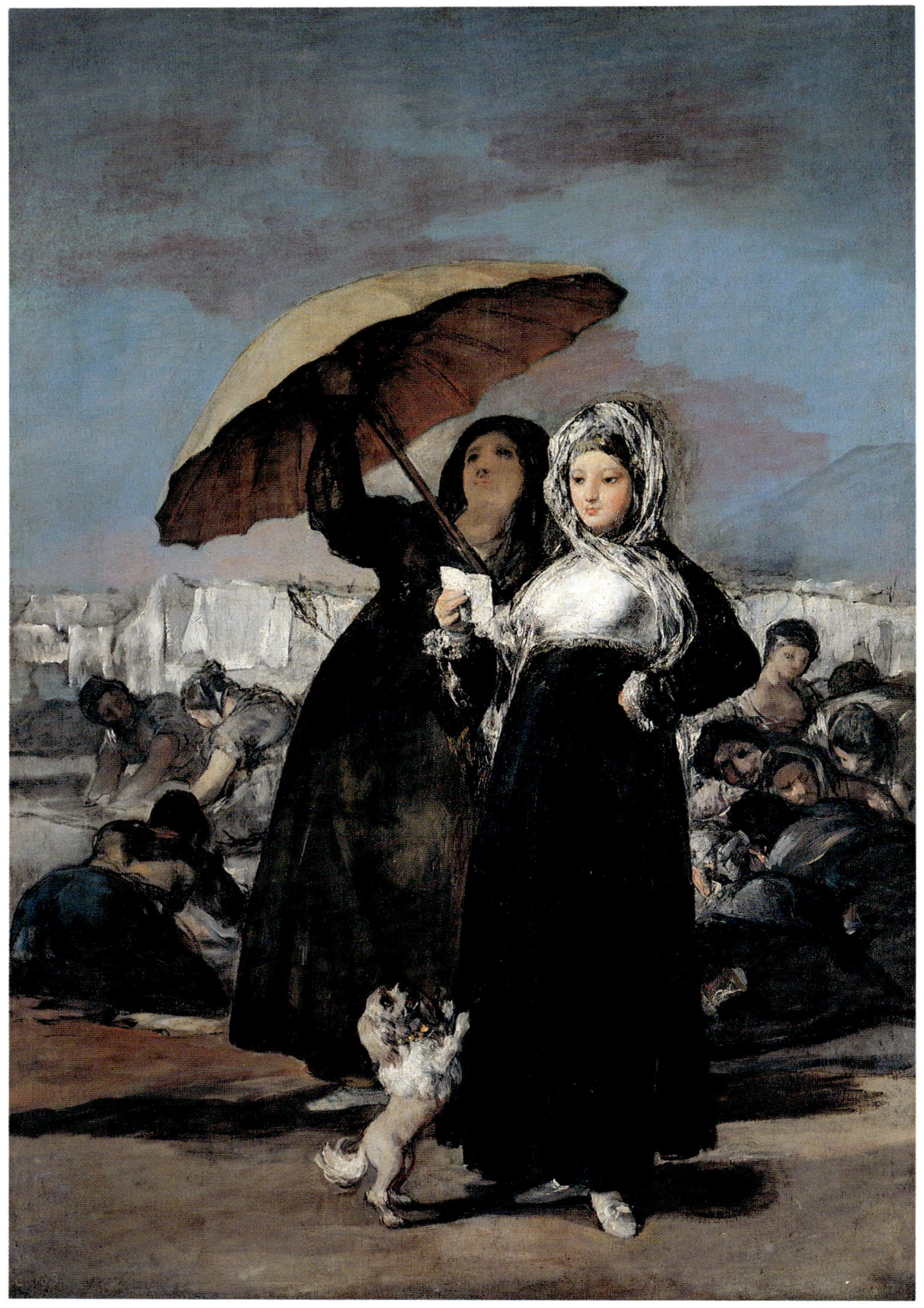

Goya (Francisco de Goya y Lucientes, known as) 1746-1828
The young ones
Lille, Musée des Beaux-Arts

Interiors

An interior is made up of trifles, those unconsidered trifles that give life its zest. Bonnard wanted to paint the zest that is derived from the humblest things. An interior is a world in miniature, a universe on the scale of the person who created it: the peace of inside as opposed to the always dreaded tumult of the external world, a space that is confined but understood, where the object betokens its harmony with the human figure, even when no human figure is present. The object then appears as the material echo of human presence: the object indicates the person, is his or her intimate, temporary substitute. The first message carried by an interior scene relates to the enigmatic connivance between the object and the human being, a concrete, lived-in harmony, the opposite of the abstract harmony of the ideal – or perhaps not opposite, just different.

At first sight the painter's eye appears to be content with restating reality. The domestic scene is a modest, elliptical genre, with everything understated, at the opposite end of the spectrum from declamatory art. There is no attempt to prove or even demonstrate, just to remind. Both Bonnard and Vermeer cultivate a kind of memory of the present, not going back over the past or looking forward to the future, with no anguish or regret: the memory of all the moments that were lived in the present, with no thoughts of the past or planning for the future. The silence of the objects is first and foremost the silence of the soul, a silence totally different from emptiness: it is a kind of plenitude, capturing an instant when existence takes on sufficient density for human consciousness not to feel the need to project beyond itself in order to go on existing. This is what is really striking in these scenes: a sort of undefinable presence-absence of the object and the human, their images bouncing back off one another in a fragile suspension of the passage of time. An interior scene is both existence and the opposite of existence. It is life in between brackets, an enclosed area, deliberately shrunk in a way that offers us something approaching the quintessence of the world. Bonnard seems almost to express the savor of his familiar world in the regular palpitation of whites and reds on this checked tablecloth, just as Vermeer's pictorial scheme condensing his art and existence might be the ray of sunshine casting its fair light on the inoffensive movements of a woman absorbed in her activity, like a precious splinter captured from the passage of time: a morning in Vermeer's house, lunchtime at Bonnard's.

This genre inevitably makes us think of still-life, but differs from it in one crucial aspect: in a still-life the object always remains external to the painter, whereas the artist is present in each and every one of the objects in his domestic surroundings. The interior here operates as a metaphorical self-portrait. In the words of Tériade, "With Bonnard the painter is reintroduced into his picture. He is no longer reporting impressions. He is present himself in the plastic action of the image. The objects, space and light attest to his presence."

Bonnard (Pierre) 1867-1947
The red check tablecloth, 1910
Switzerland, private collection

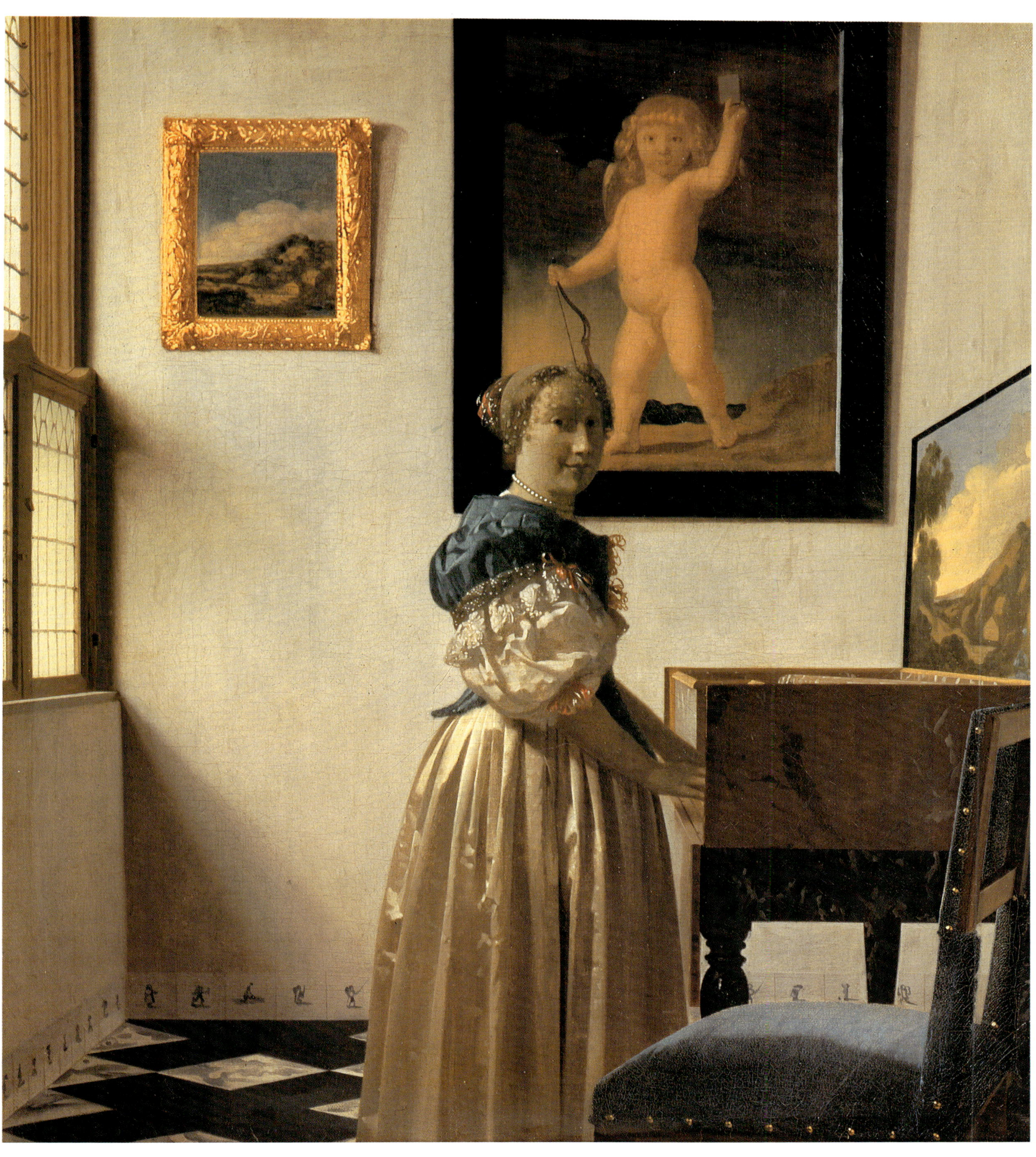

Cupid's bow meets the curve of the young woman's fair hair. Standing in front of her virginal, she thinks of the man she loves while Cupid, waving a playing card, symbolizes constancy.

Vermeer van Delft (Jan Vermeer, known as) 1633-1675
Lady standing at the virginals, 1670
London, National Gallery

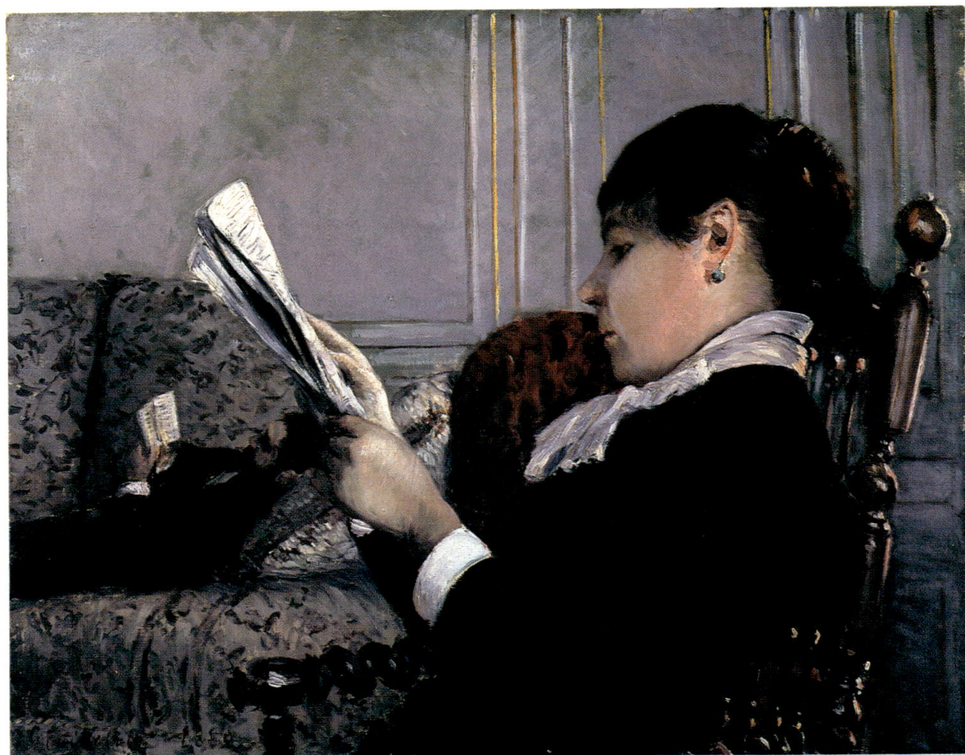

The eye of the woman reading

The woman reading is somewhere else, and the painter cannot be seen. Yet everything speaks of presence. It is the presence of the gaze on intimacy: the painter is looking at the woman reading, the woman reading is looking at the pages of her book. The book, apparently objective, is made to be read, and the reader, seemingly so unaware, is there to be painted. Everyone is pretending not to see the person looking at him or her, but everyone knows that he or she is being observed: the painting by the viewer, the woman reading by the painter and the book by the woman reading. In subdued tones, people are playing games, predicating what is untrue to discover what is true: existence and the opposite of existence.

The painter loves the model as he paints him or her. The model loves the author as she reads him or her. Dreams are catching up on life – and on love, which is saved through art: art telling us in a kind of way that a truly complete existence is impossible, art which may perhaps be that very "real life" which other people look for in vain elsewhere. In *A la Recherche du Temps Perdu* Proust writes: "The work the artist does in trying to perceive something different beneath matter, beneath experience, beneath words is the very opposite of what self-conceit, passion, intelligence, and habit too contrive within us every minute that we live alienated from ourselves, piling up on top of our true impressions in such a way as completely to conceal from us the names and practical objectives we mistakenly call life."

Yet it is said that Renoir was passionately fond of life. No doubt he was, but he loved it as only an artist can. For a person wholly committed to existence will never know more than one world. The practical man is a consumer, whereas the artist always remains fundamentally a spectator of the world, and thereby the creator of another world. To quote Proust again, "Thanks to art, instead of seeing just one world, our world, we see it multiplying itself, and we end up having as many worlds as there are original artists, differing more from one another than the spheres that rotate in infinity."

The interior and the woman reading are simple symbols of that other world: rather than being a closed universe they are a door opening onto a possible other place, the world of meditation, contemplation and reflection, in the original sense of the word. The interior is a subjective reflection of the world.

Caillebotte (Gustave) 1848-1894
Interior, woman reading, 1880
Private collection

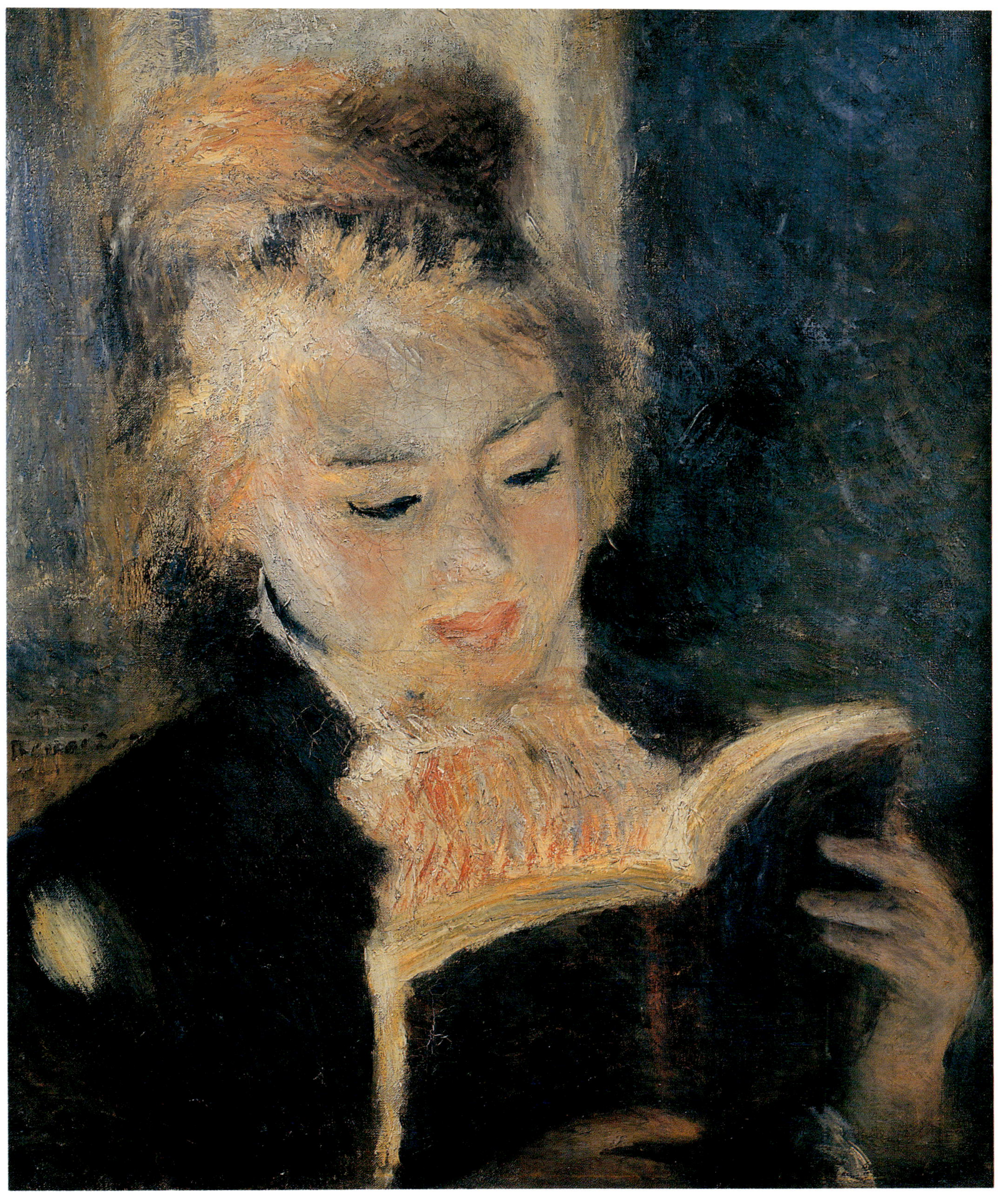

"Renoir's women are bewitching. If you have one of them in your house, she will be the person you look at last when you go out and first when you come back in. She will take up room in your life."

Théodore Duret
Les Peintres impressionnistes

Renoir (Pierre-Auguste) 1841-1919
Girl reading, 1874
Paris, Musée d'Orsay

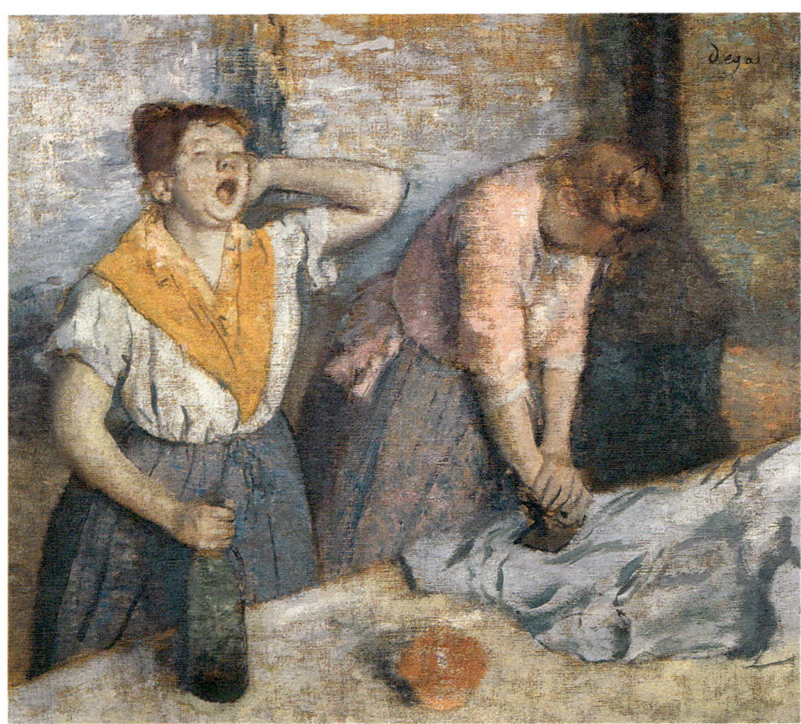

Dialog between theme and style

All figurative painting develops a dialog between theme and style. Painting life may mean painting the life of one's model, but if the model is to come alive, then the painting must also be alive, and this cannot be reduced to a simple question of technique – style is much more than that. It is technique harnessed to the service of a unique and personal vision.

When Degas painted a woman ironing or a woman at her milliner's, his attempt to suggest naturalness depended as much on the way he treated the figure as on his choice of figure. It is very tempting to regard the anecdotal nature of the figure as an indication of its unimportance and to analyze his works from a purely plastic point of view, highlighting the painter's modernity in the process, but in our opinion such an option would be a mistake. Considering only Degas's style without reference to his subject matter will impoverish any analysis, even if doing the opposite and considering only his themes without talking about his style is an even bigger fallacy, amounting purely and simply to negating the work as a work of art.

Thus we cannot say that realism in Degas's work is just a pretext, even if subsequent developments in modern art tempt us to do so. While he did not set out to copy nature as Courbet did, reality for him was still a necessary point of departure and the artist had to struggle to come to terms with it. Style does not exist independently: the "other world" is not an anti-world, but rather the subjective exaltation of this world. To sum up, seeing the work of art as being at odds with reality amounts to obscuring its genesis and so preventing oneself from understanding it in its totality: the "other world" is still the world. What changes is not reality, but the way in which it is seen and represented, i.e. understood. A representation is not right or correct in itself: it is right because it conveys a vision correctly. And there can be no vision without an object. The greatness of a figurative work lies in achieving an equal balance between the figure, the vision and the style that conveys it.

That balance is present in Degas's work. "In style he seeks only truth, and in truth only style," Valéry said of him. Degas set out to capture truth in fragments. In his view, life could never be a finished totality, it was a disjointed compilation of moments; it was up to art to try and rediscover their coherence using memory and imagination. The whole is shown by a virtual nothing, all of humanity is suggested through an anonymous figure, a life through an attitude, color through a touch, time through an instant, and space through a fragment: that is the path Degas chose to follow, with style becoming the accurate interpreter of a certain concept of the world.

Degas (Hilaire Germain Edgar de Gas, known as) 1834-1917
Women ironing, 1884
Paris, Musée d'Orsay

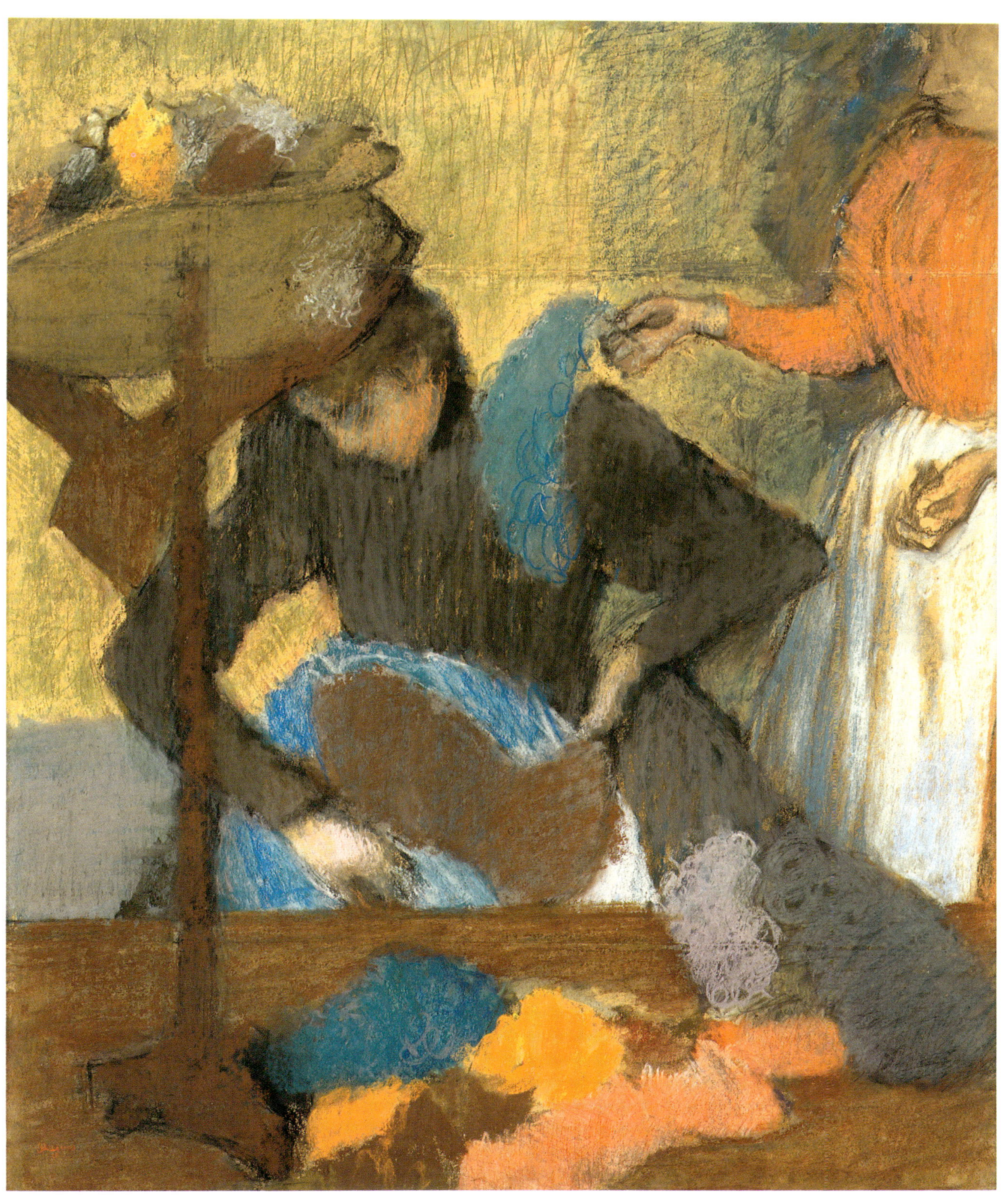

"Despite the amazingly precise way he notates those professional reflex movements, leaving them looking vividly alive, Degas remains a haughty observer, showing no liking for his models."

Georges Riviére
Degas

Degas (Hilaire Germain Edgar de Gas, known as) 1834-1917
At the milliner's, 1905-1910
Paris, Musée d'Orsay

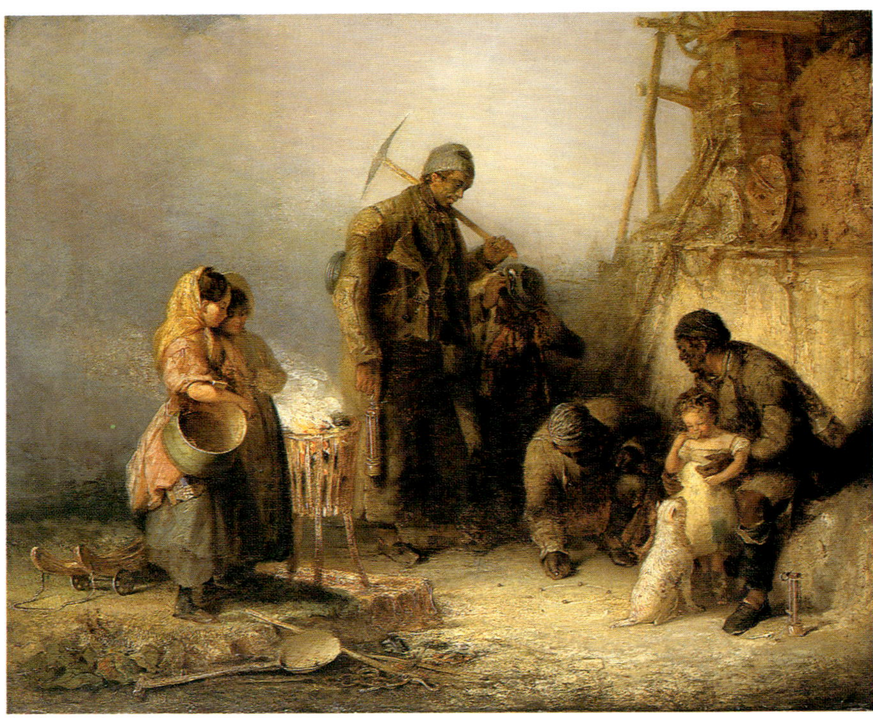

The snare of good intentions

When subject matter takes over from style, the subject of the painting becomes more important than the artist. This is what happened to 19th-century social realism, and with Socialist Realism in the 20th century it degenerated into caricature. Yet the intentions were praiseworthy. To put it very simply, the artist set out to serve life by denouncing injustices and depicting the sufferings of the poor and humble and the selfishness of the well-to-do.

The question this raises is a huge one. Can art serve anything other than itself, can it become an instrument of political struggle, without becoming alienated from itself and losing its way? Can the artist commit himself without losing his identity as an artist? Can committed art avoid degenerating into partisan propaganda?

When questioned about this in March 1945 Picasso gave a vehement answer: "What do you think an artist is? An idiot who only has eyes if he is a painter, ears if he is a musician [...]? Far from it, the artist is also a political animal, constantly alive to the heart-rending, passionate and tender events of the world [...]. No, painting is not made to decorate people's walls. It is an offensive and defensive weapon for use against the enemy."

While this is true, if style is eaten up by the political or social intentions of the work, the artist's creative power is sacrificed on the altar of political power. Because both cherish universalizing ambitions, these two powers cannot coexist in the long term without one or other of them ultimately losing its freedom. Moreover, political power is essentially normative, while art's reason for being consists not in fixing norms but in smashing them, or at least overstepping them. Finally, creative power comes into the sphere of the individual, unlike political power which purports to be the legitimate image of collective interests. Thus harnessing art to a social, political or philosophical doctrine is not a neutral undertaking. Does this amount to saying that the artist cannot venture onto the field of history in any way? Not necessarily. But the conditions justifying such a venture, which presuppose that the artist's individual reality coincides with the collective reality of history, occur virtually only at cataclysmic periods of revolution when individual destinies very briefly converge into a collective destiny at the very heart of the vacuum in political power. Only then does political power, no longer being a counterforce, become a living art, and art an extraordinary means of making a political statement: extraordinary but fleeting, because revolution unlike art does not set out to deny the norm. All it does is destroy a norm that has finished serving its purpose so as to substitute another, better suited to the needs of the day. Therefore the objectives of art and those of political power remain fundamentally contradictory. These are no doubt the profound reasons why every attempt to set up social art and the libertarian utopia of collective creation have failed.

Parker (Henry Perlee) 1796-1873
The miner's stance: the game, c. 1836
Great Britain, National Coal Board

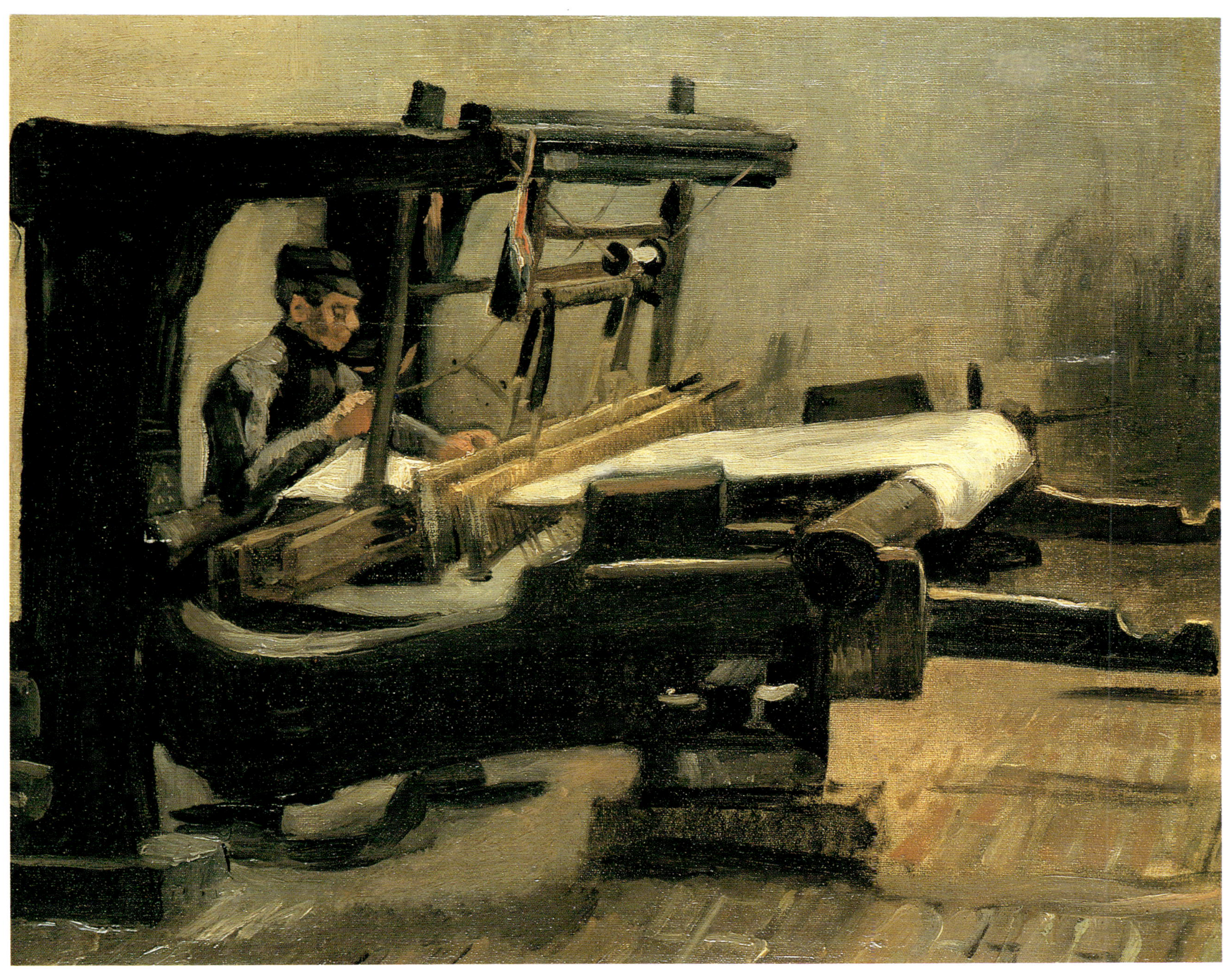

Van Gogh's first period, dark realism – peasants, weavers, a whole world of browns: earth, leather and wood. Van Gogh was 31 years old, and had six years left to live.

Van Gogh (Vincent) 1853-1890
The weaver
London, Christie's

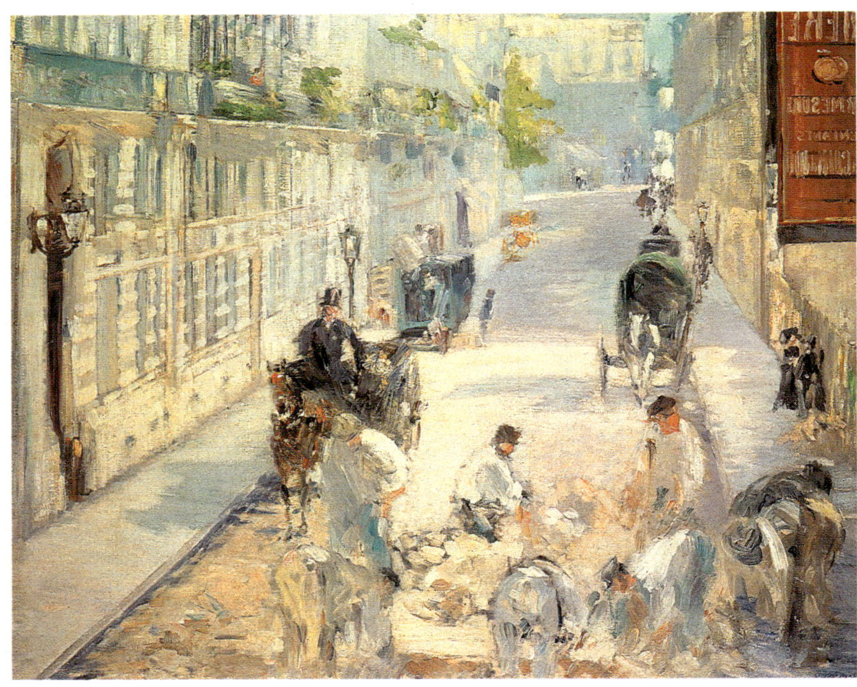

The painter of modern life

Manet's *Execution of the Emperor Maximilian* stands out as an exception in a body of work which is very remote from militant commitment of any description. In any case Manet was thinking less of poor Maximilian than of Goya and his *Tres de Mayo*, to which he pays obvious tribute. History here is used merely as a pretext. The few sketches he produced during the Commune in 1871 are not enough to make Manet a politically committed artist. But like Pissarro he wanted to be a painter of his time, a painter of what Baudelaire defined as "modern life," so in one way he was a committed painter after all.

The first hazard for a painter who ventures on to the ground of social issues is the event. A theme with too many historical connotations pushes the artist into the background. There are very few paintings where this is not the case – by its very celebrity, Picasso's *Guernica*, one of these rare exceptions, proves how difficult it is. So an artist has to contrive to paint life without painting major events, and that kind of reality – no less "true" than the event – is everyday life.

Above we considered what was meant by the daily round "inside," representing intimacy and in some ways attempting autobiography through objects, as the self-portrait can be an autobiography recounted by the face. Daily life "outside," a street scene, is something different, threatened by two dangers: anecdote and social allegory.

Anecdote is some little detail which sets out to lend authenticity to the scene – the picturesque invading the canvas, a search for something that will catch the eye, a desire to charm the spectator at the cost of skewing observation. What is required is not to "look true" but to "see true." Someone setting out to achieve the former hopes the effect of truth will come from the subject itself, which is deliberately overstated; in the second case the effect is produced by style. Social allegory, on the other hand, freezes observation into theory, transforming individuals into types; here ideology precedes observation which becomes no more than a tool in the service of a cause external to the problems inherent in art.

In his painting *Roadmenders in the rue de Berne* Manet steers clear of both these dangers: with no inappropriate use of the picturesque and no wish to prove anything, he is content to give an account of the world looked at in a certain way. If reality strikes an authentic note it is because the relationship between subject and object, i.e. observer and theme, recognizes itself as subjective, in this context meaning also artistic. The artist's way of looking at the world differs from the philosopher's: the former shows, while the latter demonstrates. The painter sets out to record the fleetingness of existence: Baudelaire wrote that "Modernity is the transitory, the fleeting, the accidental [...]. You are not entitled to despise or dispense with that transitory, fleeting element which is so frequently metamorphosed."

Everyday life is a story that unfolds quietly, with no notable ups and downs, a slow, almost impalpable mutation which only the true artist – painter or novelist – can show us without traducing it.

Manet (Edouard) 1832-1883
Roadmenders in the rue de Berne
Private collection

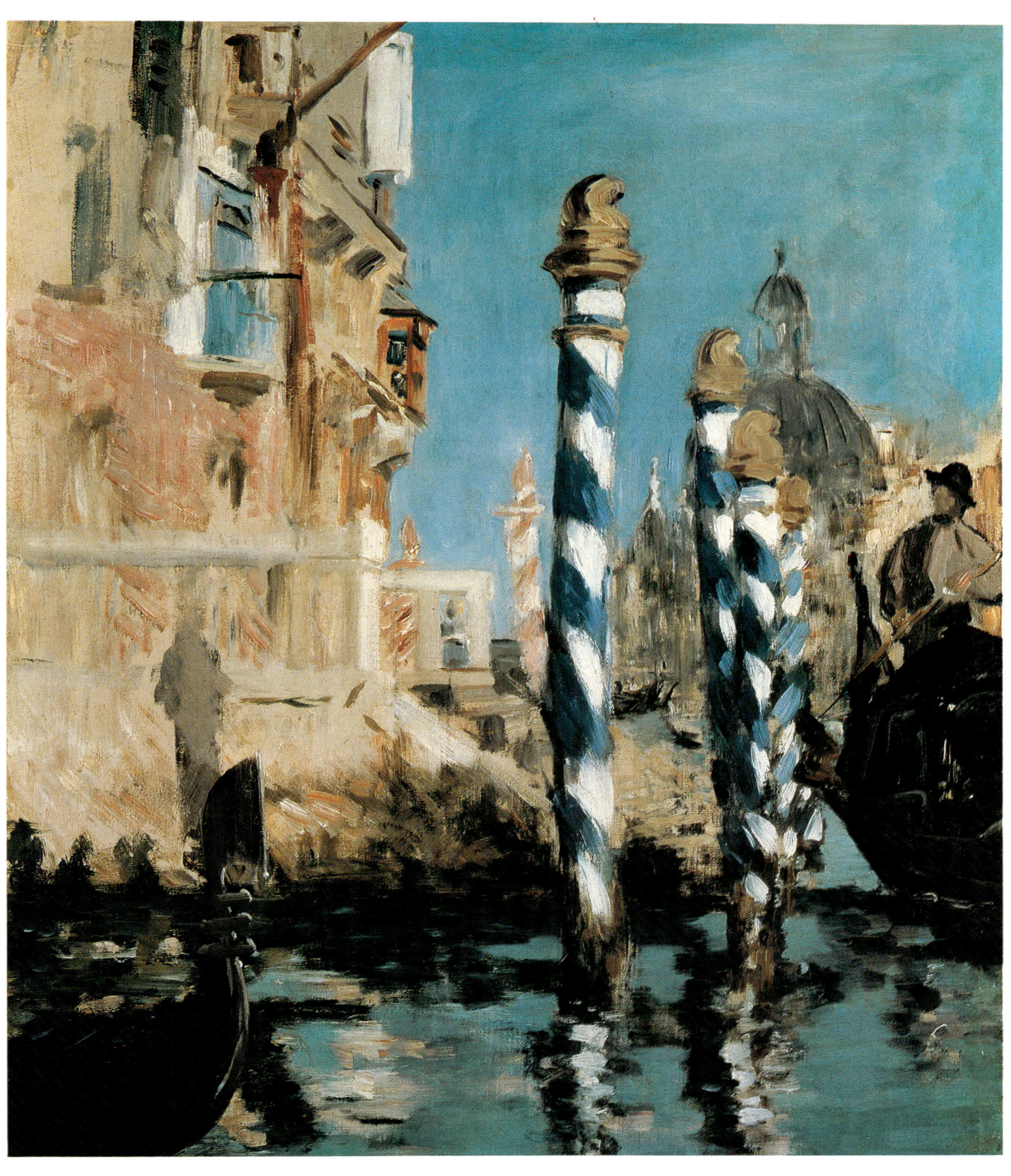

"The first impression produced by one of Edouard Manet's paintings is slightly hard. We are not accustomed to seeing such simple, sincere statements of reality. Then as I have said there are a few examples of elegant stiffness which take one by surprise."

Emile Zola
Edouard Manet, étude biographique et critique

Manet (Edouard) 1832-1883
Grand Canal, Venice
San Francisco, Provincial Security Council

The soul of a town

Towns are artificial places, artificial in the sense of "made with art," in contrast to the countryside which is the work of nature (obviously we know that much of our countryside is hardly any more "natural" than our towns, but that is irrelevant in this context).

"You can have the natural life," Degas told his Impressionist friends, "and I will keep to the artificial life," by which he meant town life. The artificial (made with art) nature of the town thus poses the double problem of its links with architecture, and the links between architecture and painting. In other words, what is the significance of architecture's entry into the town, and of the town's entry into painting? Is it just a decorative setting or does it really have a role of its own to play? For a painter like Mantegna or an architect like Giuliano da Sangallo it is clear that a work of architecture would have to be more than a simple setting. To give a very brief résumé, we can take it that up until the 15th century towns were built without any overall plan, expediency determining how they turned out, hence the extraordinarily anarchic nature of medieval towns. The true break occurred between 1400 and 1450, when men like Alberti and Brunelleschi set out to rationalize the art of building. With them and the rediscovery of the laws of Antiquity, architecture again became the intellectual discipline it had been in Pericles's Greece: a work of reason, conceived rationally for man by man, and made to his measure. With architecture reason came to be inscribed in the very body of the town.

Renaissance architecture went beyond pure utilitarianism. It was based on a program and led logically to the reinvention of town planning. Such a development can obviously be explained by the upsurge of the towns, their dominance over rural areas and the decline of the feudal system, but also by the fact that Italy, even at the height of the Middle Ages, never ceased to be an urban civilization.

The geometrical arrangement of space thus conveys reason's increasing grip on nature. The town became the concrete realization of a concept, a thought, an ideology. But oddly enough, whereas the reemerging discipline of town planning seemed to be linked with the humanist cosmology based on man's harmony with the universe, the town that was invented rejected nature as if it were something impure and soon dwindled into being no more than a rational case containing rational creatures. Unquestionably this reduction of space to pure rationality is disturbing, more especially when towns are displayed before our eyes devoid of any human presence.

The ideal town rejects chance, nooks and corners, anything that is not useful or rational. That is why it is not alive. It is paradoxical that St. Christopher's body being transported through the town seems like a spark of life in the center of a ghost town, more living in its death than the ideal form of life. Reason without soul can yield only withered fruit. It is a mistake to look for a town's soul in its architecture. You will find its history there, possibly its rationale, but its soul is elsewhere: the soul of a town is its people.

Sangallo (Giamberti Giuliano, known as) c. 1443-1516
Architectural scheme for an ideal city
(formerly attributed to Piero della Francesca), after 1470
Urbino, Galleria Nazionale delle Marche

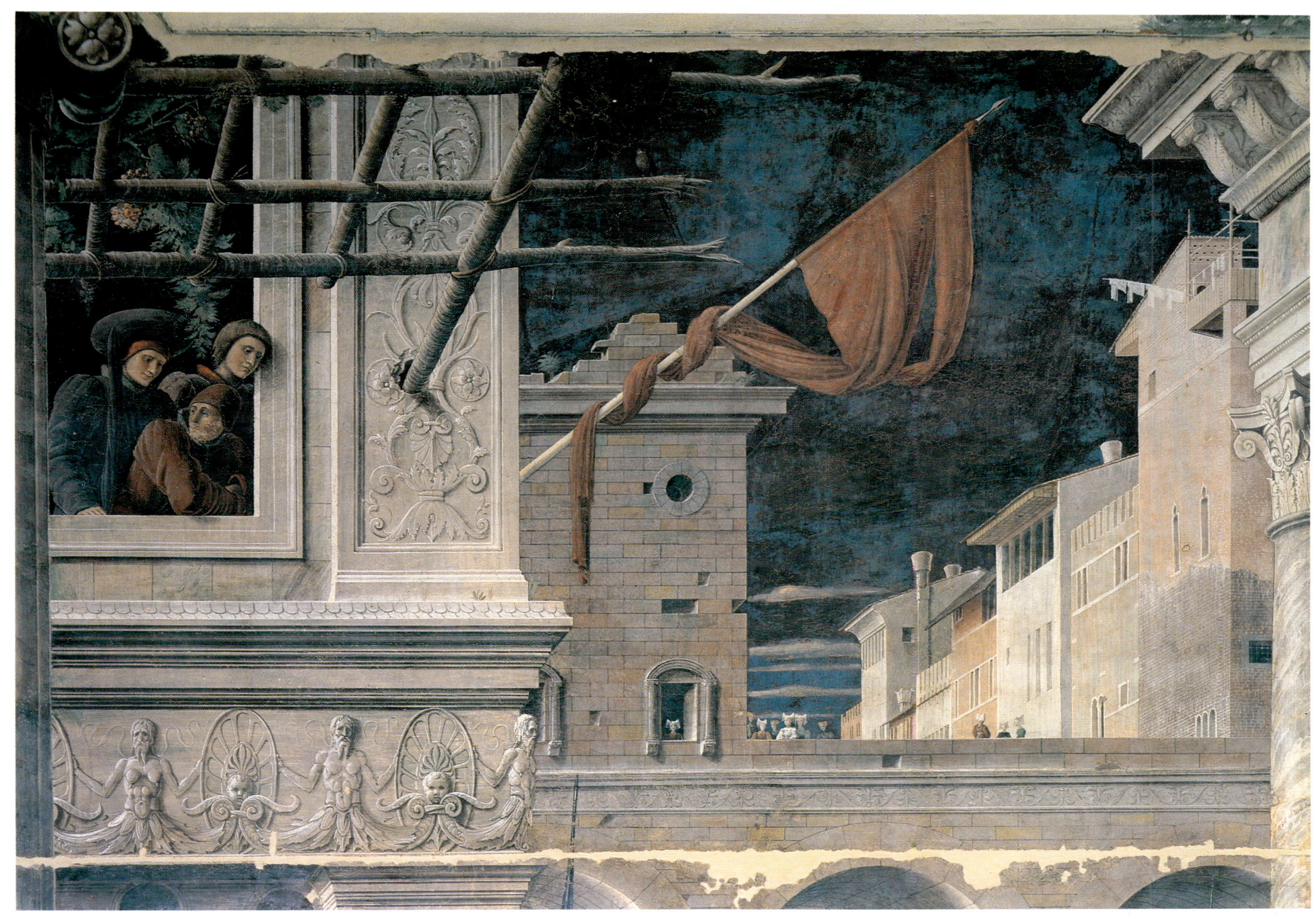

"For Renaissance theorists the ideal city could never be created by working on the urban structures already in place [...]. The ideal city, regulated, harmonious, beautiful to look at and attractive to live in, started from the presumption of a virgin space on which [...] its purely geometrical plan could be inscribed."

Roger Chartier
La Ville classique, de la Renaissance aux Révolutions

Mantegna (Andrea) 1431-1506
St. Christopher's body being dragged away after his beheading
Detail: buildings in the upper part with onlookers at the windows, c. 1450/1456
Padua, Chiesa degli Eremitani

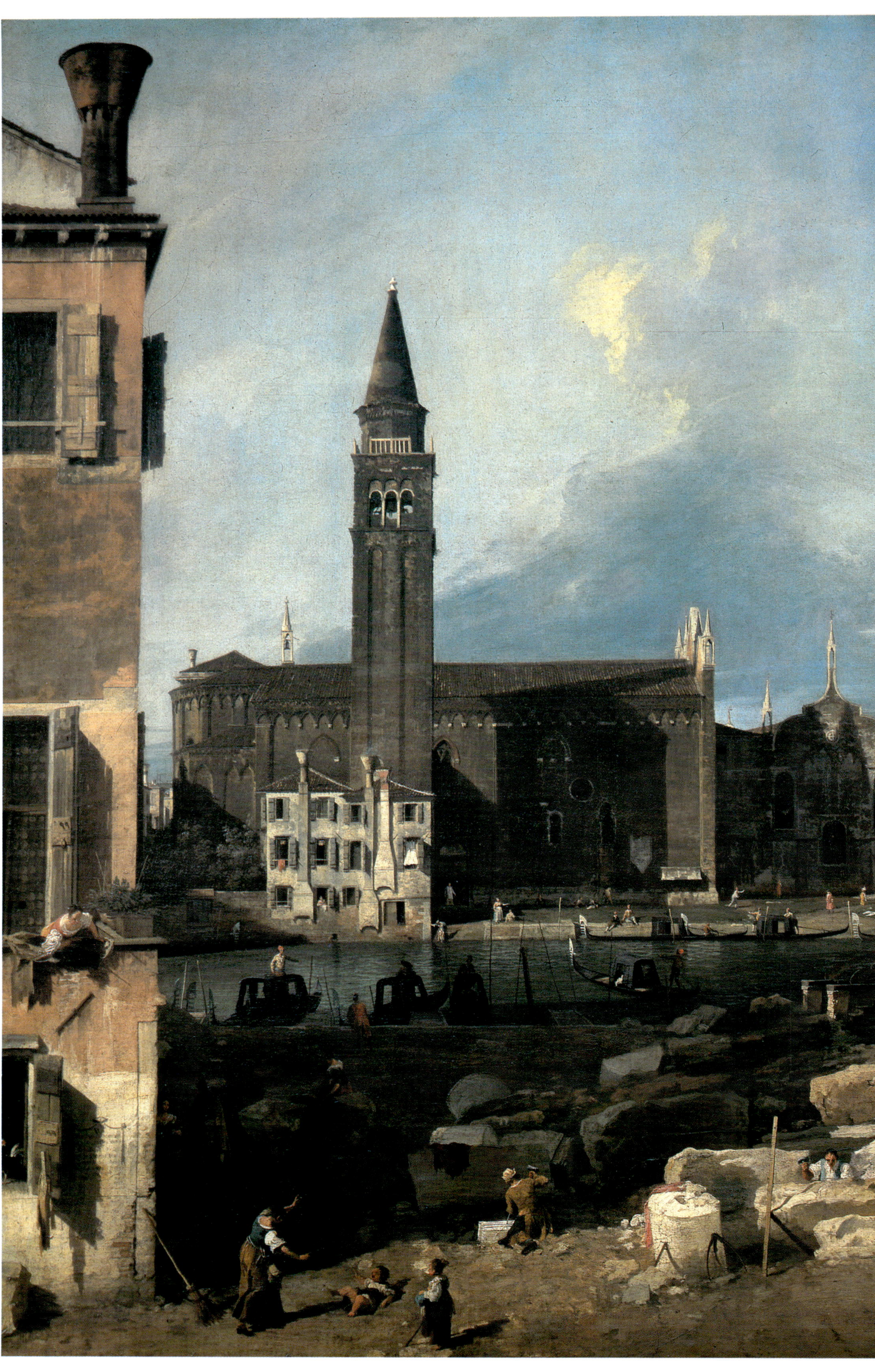

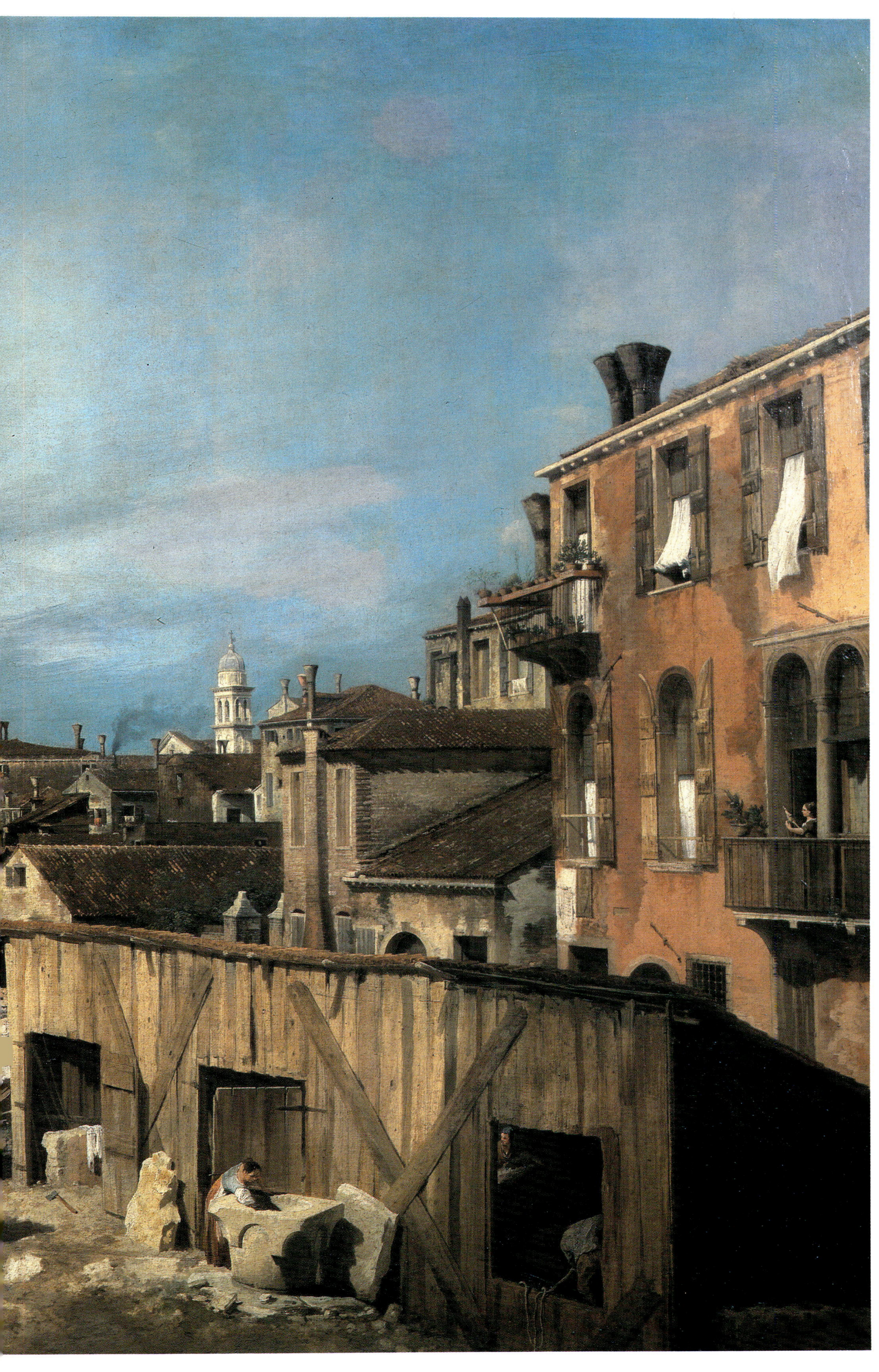

Canaletto (Antonio Canal, known as) 1697-1768
Venice, stonemason's yard, stonecutter; on the other side of the Grand Canal, the church of S. Maria della Carità
London, National Gallery

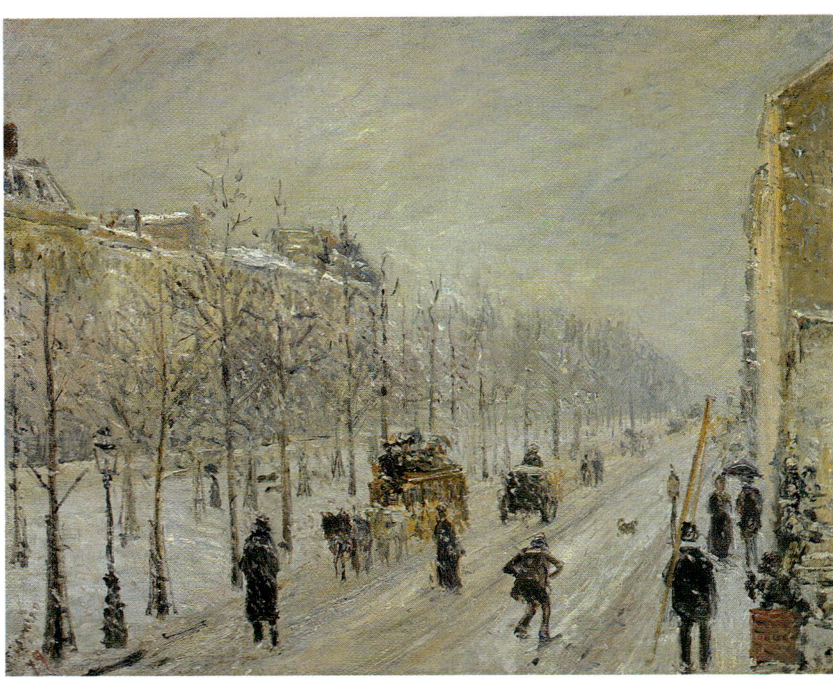

The moving town

"We know that the form of a town changes more quickly than the human heart," Julien Gracq wrote. It is a moving form, both physically and psychologically. Towns change, not only because of the permanent evolution of their morphology, but also because the memories of those living in them are continually reconstructing them. A town – and this is what the Renaissance architects tried to ignore – is a living place. Even before it is a group of monuments, organized to a greater or a lesser extent, a town is first an extraordinarily complex tangle of individual destinies. The impression given by looking at a plan, for example, that the town has an objective existence is an intellectual illusion. For the person going about it every day the town is a subjective space. The form of a town in the mind of each individual results from his personal movements through it, what he does in it and the clever or not so clever remodeling which his memory has worked on the image he thought he had of it. The subjective town has its dark and its bright areas, lending itself in our thoughts to the most unexpected anamorphoses. To sum up, the town is a plastic reality.

Reason often plays just a secondary role in all this. Passion and sensation are much more important. A town is composed of the sum of the lives that have cut across one another in it. As a moving form sheltering moving destinies, anyone painting it would need to convey both its ephemeral character and the fusion taking place between the architectural and the human elements. For these two elements are constantly interacting in the always precarious equilibrium of a town.

Thus the painter has to merge the architecture and the crowd, the set and the actor, into a single pictural substance, and – which amounts to the same thing – he has to express the contradictory natures of the stable and the unstable, movement and permanence, using identical means. In effect he would need to invent a language that could convey by means of color and touch the idea of an order underlying the apparent reign of confusion.

At first glance the rue Montorgueil and the rue Saint-Denis painted by Monet on the festival of 30 June 1878 convey that very disorder or confusion. The touch is disparate, the line chaotic and the color schematic. Then slowly, as our eyes get accustomed to the picture, the elements become organized and regroup themselves without ever ceasing to participate in the whole. The same light-colored touch conveys both the crowd and the façade of a building: a façade that lights up like a face as the flags flap over it, almost more living than the human tide moving down below, darker, more compact, as if the better to challenge the normally accepted hierarchies and categories, and the better to convey, by upsetting our way of seeing, the profound identity of a town and its people: not living creatures and things, but a single historical, cultural and emotional substance, translated on the canvas by a single pictural substance. In short, here we have the very opposite of the classical town.

Pissarro (Camille) 1830-1903
The outer boulevards, 1898
Paris, Musée Marmottan

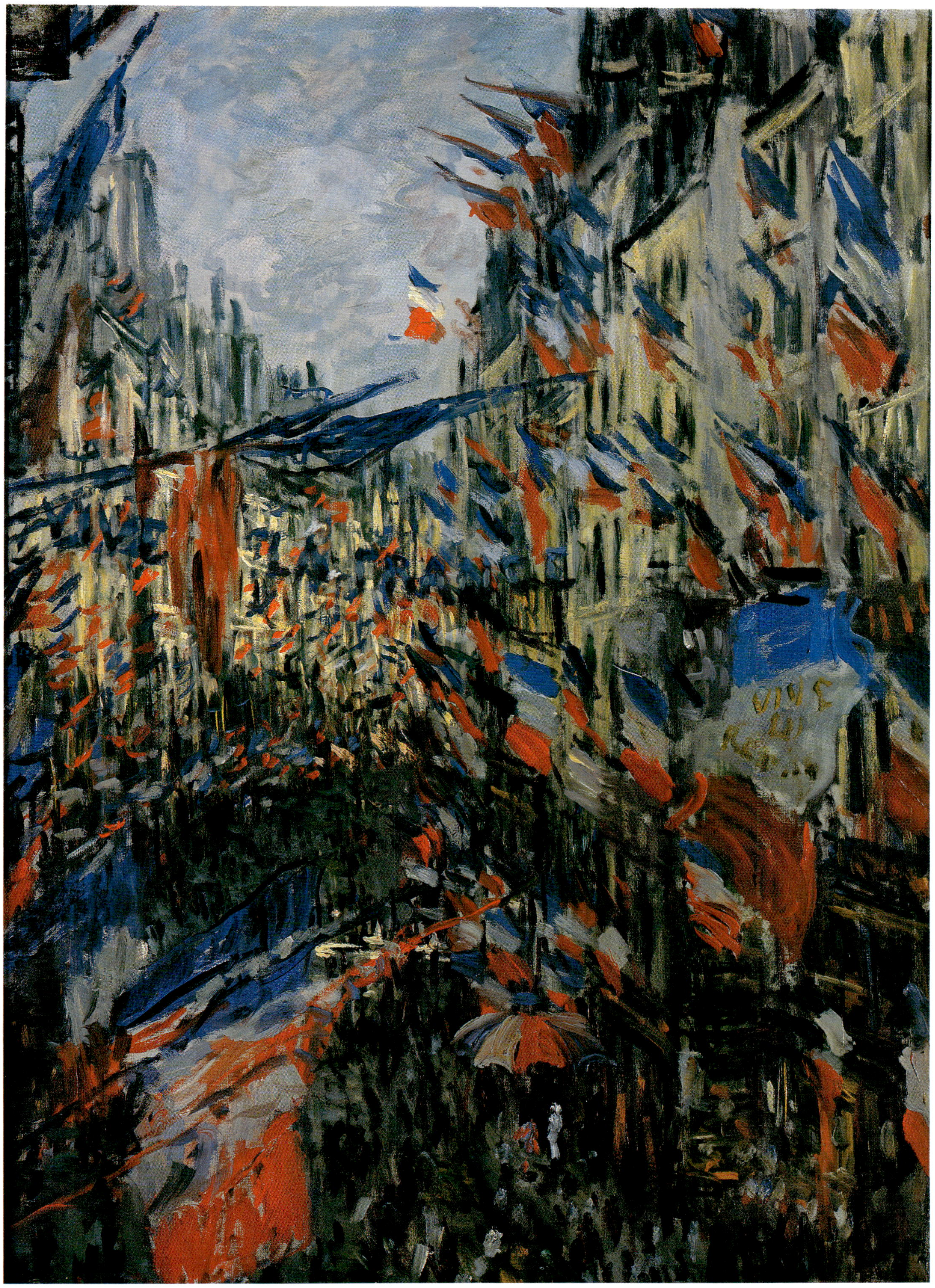

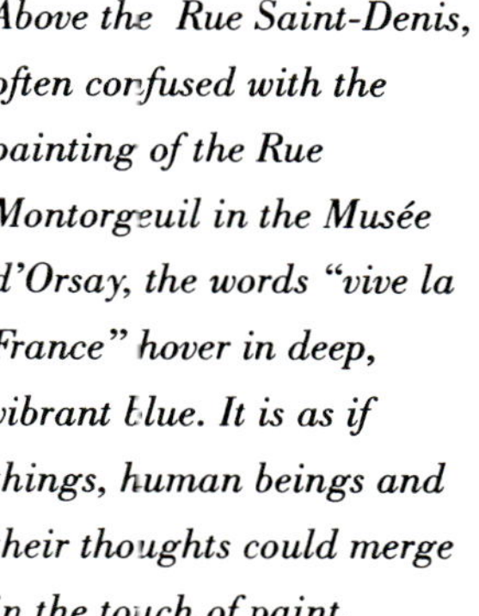

Above the Rue Saint-Denis, often confused with the painting of the Rue Montorgeuil in the Musée d'Orsay, the words "vive la France" hover in deep, vibrant blue. It is as if things, human beings and their thoughts could merge in the touch of paint.

Monet (Claude) 1840-1926
Rue Saint-Denis, festival of 30 June 1878, 1878
Rouen, Musée des Beaux-Arts

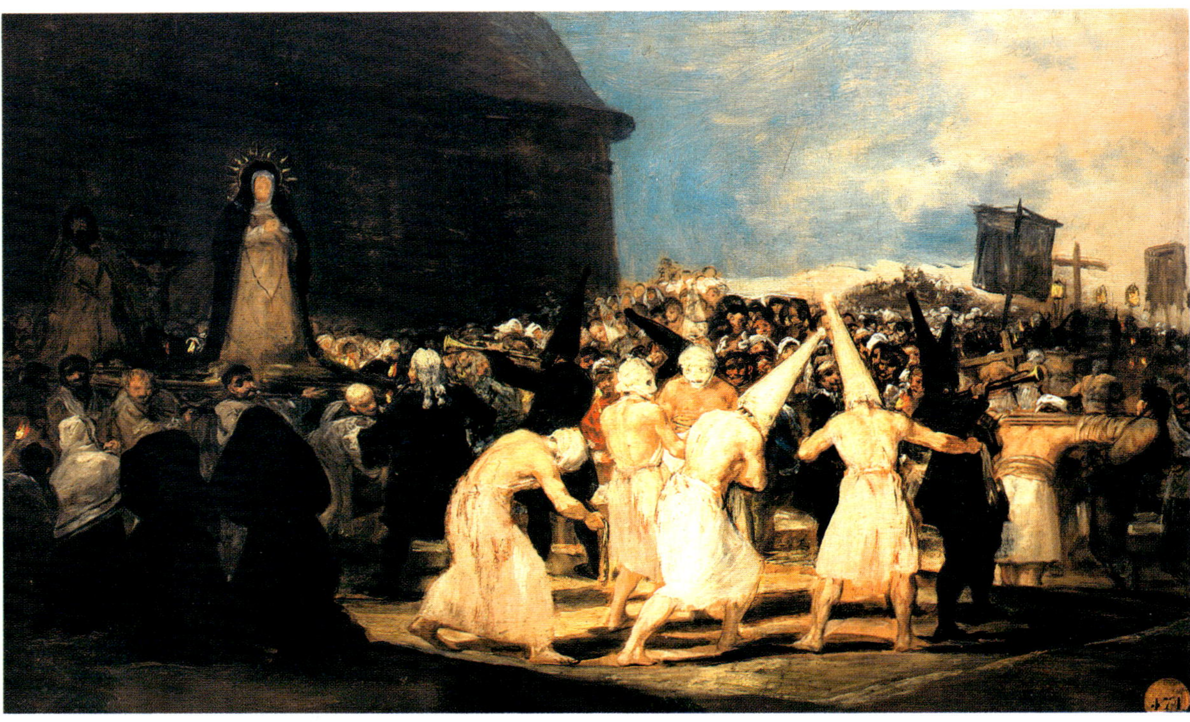

The theater of irrationality

Because the town is a faithful mirror of the human condition it may be defined as a work of reason, with irrationality working away beneath the surface. Goya said, "The sleep of reason produces monsters." The town has two faces. We can choose to see only the reassuringly organized order of the façades, but behind this ordered image another town continues to exist. The dark corners of backyards and alleyways are the parts of the town that have not been thought through, from which the ordering power of reason seems to have turned away, content to cover them up with the illusionistic set provided by the street.

But the madness that the set denies is there, and cannot always be kept out of sight. From time to time, on such occasions as festivals or carnivals, things are reversed and the backyard takes over the street, the respectable citizen becomes a penitent, and the crowd makes the fool king.

The anonymous people behind their masks become symbols. The invisible face of the town and the humanity that constitutes it can be seen in all its strangeness. The most astonishing aspect of this abrupt emergence of the irrational is not its suddenly revealed existence but the fact that it erupts at the very heart of reason. Madness is not a different reality: it is the other face of reason.

Malraux wrote that in Goya's work "the forms intermingle, or become allusive. The hat worn by the Inquisition is the magician's hat." And further on: "Goya wants the world to recognize that it is only appearance, possibly a sham [...]. In order to destroy not only that reality but even the style through which it sets out to magnify itself, Goya [...] transforms every one of the crucial accords on which the order of the world is based into dissonance."

Behind the jarring gaiety of the carnival, the conventional happiness of the wedding, there is "the thousand-year-old religious accent of pointless suffering," as behind the glow of the colors there is darkness, its other truth.

But the town, since it is conceived as a stage, turns its very madness into theater, recuperating even the transgression of order in the name of the supreme imperative: appearing. Dissonance is embodied as the counterpoint of harmony, not as its negation. To put it another way, since the transgression of its apparent order emphasizes the fundamentally artificial nature of the town, it ultimately reveals its profound truth. For a town to exist and to exist in a town every person must accept himself not as an individual but as an element of the community to which he is attached, less perhaps through adherence to the norm than a secret attraction to an underlying madness, a mute burden allocated to living creatures.

Goya (Francisco de Goya y Lucientes, known as) 1746-1828
Procession of penitents, c. 1812-1819
Madrid, San Fernando Academy of Art

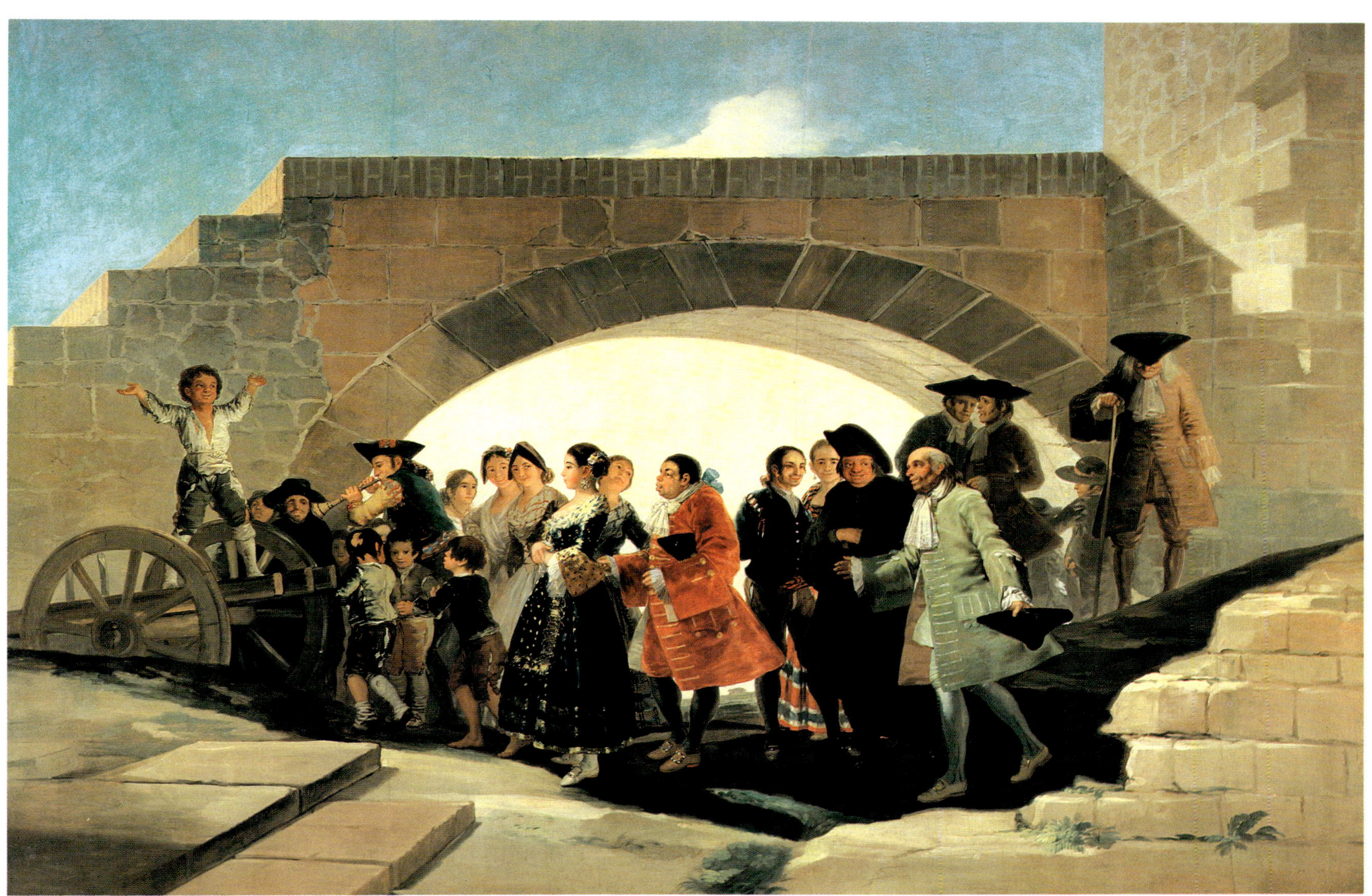

This cartoon is one of a series on popular themes intended for the king's study at the Escurial Palace. We see a wretched bride dragging her ape of a husband behind her with touching resignation: Goya has unkindly placed him in the center of the composition in a dazzling red coat.

Goya (Francisco de Goya y Lucientes, known as) 1746-1828
The wedding (tapestry cartoon), 1790-1792
Madrid, Prado

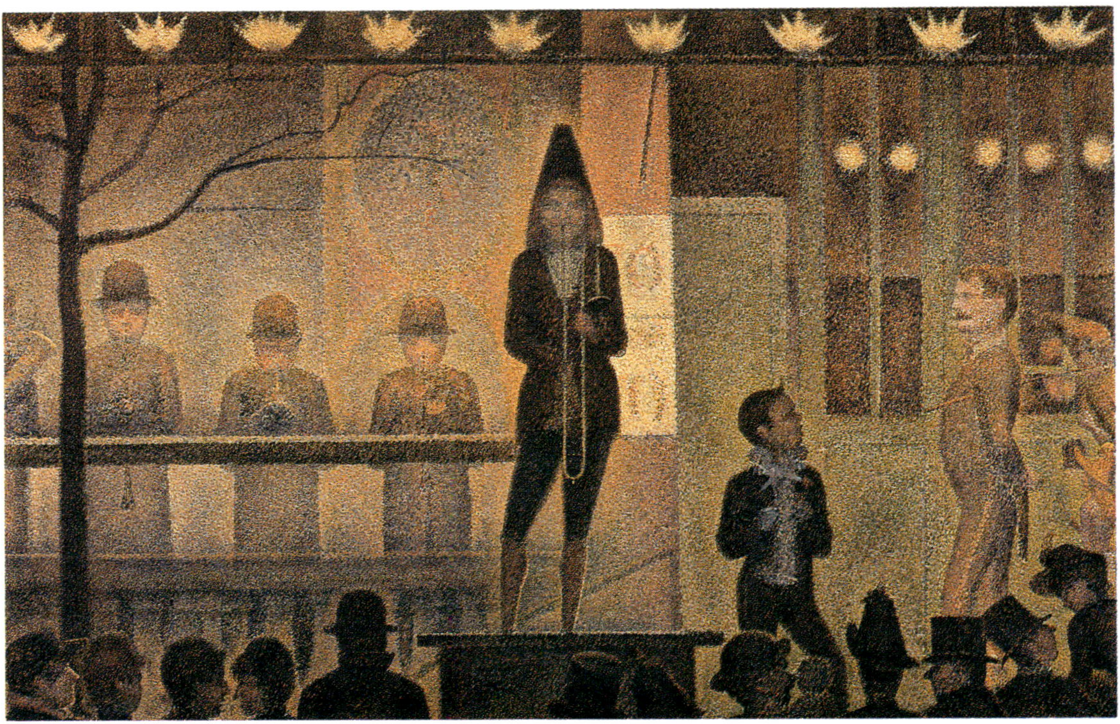

Artifice on display

The town can be seen as a woman wearing make-up. Still more cruelly, it can be compared to a grocer's shop with all its wares spilling out on to the pavement. Modern towns have become endless shop windows extending beneath the gaze of the passer-by. To parody current style, we might say that the town is a "visual space."

Everything connected with the town is linked with stage setting. The town does not exist without spectacle, and the spectator himself is part of that spectacle. That is why everything in it can be summarized in these two activities: trade and celebration – the latter being no more than the ultimate transformation of a reality that has totally turned into trade.

Looked at in this light there is no break between Degas's dressmaker and Toulouse-Lautrec's frivolous dancers. The shop by day, the cabaret by night: cabarets which flourished all round Montmartre, interspersed with other amusements like Fernando's circus at the corner of the rue des Martyrs and the boulevard Rochechouart. Renoir lingered there when the Bal du Moulin de la Galette was on. Degas painted the portrait of Miss La-La the acrobat there. Toulouse-Lautrec used it as the basis of a series called "Le Cirque" and Seurat found the material for two of his greatest works, *Parade* and *Le Cirque*, there.

If we forget the immediate obviousness of celebration for a moment and probe more deeply into works of this nature, two concepts emerge: artifice and voyeurism. Artifice here is not simply associated with costume and decor. First for Degas, then for Toulouse-Lautrec, artifice was more than a situation, it was a way of seeing and letting other people see, an attitude towards life which consisted of lighting up only certain aspects so as to allow their true nature to emerge, which many people then thought of as unnatural. This way of seeing, which was no doubt connected with the increased use of gas lighting, transformed everything into a show. Night light changed the spirit of the town. The narrow old alleys took on an alluring appearance. But the new, modern light was not equivalent to daylight: it did not show everything equally. The angle of lighting operated a real selection over what could be seen – which brings us on to the second concept mentioned above: voyeurism.

The voyeur or peeping Tom does not see everything either. He sees only what his obsession asks him to see – the rest does not exist, it has no reality. The fact that what his phantasm shows him has no reality other than his own desire is beside the point.

The town sells everything. Like "the girls who wait at night at the street corner," it adapts to suit the customer. Everything is up for sale, including love. Ruled by the law of supply and demand, reality is transformed to suit the needs of the market. Light no longer flows from God, spread uniformly across the world. It is reduced to a narrow beam which everyone directs to suit himself, making Zola's famous reality extraordinary, malleable and subjective.

Seurat (Georges) 1859-1891
Parade, 1887
New York, Metropolitan Museum of Art

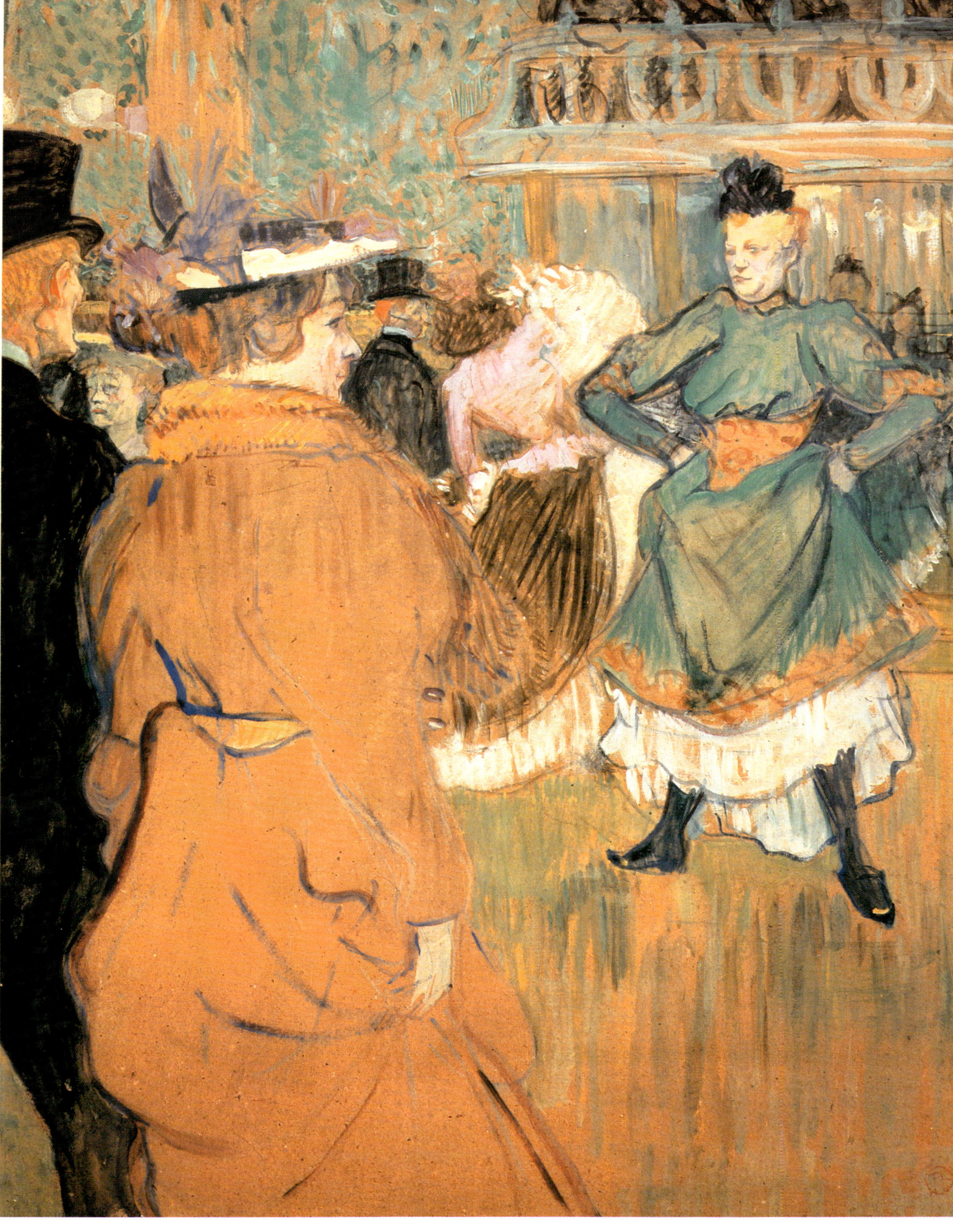

Toulouse-Lautrec, who had been cut off from ordinary people by his disability, chose to live among those on the margins of the society of his day. At the conjunction of Impressionism and Fauvism, he left behind the uncategorizable oeuvre of a professional peeping Tom.

Toulouse-Lautrec (Henri Marie Raymond de Toulouse-Lautrec-Monfa, known as) 1864-1901
Quadrille at the Moulin-Rouge, 1892
Washington, National Gallery of Art

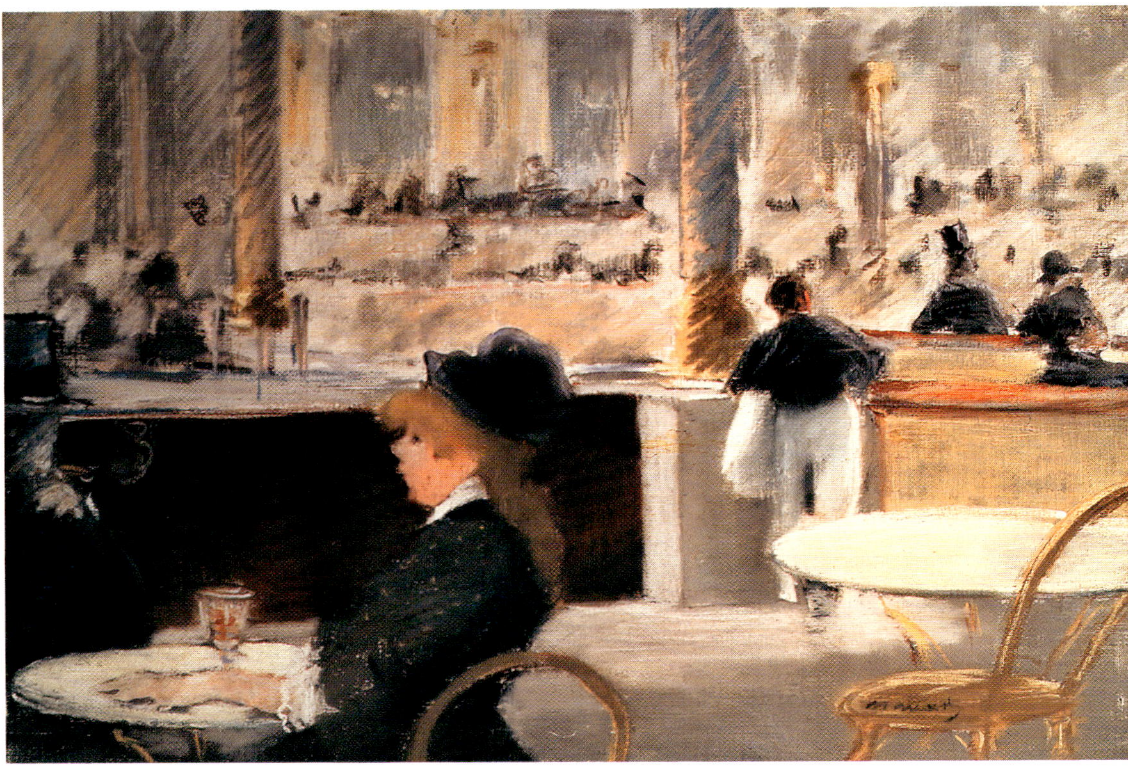

Rootless people

As Millet had divined, the drama of the urban world was that it had no roots. In order to exist the town must constantly live a life of artifice. Behind the entertainers' patter is the empty gaze of Degas's woman drinking absinthe. There is the dismal interior of a café. The Impressionists have been praised for their ability to exalt color and turn away from the gray harmonies of Academicism, and rightly so. Even so, we should not forget that they could also paint the grayness of gray moments in gray.

Too many individuals cross each other's paths in the town for everyone to be able to hope to recognize one another. The town and its cafés are the refuge of the anonymous. The entertainer comes forward wearing his mask, playing his role of entertainer for the crowd. The spectator applauds, as he is supposed to do. What then?

The café is not only an appropriate place of exchange, the heart of life, as it is always portrayed. It is also a beaching strand of the kind found at the end of some bays. Each café has its jetsam, its down-and-outs, for whom it is a final port of call. We think again of Degas, but why look so far? This little oil painting by Manet says it all, as do Tiepolo's Puncinellos at the other end of the scale. Puncinello is mad; he has lost his reason. But the laughter he provokes sometimes has a bitter ring. His ridiculousness has a tragic note. The sight of madness, even when it is mimed, causes no more than a moment's laughter, for here we are touching one of the secret wounds of a world which claimed it could overcome everything by technical means, but which has paid a high price for its victory by brutally cutting itself off from its roots.

Both the café and the troop of entertainers serve as a substitute family. The Impressionists met at the Guerbois before 1870, then later at the Nouvelle Athènes to exchange ideas, come to terms with their experiences and above all to forget their respective solitudes for the duration of an evening. For, like the unskilled worker newly arrived in the city from the depths of the country, the artist has no family. He has to reinvent all the conviviality he has lost, starting from scratch.

Talking about the Nouvelle Athènes George Moore wrote: "I remember the smell of every hour of the day; in the morning the smell of eggs cooking in butter, of acrid cigarettes, coffee and cheap brandy; at five o'clock the vegetable smell of absinthe; [...] and as the evening moved on, the mixed smells of cigarettes, coffee and watery beer."

Anyone who has experienced solitude in the heart of a city will understand the solace such sensations can bring.

Manet (Edouard) 1832-1883
Interior of a café
Glasgow, Art Gallery and Museum

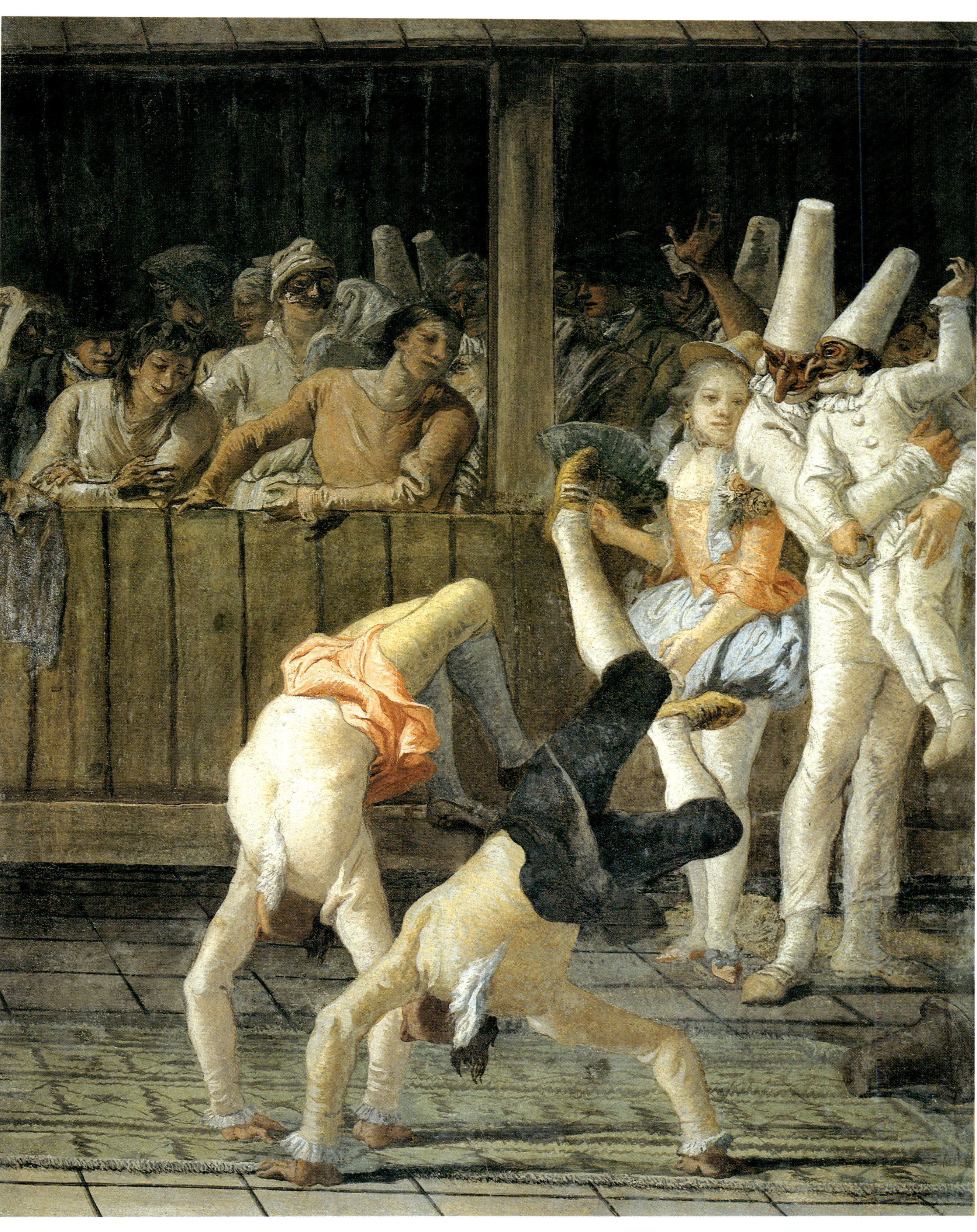

Tiepolo (Giovanni Domenico) 1727-1804
Pulcinellos and tumblers also known as The house of tumblers, c. 1793
Zinnigo, Villa Tiepolo

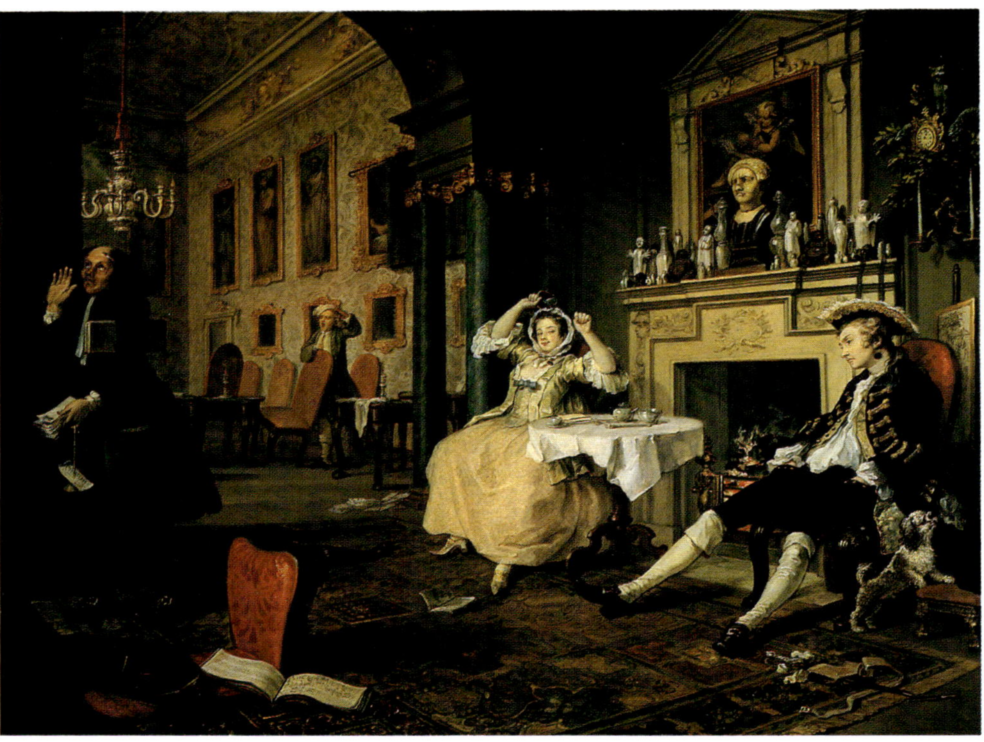

Behind closed doors

"My picture is my stage, and men and women are my players," Hogarth said. The theatrical character taken on by urban life cannot be stated better. The town is the theater of the middle classes, a world made to their measure, a decor made in their image. It is their world, their stage. They are at home within its walls: they own it.

The artist and the laborer who are not at home anywhere feel the need to congregate in cafés or bars, no doubt because solitude and rootlessness awaken within them an ancestral memory of the group. The gregarious instinct is also a survival reflex. But members of the middle classes need no such subterfuges. In a way, after building the town to their measure, they can feel free to leave it to others and dig in behind the thick velvet curtains of their private rooms. The street is used only for show. Real life goes on in private, shielded from prying eyes, for the comedy of power, except in the rare event of revolution, is better enacted discreetly behind closed doors than in the wide open spaces of outdoors. Even in its topography the middle-class town is truly happy only in enclosed spaces.

The interest of a painter like William Hogarth – his intentions are avowedly moralistic, but he is nonetheless a keen observer of his contemporaries – lies in the fact that he shows us the other side of the stage set, taking us behind the scenes of a world falsely fixed in its appearance. Of course there is a difference in style and subject matter between the popular tones of *Beer street* and the frivolities of *Marriage à la mode*, but there is also, deriving from the coherence of one man's gaze, the affirmation of the existence of a social fabric that constitutes the very web of urban reality, beyond its breaks and contradictions.

As for Nana, the central character in the ninth volume of Emile Zola's Rougon-Macquart cycle, she embodies the fate of the Second Empire. After starting from nothing and rising to the top, she dies alone, disfigured by smallpox, just as war breaks out between France and Prussia, a scant few weeks before the disaster of Sedan.

In the 18th century the painter who ventured inside respectable homes found the victorious, sometimes unsophisticated face of a middle-class group that could hardly wait to take control. A century later the middle classes had aged. Cynicism had replaced generosity. Like a body running out of breath, they sought new blood elsewhere, going to look for it in the slime of dark back streets.

The middle classes survived Sedan. They did more: they profited from it by proclaiming a Republic that was entirely devoted to them. The real victim was Nana: the true image of their baseness could not be reflected back to these replete worthies with impunity. Nana paid the price, not for her own wrongdoing, but because, in spite of herself, her artless body went on telling the men who came to make use of it a truth that did not bear hearing. In the same way Olympia told the public in the Salon a truth that people could not bear to see.

Hogarth (William) 1697-1764
Marriage à la mode
London, National Gallery

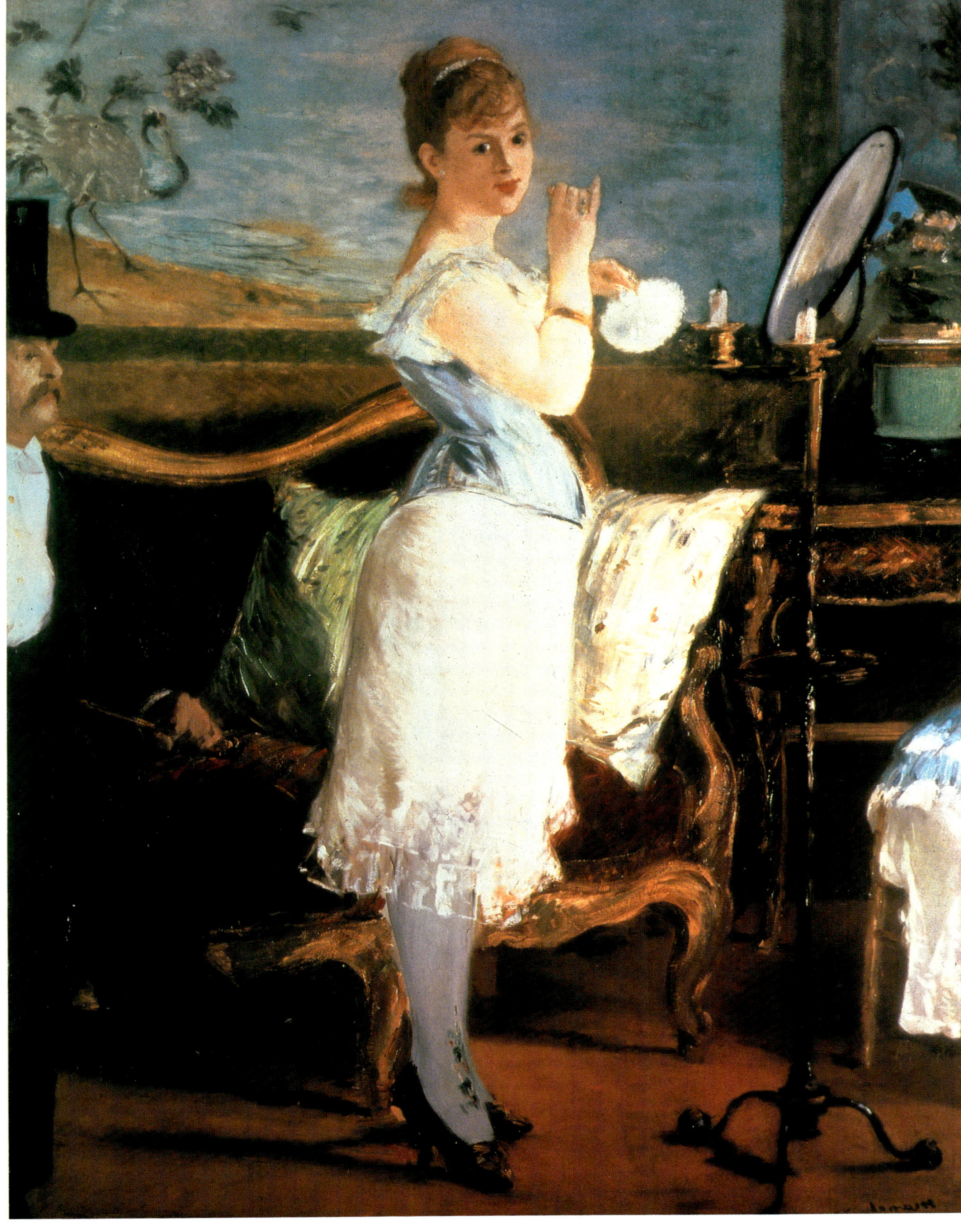

"The district put on its finery at the time [Gervaise] turned towards ruin [...]. The beautiful pile in the Boulevard Ornano made her ill at ease. Houses like that were for whores like Nana."

Emile Zola
L'Assommoir

Manet (Edouard) 1832-1883
Nana, 1877
Hamburg, Kunsthalle

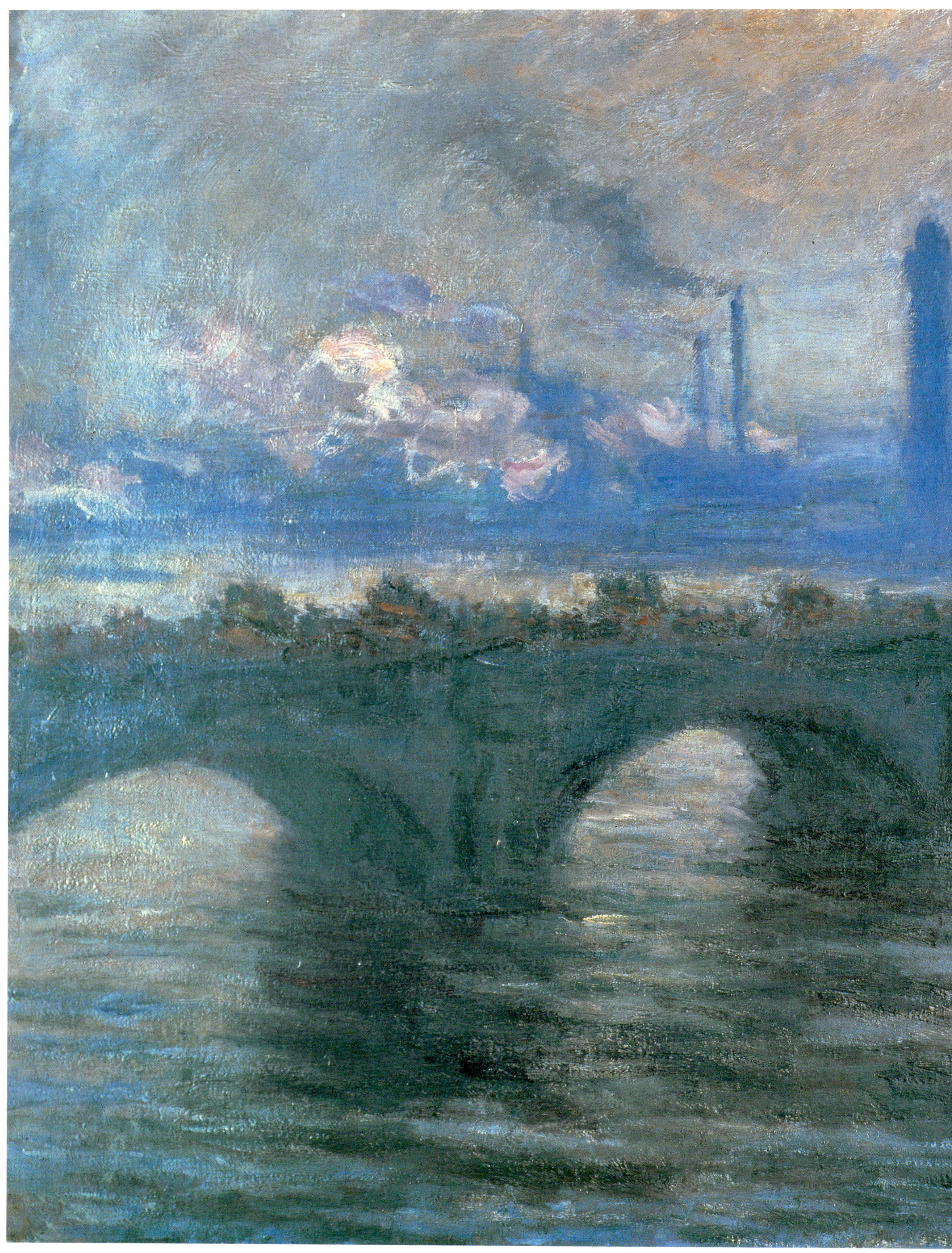

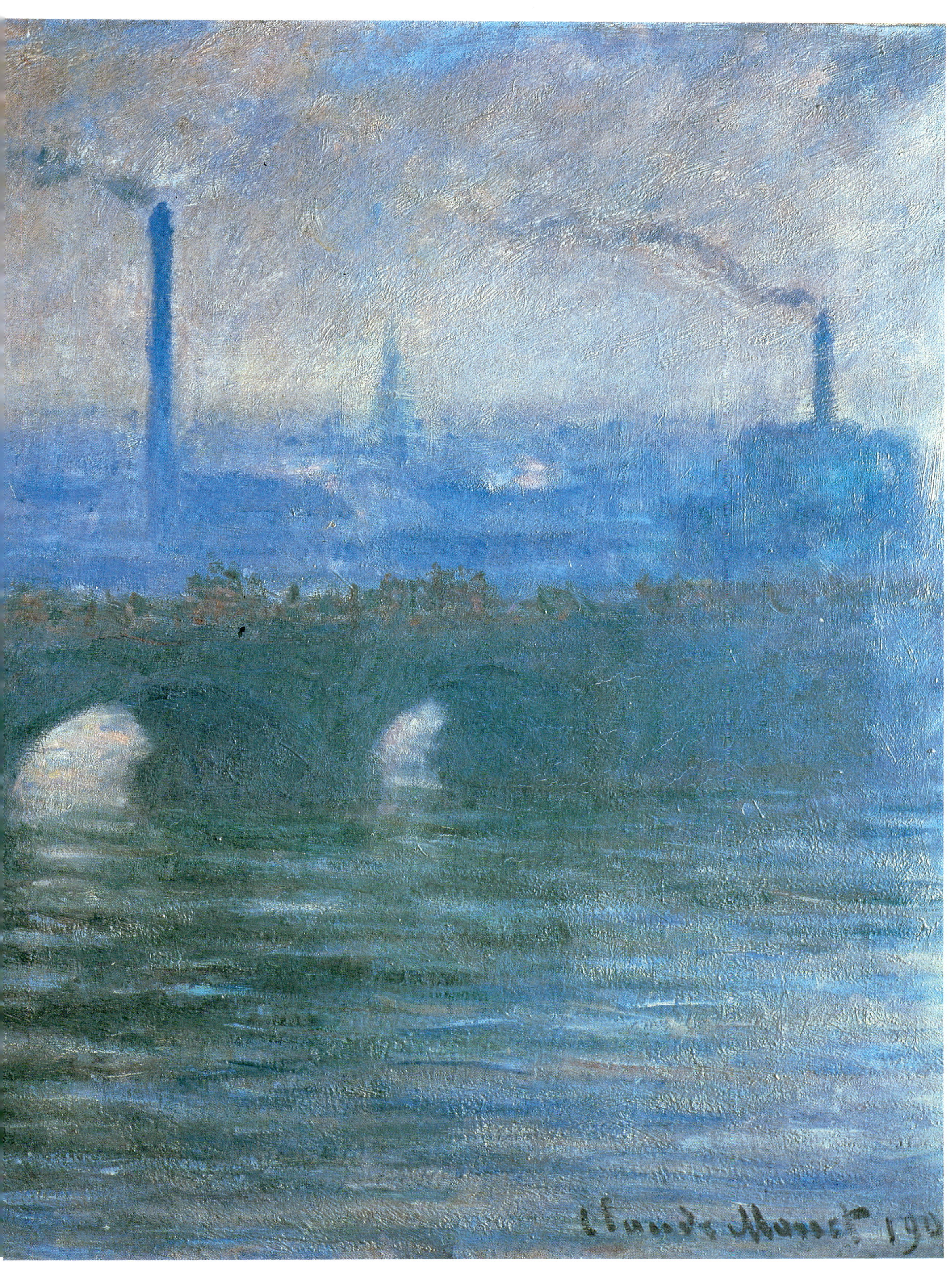

Monet (Claude) 1840-1926
London, Waterloo Bridge, a gray day, 1900
Dublin, Hugh Lane Municipal Gallery of Modern Art

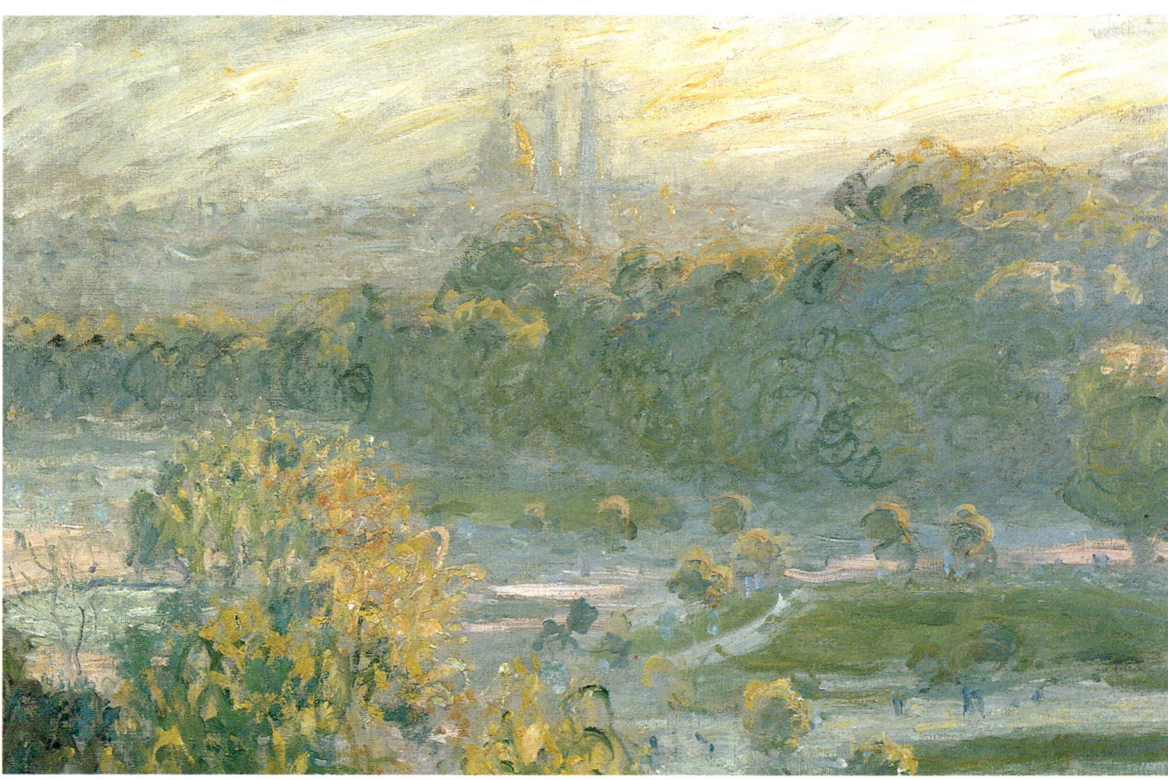

Monuments of light

Every century has looked at the town in a different way. The Renaissance saw ideal architecture, the Classical period an allegory of monarchical power, the 18th century a tableau of morals and manners and the 19th a portrait of society.

Impressionism did not initially seem to go against the lessons of Realism – which had become naturalism in the writing of Zola. It was Zola, too, who was incautious enough to write the following about Monet, describing the 1868 Salon: "He has sucked the milk of our age, growing up adoring what surrounds him, and he will continue to do so. He loves the horizons of our towns, the gray and white splashes houses make against a light sky; he loves people scurrying through the streets in their overcoats, intent on their business; he loves racecourses, aristocratic promenades full of the noise of carriages; he loves our women, their sunshades, their gloves, their frills and furbelows, even their hairpieces and face powder, everything that makes them women of our time [...]. Like a true Parisian he takes Paris to the country and cannot paint a landscape without inserting smartly dressed men and women. As far as he is concerned nature seems to lose its interest directly it ceases to bear the imprint of our civilization."

Looking at Monet's paintings of Rouen cathedral, we may feel tempted to smile at this piece of fine writing. But almost a quarter of a century lies between the Rouen paintings and the women in the gardens. Between 1868 and the series painted in 1893 Monet's ideas had matured. The original misconception which led Zola to think that there was a kinship between naturalism and Impressionism had been cleared up. When Monet's painting ceased to be narrative it turned away from any message other than a pictural one. His only intention was to translate light into color and to show that color changes according to the quality of light; to show that color does not exist in itself and perhaps even that matter does not exist, only the changing illusion of the existence of matter. For Monet the town does not exist, or rather it does not exist in the sense that we normally mean. In his eyes, it was only an object like any other – say a water-lily or a haystack; a simple object to be painted, a pure surface, with no social background or historical depth, having no existence beyond that of the work itself.

Monet (Claude) 1840-1926
Les Tuileries, 1875
Paris, Musée d'Orsay

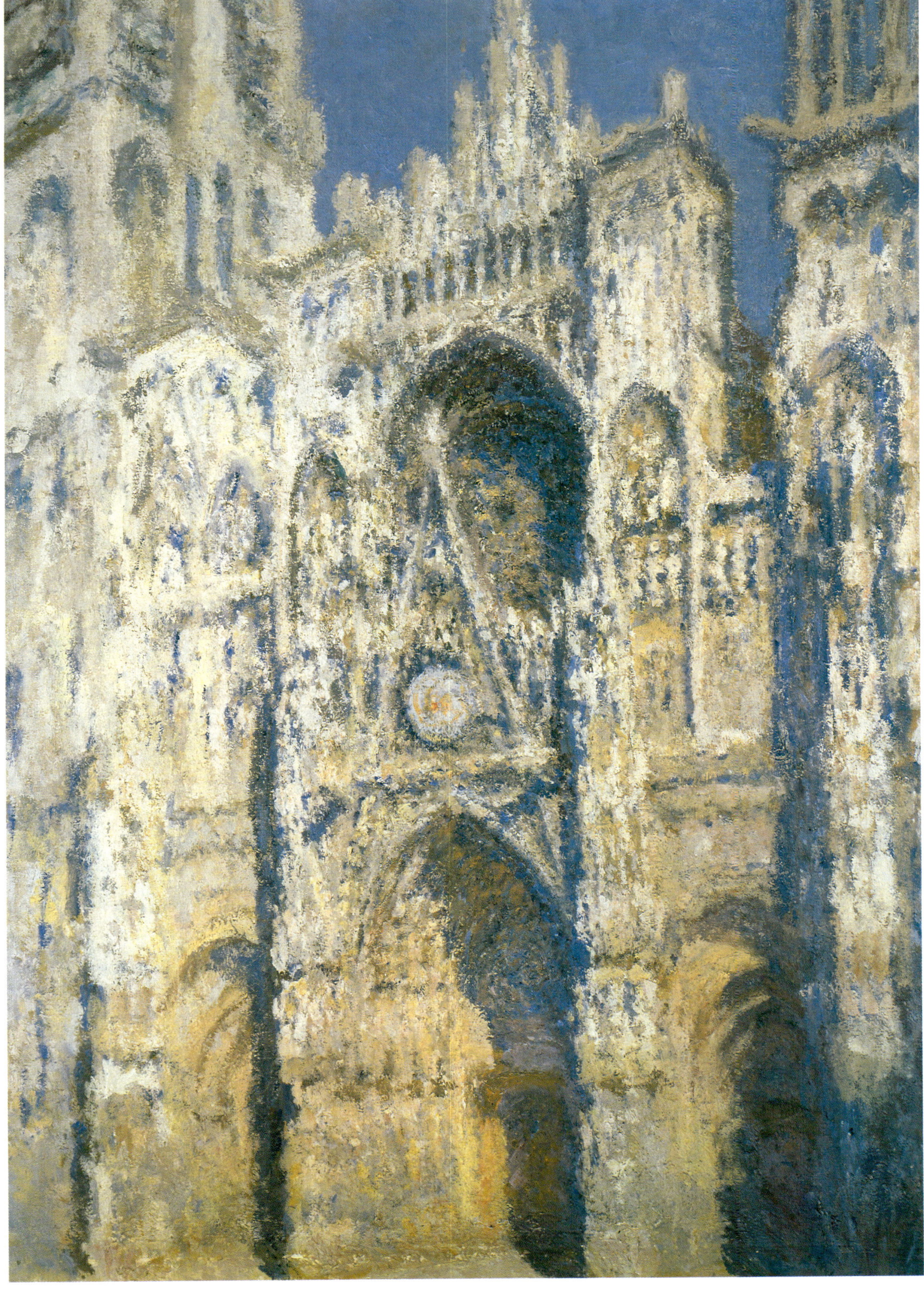

There is no doubt something crazy about Monet's desire to transform this huge mass of limestone into a pure vibration of light. But when it comes down to it, was that not what the builders of cathedrals had originally set out to do? Their program could be résuméd in these three words: "God is light."

Monet (Claude) 1840-1926
Rouen cathedral. Harmony in blue and gold, full sunlight, 1894
Paris, Musée d'Orsay

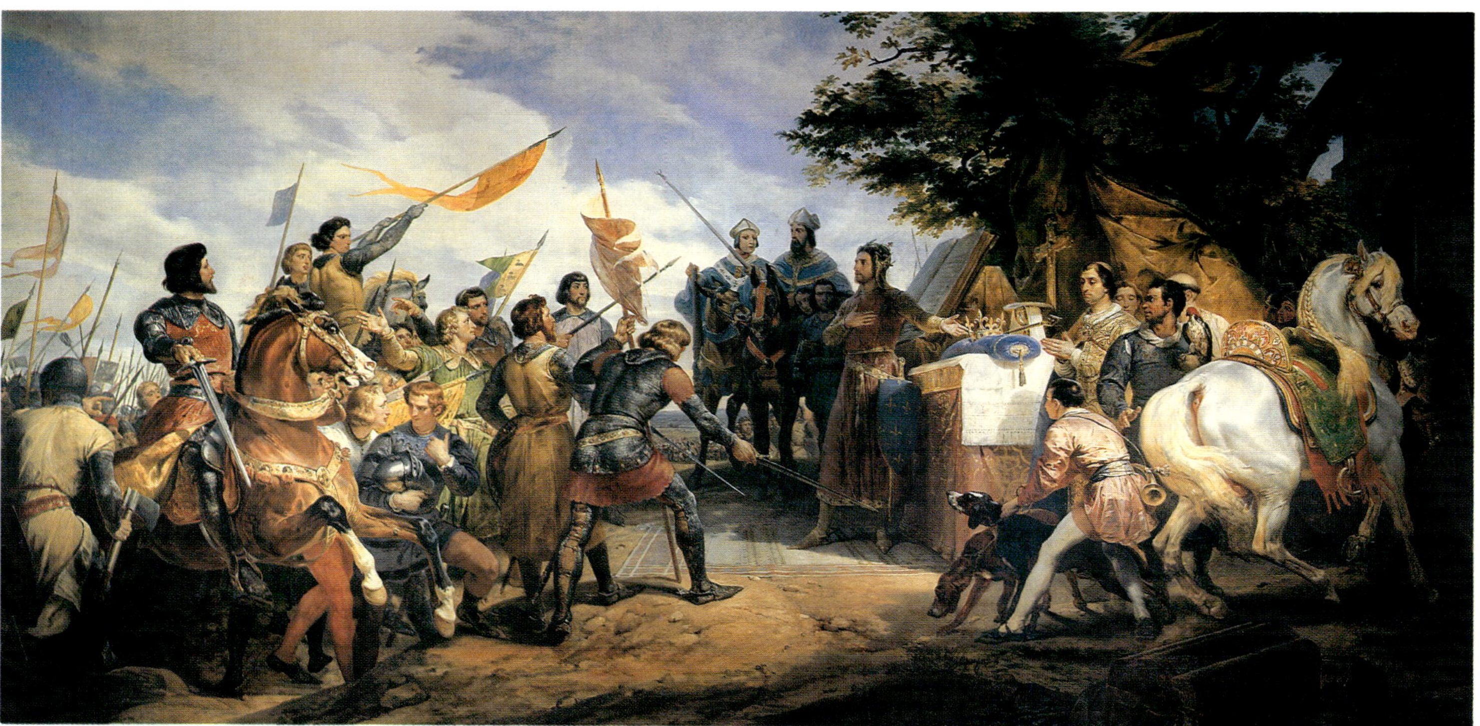

Vernet (Horace) 1780-1863
Battle of Bouvines, 27 July 1214, 1827
Château de Versailles, Galerie des Batailles

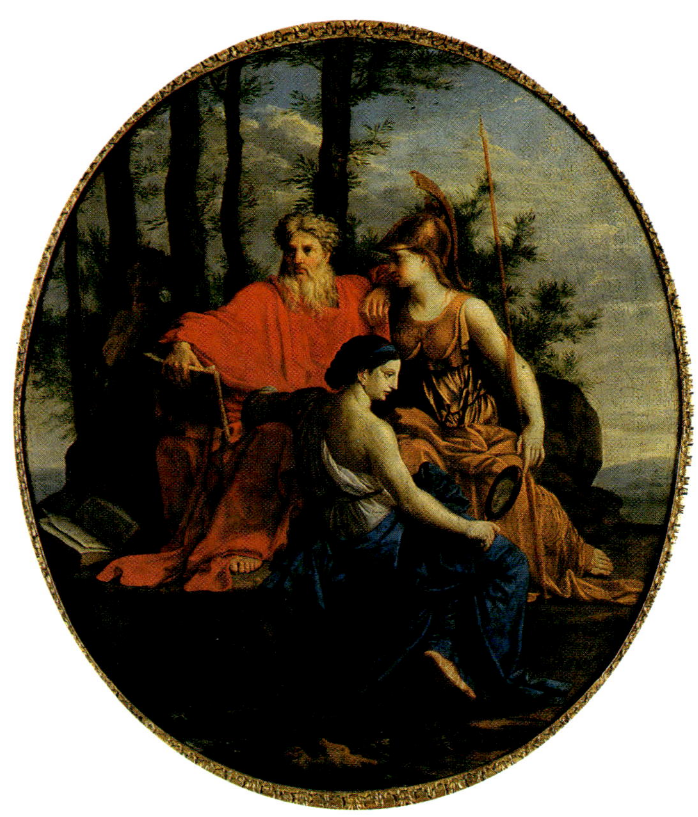

The allegorical vision

We have already mentioned in earlier chapters the difficulties that arise when painting and history meet. And yet the history of painters, if not that of painting, has always been linked to power. Painters cannot exist without patrons. And the painter's closeness to, not to say dependence on, his protector necessarily implies that his work will contain some celebration of political power.

In France the century of Louis XIV marked the apogee of the artist's subjection. The pictorial arts under Le Brun's control were reduced to being a simple celebration of monarchical power. But no doubt because that power claimed to be divine in nature, its legitimacy could not derive from history. Thus it became part of the painter's remit to act as the prince's herald, celebrating his great feats, but without ever letting it seem that the monarch's power depended on this. History was deduced from the nature of the prince, not the other way round.

In such a system the whole of history ceases to be based on events and becomes allegorical. The event, the minister and perhaps the king himself can no longer be apprehended other than as figures of a higher will, each of them contributing to the expression a central truth, namely the divine origin of royal authority and – resulting from it – the infallibility of the king's word.

Just as etiquette imposed the rules governing the behavior of the nobility, the Academy took control of pictorial language, setting a certain number of fixed stereotypes for it. History as a process of development had no place here since it was impossible that the king's absolute power should be capable of being perfected.

Despite this – and this paradox deserves a few moments reflection – history painting was regarded by 17th-century theorists as the most elevated genre, greater than landscape and portraiture. In the words of Félibien, "Both history and fable should be painted; great actions should be depicted as historians would describe them, and pleasant subjects should be treated in the manner of poets; and going higher still, allegorical compositions should be used to describe the virtues of great men and the highest mysteries in the guise of fable. Someone who acquits himself well in undertakings such as these may be called a great painter."

Understood in this way there is hardly any difference between history and fable. The work of the painter which is close to that of the poet consists of drawing a moral lesson with a general application from an action. The meaning of history does not belong to history, but to the morality governing it. That is why the event depicted cannot have any meaning in itself, or in relation to other events, for it exists only in its moral dimension. Thus in 17th-century France history was fundamentally perceived as an allegory. And even portrait painters like Rigaud, quite capable of psychological penetration when the model lent itself to it, had to conform to the ceremonial style of which this portrait of Louis XIV is a perfect illustration.

Lesueur (Eustache) 1617-1655
Allegory of a perfect minister or The Minister of State with his attributes, 1653
Dunkirk, Musée des Beaux-Arts

"Fulfilling a completely divine function on this earth as we do, we must appear incapable of the agitations that might demean it."

Louis XIV
Mémoires

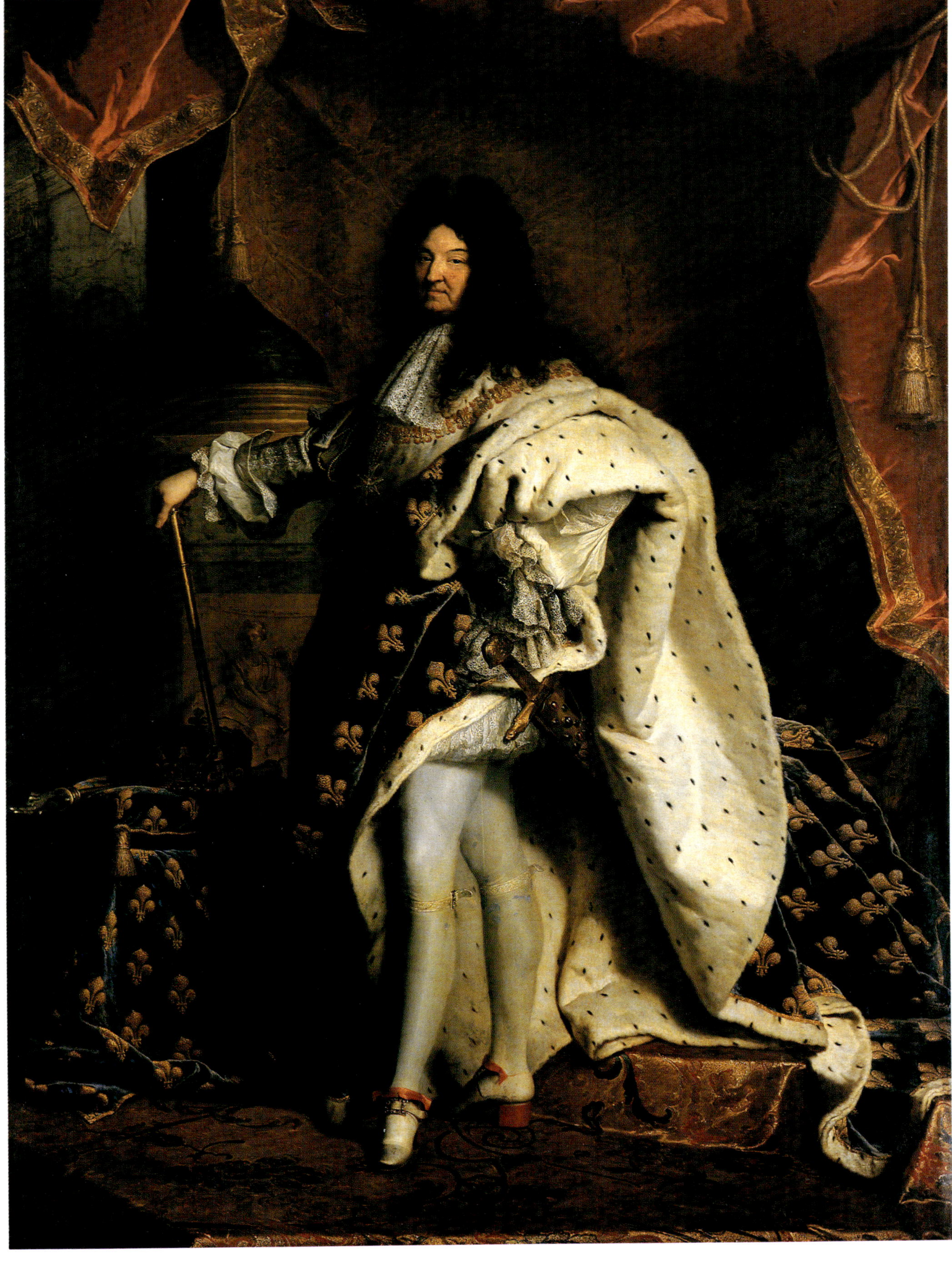

Rigaud (Hyacinthe) 1659-1743
Louis XIV in full regalia, wrongly described as in his Coronation robes, 1701
Paris, Louvre

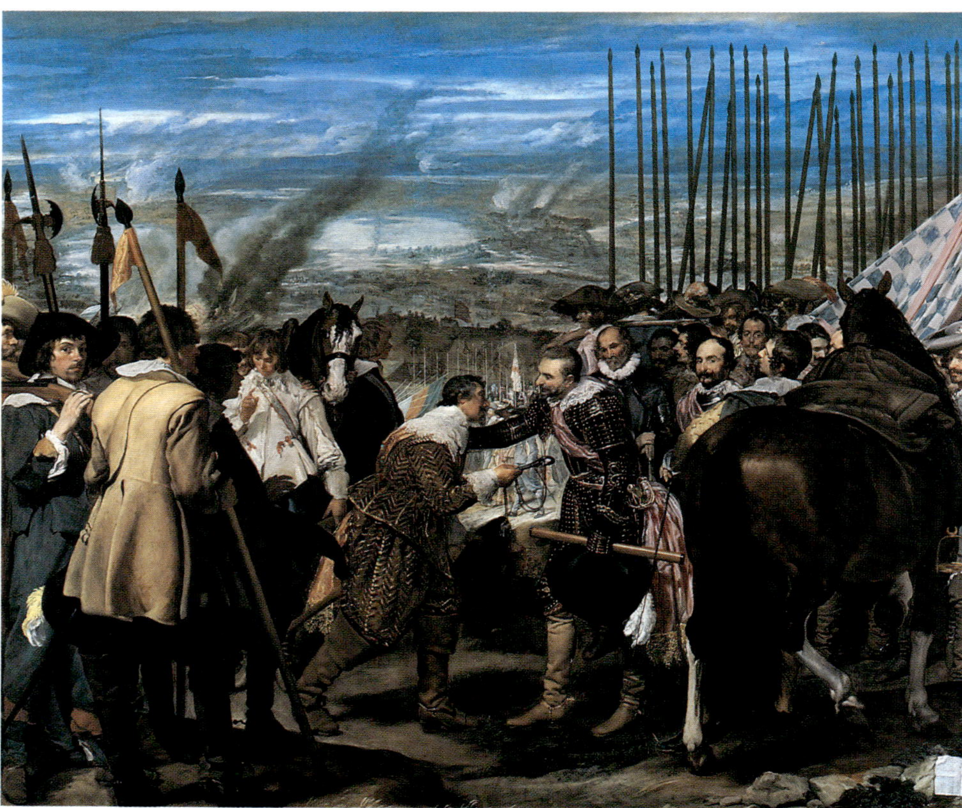

The event as opposed to allegory

The allegorical representation of history has some strange merits, just the same. If Titian and Veronese had not chosen to devote a work to the Battle of Lepanto, no doubt it would today have been forgotten behind the long series of more recent and famous battles.

In 1571 the fleet of the Holy League, consisting of Spanish, Venetian, Genoese and Papal galleys, met and defeated Ali Pasha's Turkish fleet in the Strait of Lepanto, which controls access to the Gulf of Corinth, thus preserving the Ionian coast from Ottoman occupation for the time being.

Two great Venetians paid homage to their native state, but the paintings celebrating the victory do not stand out as landmarks in their work, unlike the Surrender of Breda painted fifty years later, which is regarded as one of Velazquez's masterpieces. Yet the importance of the event was slight, even slighter than that of the Battle of Lepanto. So what is it that caused this surrender to make a greater impression in the annals of painting than the two versions of the Battle of Lepanto? The genius of all three painters is not in dispute: we are dealing with something else. Velazquez set allegory aside. His vision was theatrical, but still realistic. Moreover, ceremonies of this kind were intrinsically staged events, and the painter still remains true to his realistic vision in schematizing the composition.

On the left are the Dutch who capitulated on 25 May 1625 (the keys of the town were handed over on 2 June) with the town's governor Justin of Nassau at their head; on the right the Spanish troops commanded by the Marquis of Spinola, who places a magnanimous hand on the shoulder of his defeated enemy. The governor bows, but his knee does not touch the ground. The Marquis of Spinola accepts the keys and bows in turn, as if to avoid taking advantage of his patently superior position. In the distance, however, plumes of smoke attest to the bitterness of the struggle. Obviously there is a political message here, but it is expressed using means that belong exclusively to painting; it is contained not in the pasted-on meaning of the allegory but in the internal meaning given to the painting by the composition.

That is why this is really and truly a history painting: the painter conveys a message of a historical, political nature using plastic means, without borrowing anything from the traditional figures that derive from poetry. Thus he constructs a truly autonomous language.

The message might be read as follows: history is a series of events the outcome of which is always in doubt, and not a series of allegorical enactments of eternal truths. This leads to a rehabilitation of the event as a particular event, and of those caught up in it as flesh-and-blood creatures. Here order is obviously on the side of the Spanish lances, while doubt hovers over the Dutch camp. But beyond this clear dissymmetry, the technique of harmonious counterpoint reestablishes the equilibrium between the two armies. The foreground of the picture is given over to the victors. This is not just a technical procedure, it emphasizes the homage being accorded to the enemy.

Velazquez (Diego Rodriguez de Silva y) 1599-1660
The lances or The surrender of Breda in 1625, before 1635
Madrid, Prado

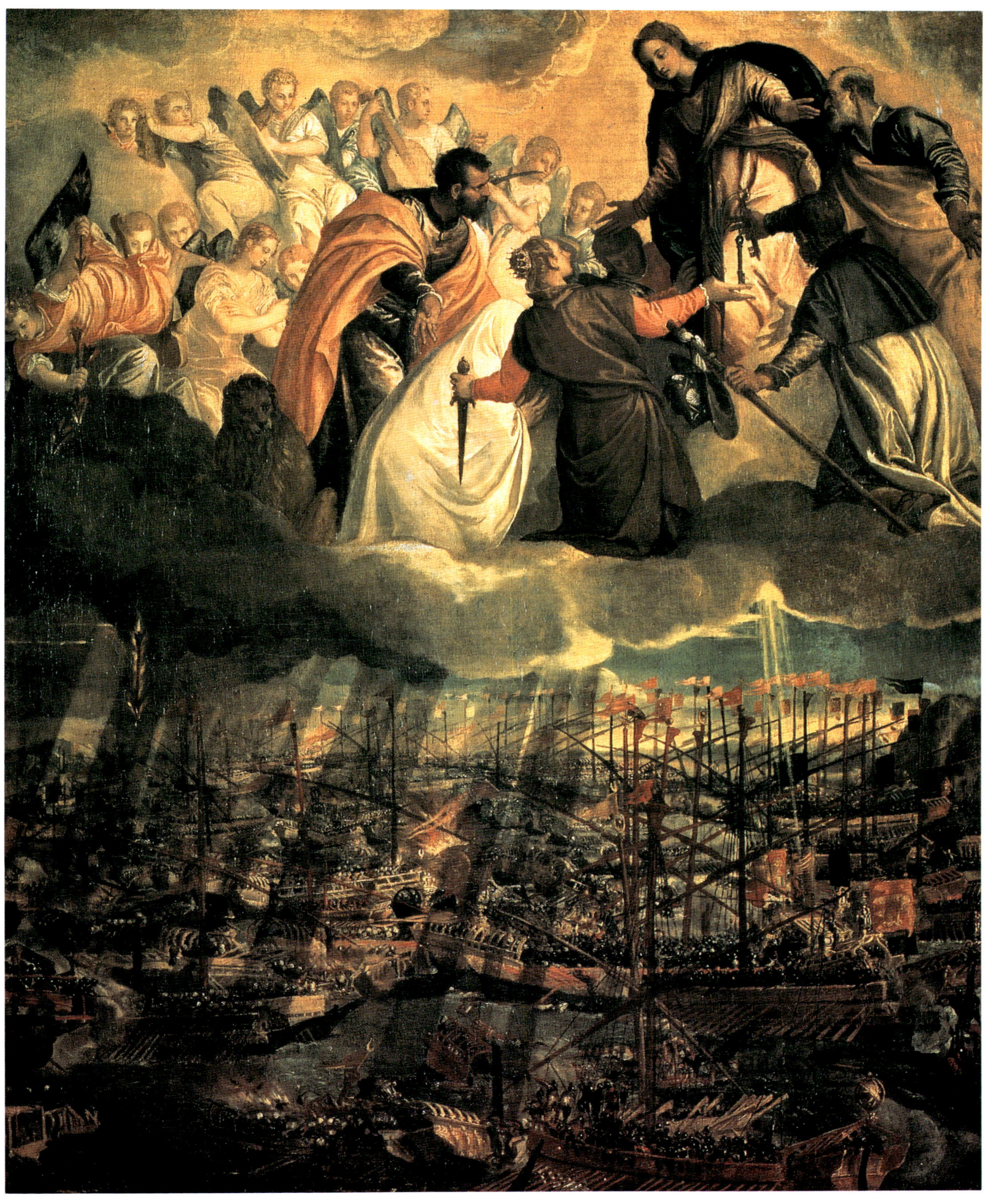

"With a gift for setting the scene which would be equalled only by Tiepolo, Veronese organizes huge compositions full of figures and tiny events which always remain under control, for he is a supreme master of the art of depicting great spectacles without seemingly sacrificing anything and without confusion."

André Chastel

Veronese (Paolo Caliari, known as) 1528-1588
Allegory of the Battle of Lepanto
Venice, Accademia

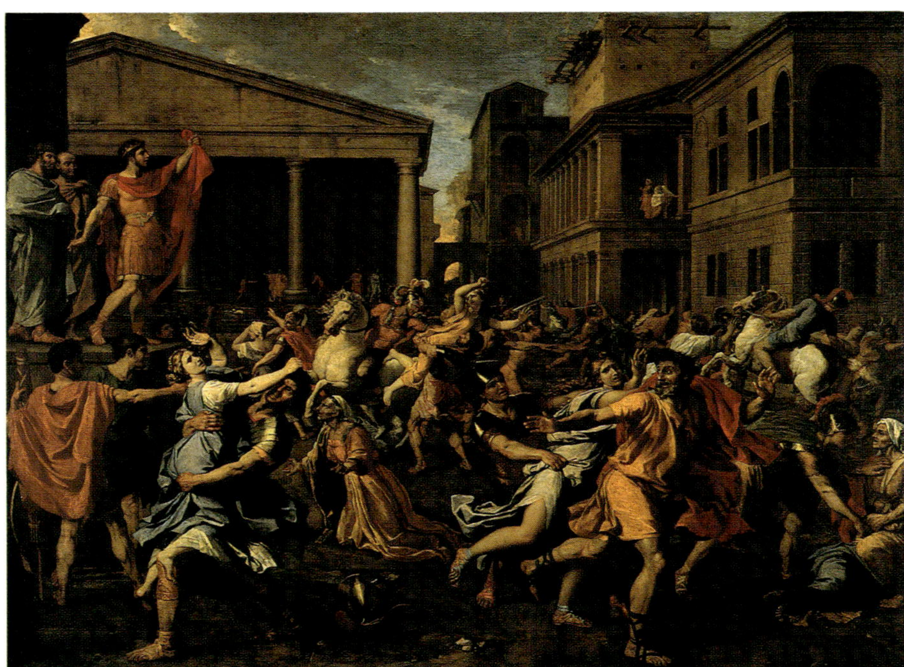

Where history begins

The French school, for reasons connected with the development of absolutism, was not able to take the same liberties as Velazquez. But painters such as Poussin in Louis XIII's reign and David in Louis XVI's did weigh up the danger of awful insipidness to which their work would be exposed if they resorted too systematically to allegory.

By its nature allegory is unsuited to the language of history, for it denies the notion of development and change which is at the heart of the historical process. It is this very notion of a possible evolution in the world order that an absolute monarchy cannot accept. Innovative painters, caught in this subtle trap, looked to Antiquity for escape, a clever way of continuing to relate history without seeming to question the monarch's absolute authority.

According to his biographers, Poussin was extremely well versed in Antiquity, and his prolonged stay in Rome only served to strengthen his original liking for it. But for him history started with myth, as if wanting to return to the cyclical era of myth. The episode involving the Sabine women conjures up both a foundation and a reconciliation. Without denying the event the potential of existing, Poussin set out to open and close it within a single work: the event may well develop, but it is up to the artist to circumscribe it. Thus the whole of history is résuméd in man confronting his destiny, and it is that meeting we call an event. If man masters the event, time will remain cyclical (not unchanged, but predictable); if he ceases to dominate it completely, everything becomes possible, both the best and the worst. Thus whether the pursuit of a happy eternity or the plunge into history the tragic nature of which is beyond doubt occurs depends on the attitude of the hero. What is going on in the mythical event is undoubtedly the birth of history experienced as a "passion." "This word should be understood not in the modern sense," Jacques Thuillier wrote, "but with the meaning Descartes gave it, bringing together all man's attitudes when confronted with the event. The living heart of the creative work of an artist like Poussin lies there [...]. But gradually as the years pass the enthusiastic impulse becomes set and heroes try to resist the event rather than to direct its energy [...]. The conflict [...] is no longer felt only within human destiny, it becomes the cruel opposition between nature which is infinitely happy, eternal and fruitful and the fleeting, sterile destiny of man."

Thus Poussin's work reveals a certain resistance to history conceived of as ineluctable fate: resistance, but not denial. History announces its coming in myth, just as a theme is sketched out in the overture to an opera.

Poussin (Nicolas) 1594-1665
Rape of the Sabine women
Paris, Louvre

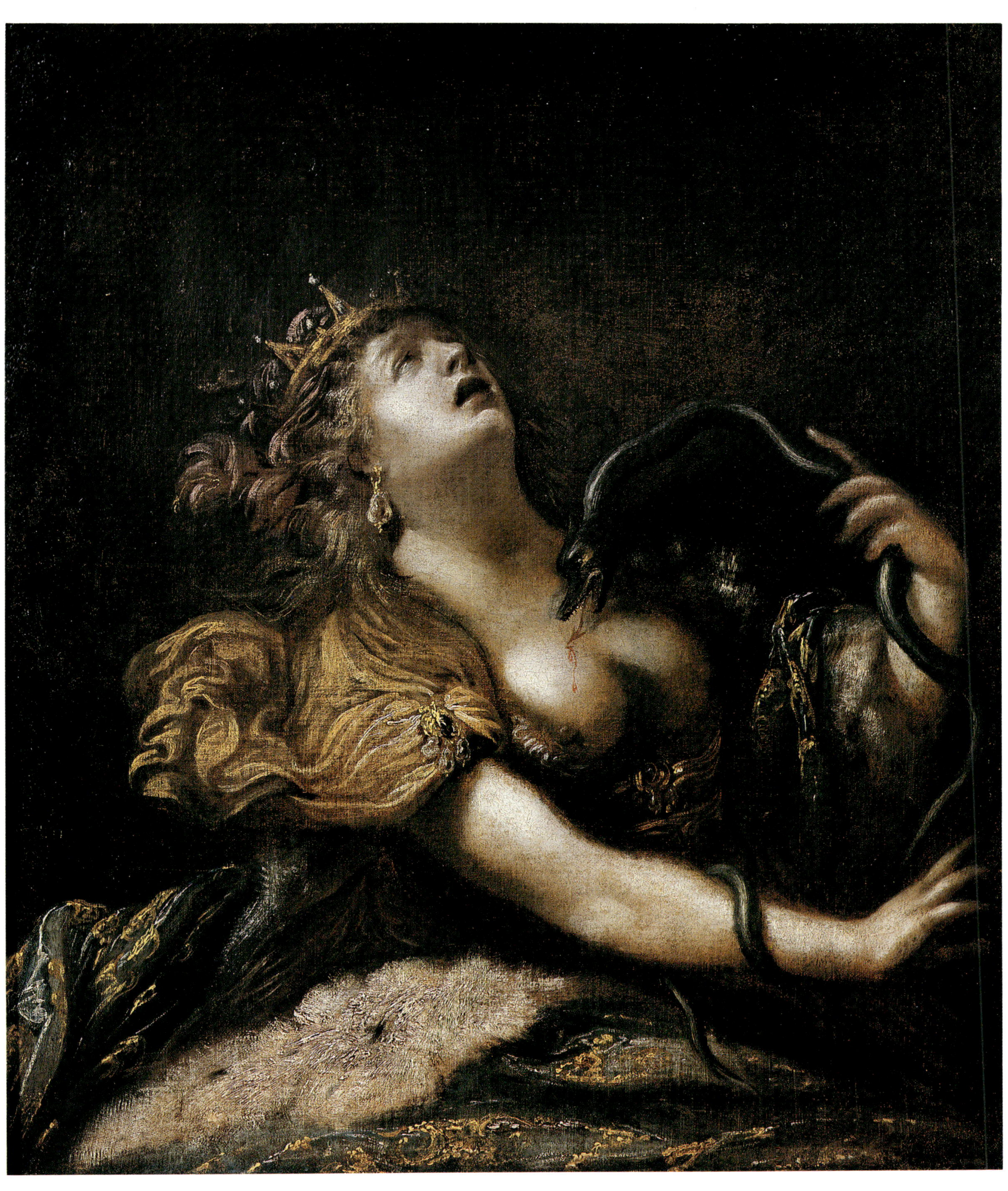

"To the very end Vignon remained what his first pictures had shown him to be: he had imagination, endless facility, very little order and no economy."

Jacques Thuillier
La Peinture française, XVIIe siècle, vol. I

Vignon (Claude, called the Elder) 1593-1670
Cleopatra taking her own life
Rennes, Musée des Beaux-Arts

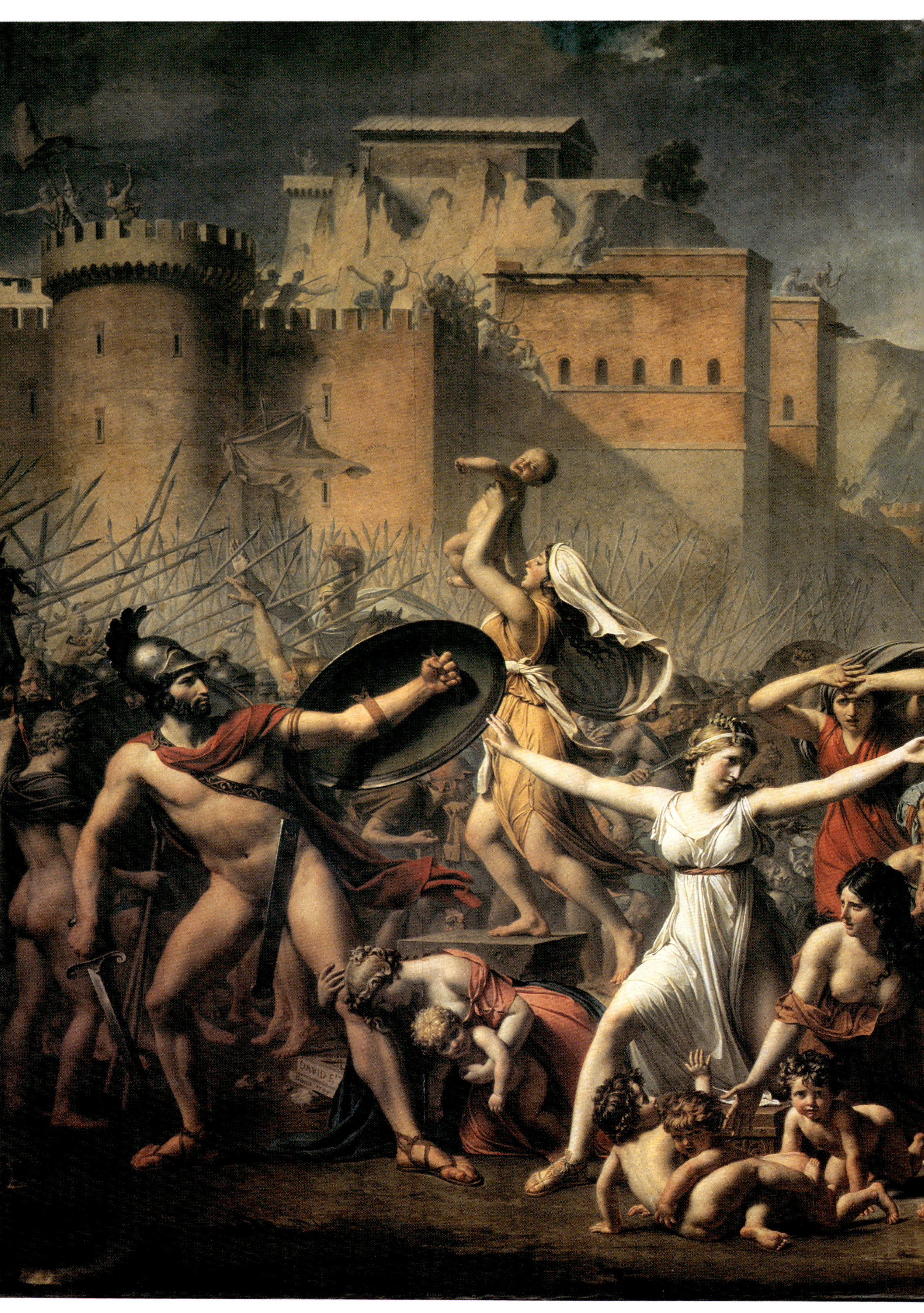
DAVID

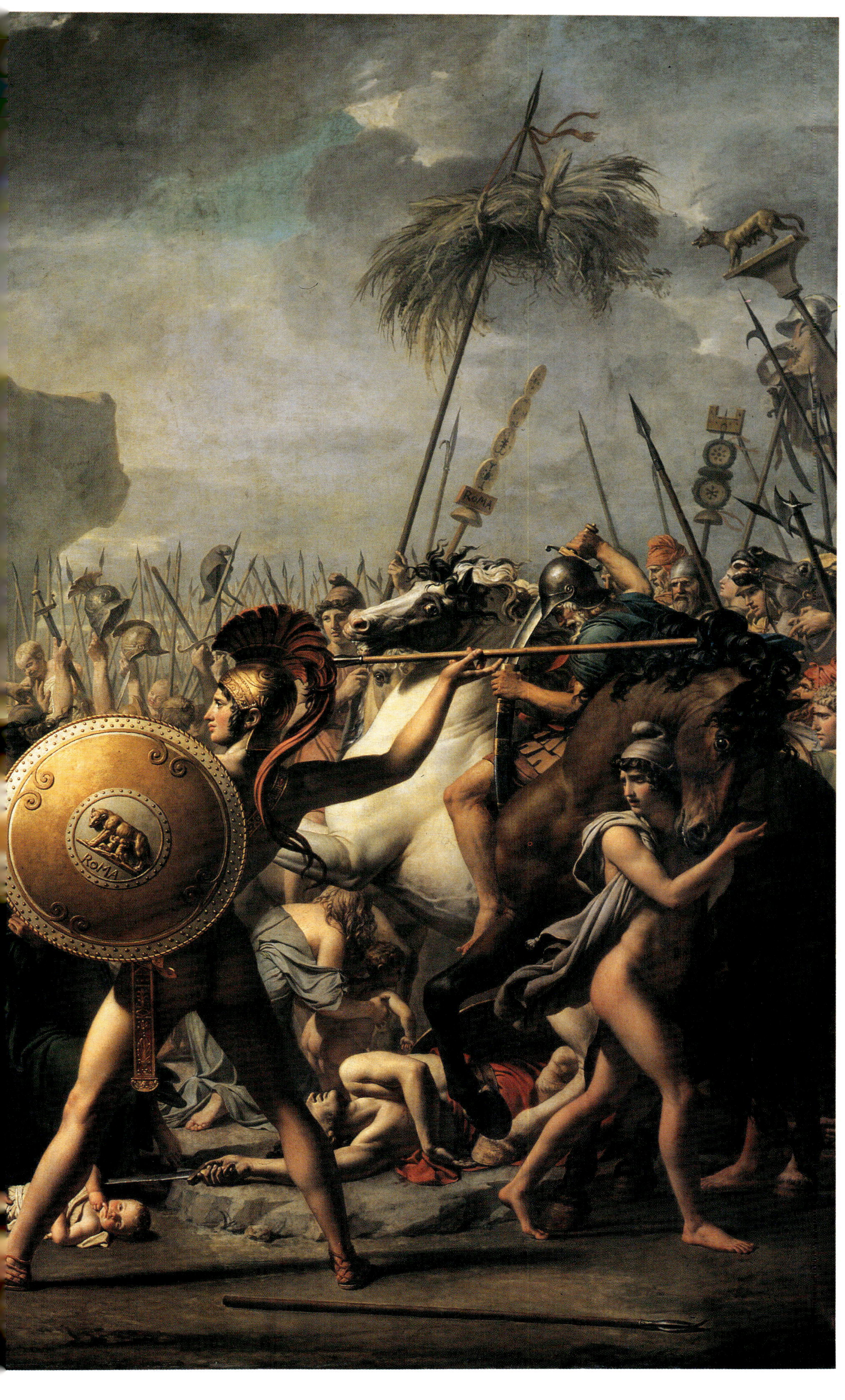

David (Louis) 1748-1825
The Sabine women ending the battle between the Romans and the Sabines, 1799
Paris, Louvre

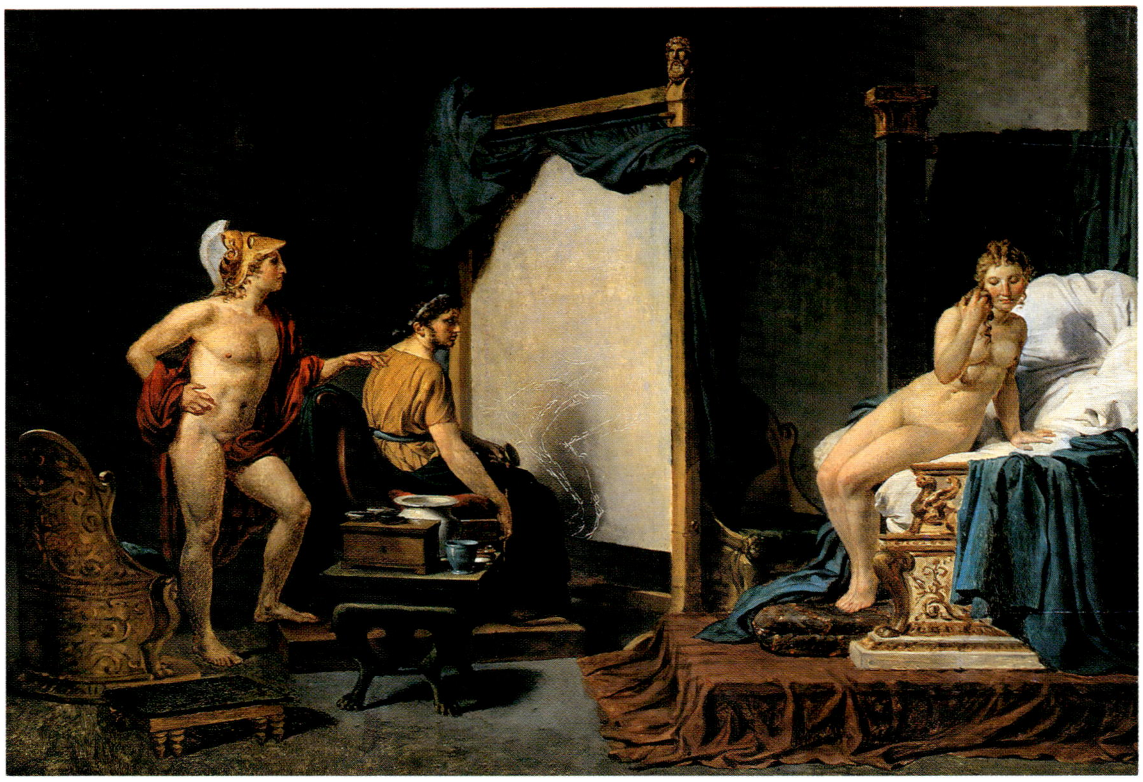

The three heroic cycles

In breaking the interdicts of the law in the name of the higher imperatives of pride, the hero disturbs the skillful balance of immobile time. His challenging of the rule compromises natural harmony, and by modifying what is possible the heroic act gives birth to history. As Paul Bénichou wrote, "The hero as Corneille had conceived him, a nature greater than nature, a type of man who is more than a man, which had been the ideal model of the aristocracy as long as they remained true to their traditions, had no worse enemy than the moral pessimism [of Jansenism] [...]. A huge current of moral thinking went with Jansenism as strictly defined and bore it along, becoming stronger in the second half of the [17th] century just as the obsolete character of the old heroic ideal of the aristocracy was becoming obvious with the triumph of Louis XIV's absolutism." In other words, caught between Jansenism, which declared that everything was predetermined, and an absolutism that tended to control events to the point of claiming to eliminate the role of chance, the hero demanded the right to go on throwing the dice. It was in this tiny margin left to chance that history could still be constructed.

The paradox of the hero in the final analysis lies in this: because he repeats the mythical action of the gods without himself being a god, he breaks the magic perfection of the cyclical mythical era. Then all the hopes and all the contradictions of humankind rush through this breach which has been opened virtually as an oversight. Seen in this light the hero is like the sorcerer's apprentice; it is far from certain that he weighs up all the consequences of his action when embarking on it.

In this connection David's painting of the Sabine women is equivalent to an admission of guilt by the artist. Conceived in 1794, when David was in prison after the fall of Robespierre, and painted in 1799 when Napoleon Bonaparte, that other heroic figure, was coming to the fore, it is an obvious appeal for reconciliation between Frenchmen after ten years of revolutionary upheaval. What the hero has unleashed, it is up to him to stem. The three movements in the great cycle of the hero who sacrifices himself for the happiness of his people are these: the cycle of myth (Leonidas); the cycle of revolution (Robespierre and Marat); the cycle of peace sealed by an oath that is the basis of a new order (Napoleon).

We know how Napoleon's peace turned out, but that is irrelevant here. David's error of judgment is an error of a political nature and does not alter the general coherence of his oeuvre. Moreover Leonidas (alias Napoleon) fought for peace. He sacrificed himself at Thermopylae at the head of his thousand hoplites against the troops of Xerxes in the name of civilization. The Barbarians were the Persians, i.e. the Austrians, Prussians and British. Symbolically Leonidas and Napoleon represent the last bulwark of common law against the arbitrariness of the despot. For the new law, resulting from a solemn oath taken by the whole nation, had become a human law (the *Oath of the Horatii*, the *Serment du Jeu de Paume*) forbidding anyone from ever again claiming to act by divine right ....

David (Louis) 1748-1825
Apelles and Campaspe
Lille, Musée des Beaux-Arts

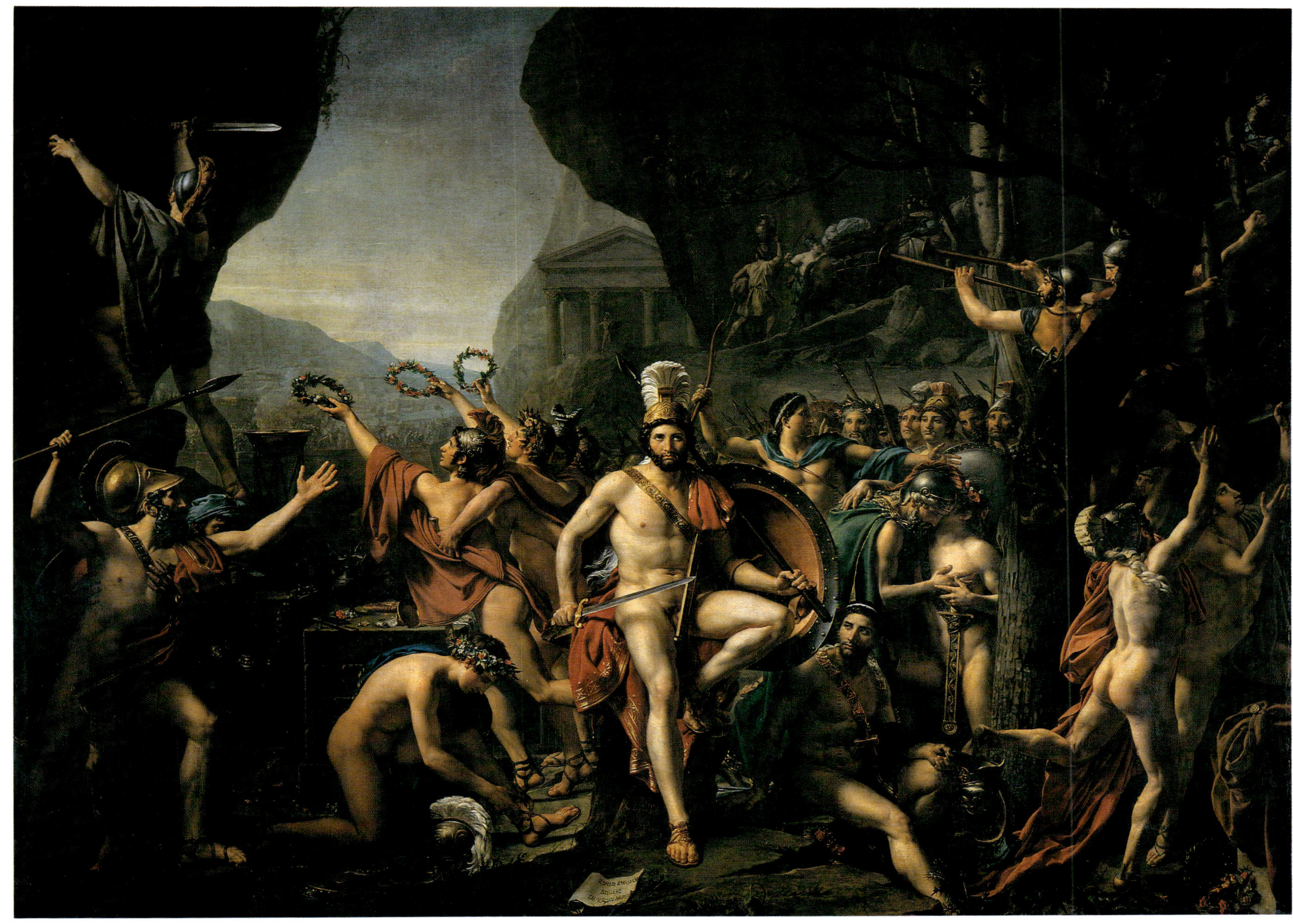

David (Louis) 1748-1825
Leonidas at Thermopylae, 1800-1814
Paris, Louvre

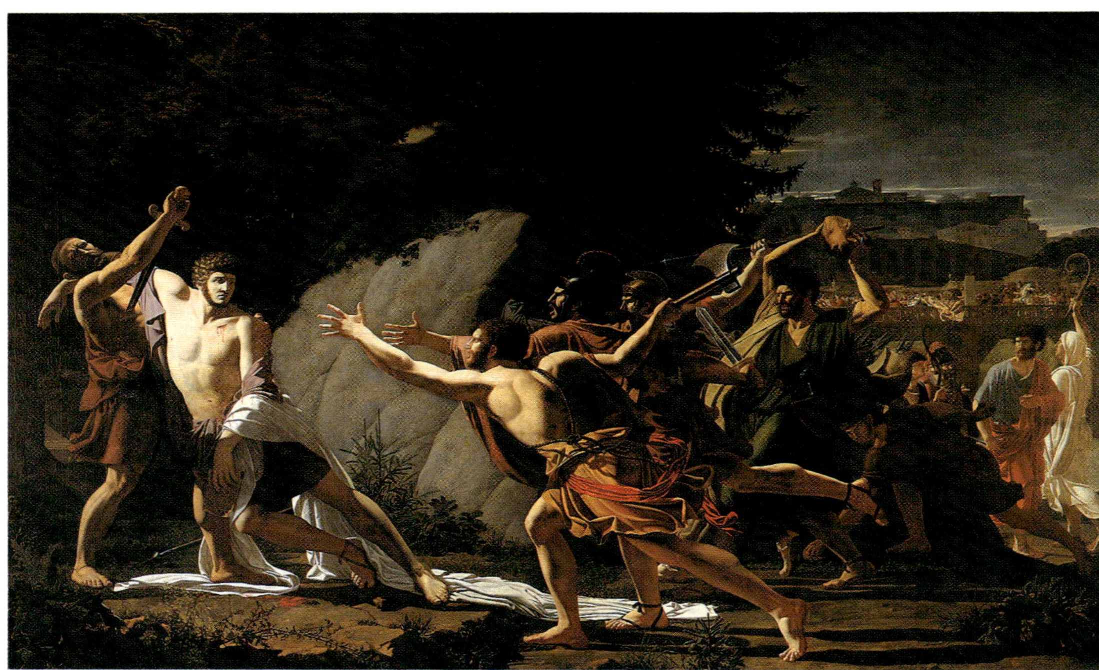

The death of the hero

History feeds on heroic figures. To enter history the hero has to die for it. What would we know of Babeuf and Marat if they had died in their beds? The hero's glory lies not so much in his deeds as in his death. "I could conceive of no other way of making you happy than through the common weal," Gracchus Babeuf wrote to his wife when preparing to go to the scaffold. "I failed; I have sacrificed myself; it is for you too that I am dying."

The hero, a heightened version of the individual, claims to fight for a collective which it is hard to define. At a point in history when the universal can no longer be formulated, when the old norm has been declared obsolete and the one that will replace it has still to be formulated, the figure of the hero aims to alleviate this absolute dearth. Like a captain on a ship that is about to be lost he shows a way through the storm but dies before land is reached.

There is an obvious relationship between the revolutionary hero and the Christian martyr. David's painting of Marat assassinated is modeled on a deposition from the Cross. The mark left by Charlotte Corday's knife makes us think of the stigmata of Christ, for the hero at that moment embodies the new transcendence; and revolution which realizes it is a new religion based on the cult of reason, which claims legitimacy by canonizing its first martyrs through the genius of David. "When the sans-culottes say that Marat is immortal," Jean-Paul Bertaud wrote, "by that they mean he is a saint: whereas the Republican middle classes understand being immortal as living for ever in the memory of patriots, so supporting them in their undertakings, the sans-culottes, most of them still nurtured in Catholicism, think of immortality as the immortality of the soul and believe that in the after-life a martyr has the power of a saint: his shade can come to the help of those who invoke him on this earth."

The hero must die, for his heroism is very closely linked with the state of affairs current at that moment. Times are abnormal, in the true sense of the word, and the hero serves as an "escape agent." The concept of truth, cut off from any stable point of reference, hangs only on him, as if suspended above the void. Thus the hero is the transitory and so ephemeral form of the truth. But immediately a new norm or a new order has been established (the overthrow of 9 Thermidor and the Directoire from 1794), his existence becomes not just superfluous but dangerous. Saintdom, whether revolutionary or religious, always represents a serious threat to the established order, for it is a constant appeal to the individual to be idealistic and excel himself, two highly destabilizing concepts. Babeuf, who was executed in 1796 after the failure of the Conspiracy of the Equals, was the victim of the very people who claimed to want to save the Revolution. His egalitarian logic had become unacceptable to the middle-class majority in charge of the Directoire. But through his death he contributed to strengthening the myth of revolution which his executioners would themselves exploit and abuse.

Topino-Lebrun (François Jean Baptiste) 1769-1801
Death of Caius Gracchus, 1797
Marseilles, Musée des Beaux-Arts

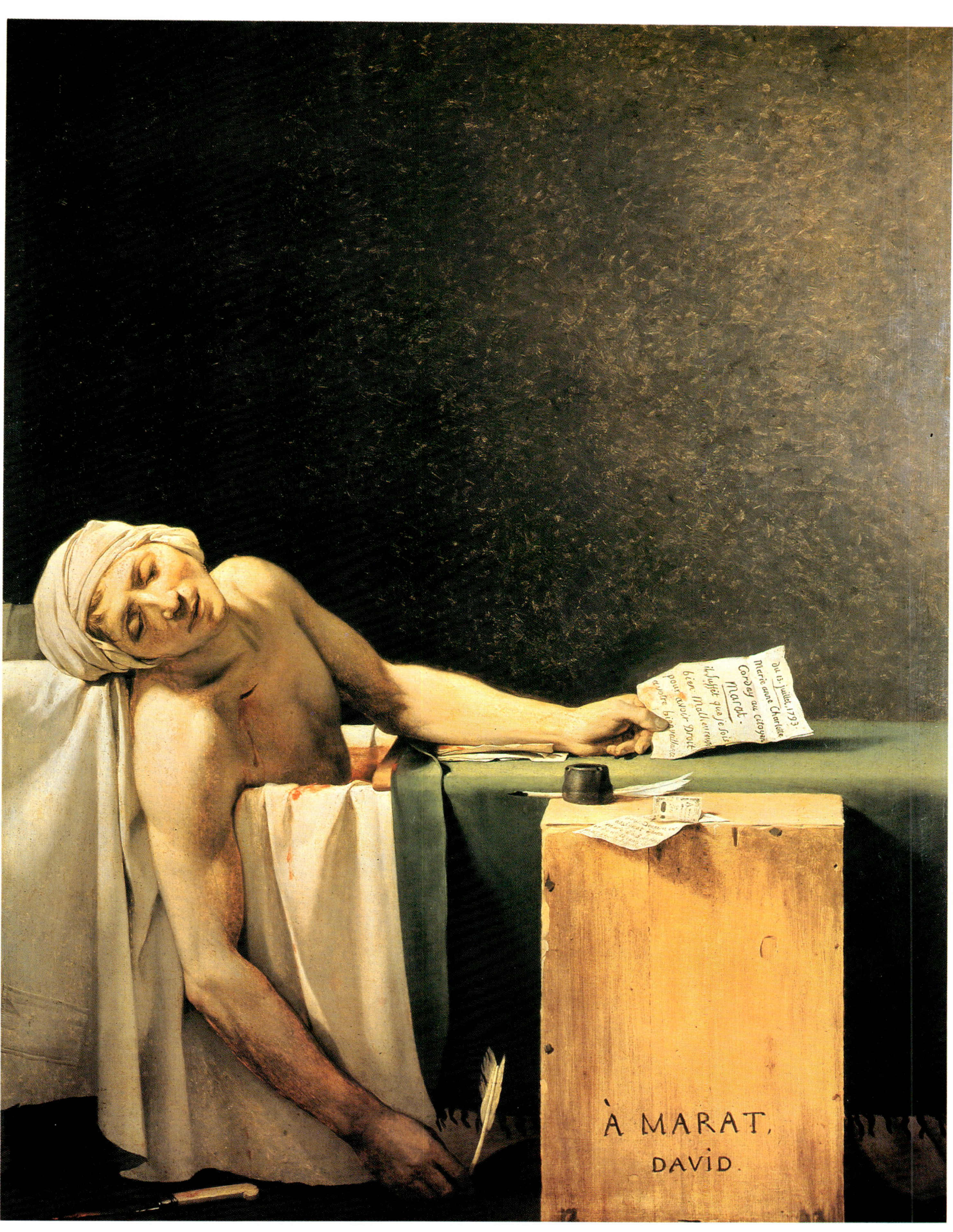

"In Paris Marat's death is sorely felt. His heart has been placed on an altar in the Club des Cordeliers. People invoke it saying, 'Heart of Jesus, heart of Marat, have pity on us.'"

Max Gallo
Robespierre

David (Louis) 1748-1825
Marat assassinated, 1793
Brussels, Musées Royaux des Beaux-Arts

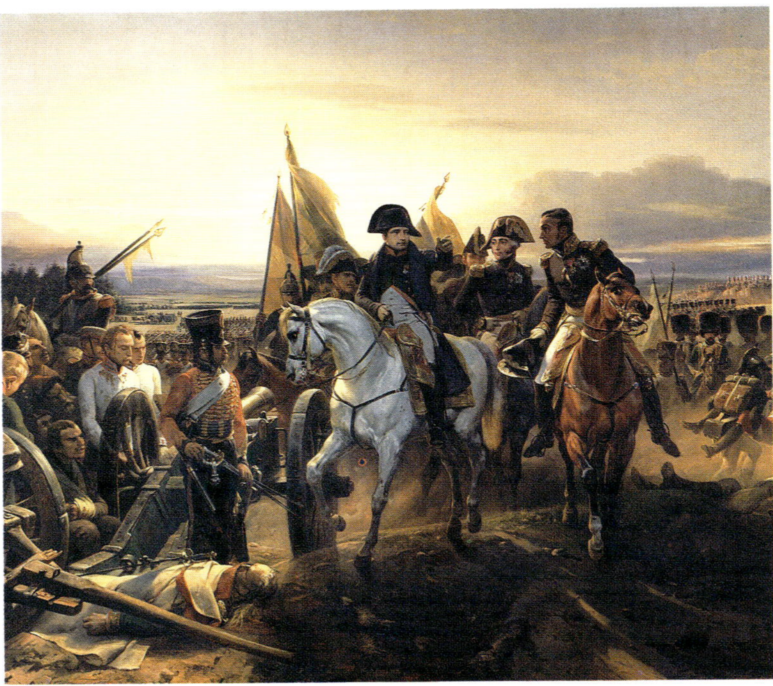

The monarch and the conqueror

"France deserved Austerlitz, the French Empire deserved Waterloo," Victor Hugo wrote. In the great gallery of heroes and martyrs of the Revolution, Napoleon is the greatest, the most terrible and the most ambiguous. His stature eclipses that of all the others. Italy, Prussia, Spain and Russia: for twenty years his armies drove through, liberated and devastated Europe. For the duration of an empire Napoleon – a new Alexander, a new Caesar – subjugated the world to his own law. In the process his destiny surpassed the strict attributions of the hero. Alexander was a pure hero because he conquered without reigning. Napoleon did both; that often contradictory mission resulted in a sort of doubling which lends him a depth and richness that the other emblematic figures of the Revolution do not have.

In Napoleon there is an essential contradiction between the conqueror, the man who carried the day at Ulm, Austerlitz and Friedland, and the legislator and administrator, a sort of petty bourgeois anti-hero, closeted in his office looking after his property with the maniacal attention to detail of a dedicated bookkeeper. The best the petty bourgeois could do for himself was to become monarch, marry Archduchess Marie-Louise in 1810 to found a dynasty (Napoleon II was born in 1811) and dream of seeing his title to the throne recognized by the great dynasties of Europe. But he was very ill adapted to that role, and David made a complete mistake in his portrait of the emperor in his study. Rather than painting him as a sovereign, he should have dwelt on what set the hero apart from the monarch: his exceptional, unique character, his lack of noble ancestors and the impossibility of a posterity. But no doubt the painter only complied with the wishes of his model, who could no longer be satisfied with the gratitude of an entire people.

However, at Waterloo history took over, recalling the hero to his destiny. Victor Hugo wrote these famous lines on the occasion:

"Waterloo! Waterloo! Waterloo! dreary plain!
Like a wave that boils up in a brimming urn,
In your circus of woods, slopes and valleys,
Pale death intermingled the dark battalions.
Europe on one side, on the other side France.
A bloody crash! God disappointed the hopes of heroes;
Victory, you deserted us, and fate was weary."

He may lament the defeat, but he knew it was necessary for the birth of the myth that would feed a whole sector of 19th-century political and literary thinking. The Napoleonic epic cannot in fact be reduced to the history of an idea or an ideal as was the case with Robespierre or Babeuf. It is a strange adventure verging on genius because it dragged a whole people in its wake. Napoleon is not a classical hero, torn between an ideal and a passion. In the final analysis the pure passion that fired him when the conqueror finally took over from the legislator met no other obstacle than its own end, making him the first great Romantic hero.

Vernet (Horace) 1780-1863
Battle of Friedland, 14 June 1807, 1836
Château de Versailles

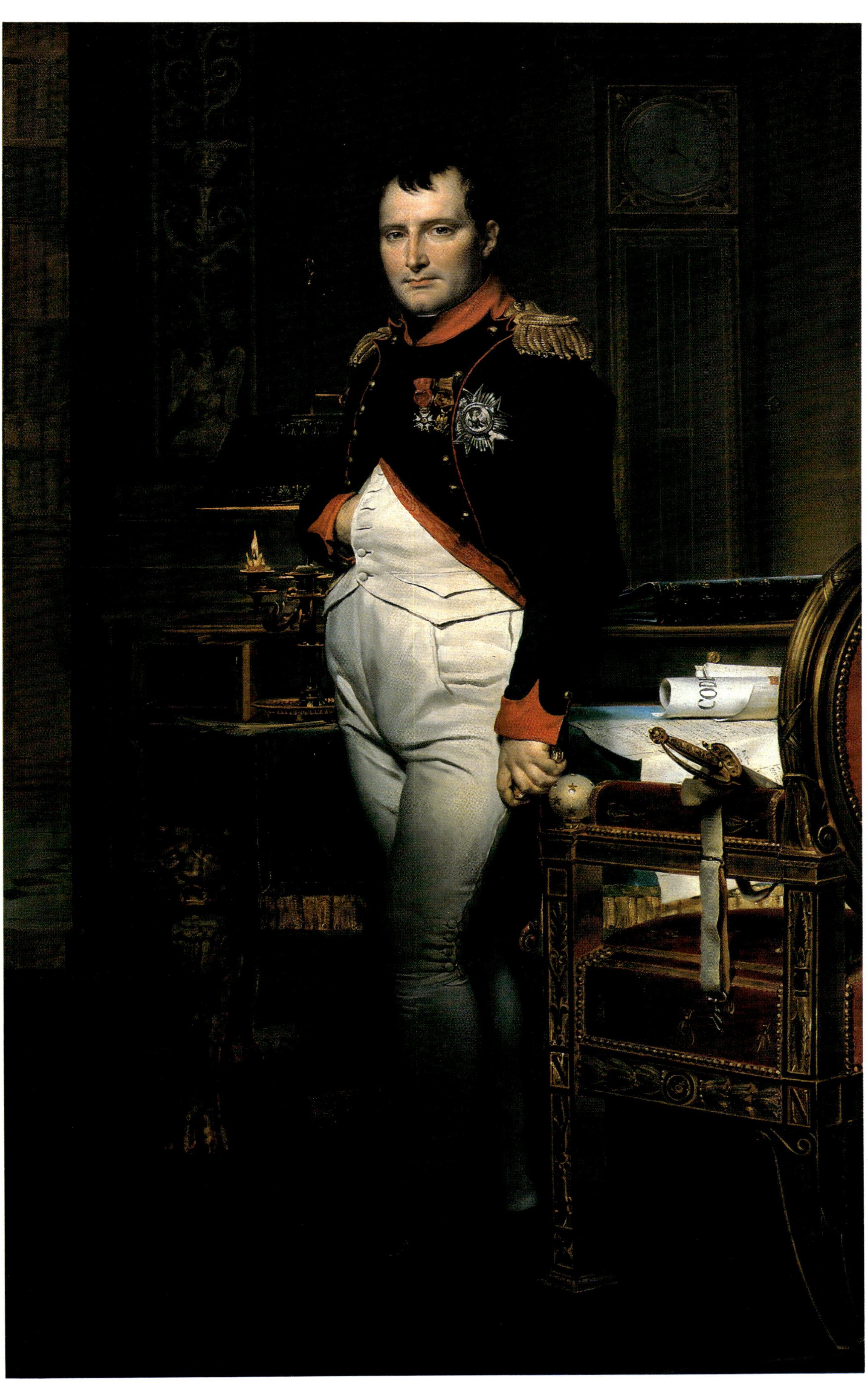

"Everything seemed to have been achieved; Bonaparte had obtained the only thing he lacked: [...] he mixed the last race on the scene with the blood of great kings; the past was linked to the future. [...] But though he had the power to stop the world, he had not the power to stop himself: he went on until he had conquered the final crown [...], the crown of misfortune."

Chateaubriand
Mémoires d'outre-tombe

David (Louis) 1748-1825
Napoleon in his study at the Tuileries, 1812
Collection of Prince and Princess Napoleon

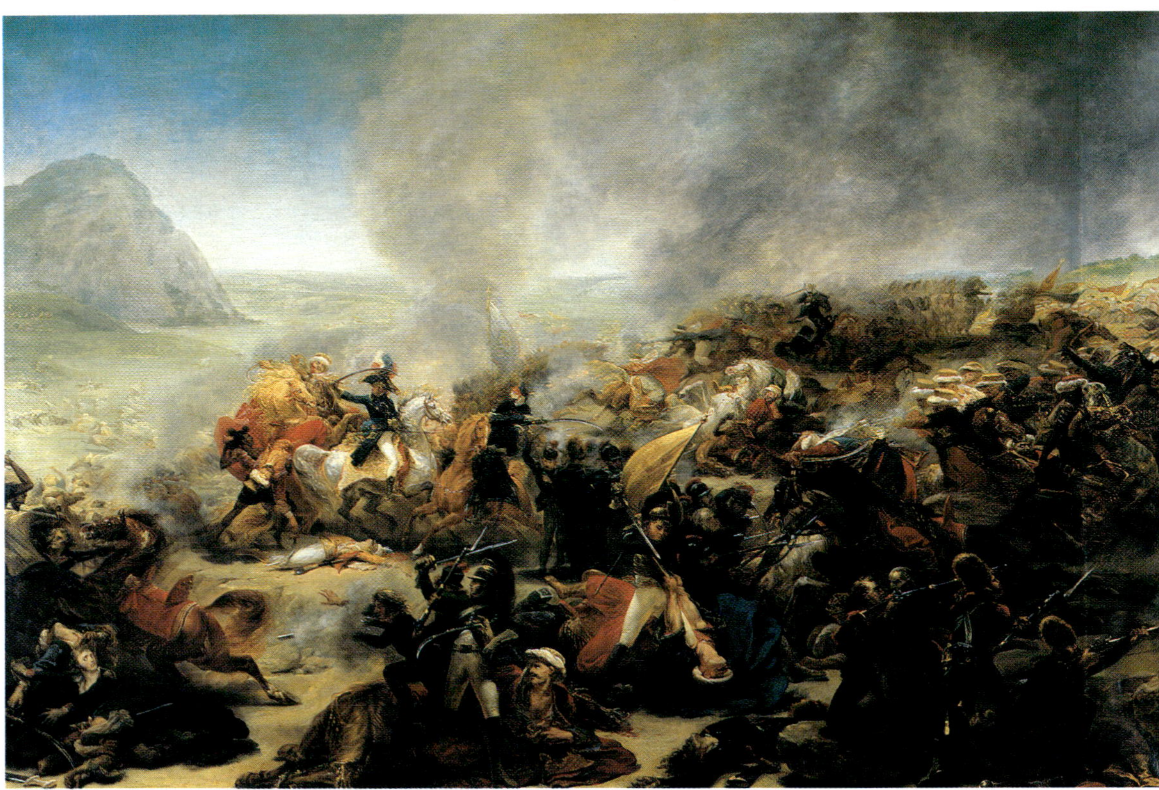

Orgies of blood

Antoine-Jean Gros was a pupil of David. It was thanks to him that he traveled in Italy between 1793 and 1800, where he worked for Josephine de Beauharnais and Bonaparte, then leading the Army of Italy. From the very outset he understood the epic nature of Napoleon's adventure better than his master.

David's classical language presupposes a morality which superimposes itself on the action, freezing it into a certain structure which has more to do with ethics than esthetics. David never painted action, preferring its genesis (*The oath of the Horatii*), its end (*Mars disarmed by Venus and the three Graces*) or its suspension (*The Sabine women*). As a faithful disciple of Rousseau he dwelt only on the educational, civilizing and moral implications of action. His work is a blueprint, and its greatness lies in that. But in the process he omitted an entire different aspect of the work of reason, namely its confrontation with chaos: the epic moment when the world is shaken.

Gros, who deeply admired David, continually proclaimed his faithfulness to his master's teaching, and yet, in spite of himself, he continually betrayed it. This personal drama culminated in his suicide. Gros wanted to be a Classical painter, but his painting invented Romanticism. Perhaps he thought that in betraying David he was also betraying Napoleon, whereas his language, which lit the path for the new generation of painters such as Delacroix and Géricault, was indubitably better adapted to conveying the epic nature of that terrible period of European history. In the *Battle of Nazareth* Gros's intention is to show only the grandeur of the action, the fury, heroism and self-forgetfulness. Standing in front of this work (as opposed to one of David's) we really feel that morality has been postponed to a later date and now is not the time, with death not just prowling but positively unleashed, to think of any future whatsoever. The truth here is not moral, but purely physical. These are bodies that are dying, or killing so as not to die: bodies, not souls.

Behind the ideals proclaimed by the Enlightenment the painter seems to sense a much darker and more painful truth. Writing of this work, Michel Le Bris asks: "Pulsating with the fury of cavalcades, in the eddies of smoke and sand, [does this work] which won Gros the competition organized to celebrate the victory of Junot's five hundred soldiers over an army of six thousand Turks in 1801 simply celebrate heroic virtues, the courage and intoxication of conquest, or do we stand in front of it in fascinated contemplation of an orgy of blood?"

While the deadly plumes of smoke from the combat gradually obscure the clear Oriental sky, in spite of the intoxication, in spite of the victory, the foreground plunges little by little into a confused half-light. And the idea then arises that perhaps, behind the esthetic fascination with the epic, a formidable questioning of its true nature lies hidden. For in spite of its promises, the Enlightenment in arms went on and on producing more darkness.

Gros (Antoine Jean) 1771-1835
Battle of Nazareth, 1801
Nantes, Musée des Beaux-Arts

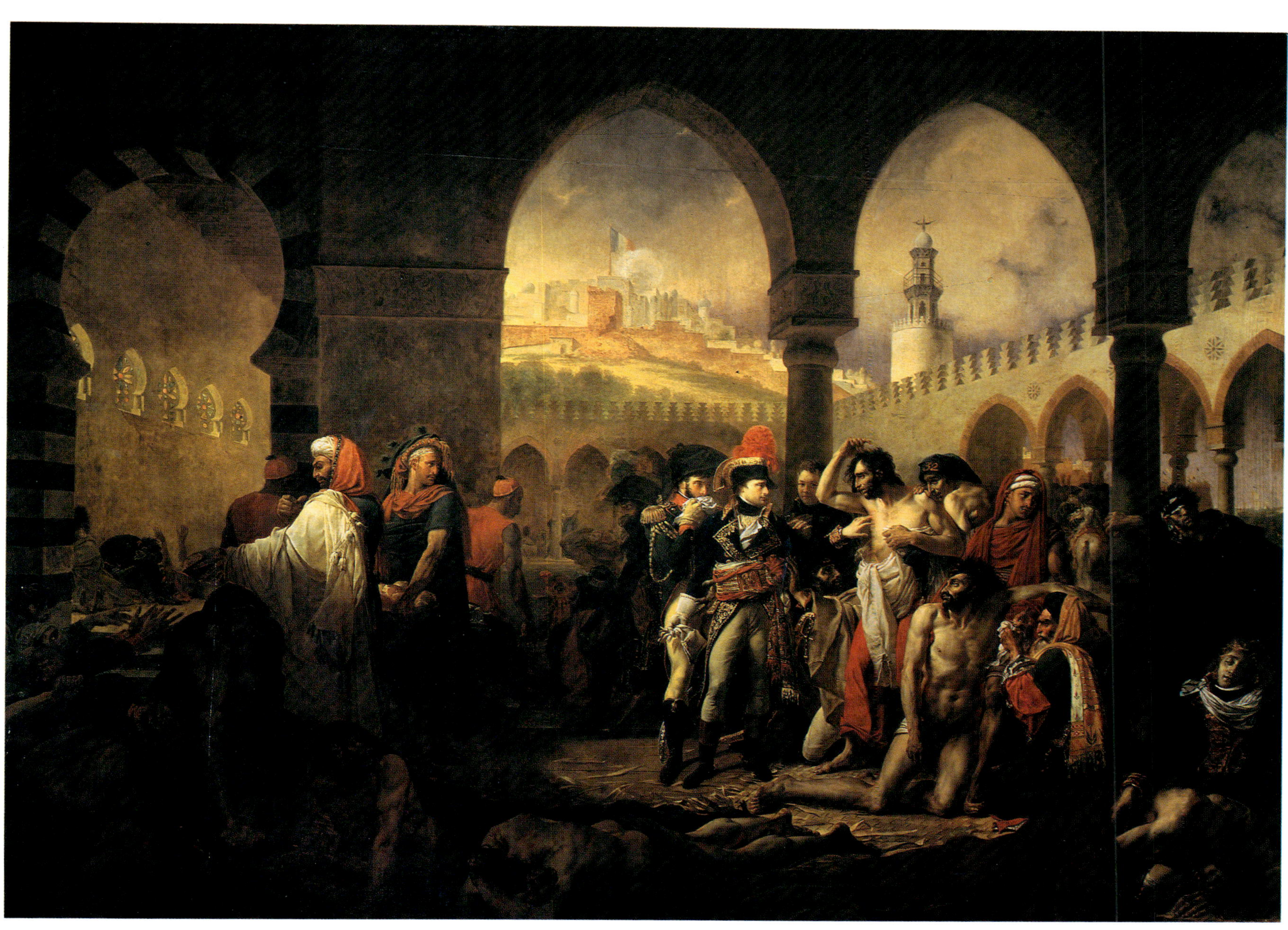

"Bonaparte's Egyptian policy has long been celebrated [...] as being in advance of its time [...]. If it is examined more closely it contained, alongside aspects that were incontrovertibly innovative, very traditional responses to eternal problems."

F. Furet and D. Richet La Révolution française

Gros (Antoine Jean) 1771-1835
Napoleon visiting the plague stricken at Jaffa (11 March 1799), 1804
Paris, Louvre

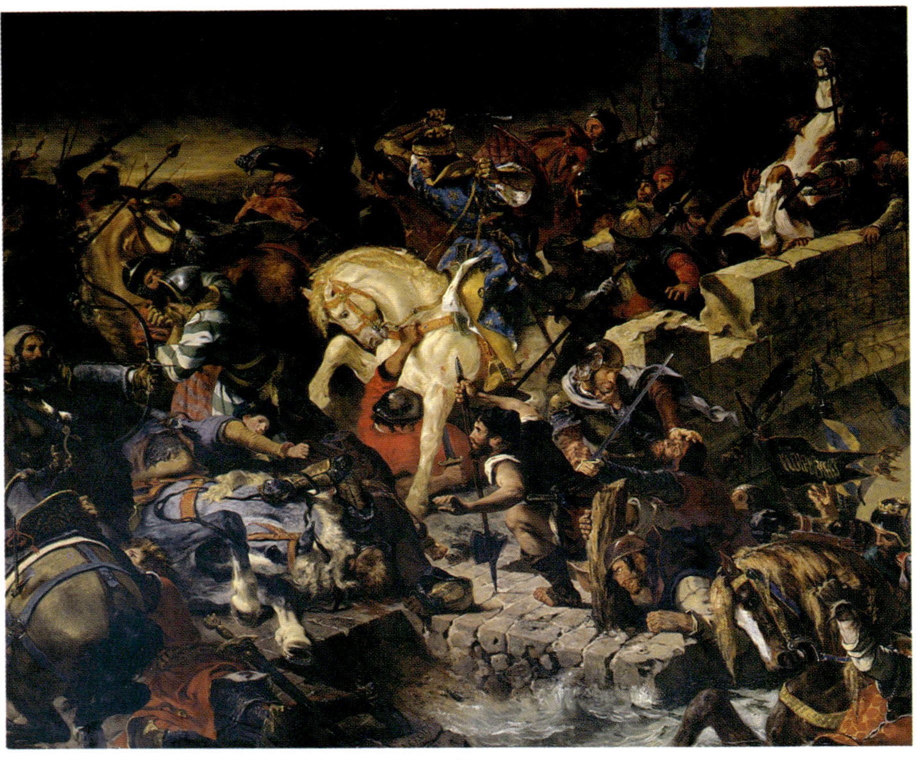

The people shipwrecked by history

"What is Romanticism?" Baudelaire asked himself in his *Salon de 1846*. "[...] We can make Romantic Romans and Greeks if we are Romantic ourselves [...]. Romanticism in fact lies neither in the choice of subject nor in the precise truth, but in the way we feel." Without wishing to reduce Romanticism to that, we cannot deny that it was born of the failure of the French Revolution. There could be no further doubt as to the tragic outcome of revolutions. The hope of communal happiness had died under the combined onslaughts of Robespierre's Reign of Terror and Royalist reactionism. Salvation henceforth seemed to be up to the individual. The very notion of art moved away from schools to center on the concept of individual talent. History as a collective aspiration had failed. Yet there was no question that the solitary epic feats of the Eagle had left their mark on the imaginations of artists of the younger generation.

To quote Baudelaire again, "Thus Delacroix starts from the principle that a picture should first and foremost reproduce the intimate thinking of the artist who dominates his model as the creator dominates creation." Or these unequivocal words: "For a man of this stamp, endowed with such courage and passion, the most interesting struggles are those he has to engage in with himself; horizons do not need to be wide for battles to be important; the strangest revolutions and events take place beneath the sky of the skull, in the narrow, mysterious laboratory of the brain."

So history deserted reality. The middle-class 19th century wanted to be a century without a history – if it did not succeed, this was not its doing, at least not directly, but the result of the awakening of nations and the birth of the proletariat. Confronted with this official resistance, history, perceived as fermenting terror and disorder, took refuge in individual exploits. "Every individual is a history in himself," we have written elsewhere, "and the instant of fusion welding all these individual destinies into a potential single-voiced history of the human race is quite simply inconceivable."

In contrast to Neo-Classical idealism, Romantic history opted for individualism in order to rediscover – at the very heart of the century of bourgeois conformism – an epic meaning which would give works of art a new lease of life just as they were running out of breath. But in its pursuit of the epic Romanticism opened the door on tragedy; tragedy which no longer had the proud aristocrat rising against the law of the monarch as its hero, but the people, humiliated and enslaved by the upper middle classes who now revered one value and one value only: money.

In painting the poor and humble Géricault set out to rediscover through them "the whole epic of the modern world."

The shipwrecked figures on the *Raft of Medusa* are those whom history has forgotten and he wished to celebrate. But what was lacking in this epic tale were an ideal and hope which would not take shape until later in the century. For the time being the people, when not purely and simply excluded from the theater of history, were shoved into the background of a stage once again occupied by allegory, as in Delacroix's famous masterpiece, *Liberty leading the people.*

Delacroix (Eugène) 1798-1863
Battle of Taillebourg, 21 June 1242, 1837
Château de Versailles, Galerie des Batailles

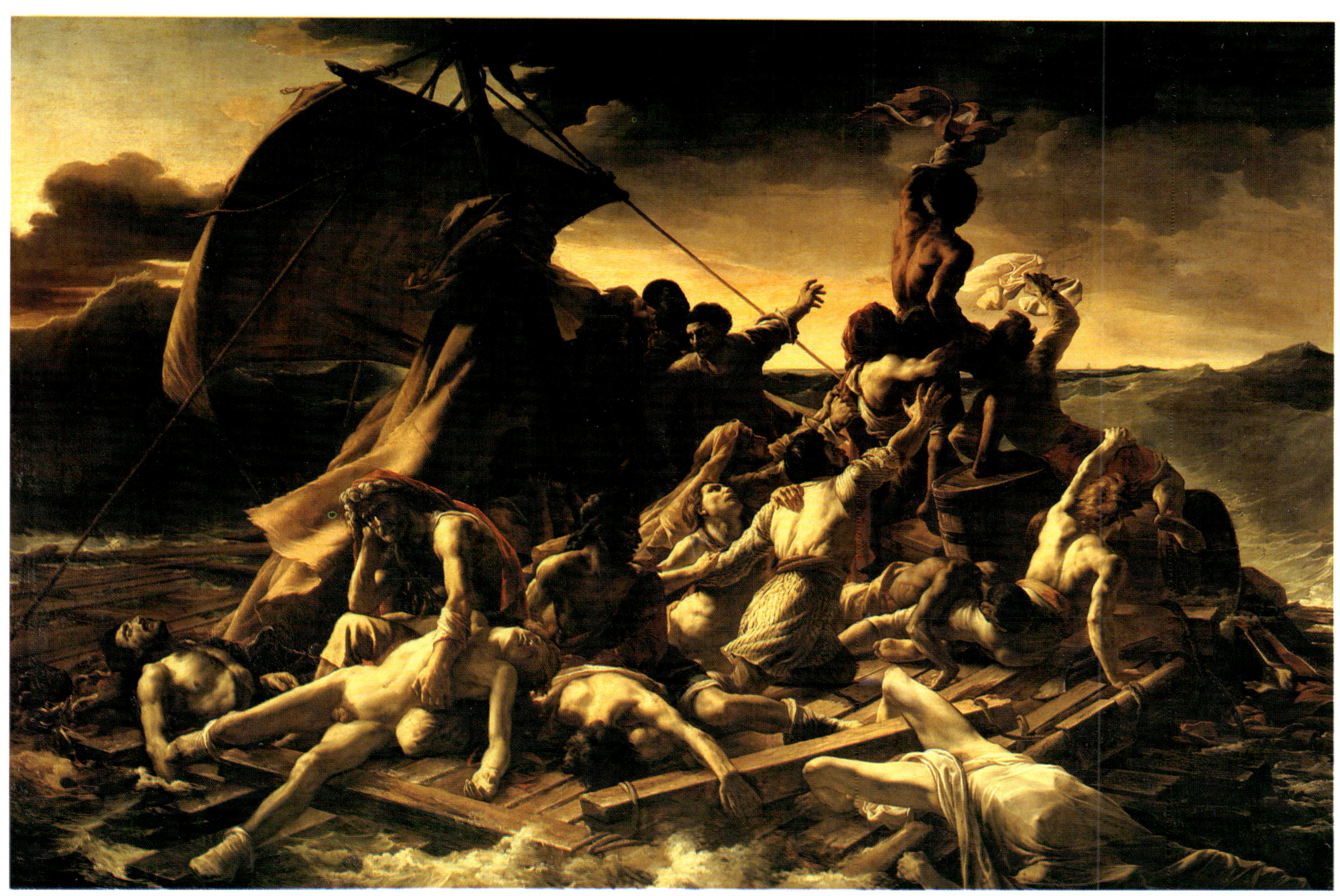

"I plunged into the stormy sea of life; [...] while you were admiring the surface, I saw the debris of shipwrecks, bones and Leviathans."

Alfred de Musset
Lorenzaccio

Géricault (Théodore) 1791-1824
The raft of the Medusa, 1819
Paris, Louvre

"The impartiality of history is not that of the mirror which reflects only objects [...]. Annals are not history: to merit its name history has to have a conscience, because that conscience later becomes the conscience of the human race."

Lamartine
Histoire des Girondins

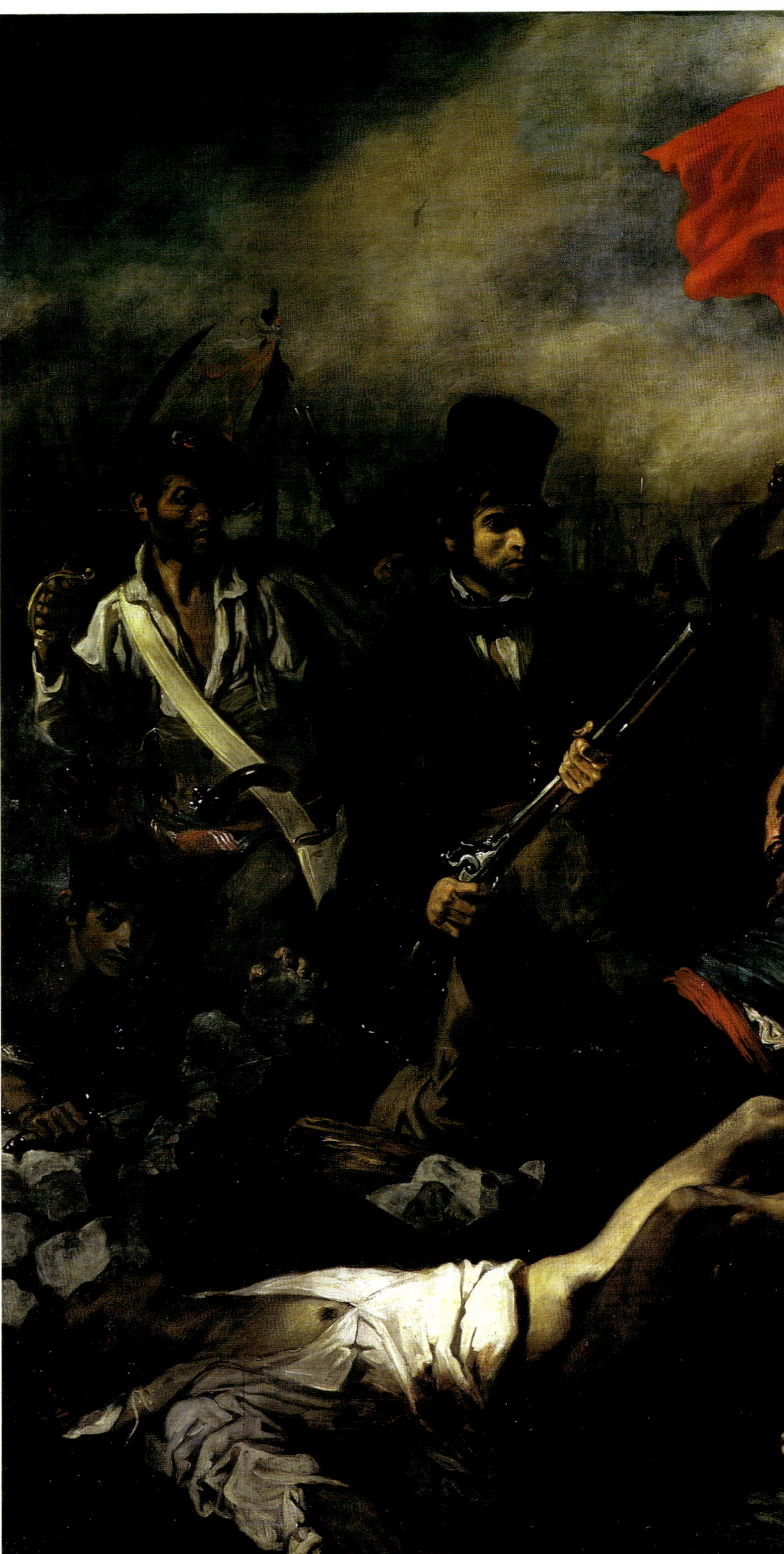

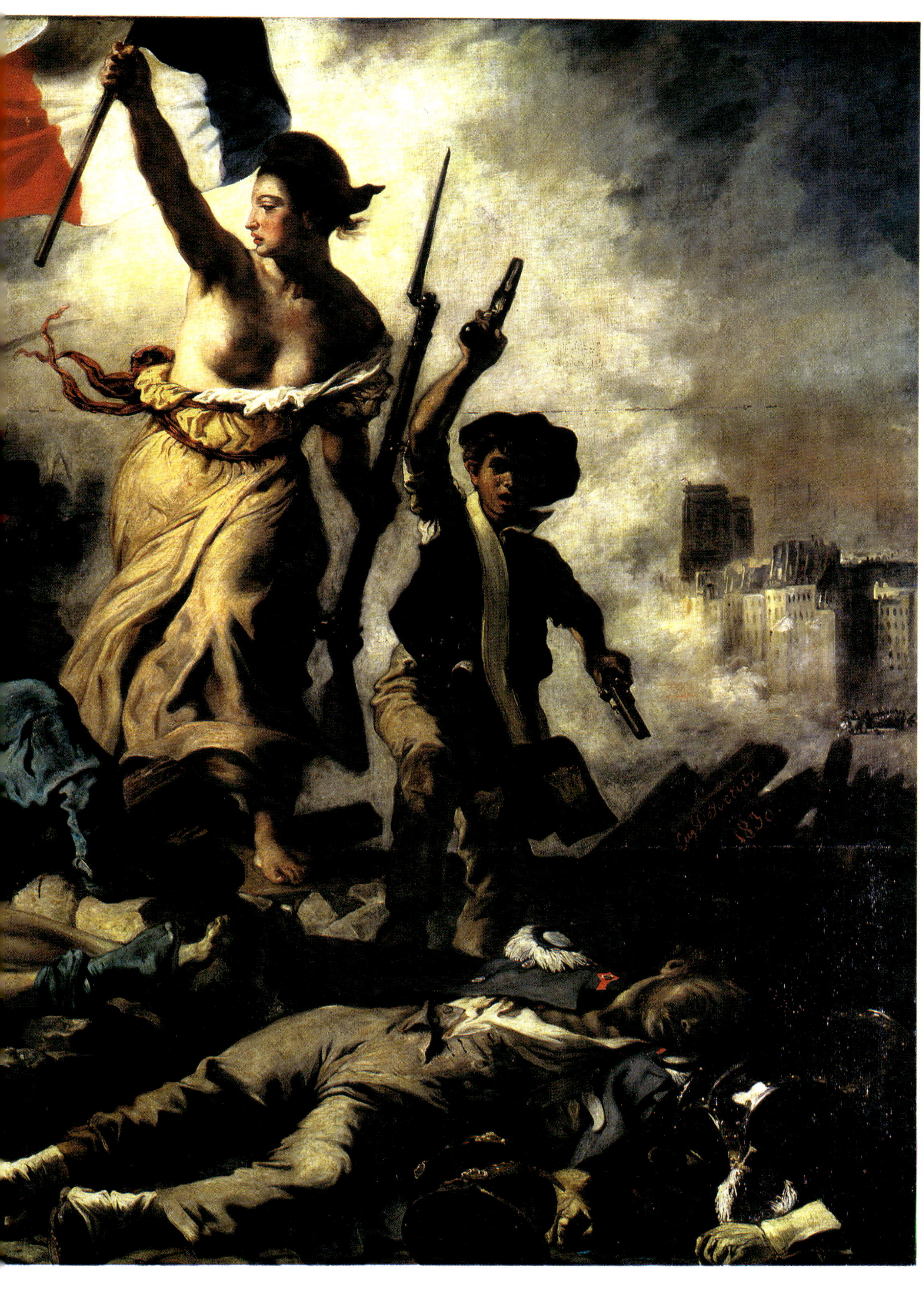

Delacroix (Eugène) 1798-1863
Liberty leading the people, 28 July 1830, 1830
Paris, Louvre

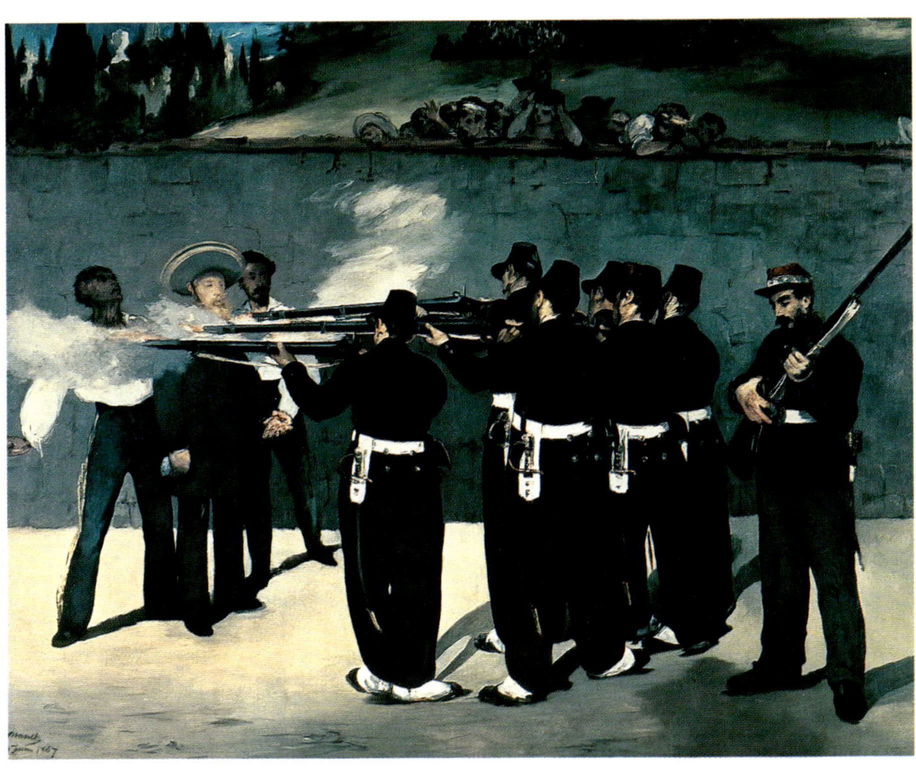

The individual as against history

Thirty years later, perhaps because the memory of Napoleon's epic was becoming more distant, and perhaps the Second Empire – a caricatured double of it – was also to blame, Romanticism as a lyrical vision of history had given way to a more prosaic way of seeing the world which the critics baptized Realism.

What is the difference between the vision of an artist like Courbet and that of someone like Delacroix? Apart from style, for each artist has his own, the fundamental change lies in the loss of a sense of the epic. Historically the break took place in 1848 in the June revolution, when the bourgeoisie decided to open fire on the people. In the plastic arts the change was subtle and slower. Those who carried on the epic genre sank into academicism. Others, including Courbet and Manet, tried to rediscover the note of lost truth through observing reality. But reality can be captured more accurately in the permanence of everyday life than in the flashing eruption of the event. And the Realist painter nurtured some claim to being objective, mistrusting those aspects of the historic event that risked plunging him back into Romantic lyricism or Classical allegory. Historically speaking, the event is inevitably something out of the ordinary. But the Realist painter had set himself the task of transforming the ordinariness of life into a work of art. There was an essential contradiction between these two positions.

Manet produced very few historical works, and it has been said that their rarity is indicative. If we analyze the most famous, the *Execution of the Emperor Maximilian*, we will find confirmation that art and history were keeping their distance. Maximilian of Austria was the younger brother of Emperor Franz Joseph. In 1864 Napoleon III offered him the crown of a new empire he wanted to set up in Mexico. But when Maximilian made a clumsy attempt at rapprochement with the liberal forces led by Juarez, Napoleon very quickly abandoned him. Isolated and besieged by the liberals at Querétaro, Maximilian capitulated on 14 May 1867 and was executed on 19 June.

The work Manet based on this is both a political manifesto and a denunciation of the cynicism of the politics of which Maximilian in his naivety became the victim. Thus any interpretation here has to be double. The composition stresses its homage to Goya, but at the same time it can be seen as an upside-down vision of the *Tres de Mayo*, copying it only in appearance. In Goya's picture it was the imperial forces that fired on the Spanish people. In Manet's it is the Mexican liberals who are shooting the would-be empire: the naivety of one man alone against the brutal force of history. All the grandeur in Goya's painting has been stripped away by Manet, who gives an uncompromising portrait of the lies of history. Of course, the work was initially interpreted as a violent denunciation of Napoleon III's cowardice. But does it allow us any more to believe in the virtues of liberalism? Manet confronts both sides with the image of their own Machiavellism.

Manet (Edouard) 1832-1883
Execution of the Emperor Maximilian, 1867
Mannheim, Städtische Kunsthalle

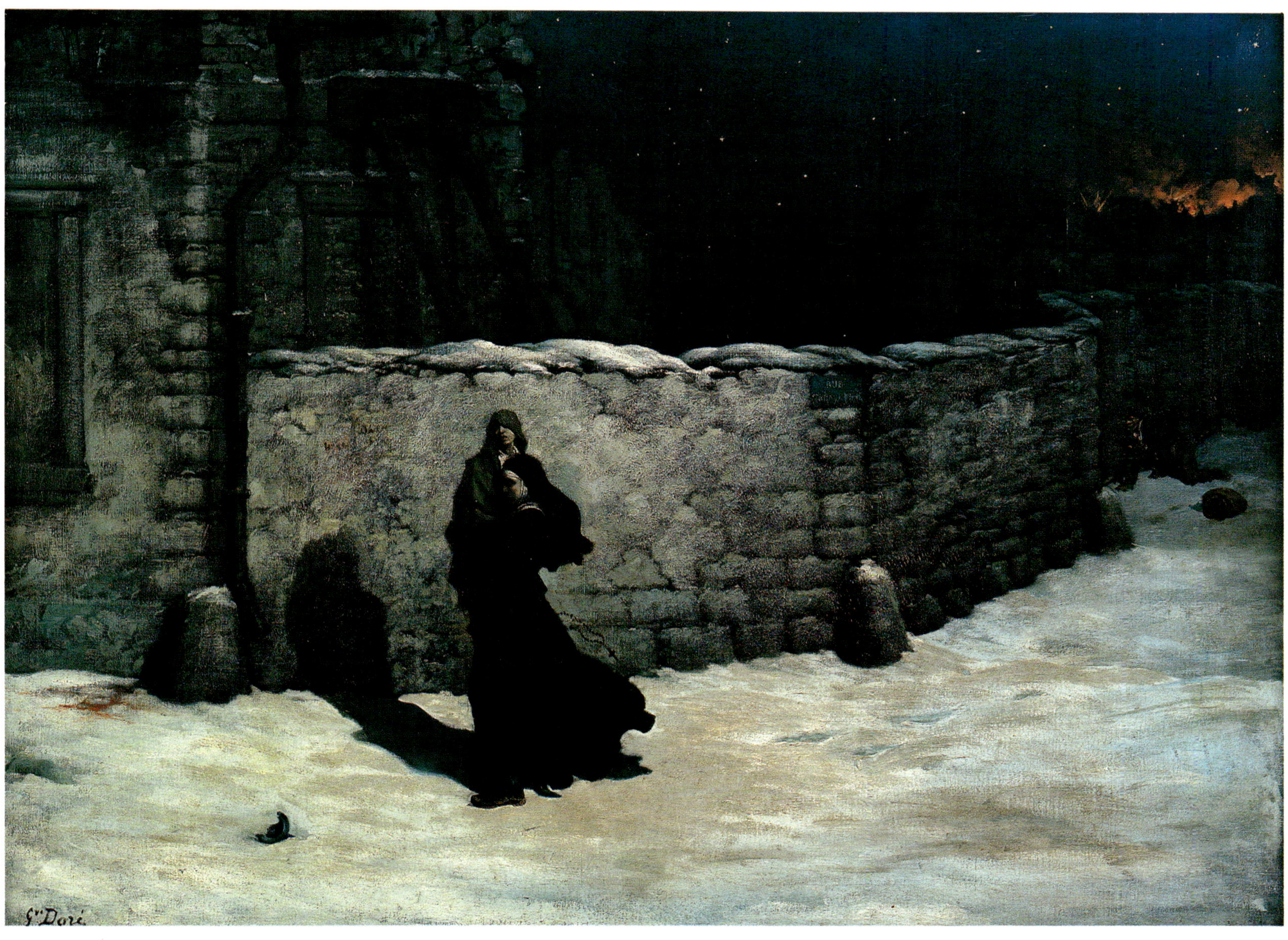

Doré (Gustave) 1832-1883
Episode from the siege of Paris in 1870
Le Havre, Musée des Beaux-Arts André Malraux

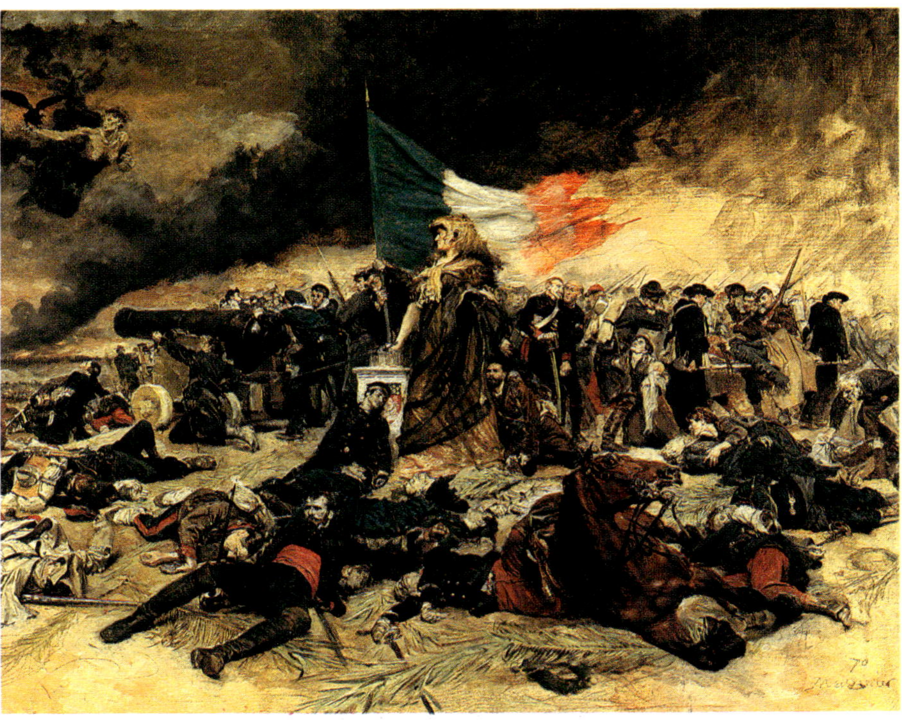

The Futurist Utopia

Meissonier's work is a perfect illustration of the kind of divorce that took place between art and history in the second half of the 19th century. By going back to the very sources of myth, he tried to endow the Second Empire with the greatness it lacked. In so doing he became rich and famous, and lost the right to feature honorably in histories of art. For all he did was paint a detailed, slavish caricature of the Napoleonic epic. If that had been his only achievement he would deserve to be forgotten. Fortunately a few sorties into the field of current events in 1848 and 1870 allowed him to demonstrate that he was also capable of a more liberal approach to historical reality. But as the truth of that reality became evident, the iniquitous nature of history seemed to be unmasked alongside it. And in order to go on existing, art had then to cut free from history.

In 1909 Italian Futurism, the culmination of that development and the most extreme manifestation of the refusal of history and the absolute rejection of any reference to the past, was born, with the first Futurist manifesto being published in Paris by the poet Marinetti and supplemented in 1910 by the manifesto of the Futurist painters signed by Balla, Boccioni, Carrà, Russolo and Severini. Futurism was a radical program centered on the idea of a break with the past. It was not content with demanding total autonomy for art (the theory of art for art's sake which had already been developed by the Symbolists), but challenged the whole artistic heritage en bloc. Therefore it was not just history as a distinct entity, but the history of art too that was rejected lock, stock and barrel. Since the historic perspective is based on reflection, it was almost logical that Futurism would prize action above reflection, movement above permanence, and form above content.

Futurism, which started off initially as an anarchical rebellion against the oppressiveness of middle-class traditionalism, was to veer towards being a pure esthetic of movement with Nietzschean overtones. An apologia for speed and the machine, a condemnation of humanism, and soon a glorification of war, which was conceived of as a huge process of purification, after the First World War was over Futurism offered Mussolini's incipient Fascism a made-to-measure esthetic.

Severini for his part moved away from the movement by reverting to Classicism in the '20s (*Du Cubisme au classicisme*, 1921), but this "return to order" itself, because it took a narrowly nationalist form in the context of the Novecento movement (the glorification of "a purely Italian art drawing inspiration from the purest sources and free of all imported tendencies,") was in turn hijacked by Fascism from 1924.

The mishaps encountered by the Italian avant-garde did at least have the merit of highlighting (sometimes cruelly) the very complex nature of the links between art and history, which might be more correctly described as the links between art and political power, raising the question of the content of works of art. The Futurists proved through absurdity that it was impossible to leave that aspect of creativity empty with impunity.

Meissonier (Ernest) 1815-1891
Siege of Paris, 1870
Paris, Musée d'Orsay

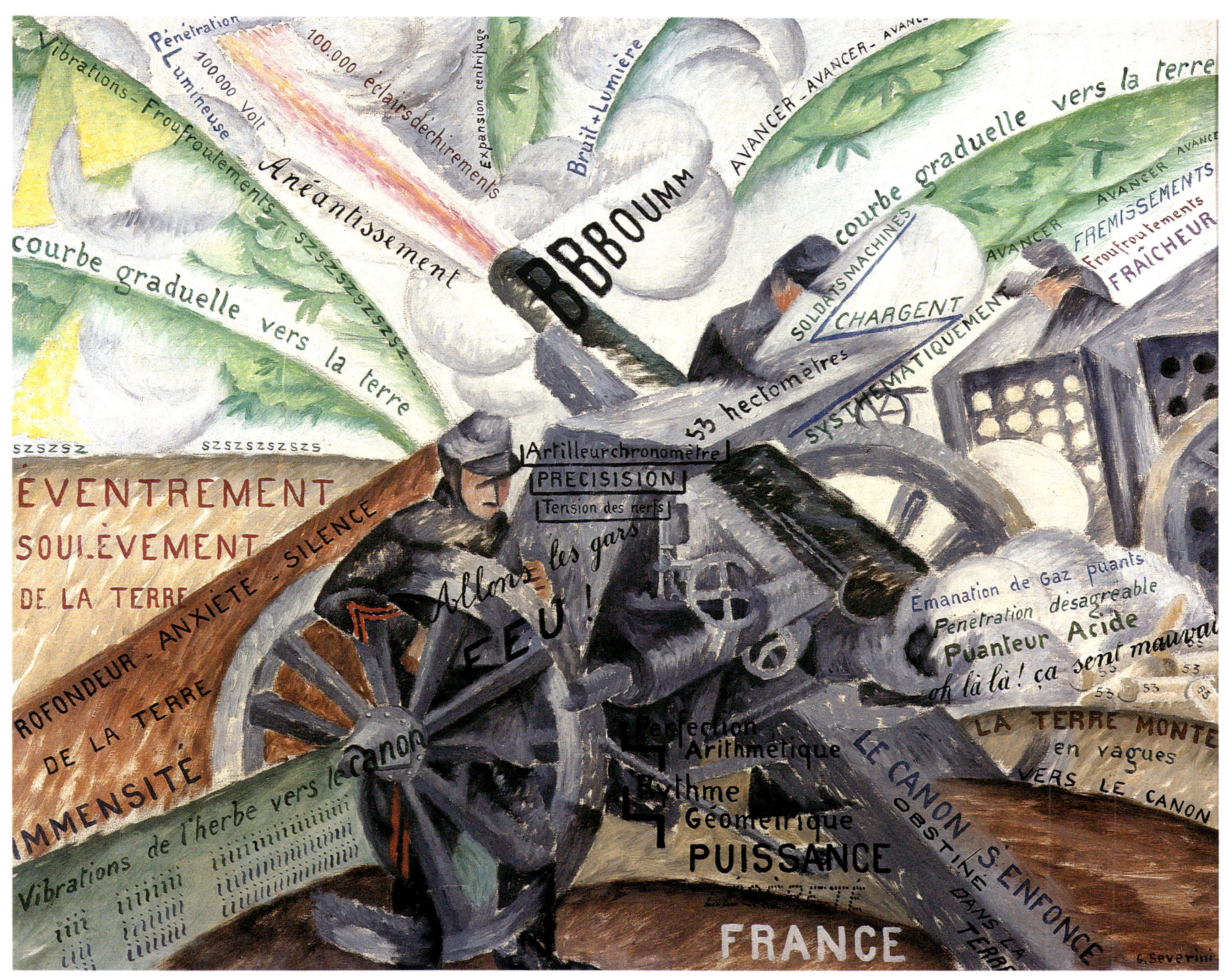

"War, the world's only sanitation."

Marinetti

Severini (Gino) 1883-1966
Cannon in action, 1915
Milan, P. Guarini Collection

"So there was no mistake? What we were doing firing on one another like that without even seeing each other was not forbidden! [...] We had just lit the war between ourselves and those across from us and now it was burning! Like the current between the two carbon electrodes in the arc light. And the carbon was nowhere near burnt out!"

Céline
Voyage au bout de la nuit

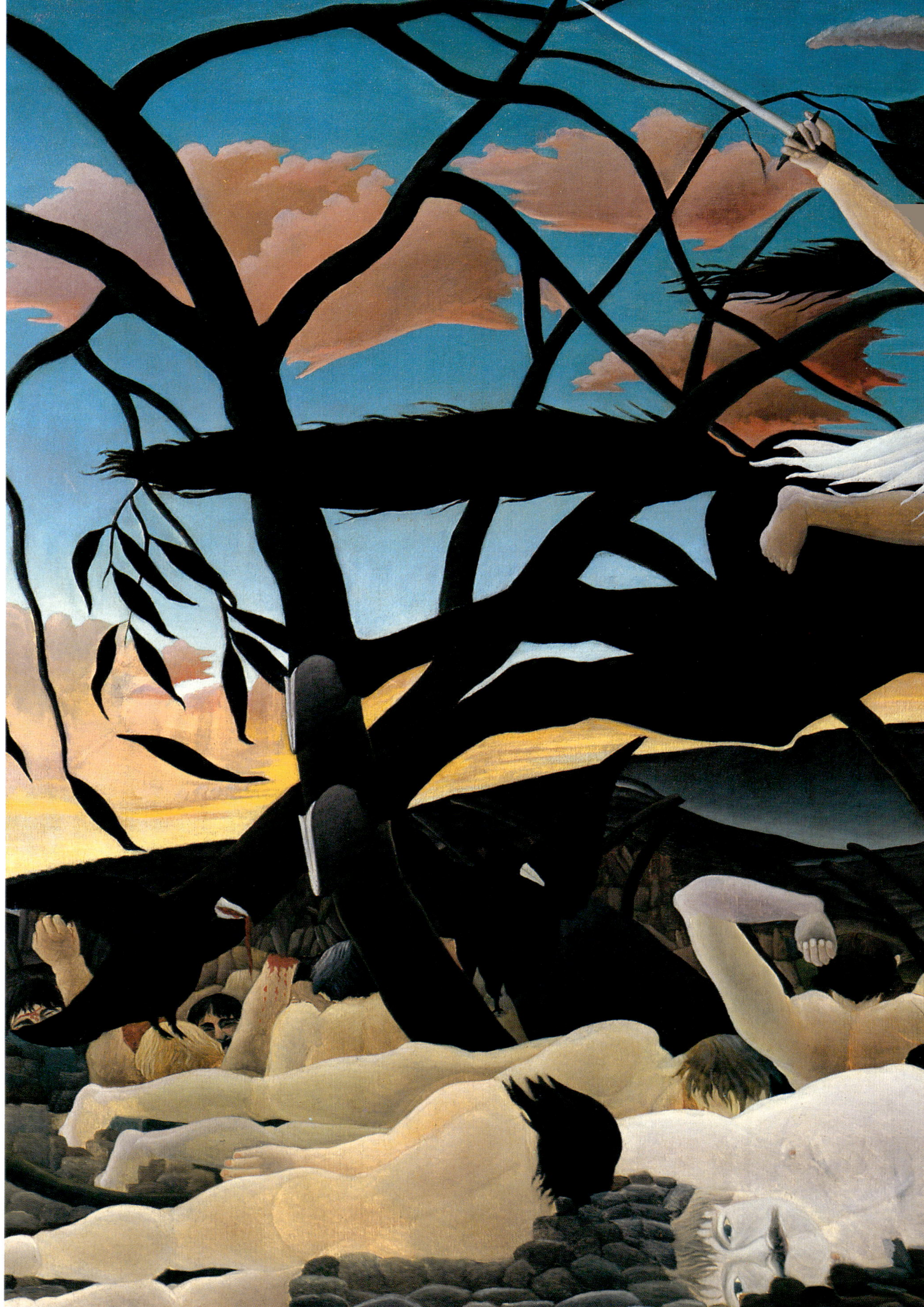

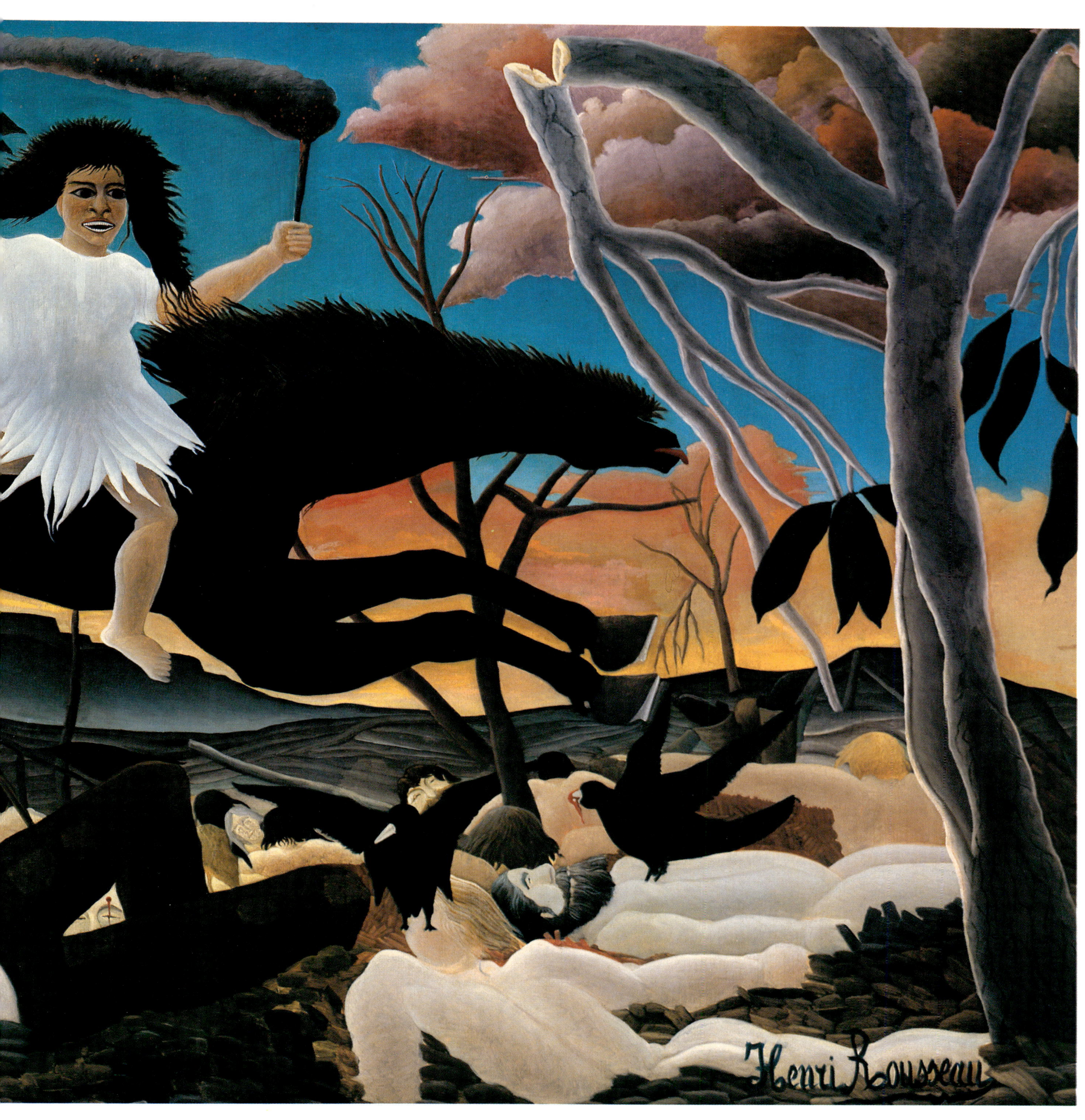

Rousseau (Henri, known as Douanier) 1844-1910
War or The ride of discord, 1894
Paris, Musée d'Orsay

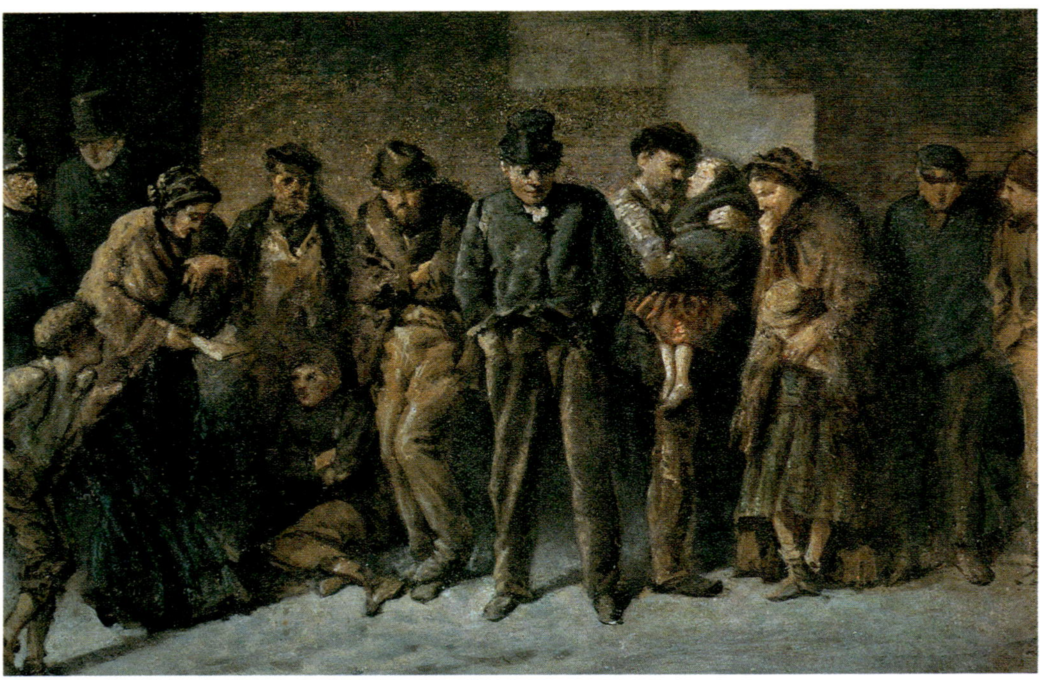

The endless debate

A certain tradition of social painting had been in existence since the 19th century. It had no real impact on the general course of the history of art, illustrating the failure of a pictorial transcription of the type of undertaking Zola had attempted in the field of literature. The fate of the working classes was a matter of indifference in artistic circles, or, to be more accurate, the presence at the heart of a work of art of any social content whatsoever was regarded as prejudicial to its development. "Class struggles should be sorted out at the circus to protect art," Kokoschka declared after a working-class riot in Dresden which left thirty-five dead and during which a stray bullet had gone through a picture by Rubens on display at the museum. "Kokoschka's remarks are the typical expression of the whole bourgeois mentality," the Dadaists Grosz and Heartfield riposted. "The bourgeoisie values its culture and art more highly than the lives of the working classes." In his *History of Dadaism* published in 1920 Huelsenbeck enlarged on this by writing: "Art in general deserves a good flogging."

It was in Germany, traumatized by defeat, crushed by the economic crisis and humiliated by the Treaty of Versailles, that the question of the artist's social commitment was violently raised yet again. Artists like Dix and Grosz fiercely denounced "the role of parasite and prostitute imposed on the artist by capitalist society." In their work Realism became an instrument for denouncing the reality of the present: a reality that they denounced not in the name of some aspiration towards the ideal, but on the contrary in the name of a profound attachment to that reality, refusing to accept that it should be confiscated for the profit of the capitalist minority.

So here we have a militant art in the service of revolution, and also, when understood in this sense, art against art. In Huelsenbeck's words, "Dadaism sees it as necessary to demonstrate against art because it has stripped the mask off its fundamental imposture which sets it up as a valve for moral safety."

However, this attitude was not shared by all Dadaists. Kurz Schwitters with his Merz version of Dada counter-attacked in 1923 in the *Manifesto of Proletarian Art* writing: "There is no art made by members of the proletariat because a proletarian who creates art is no longer a proletarian but an artist. [...] The proletariat is a state which must be left behind, the bourgeoisie is a state which must be left behind. But insofar as they imitate the bourgeois culture with their proletarian culture, members of the proletariat are in fact the very people who are supporting the rotten culture of the bourgeoisie albeit unawares; [...] Consequently the proletarian artist is fighting neither for art nor for the new life ahead but for the bourgeoisie."

It is of course an endless debate, continually taking up the two terms – art and history, art in history, history in art – without being able to decide one way or the other, bring them together or prize them apart .... Inseparable and incompatible for ever and ever ....

Fildes (Luke) 1844-1927
Houseless and hungry
New York, Forbes Magazine Collection

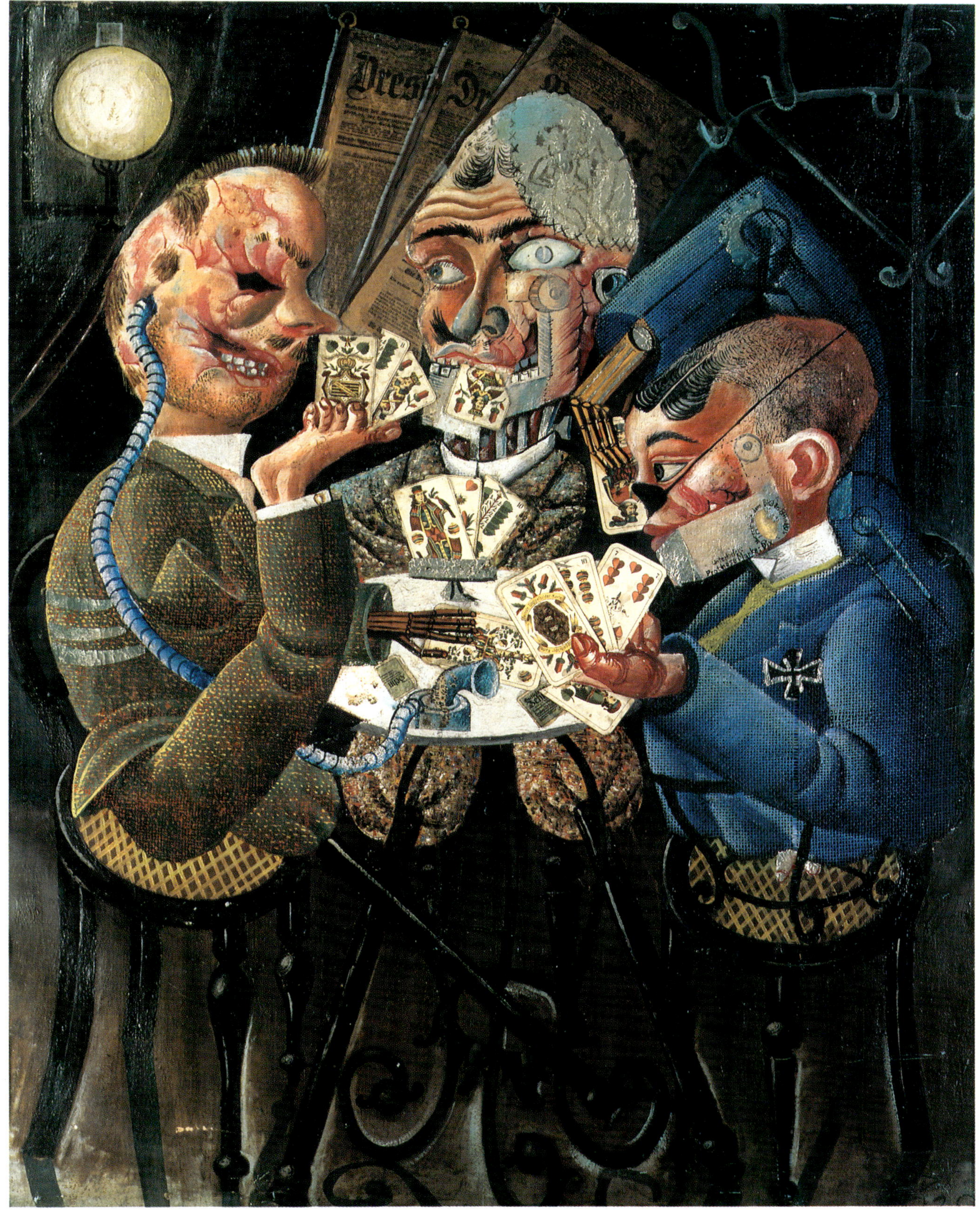

"The highest art will be that which represents the multiple problems of the day in the content of its consciousness; [...] The finest, most peerless artists will be those who every hour pick up the shreds of their bodies in the racket of life's cataracts."

R. Huelsenbeck Dadaist manifesto, 1918

Dix (Otto) 1891-1969
The Skat-players, 1920
Constance, private collection

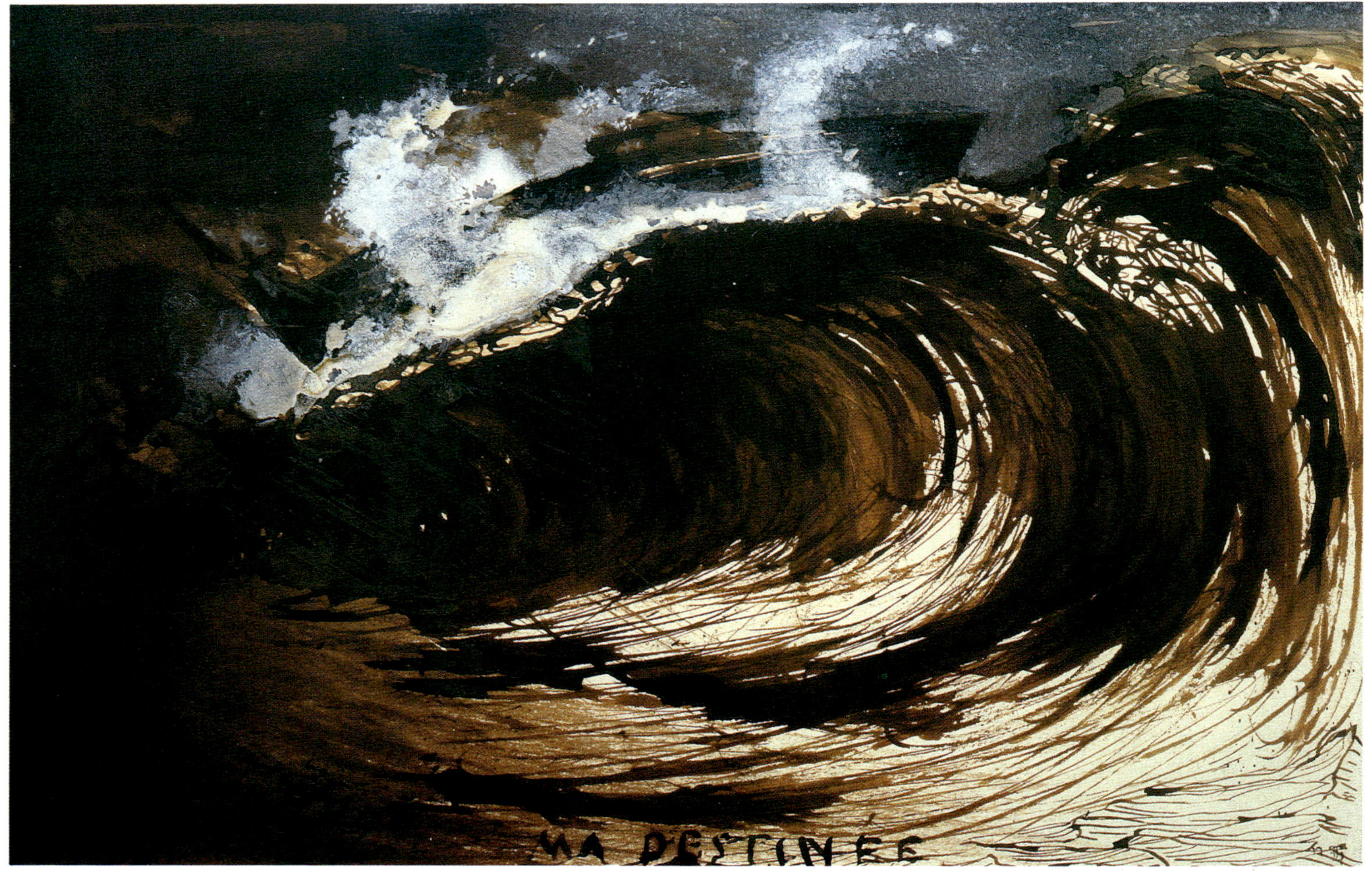

Hugo (Victor) 1802-1885
Ma Destinée, 1857
Paris, Maison de Victor Hugo

Inner monsters **1**

Mysterious symbols **2**

The icons of modernity **3**

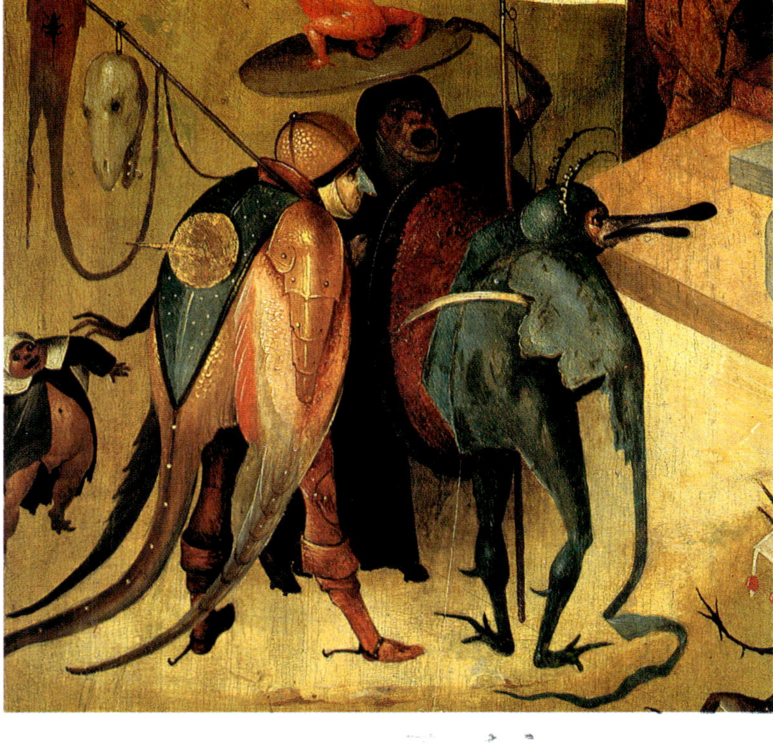

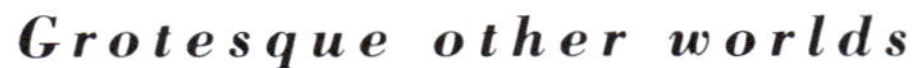

Grotesque other worlds

Hybrid creatures, nightmarish figures, fantastic animals: Hieronymus Bosch's painting has been a source of fascination for five centuries without its mystery having been wholly penetrated. As there are great gaps in our knowledge of his life, it will probably never be possible to give a definitive interpretation of his work.

The grotesque forms that emerged from his imagination had their antecedents in medieval illuminations, and obviously carry a moral lesson, but they are equally valid as strange forms, testimonies of a completely personal inner world. Walter Bosing writes: "The love of the monstrous which Bosch held so dear was very widespread in his period, when people were fascinated by all grotesque, unnatural forms [...]. However, in his sketches Bosch is less a medieval moralist than an artist struggling with the creator, in search of new forms 'never before seen or imagined' as Dürer would later put it when describing the products of the artistic genius."

That is perhaps the first interesting thing about Bosch's monsters: they have a properly identified father, unlike the medieval gargoyles on the roofs of our cathedrals which seem to have emerged from the stone purely through the grace of the genius of time. For while Bosch drew inspiration from a bestiary shared by popular imagery, he added his personal touch to it in the process. In his work fantastic art, by becoming individual, took a crucial step from one state to another, a move which also marked the end of the collective creativity which had been predominant throughout the Middle Ages. For the artist the advent of the Renaissance also corresponded with recognition of his own creative power.

The second peculiarity of this inner world which recurs throughout Bosch's work is associated with the proliferation of mysterious figures. In his work monstrousness is multiple, protean and incomplete. Unlike the Leviathan or the dragon which condense all the monstrousness of a world into a single figure, Bosch's monstrosity seems to surge up from every nook and cranny of his work, very subtly mixing with what we might hesitate to call normality: for example, what difference is there between the decapitated head of a condemned man and the bodiless head that is walking on its left (*Last judgment, Vienna*)? What difference between dream and reality?

The third peculiarity comes from the hybrid nature of the monsters. Our consciousness does not produce monsters from nothing, it draws its forms from reality, the monstrosity resulting not from the form itself but from the incongruity with which several forms are combined (a two-legged rat-fish, for example). What is worrying is less the difference than the closeness which is established between the normal and the fantastic universe. Which is the lie? Which is the truth? It was then, as the Middle Ages gave way to the Renaissance, that the central question of humanism started to be asked, relating to the confrontation between consciousness and the unknowable.

Bosch (Hieronymus Van Aecken, known as) c. 1453-1516
St. James of Compostela and the sorcerer
Valenciennes, Musée des Beaux-Arts

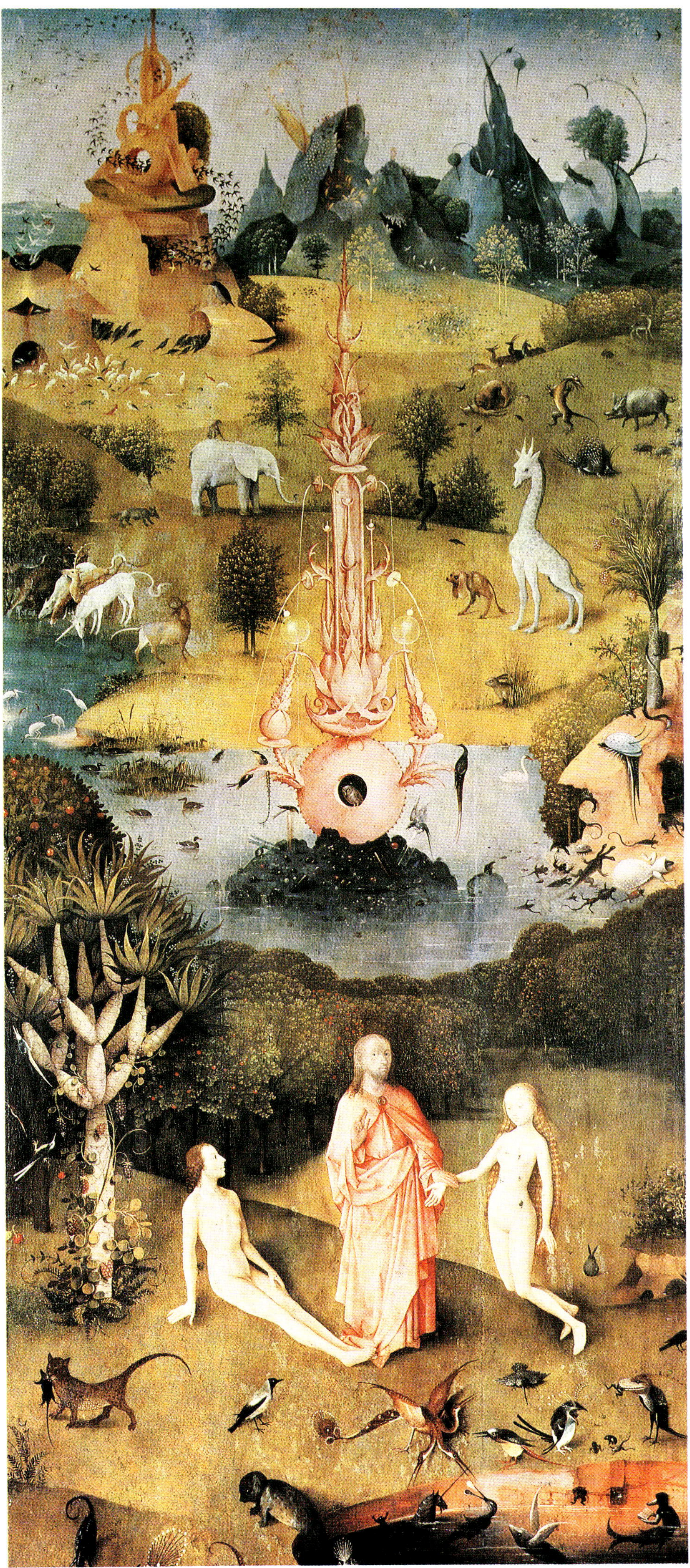

"In his art Bosch is the typical representative of his own very troubled times which saw a civilization that had lasted many centuries ending, a Church which had hitherto been homogeneous tearing itself apart, and old values being dethroned and rejected in favor of new, untried qualities."

J.J.M. Timmers
Le Gothique tardif

Bosch (Hieronymus Van Aecken, known as) c. 1453-1516
The garden of delights (triptych)
Left wing: Creation, c. 1500/1516
Madrid, Prado

Visionary disquiet

Paradoxically, when we peer into the "labyrinth of fantastic art" it is reality rather than the phantasm that causes difficulty. The idea of horror applies only when set against a certain scale of reality that we accept. A mutilated body is not horrible in itself, but only in relation to a reference point which we call reality and from which it is far enough removed for us to be able to recognize a distance, but not so far removed that the distance makes comparison difficult. A skeleton is acceptable; a putrefying body never will be.

Grünewald's power, more insidious than that of Bosch, lies in conjuring up monstrosity at the very heart of reality. Better still, since it is the figure of Christ that he is dealing with, the artist manages to conjure up the notion of unrealness by showing us the body of Christ at the furthermost point of earthly decline. He is never more human than when all he offers is the awful appearance of a tortured body; and yet never does he appear to us so far removed from what we ourselves know of the human condition. The unreal is in the real. This means that what we know of the story of Christ transfigures his body, but also, if we want to make a metaphor of this vision, that the artist's imagination too transfigures our vision of the world. All representation is intrinsically an apparition of something unreal pretending to be the real thing. And all art is intrinsically fantastic since it achieves its objective only if it succeeds in making its vision acceptable to us as a possible world.

In Grünewald's work the presence of the fantastic lies in the omnipresence of death in life, but also, when resurrection comes into play, in the life which rises at the very heart of death. To quote Elie Faure, "This patient, exact art, complicated though poetic, sincere to the point of self-immolation, full of tormented fantasy and deep symbolism that is sometimes so obscure that it appears not to know itself, in spite of the concentrated brilliance of a powerful vivacity and its tremendous sensuality, is overbrimming with the irreparable sadness of the man who cannot choose." Macaber violence alongside the naive hope of salvation, radical pessimism and sincere faith: faced with these two antinomous extremes the artist makes no choice, preferring to express all the complexity of the world and of man facing the world in a work which, like dreams, feeds on absurdity rather than trying to explain it.

Grünewald (Mathis Gothart Nithart, known as) c.1475/80-1528
Issenheim retable. The temptation of St. Anthony
Detail: demons armed with sticks, c. 1512/1516
Colmar, Musée d'Unterlinden

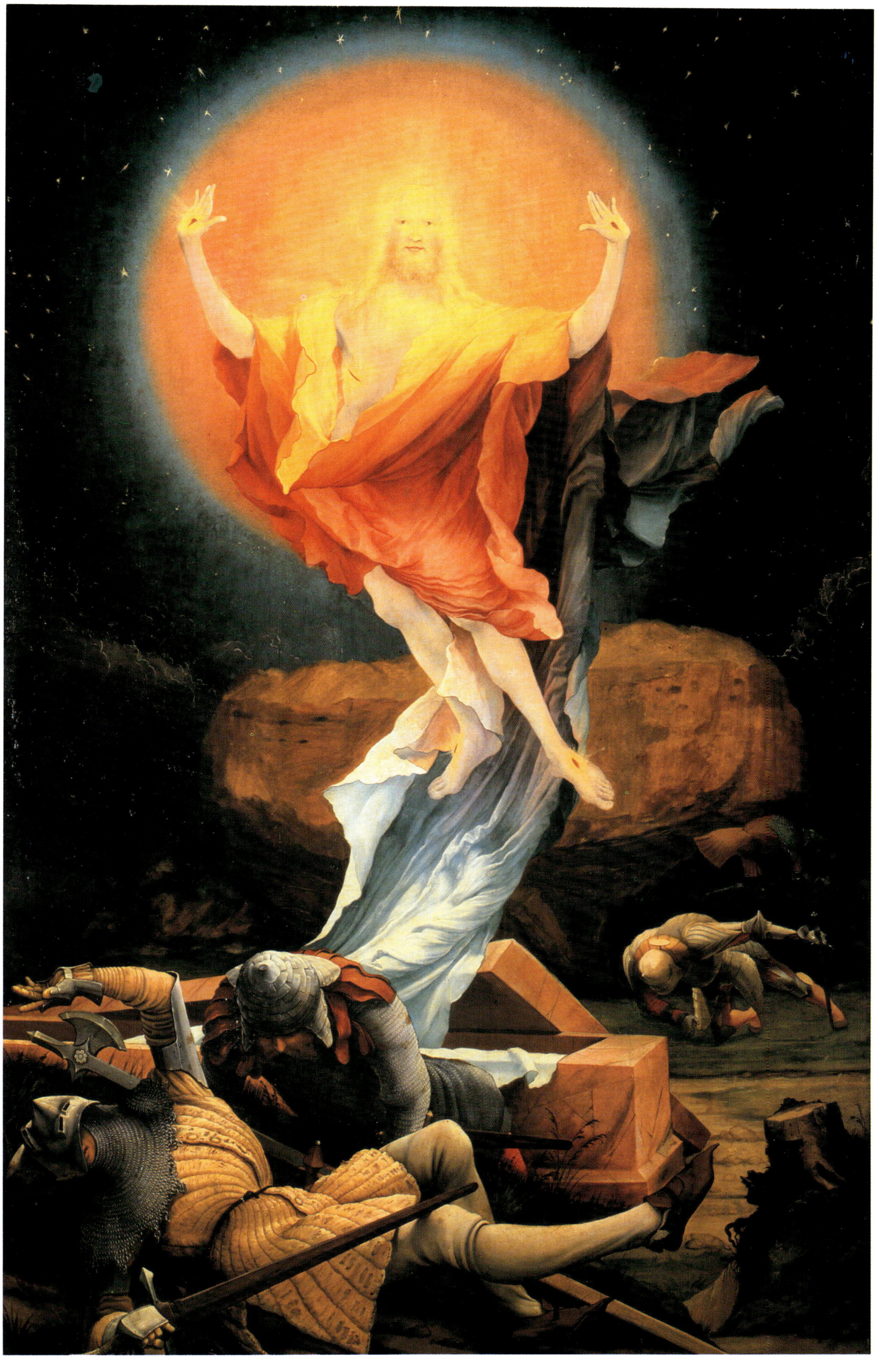

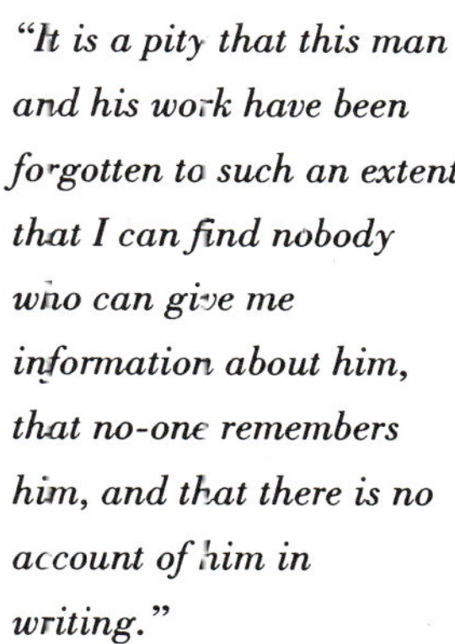

"It is a pity that this man and his work have been forgotten to such an extent that I can find nobody who can give me information about him, that no-one remembers him, and that there is no account of him in writing."

Joachim von Sandrart Deutsche Akademie, 1575

Grünewald (Mathis Gothart Nithart, known as) c.1475/80-1528

Issenheim retable. Resurrection of Christ, c. 1512/1516

Colmar, Musée d'Unterlinden

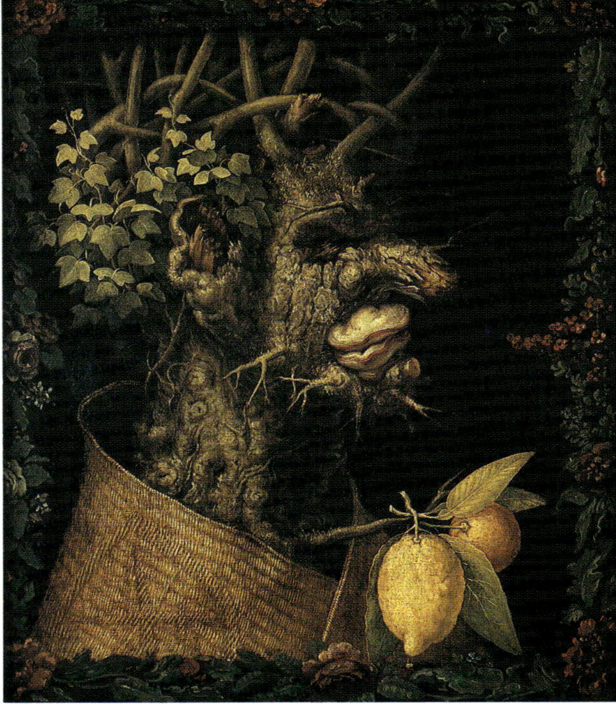

Terrifying oddities

Arcimboldo was rediscovered by the Surrealist painters at the beginning of the 20th century. However, his painting, which is both Mannerist and allegorical while going beyond both these late 16th-century artistic categories, did not attract followers. At the time when nature was beginning to yield up some of its secrets and Emperor Rudolf II in Prague was surrounding himself with scholars like Tycho Brahe and Kepler, and artists like Arcimboldo, it would seem that their discoveries, far from reassuring man concerning his place in creation, aroused a disquiet that was all the deeper because these men freed themselves of the yoke of religion to exercise their art. In rejecting the medieval recourse to the supernatural and subjecting nature to scientific scrutiny they discovered a still more fantastic nature: a discovery which inevitably aroused a certain feeling of anguish in human beings.

Thus in Arcimboldo's work it is nature itself which appears fantastic. But unlike Hieronymus Bosch, who put together elements deemed to be irreconcilable, or Grünewald, who resorted to exaggeration, the fantastic in Arcimboldo comes from a doubling of meaning. As Roland Barthes put it, "It is as if Arcimboldo disarranged the pictural system, doubling it improperly, enlarging the signifying analogical virtuality in it so as to produce a sort of structural monster, giving rise to a subtle (because it is intellectual) unease [...]: it is because everything has significance at two levels that Arcimboldo's painting functions as a somewhat terrifying denial of the pictural language."

Looking at a painting by Arcimboldo we experience the same fascination and the same disgust as when confronted by carrion being eaten by maggots: the swarming movement of life feeding off the decomposition of another life. Behind the seeming classical harmony of the human body his portraits – where the figures appear to have been flayed – uncover a different sort of harmony, a different order of nature, all the more disturbing because it seems to threaten the distinction which was thought to be absolute between man and other forms of life. Gustav René Hocke described Arcimboldo's art as being on the "boundary"; we might equally well say that it is an art that blows up the boundary.

Thus there is absolutely no need to imagine monsters in order to conjure up the fantastic, nor to seek out any monstrosities that nature may have produced. As Roland Barthes remarked, Arcimboldo "produces the fantastic from the very familiar." For when closely examined the very process of life turns out to be truly monstrous: behind every man is concealed a disgusting tangle of tepid organs and guts; and beneath our feet, in the idyllic setting of harmonious nature, a whole larval world is swarming, all the more repellent to us because it reminds us of our own biological reality.

Arcimboldo (Giuseppe) 1527-1593
Winter, 1573
Paris, Louvre

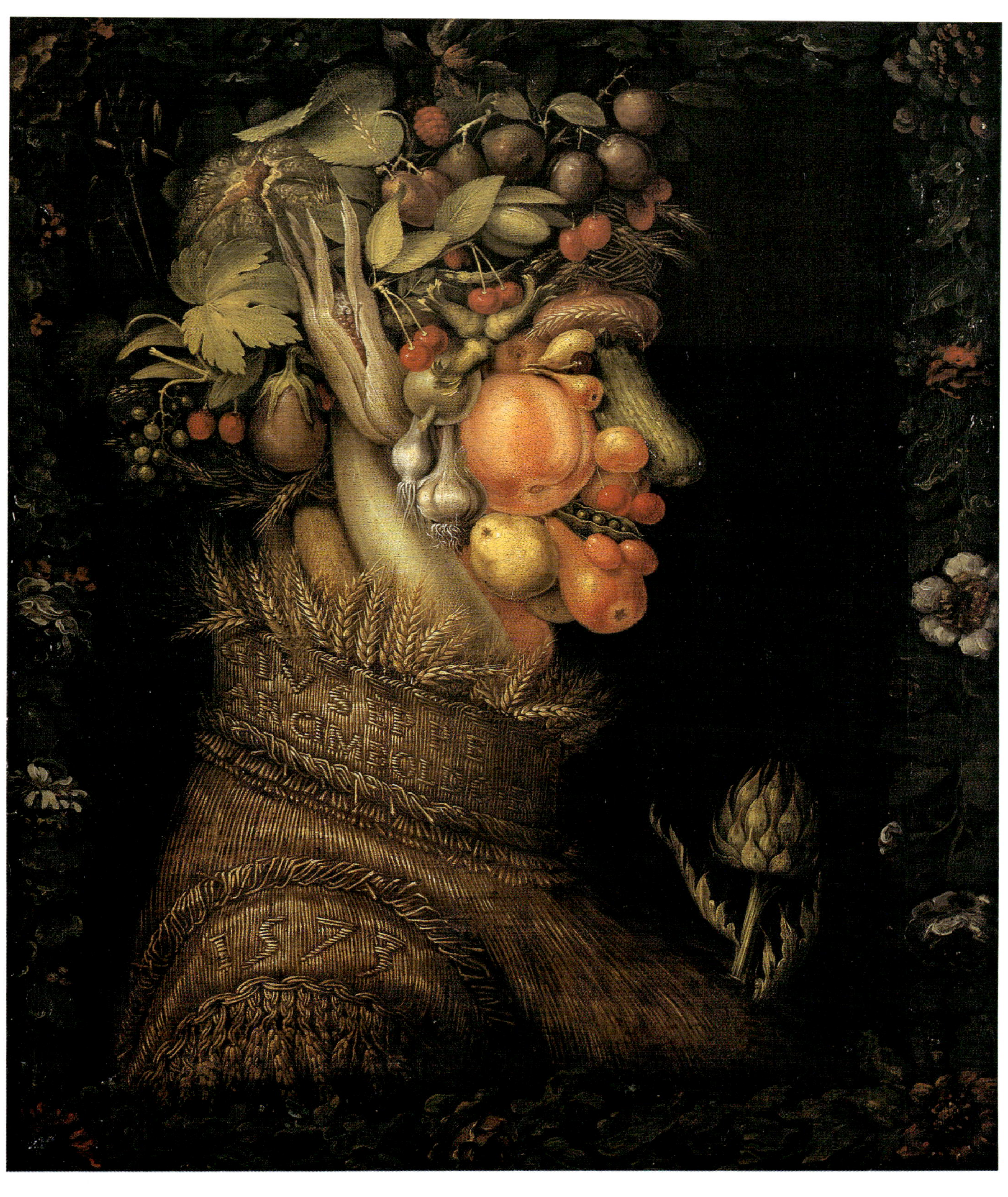

"If you look at the picture closely you will see only fruit and vegetables: if you move further away you will see only a man with a fearsome eye, a ribbed doublet and a spiny ruff; being far or near is what gives it meaning."

Roland Barthes Arcimboldo ou Rhétoriqueur et Magicien

Arcimboldo (Giuseppe) 1527-1593
Summer, 1573
Paris, Louvre

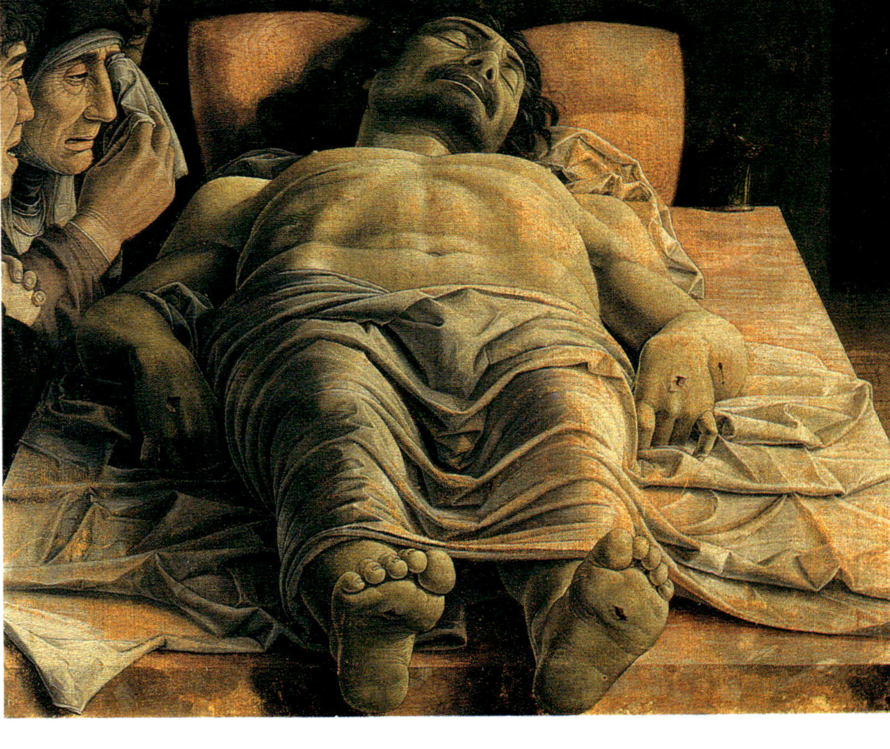

Ecstatic matter

In the late 19th and early 20th century the Expressionists chose Grünewald and El Greco as their two spiritual fathers. Lyricism, mysticism and anti-rationalism were thus seen as the attributes of both masters. Associating the two in this way obviously calls for some light to be shed on the nature of El Greco's oeuvre, the main characteristics of which are of course known: stylization, elongated forms and a rejection of the naturalistic depiction of space.

Is that enough to justify calling his painting visionary, or even mystical? While the Renaissance in Florence set about creating the illusion of depth by following strict geometric rules (Brunelleschi and Alberti), El Greco chose the opposite path: he preferred frontality and verticality (which suited the deliberate elongation of forms) to the illusion of depth – a diametrically opposite choice in fact to that of Mantegna in his spectacular *Dead Christ*. So El Greco might be regarded as visionary because he offers us his vision of the world and not the vision made official by the 16th century in Italy: a resolutely subjective vision as against an objective norm ....

While it is not irrelevant, such an argument on its own is not sufficiently persuasive. But if we examine El Greco's painting more deeply we find a constant that has already been emphasized in relation to fantastic art: the feeling of swarming movement which emanates from his tangled forms. Where the Raphaelite tradition was usually anxious to open up wide spaces and encircle forms, in El Greco's work it is as if he had elected to fill the surface of the canvas to total saturation point. When Pacheco asked him whether drawing or color presented the greatest difficulty in his art, he broke with tradition by answering that it was color. As a matter of fact such a question must have been meaningless to him, for in his work drawing exists only through color. And color is present everywhere, blacks too being colors. Everything, even a void, becomes matter, and hierarchies are blurred. This lies behind the feeling of surreality his work arouses, reminiscent of that evoked by Tintoretto. However, one crucial detail distinguishes the two. Writing about Tintoretto's *Last judgment* Sartre wrote that "the damned fall of their own accord without even being touched by the finger of God: directly creatures are left to their own weight, they topple over. Now look at the chosen: they are not proud [...], and the reason they do not fall is that they are looked after: a dark cloud is slipped underneath their feet, they are propped up and supported." In the work of El Greco everything is the other way round, and in spite of having the expected weight the figures rise as if drawn by the white arch of the dove; we divine that all this superfluous matter will melt there to become pure light: something that can never be painted. Here perhaps, because it expresses true material ecstasy, El Greco's painting verges on mysticism, demonstrating that the representation of the real cannot possibly be reduced to the Florentine vision alone.

Mantegna (Andrea) 1431-1506
The dead Christ, c. 1480-1490
Milan, Pinacoteca di Brera

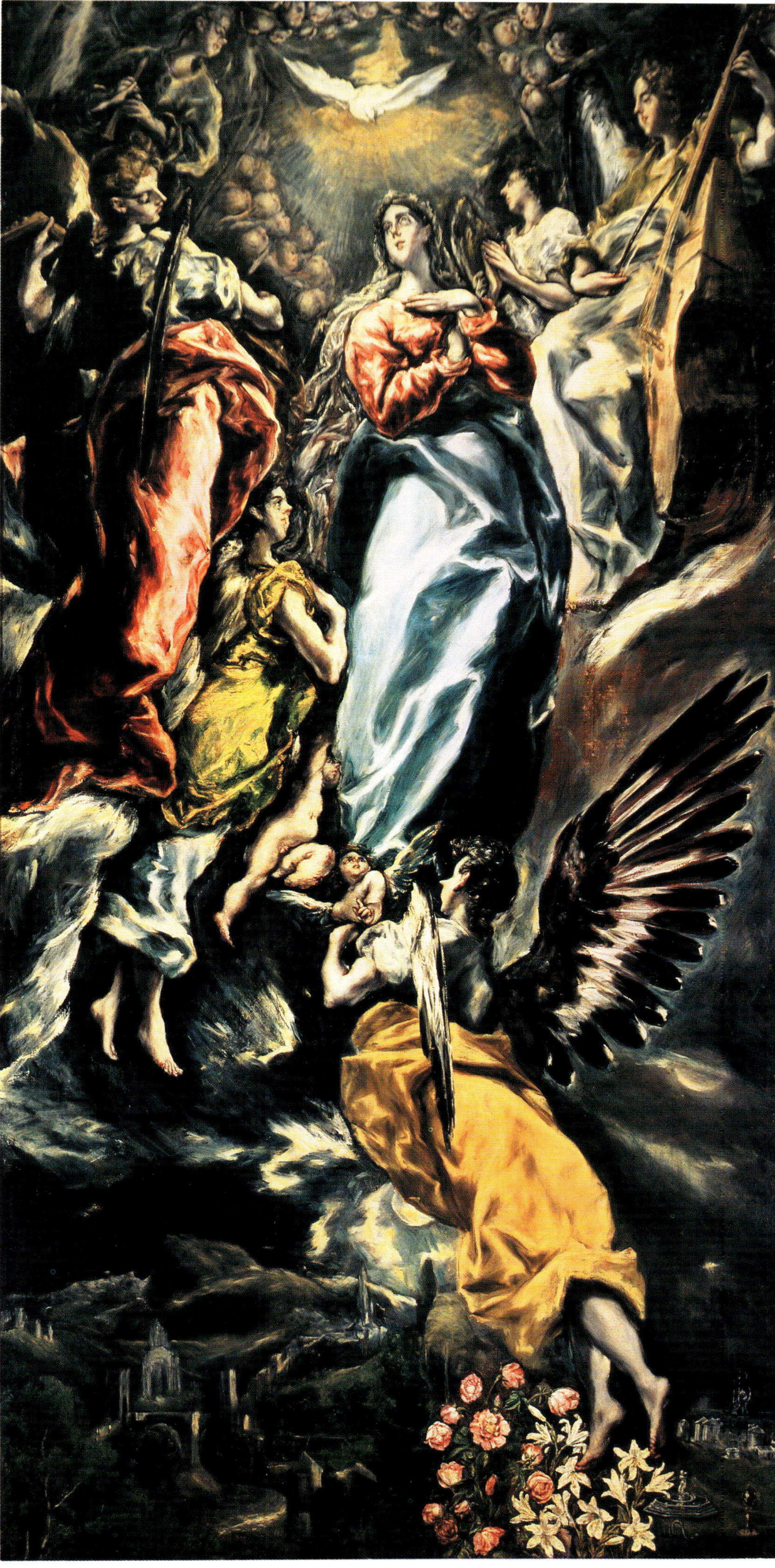

"Artists of religious themes who do not ignore 'Nature' but make it subordinate or despise it seem to be in the service of a superworld: a truer, more lasting and above all more important world than that of appearance."

André Malraux
La Tête d'obsidienne

Greco, El (Domenikos Theotokopoulos, known as) c. 1541-1614
Assumption of the Virgin, between 1607 and 1614
Toledo, Santa Cruz Museum

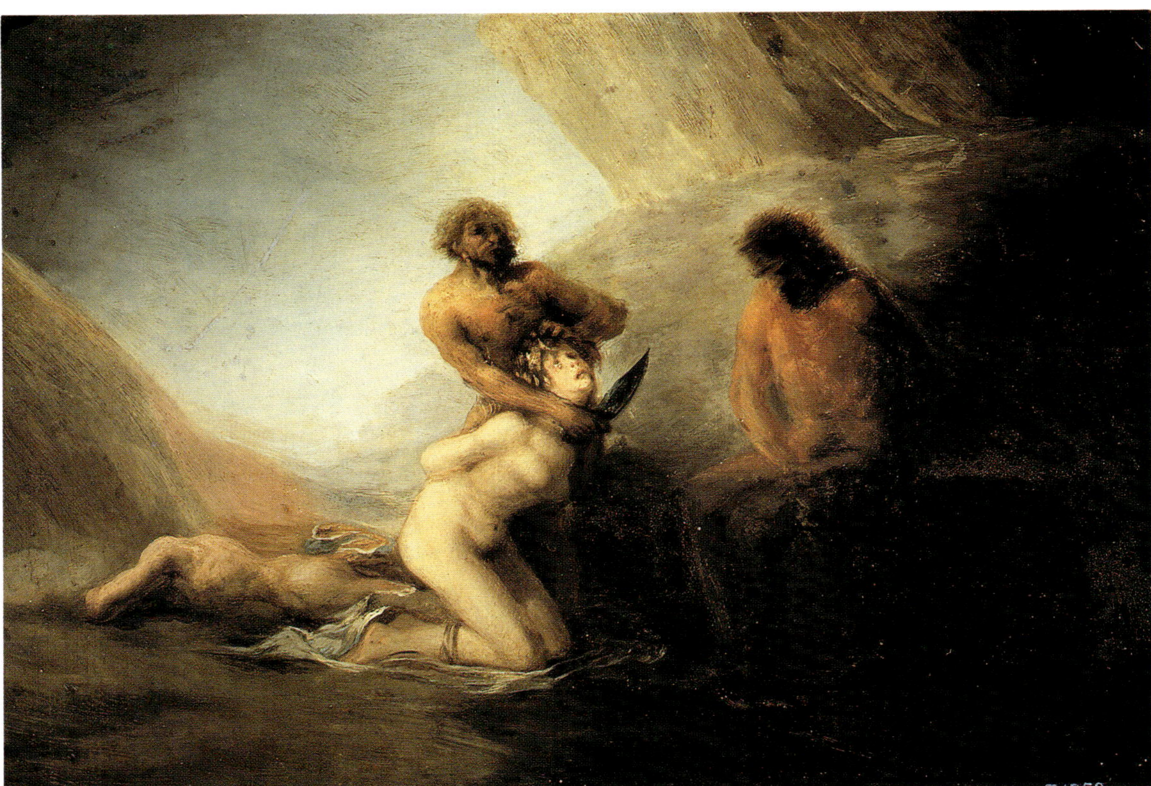

The part played by shade

"What is called Goya's realism," André Malraux wrote, "does not so much come from observation, as everyone – including himself! – claims, as from the fantastic." Further on he adds: "What [Goya] understands is that his enemy is Creation. He fights against it, following in the footsteps of the Flemish diabolists, through an ironic deployment of the fantastic." His irony and cruelty claim to be the paradoxical weapons of reason in pursuit of happiness. But there is a narrow margin between religious fanaticism and the Terror of revolution. Italy in its day had invented a credible way of representing things, i.e. in tune with that period, by uniting – still quoting André Malraux – "sensuality and spirituality." But that language which had been alive had become set into something commonplace. It was ill-suited to expressing the deep contradictions of Spain at the beginning of the 19th century. El Greco disturbed the evidence of the senses by inventing a style thought to be visionary, but he never questioned the ultimate objective of art, namely the expression of the harmony between man, nature and the Creator. But Goya no longer believed in reconciliation between man and God. No more did he believe in man's salvation without God. Wherever he looked he could see no way out. And when the mind is trapped it gives birth to madness, with irony representing a final bulwark against that madness. In the words of Cioran, "Irony is the politeness of despair."

The belief that Goya's fantasy is the opposite of reality makes the mistake of assuming that Italian Renaissance realism expressed reality better than the fantasies of Bosch, Bruegel or Arcimboldo. But Italian realism is no more true than any other representation. The degree of truth in a representation has no connection with the concept of resemblance. A work gets near to its own truth when the artist invents a language (i.e. a style) that is appropriate to his vision, and moves away from it when the artist resorts to a language invented by others to serve a different vision. The truth of a representation lies in invention and not, as people would like to believe, in reproduction.

The caricatured presence of the supernatural, violence and the absurd in Goya's work is not opposed to reality; on the contrary, it is through their presence that the reality of Spain and a people who had never managed to recognize themselves in the light-filled world of the Italian Renaissance (even when welcoming Tiepolo) is most accurately expressed. For in Spain light is nothing without the shade that gives it existence. Nor was Spain able – unlike France which could erect an altar to the goddess Reason during the Revolution – to invoke the heritage of the Enlightenment, as Goya would have wished, without all the ghosts of the Inquisition immediate rising up across its route; we will never know if the grimacing faces of these figures should be read as a threat or a call for help.

Goya (Francisco de Goya y Lucientes, known as) 1746-1828
The beheading, c. 1800-1805
Madrid, Prado

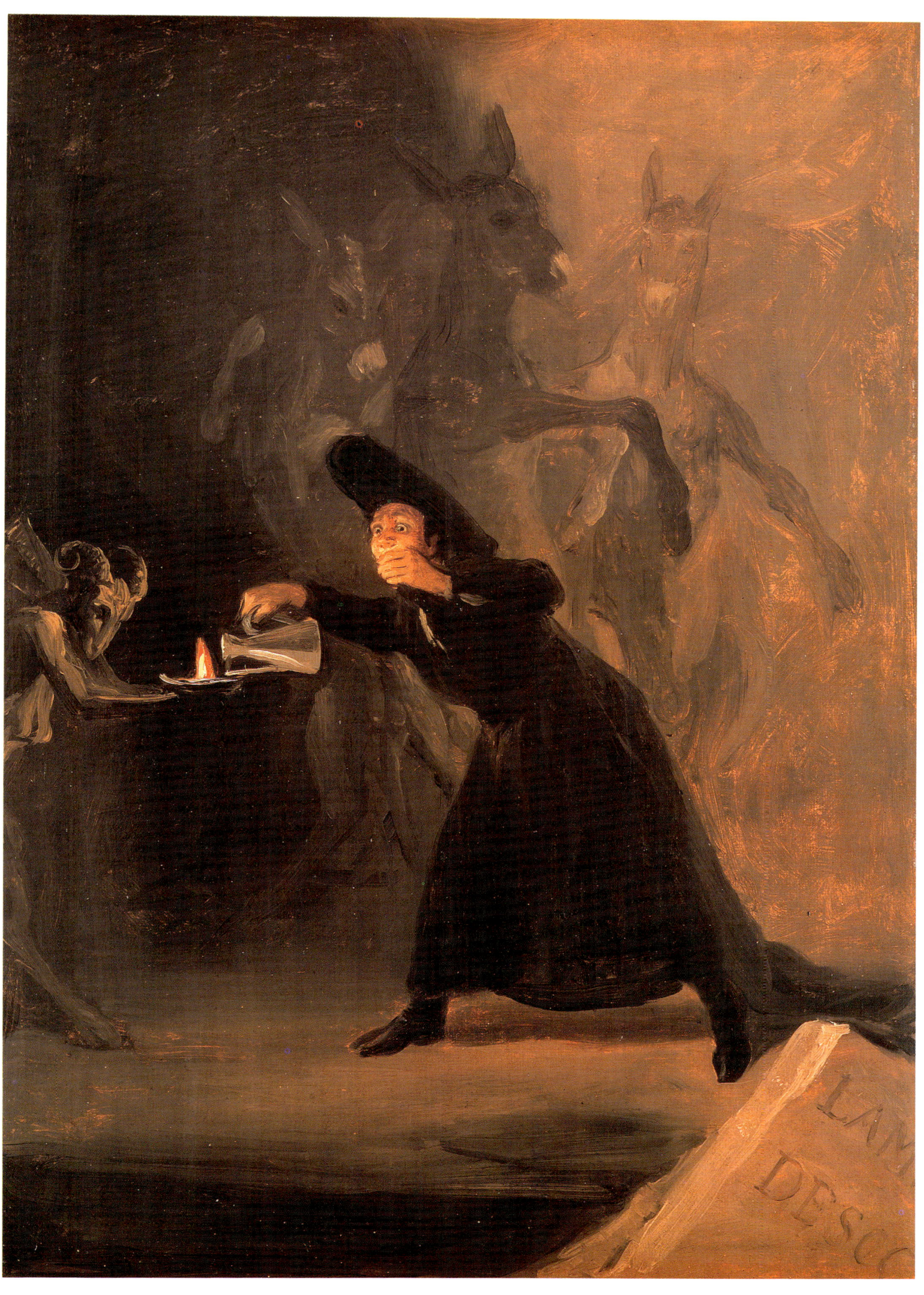

"Goya's eye sounds nothingness but does not get lost there. His faith in man is stronger than all the temptations to despair."

Anton Dieterich
Goya

Goya (Francisco de Goya y Lucientes, known as) 1746-1828
The bewitched man
London, National Gallery

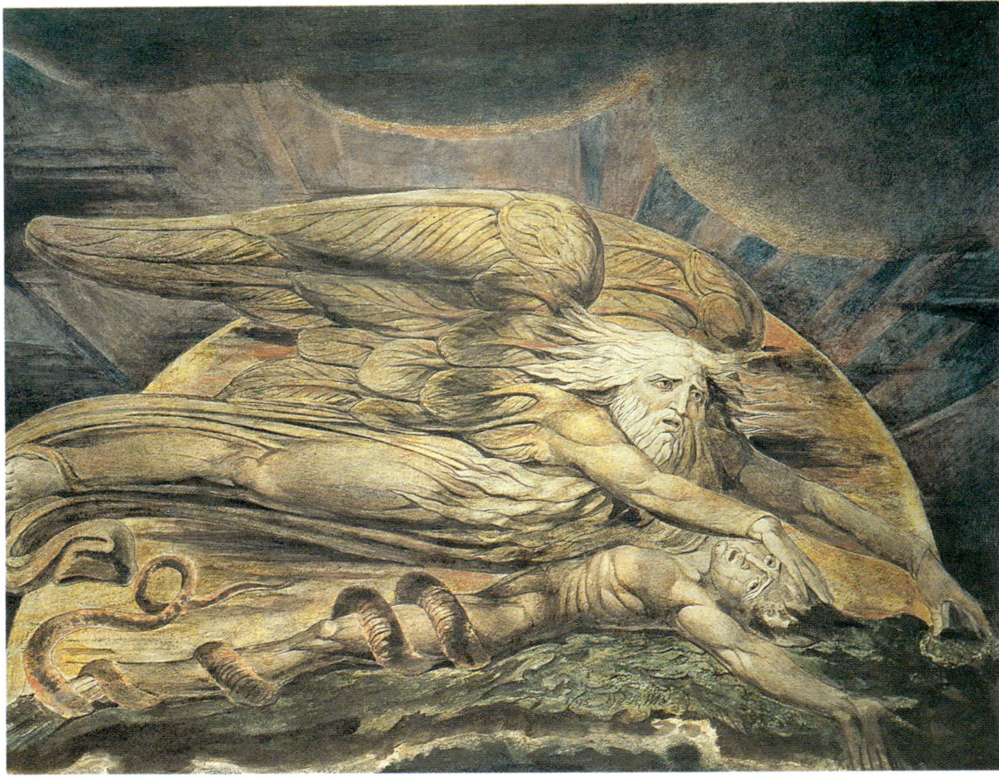

The heirs of Sturm und Drang

The whole of European thought from St. Thomas Aquinas to Kant had been forged round the question of the exercise of reason and the limits of its powers. In a way Kant set out to close the debate by assigning a limited field of action to reason. But at the same time he removed it from the province of faith, demonstrating, since that area could not be investigated by him, that the two should be clearly separated. Thus with Kant reason came of age and achieved true autonomy.

Artists and writers such as Fuseli, Blake or Goethe, the heirs of the German Sturm und Drang movement, rebelled against such a restrictive but fundamentally optimistic system. For them the question of morality was intimately associated with creation itself. The confrontation between Good and Evil was not played out purely at a metaphysical level (that of faith), but was also at work at the very heart of nature, i.e. within us human beings, the world's conscience. In other words Kant's reason which claimed a purely relative autonomy was in fact contaminated by unreason. For it was from nature as creation – which human reason claimed to investigate outside any religious questioning – that the Evil gnawing at the world derived.

With these as their premisses (profoundly heretical, since they were based on the idea that Good and Evil are consubstantial) Blake and Fuseli went against Locke in denouncing the deceptive evidence of the senses, and against Kant in denouncing the falsifying work of reason. Thus at one fell swoop they rejected the two main esthetic currents of the 18th century – with Fragonard or Watteau representing sensualism and David rationalist Neo-Classicism in painting.

These heirs of Sturm und Drang in fact envisaged nature less as something that could be known than as a moral object. Regarding reason as incapable of operating on such an object, they preferred the exaltation of the power of the imagination to reason. Only through imagination could the poet and the artist go right back to the genesis of the world to explore its mysteries. For it was at the very heart of its genesis that the question of morality had its source, at the time when the ideas of Good and Evil came together after God had placed Adam and Eve in the middle of the earthly Paradise.

In resorting to the visionary world of the imagination art acts as a catharsis, purging the world of the evil within it, and takes on a messianic character, fulfilling in the field of metaphysics the role science has taken upon itself in the field of physics.

In both Blake's and Fuseli's work, resorting to the visionary imagination was ultimately not perceived as the antithesis of rationalism, but rather as a preliminary to it, in a system which is at the very least original since it defines esthetics as the basis of physics.

Blake (William) 1757-1827
Elohim creating Adam, 1795
London, Tate Gallery

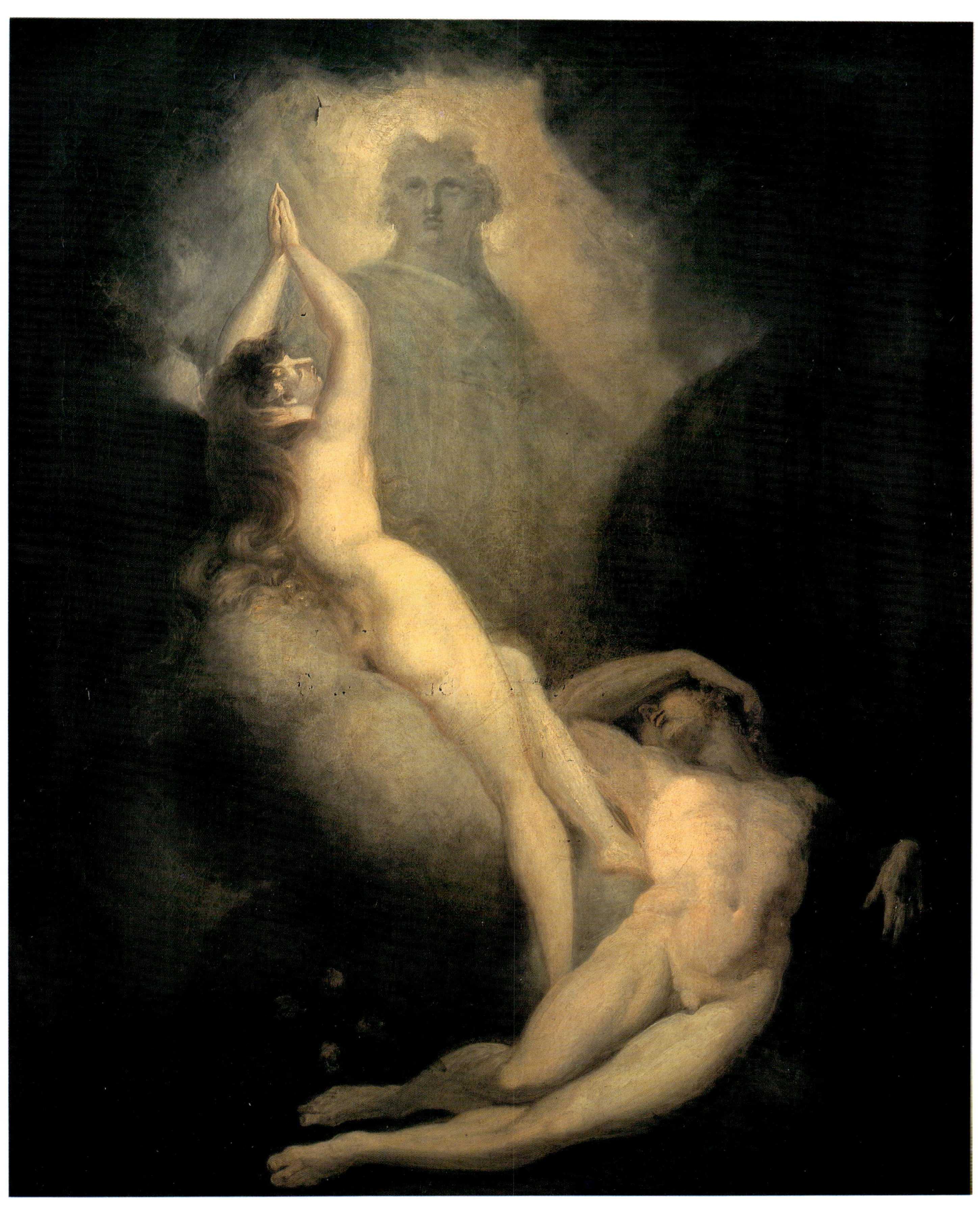

"The mortal fury which inspires and animates [the imagination] and which seems determined to strip the human condition bare down to its last secret might well be directed against the illusion on which the flight of the imagination lives [...] and signify the search for a way out other than the unreality in which [Fuseli's art] develops."

Jean Starobinski
L'Invention de la libert

Fuseli or Füssli (Johann Heinrich) 1741-1825
The Creation of Eve
London, Christie's

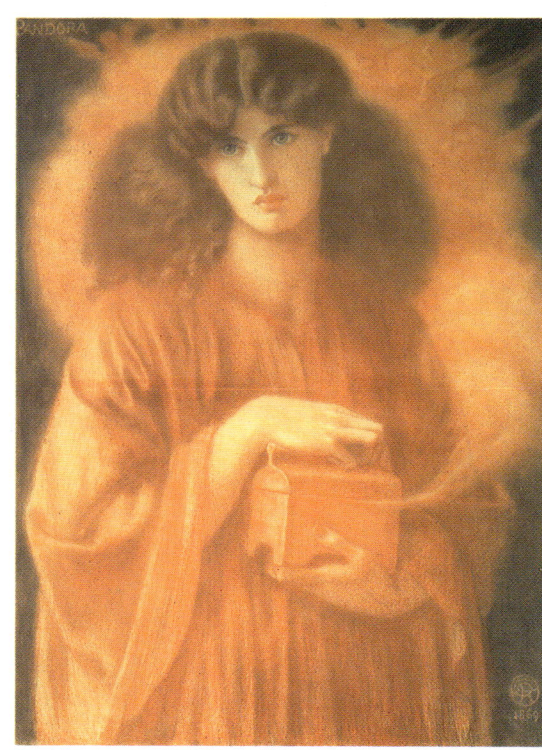

The marvelous and the real

The Pre-Raphaelite movement, which came into being in England around the mid-19th century, partly influenced by the Nazarenes, is at the opposite end of the spectrum from Fuseli's demonism. Reacting against some aspects of industrialization and against Victorian academicism the artists set out to rediscover the basis for a "sincere [attitude] towards nature" through the example of 15th-century Italian painting: an ambition that was as noble as it was vague.

Some artists in the movement followed the path of analytical realism. But the more interesting among them were those like Rossetti, who successfully enriched their work with hints of mysticism mingled with a disturbed (and disturbing) sensuality, heralding *fin-de-siècle* Symbolism and Decadence rather than reminding us of the naive purity of Fra Angelico. Subsequently Rossetti, helped by Burne-Jones, founded the second Pre-Raphaelite group, which developed a thematic area based on the New Testament and medieval legend.

When we consider these artists (the Nazarenes and the Pre-Raphaelites alike) the difficulty lies in understanding how what was initially stated as a sincere attraction towards nature, i.e. reality, subsequently turned into a search for legendary themes and ended up as pre-Symbolist painting. The painter Franz Pforr provided a partial answer to this question when he wrote: "My inclination led me towards the Middle Ages [...], the spirit of that period is so beautiful and so little used by artists. The marvelous and the real intermingle, almost always with a moral content, and everything is penetrated with an atmosphere of meditation which is extremely conducive to art." In fact the love of nature rests on a nostalgic cult of the past, a denunciation of modernity and an anti-rationalism far removed from Fuseli's demonism, rooted in extremely conservative aspirations that would lead at the end of the century to nationalistic exaltation and the often bellicose cult of one's native land. This is primarily true of the Nazarenes, however. The English Pre-Raphaelites avoided these excesses by developing a more sensual painting, though it was also more ambiguous in its symbols.

The Nazarenes' anti-rationalism was militant, while that of the Pre-Raphaelites was more relaxed. In legend they found a pretext for sometimes equivocal reverie; when confronted with modern life they adopted a detached esthete's attitude anticipating that of Oscar Wilde in Britain and Huysmans in France. Their painting offers a transition, a passage from the Romanticism of the beginning of the 19th century to the Symbolism of the end, elucidating an evolution (if such an evolution exists outside the realms of the scholarly reconstructions of the history of art – perhaps yet another illusion ...) which is more confused in its image in France as a result of the Realist reaction and the Impressionist rebellion against the post-Neoclassical academicism of the establishment masters of the Salon.

Rossetti (Dante Gabriel) 1828-1882
Pandora, 1869
Buscot, Faringdon Collection

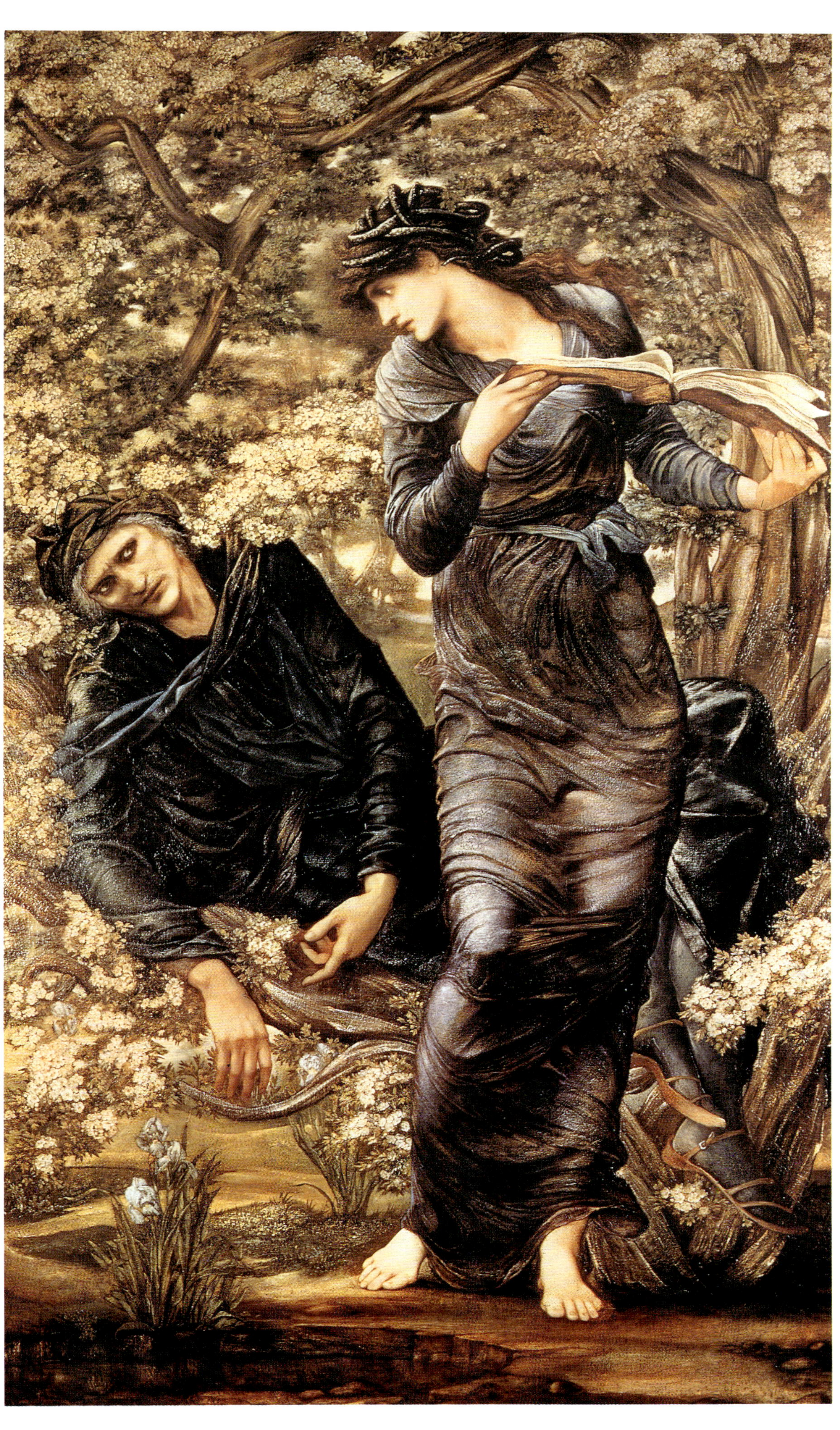

"Admiring the naive faith of the 'Primitives' and trying to recapture it are two different things. With the best will in the world it cannot be achieved. The naivety of the Pre-Raphaelites is a contrived naivety."

Ernst Gombrich
The Story of Art

Burne-Jones (Edward Coley) 1833-1898
Merlin and Vivien, c. 1870-1874
Port Sunlight, Lady Lever Art Gallery

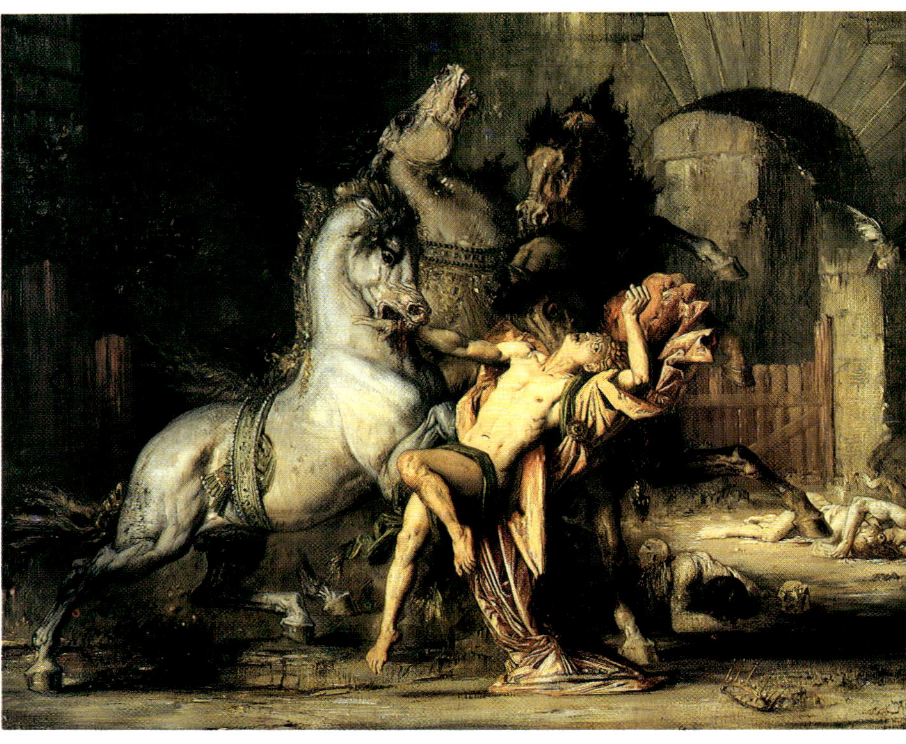

The rhythm of dreams

Turning one's back on reality and aspiring towards the sublime may be attributes of saintdom or of dandyism – the caricatural, fascinating double of saintdom. Retracing the esthetic path followed by Des Esseintes, the hero of *A Rebours*, Huysmans wrote: "After losing interest in contemporary existence [he had sought] subtle, exquisite painting suffused with old dreams, Antique corruption, far removed from our manners and morals, far removed from our days. He had sought [...] some evocative works launching him into an unknown world, unveiling the traces of new conjectures, disturbing his nervous system through bouts of erudite hysteria, complicated nightmares and uncaring, atrocious visions. There was one artist among all others whose talent sent him into long transports, Gustave Moreau.

Symbolism, which became established in the 1880s as a reaction against the Realist trends in painting, is both a rejection of rationalism and an affirmation of the metaphysical nature of art. The opposite in every respect of Seurat, who dreamt of a scientific art with his Divisionism, Moreau retackled a problem already revealed by Fuseli and Blake by asserting that the object on which the painter's eye is trained does not belong to the real world, but the surreal world of dreams. In this respect Symbolism is a subjective movement, i.e. a system that places the subject who creates at the heart of the creative act. It differs from Impressionism in that the object on which the painter's eye is trained does not belong to the world of objective realities. The object for Symbolism is the fantasy world of the painting subject. In other words, Symbolism marked an even more radical turning in on the self than Impressionism by declaring that it could make works of art by cutting itself off from reality.

The renunciation of any representation of an objective reality changed the very nature of representation. Symbolism with its phantasms established itself as a criticism of the realistic (but illusionistic) representation that had emerged from the Renaissance. It unveiled not the illusion of reality, but the reality of illusion. The radical reversal of the perspective of creation initiated a new relationship between the painter and his work in which the concept of resemblance no longer had any place; similarly, the concept of rhythm replaced that of narration, anticipating in the realm of painting the upheavals Igor Stravinsky would translate to the field of music in his brilliant, sensational *Rite of spring* .... Thus rhythms were thought to transcribe a kind of impulse of the soul towards the sublime, towards a metaphysical order that reason, i.e. science, could not reach; rhythms conveyed the music of the soul which the artist interpreted for humankind, blinded by the immediate presence of objective realities.

Symbolism, an heir to Romanticism insofar as it still assigned the status of medium to the artist, broke with it in another respect in renouncing narrative fiction to develop a concept of esthetics based on rhythm which generated a subjective sense of time like that of a dream, a sense of time that is repetitive, reiterative and cyclical.

Moreau (Gustave) 1826-1898
Diomedes devoured by his horses, 1865
Paris, Musée Gustave Moreau

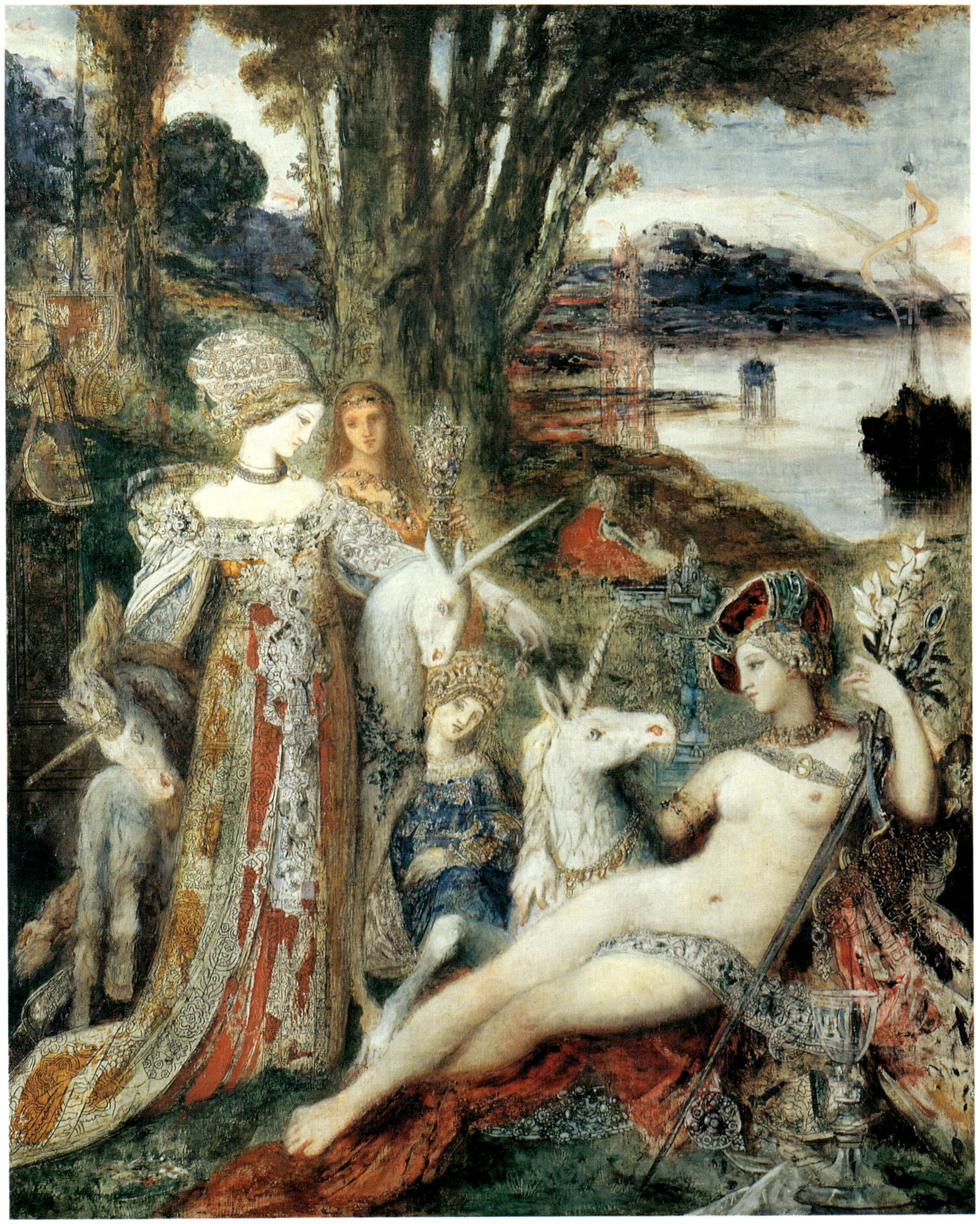

"Lost in contemplation, [Des Esseintes] examined the origins of this great artist, this mystic pagan, this enlightened being who could abstract himself from the world sufficiently to be able to see, in the heart of Paris, the glowing light of the cruel visions and fairy-tale apotheoses of other ages."

J.-K. Huysmans
A Rebours

Moreau (Gustave) 1826-1898
The unicorns
Paris, Musée Gustave Moreau

Serving the invisible

The first collection of lithographs published by Odilon Redon in 1879 carried the programmatic title, "Dans le rêve" [Dreaming]. Redon, like Moreau, was inimical to Impressionism, drawing inspiration from Goya, Poe and Baudelaire; as well as illustrating Baudelaire's work he illustrated that of Mallarmé and Huysmans.

'In *A Soi-même* (To oneself – another revealing title) Redon wrote: "No plastic form, I mean perceived objectively, for itself, by the laws of light and shade, using conventional modeling, could possibly be found in my works. [...] My whole art is limited to the resources of light and dark alone, and it owes a lot to the effects of the abstract line, that agent from a deep well that acts directly on the mind. Evocative art can provide nothing without resorting solely to the mysterious play of shadows and the rhythm of lines conceived in the mind." He went on: "Evocative art is like an irradiation of things for the dream towards which thought is traveling." And still further on he said: "My drawings inspire and are not defined. They determine nothing. Like music they transport us into the ambiguous world of the indeterminate."

Such words as these are proof of Redon's obvious adherence to the Symbolist movement. His ambition, in keeping with the spirit of that movement, was to make the invisible visible. However – and here Redon's art differs from Moreau's – he set out to do so by conveying the invisible through the visible. "I have made my own version of art," he declared. "[But] I have done so with my eyes open to the wonders of the visible world and, whatever may have been said, with a constant concern to obey the laws of the natural world and of life."

Redon was a friend of the botanist André Clavaud who "worked with the infinitely small, on the confines of the perceptible world." His discovery of the world of the microscope turned Redon away from the pure subjectivism developed by Moreau. Through observation of the plant and the animal kingdom he understood that the visible is not opposed to the invisible, to phantasms and chimeras, but is instead the prelude to them. He confided to Bonger that: "All my originality lies in making improbable beings live humanly according to the laws of probability, putting the logic of the visible at the service of the invisible as far as possible [...]. Nature, measured and infused in this way, becomes my source, my yeast, my fermenting agent. From this starting point I believe that my inventions are true."

Thus reality is conceived as what gives body to dreams. Through it creation both takes root and rises up, in its turn providing body, or matter rather, for more abstract speculation of a metaphysical nature. But that speculation must remain alien to art which, according to Redon, can have no end other than itself. If art opens the way to metaphysics, it is not itself either physics or metaphysics. So the artist then becomes "a soul in the midst of the world" who, looking at this world, can sense through it the existence of another one.

Redon (Odilon) 1840-1916
The shell, 1912
Paris, Musée d'Orsay

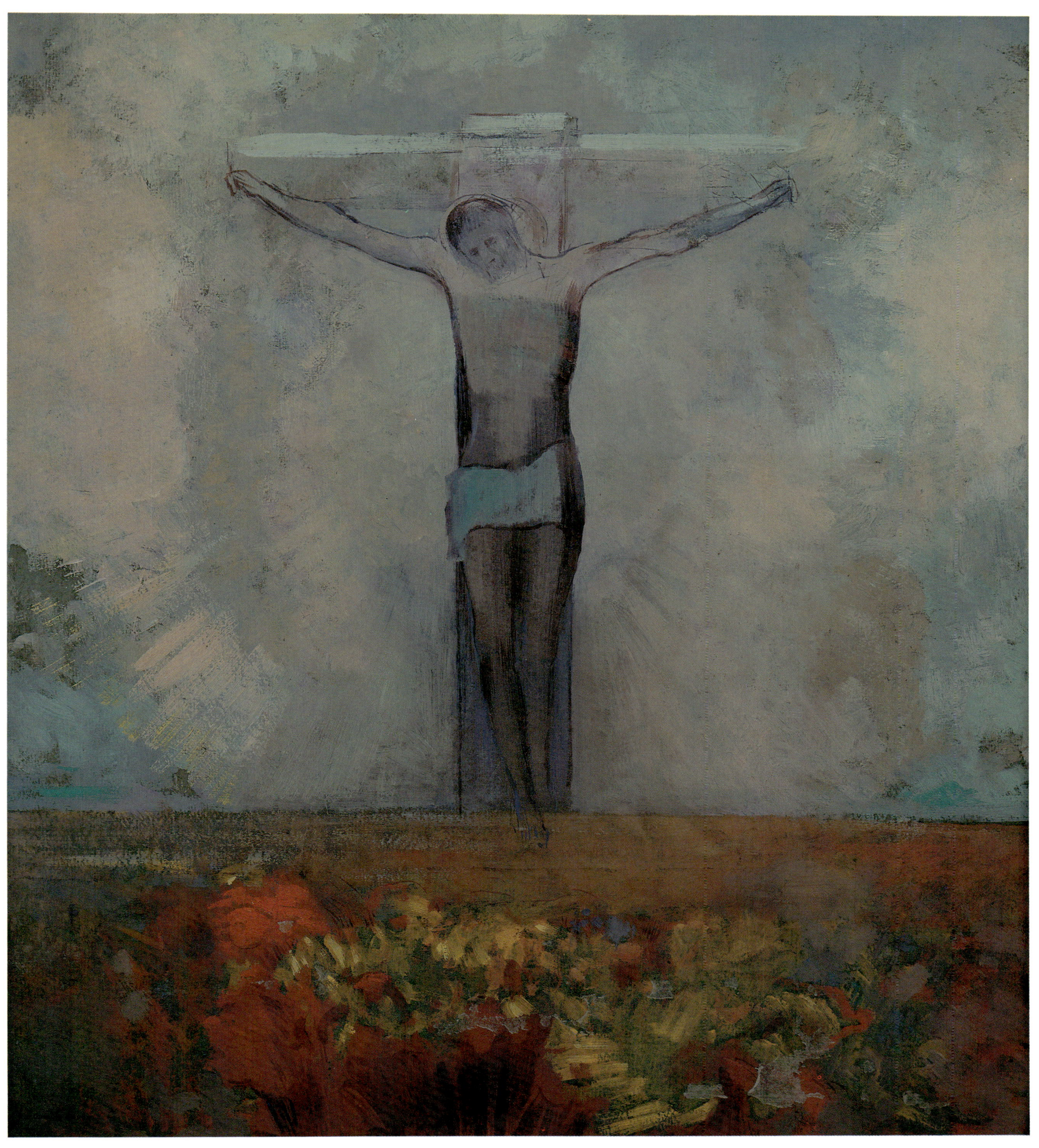

"If by genius you mean the desire to create so simply, so broadly, that nature itself is conveyed on an insensate but grandiose scale, I have genius."

Odilon Redon
A Soi-méme

Redon (Odilon) 1840-1916
Christ on the Cross, c. 1910
Paris, Musée d'Orsay

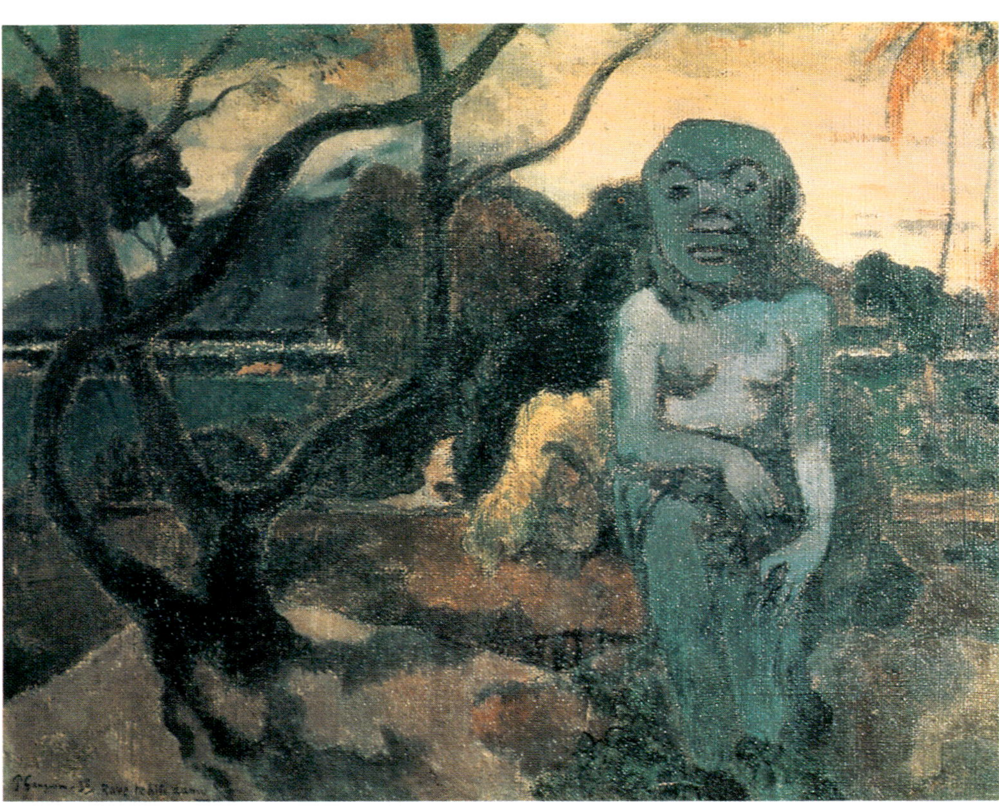

A "pure cerebral art?"

The irrational, the symbol, the proscription of nature, aspiration to the sublime: a range of themes tending to demonstrate that art, at the point when the 19th century gave way to the 20th, represented the antidote to a technological and sociological reality embracing (perhaps held in thrall by?) usefulness and efficiency as its sole values. Art no longer went hand in hand with a scientific vision of the world, as in the glorious days of humanism triumphant. On the contrary, art became a denunciation of the wrongdoings of the positivism and scientism guiding modernity. This may have given rise to some ambiguity about the exact nature of artistic work, which was contradictorily both revolutionary and reactionary: revolutionary because the reintroduction of the concept of irrationality into art opened up the way for the destabilizing experiments of Expressionism, Dadaism, Surrealism and Abstraction, but reactionary because the requestioning of the foundations of Western civilization in such a way could not be restricted, whatever artists themselves might say, to the field of art. The consequences were also political. To be convinced of this, one only has to follow Gauguin's reasoning when setting out to criticize naturalism in art: "[Nature] debases the artist by letting itself be adored by him. That is how we have fallen into the dreadful error of naturalism. Naturalism began with the Greeks of Pericles's day. Since then the only greater or less great artists have been those who have reacted more or less against this error; but their reactions have been no more than sudden starts of memory, gleams of good sense in a decline which has basically been uninterrupted for centuries." This type of reasoning, assimilating civilization with decadence, inevitably has political consequences.

We may not want to measure the full implications of such a statement, partly because Gauguin became one of the spiritual fathers of modernism, and also because he became politically involved in a brave fight against colonialism which no doubt hastened his death. Nonetheless, the thesis spelt out above amounts to condemning all humanism and in more general terms all civilization that emanates from Greek humanism. However, in spite of adopting a stance in favor of a "pure cerebral art," Gauguin continued to celebrate the mythic memory of an Eden-like nature which he believed he had discovered in Polynesia. Thus it is less nature in itself that is condemned than its degeneration in the course of history – and the fact that its ideal origins have been forgotten. Lastly, there are strong overtones of Rousseau in Gauguin when he claims to have rediscovered the happy origins of humankind through the initial simplicity of the symbol (expressed in pictural terms by cloisonnist Synthetism). "Barbarism for me is a rejuvenation," he said: which sounds dreadful in one way, if we forget that he meant not the barbarism of aristocratic power exalted by Nietzsche (that of those peoples called on, so he said, "to engender and implant a new order,") but the very opposite, the barbarism of the original innocence of peoples "without a history."

Gauguin (Paul) 1848-1903
The idol, 1898
St. Petersburg, Hermitage

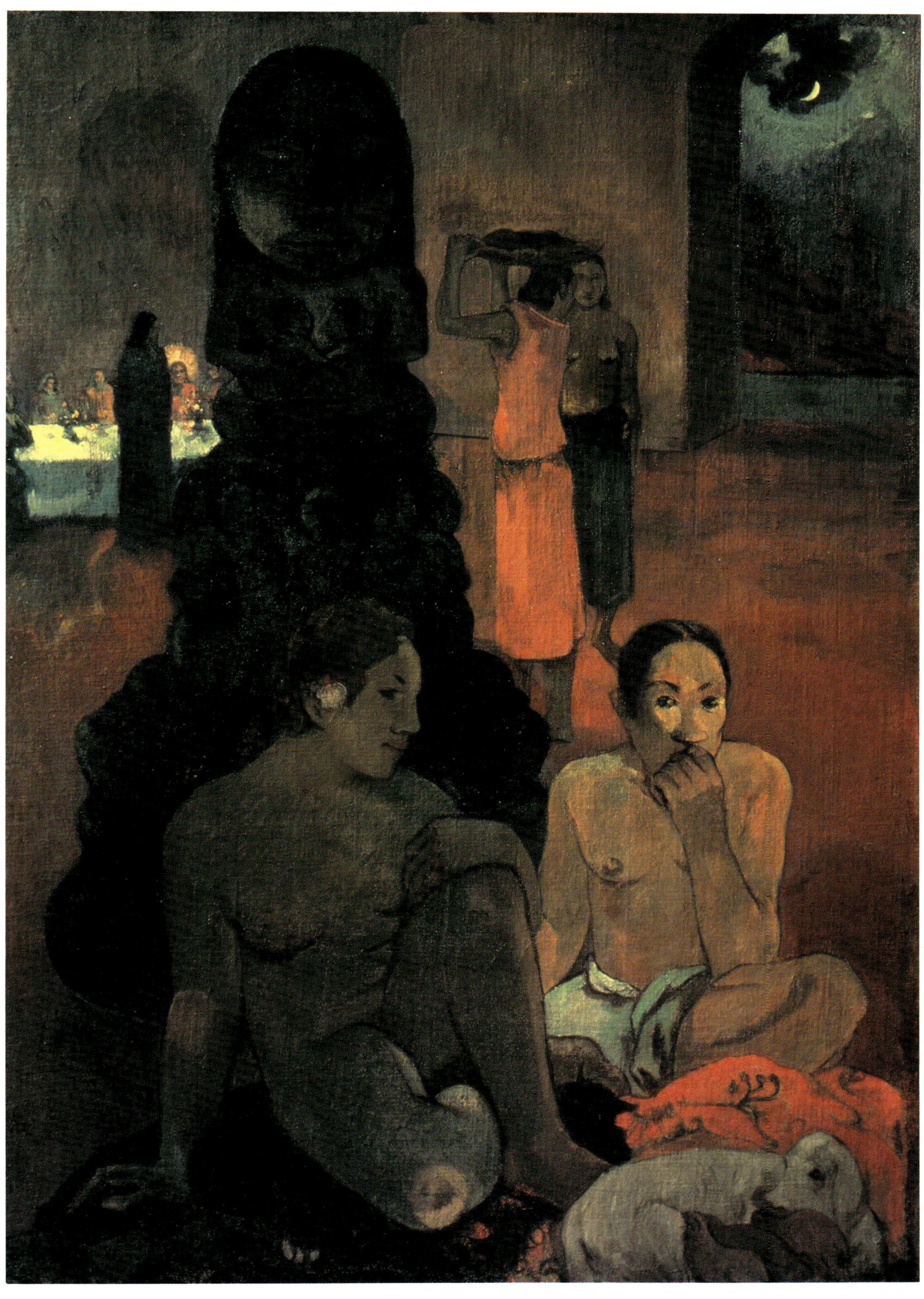

"I have traveled back a long way, even farther than the horses of the Parthenon, back to the hobby-horses of my infancy."

Paul Gauguin
Le Cheval blanc, 1898

Gauguin (Paul) 1848-1903
The great Buddha, 1899
St. Petersburg, Hermitage

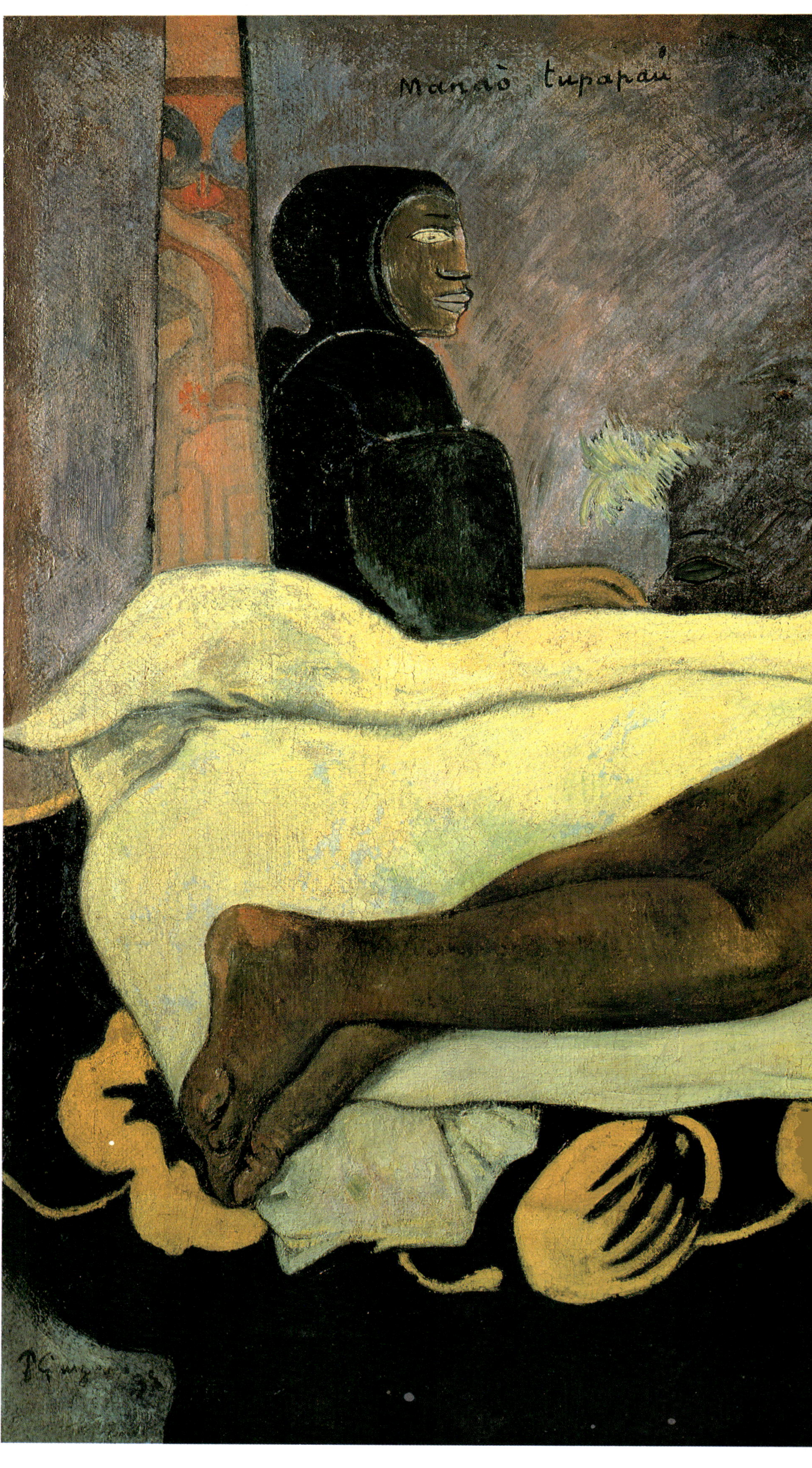
Manaò tupapaù

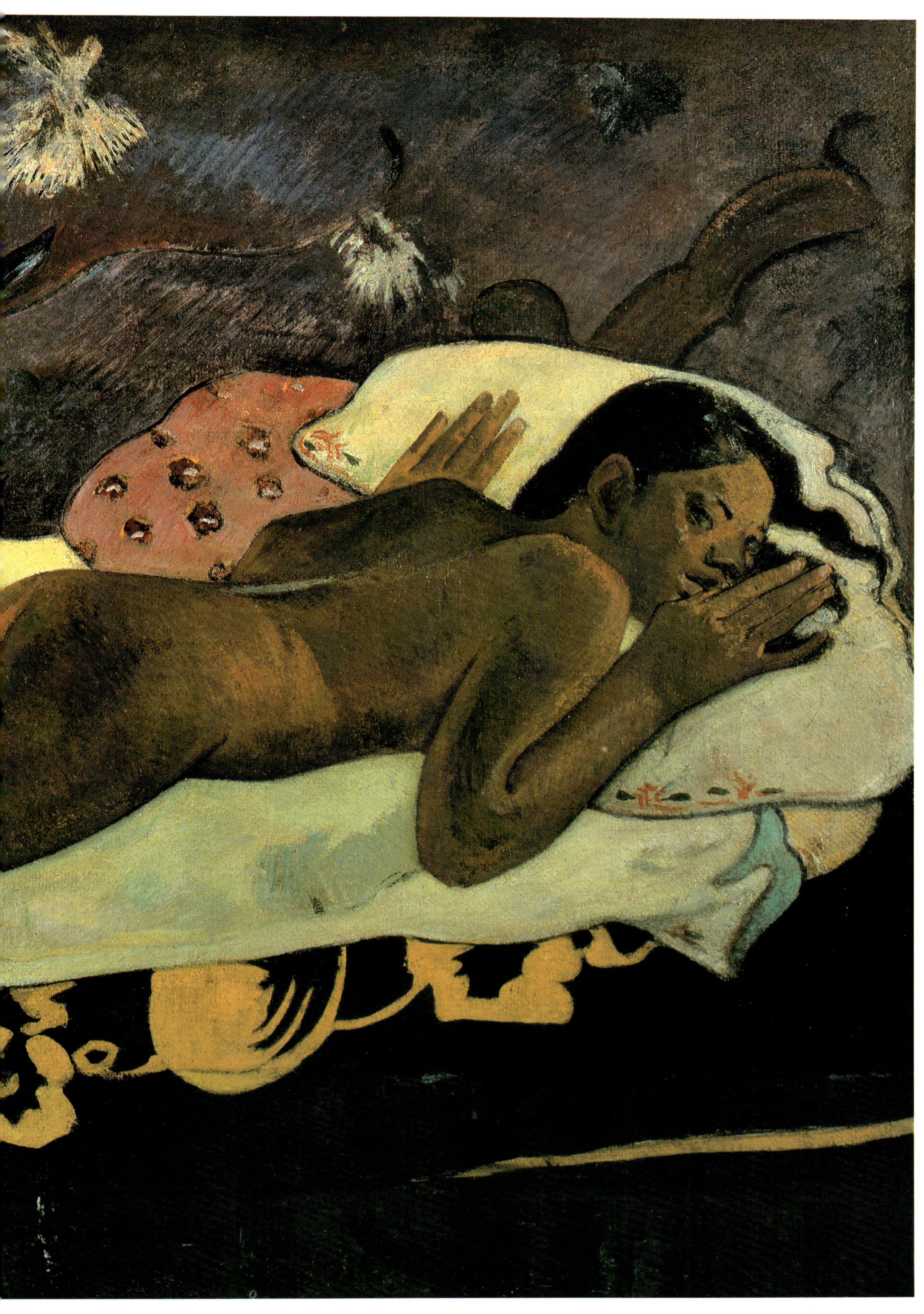

Gauguin (Paul) 1848-1903
Manao Tupapau (The spirit of the dead watches), 1892
Buffalo, Albright Knox Art Gallery

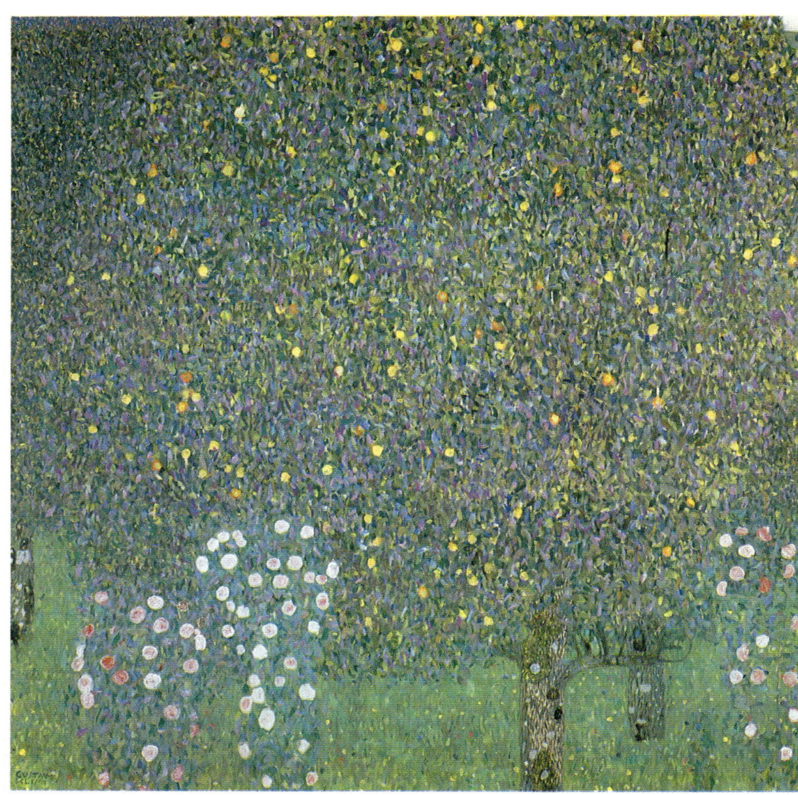

The symbol as opposed to history

"Vienna at the end of the century," C.E. Schorske wrote, "where the repercussions of political and social disintegration were keenly felt became one of the most fertile breeding grounds of ahistorical culture of our century. The great creative artists [...] more or less deliberately broke all links with the historical perspective which had underpinned 19th-century liberal culture."

In this context Klimt, who had taken charge of the Vienna Secession, expressed in the field of art what Freud was beginning to formulate into a theory in the field of scientific research. To quote C.E. Schorske again, "Klimt and Freud [...] resolutely rejected the naturalistic realism which had been accepted during their years of training. [...] Seeking to chart new waters and distance themselves from the ruins of a substantialist conception of reality, they plunged into themselves and embarked on an internal journey": an exploration of dreams and the instinctive, impulsive dimension of human beings (Eros and Thanatos), not so much denying reality as seeking to perceive its contradictory effects on the psyche. The creative instinct as against the oppressive power of civilization: here we find a major theme of Nietzschean thought, but also the point where French and German Symbolism parted company, the former rejecting naturalistic illusion in the name of formalist idealism while the latter rejected it in the name of Dionysiac sensualism.

However, just as the instincts were being affirmed, the unity of the psyche, which was progressively losing any stable reference to an objective reality, was seriously questioned by the Freudian conceptualization of the unconscious. From this confusion of one feeling with the other, and of feelings with a reality that was becoming ever harder to discern, a stylistic eclecticism – the true hallmark of Klimt – emerged, in which violently realistic elements coexist alongside geometric motifs that prefigure abstract formalism.

By tearing art away from naturalistic realism, i.e. the grip of historical necessity, and opening up the psyche to it, Klimt thought he was fighting for liberation: the liberation of art, and of the individual through art, both mixed together in the symbolic expression of the struggle between Eros and Thanatos, and both in keeping with the original program of the Secession, namely to take art back towards life. But by voluntarily cutting itself off from the historical substratum, rather than drawing closer to life, art moved towards an abstract formalism which resulted in its break with the perceptible world. Increasingly stripped of its signifying message, the symbol was reduced to its purely plastic dimension. Naturalism and Symbolism had been and gone. Painting had finally achieved autonomy. But it emerged from this century-long conflict tragically denuded.

For what is a language if it has no ultimate purpose other than to speak itself? And what is art if it does not express the world that produced it? These questions will be at the heart of the problematics of 20th-century art.

Klimt (Gustav) 1862-1918
Reeds below trees, c. 1905
Paris, Musée d'Orsay

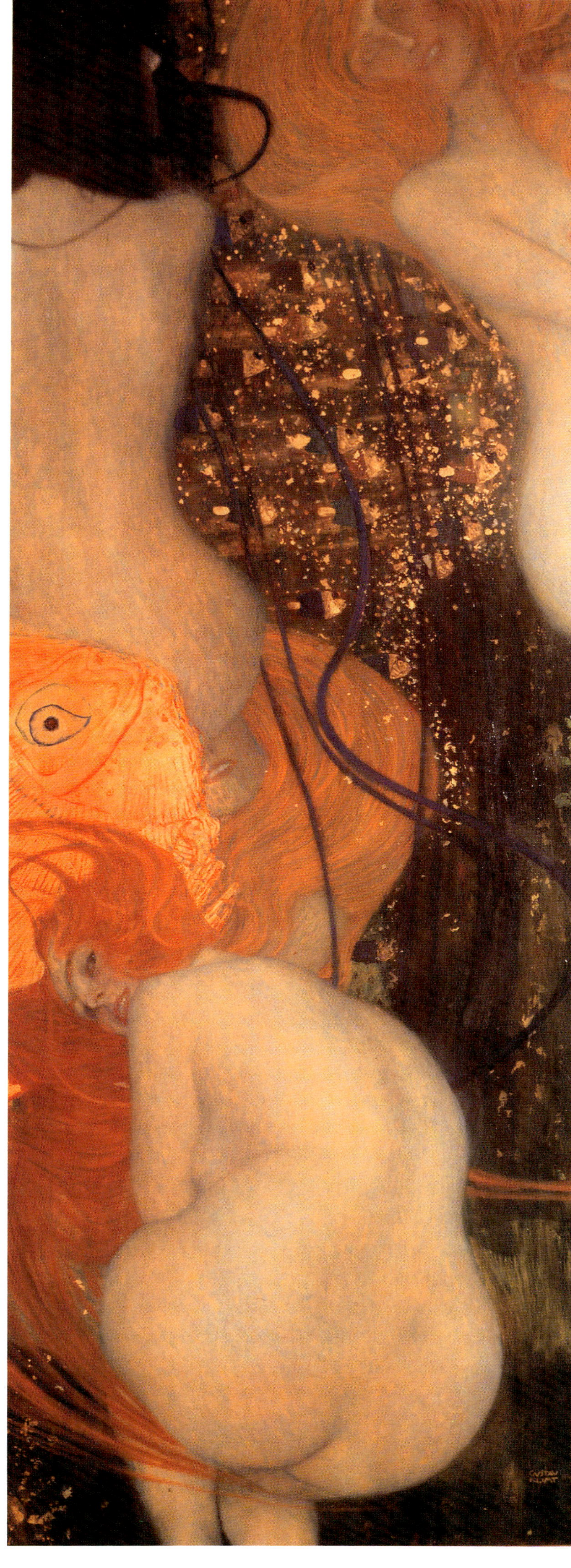

"Klimt's art is essentially inspired by the knowledge of man's subjection to his instincts. That explains the candor with which he takes possession of the intimate field of eroticism."

Werner Hofmann Gustav Klimt

Klimt (Gustav) 1862-1918
Goldfish, 1901-1902
Solothurn, Kunstmuseum, Dübi-Muller Foundation

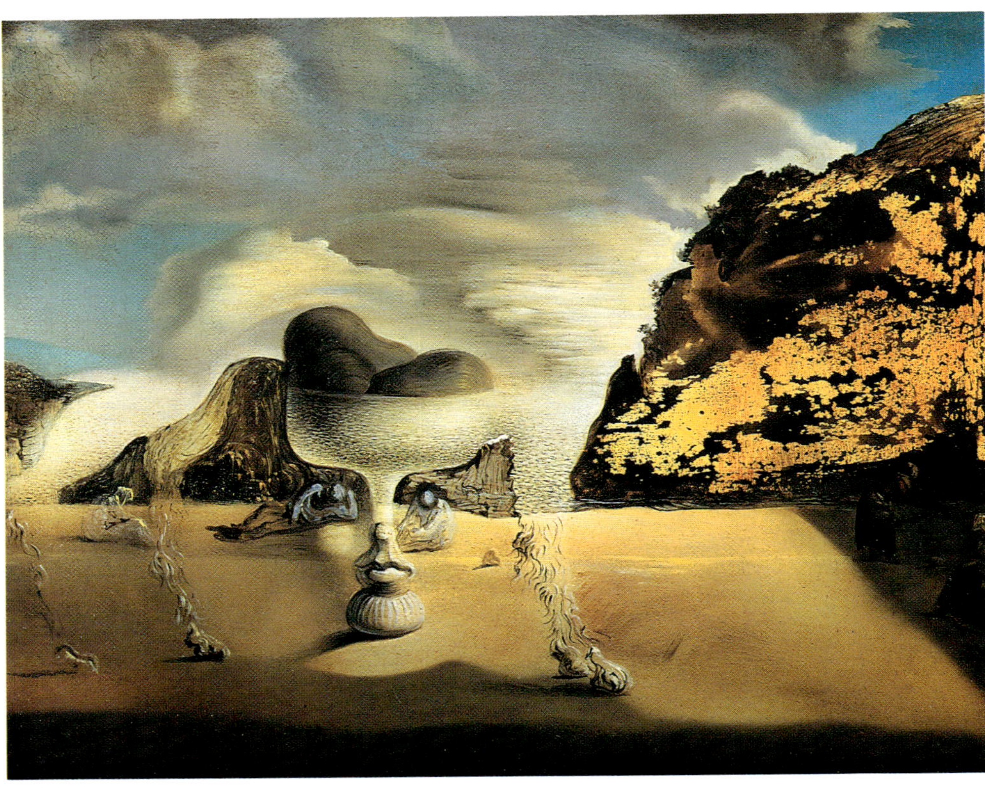

Surreal perspectives

In talking about Klimt we mentioned the indirect influence of Freudianism in the anti-naturalistic battle. But for the most part psychoanalysis was expressed in terms of the plastic arts in Surrealism (even if Freud had serious reservations about this).

As a preface to the 1924 Surrealist manifesto André Breton wrote: "Belief in life, in the most precarious aspects of life, by which we mean real life, goes so far that in the end the belief is lost. [...] The case against the realist attitude needs to be argued [...]. Imagination is perhaps about to resume its proper place. [...] Freud was very right to look critically at dreams." A little further down Surrealism is defined as follows: "A dictation given by thought, with no control exercised by reason, external to any esthetic or moral preoccupations. Surrealism rests on the belief [...] in the omnipotence of dreams, the disinterested workings of thought."

Salvador Dali was enlisted to the Surrealist cause in 1927, bringing to the movement all his peremptory fantasy and his genius for provocation. He borrowed from Chirico and Tanguy, but surpassed them through the excellence of his technique and the richness of his imagination. His method, which he took care to call "paranoiac-critical," is deemed to consist of a "handmade colored photograph of concrete irrationality and the imaginative world in general." He wrote in his *Secret life*, "All day sitting at my easel I stared at my canvas like a medium to see emerging from it the elements of my own imagination." But his attitude did not stop at the total passivity required by Breton, for Dali reorganized his figures into a whole with a meaning, or to be more precise a deliberate multiplicity of meanings. He used Surrealism rather than serving it: "At the same time as launching myself into the craziest speculations with the same passionate enthusiasm as they did," he later wrote, "with a skeptic's Machiavellianism I was already preparing the structural bases of the next historic tier of the eternal tradition. The Surrealists seemed to me to be the only people forming a group whose means would serve my action." Here again Dali's spirit of provocation no doubt leads him to caricature the depth of his commitment in 1927. The break which came about in 1939 had a variety of causes, the objective ones including Dali's guilty fascination with Hitler, and the subjective ones the painter's devastating humor, which was more often directed against his Surrealist friends than his declared enemies.

But the deepest difference was undoubtedly theoretical in nature: according to Dali, the creative act, even if it draws its material from the unconscious, is still associated with the idea of system and the question of sense or meaning. The Surrealists who came from Dadaism were fighting for non-sense. This was not true of Dali, to whom Lacan's famous aphorism might easily be applied: "the unconscious is structured like a [pictural] language." Freud understood this perfectly, and he accorded the accolade of master to Dali alone.

Dali (Salvador) 1904-1989
Apparition of a face and a fruit dish on a beach, 1938
Private collection

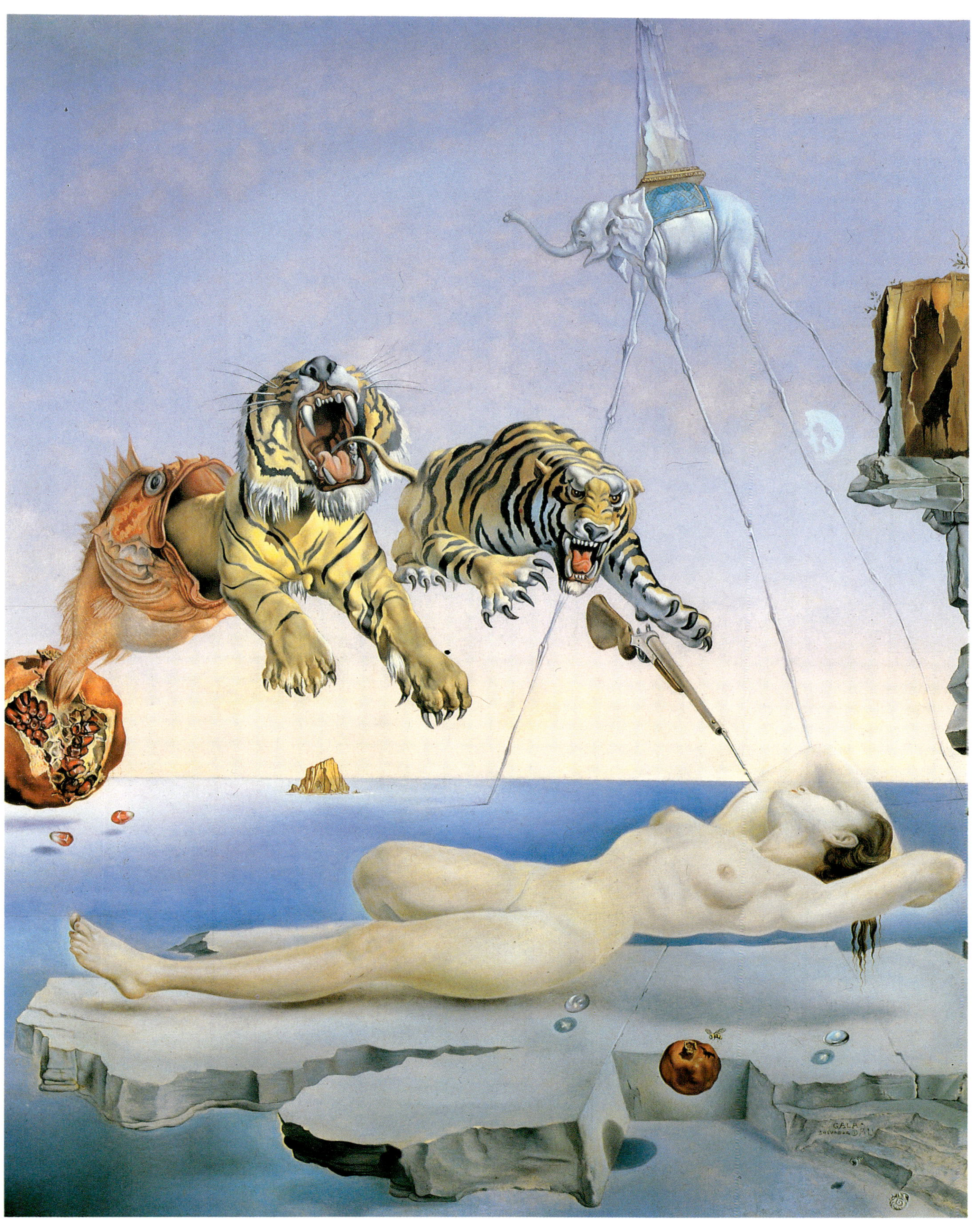

"The precautions taken to safeguard the integrity [of the Surrealist movement] have not ruled out [...] imposture, of the picaresque type, of the neo-Phalangist bedside table known as Avida Dollars."

André Breton
Troisième manifeste du surréalisme, 1942

Dali (Salvador) 1904-1989
Dream caused by the flight of a bee round a pomegranate a second before wakening, 1944
Lugano, Thyssen-Bornemisza Collection

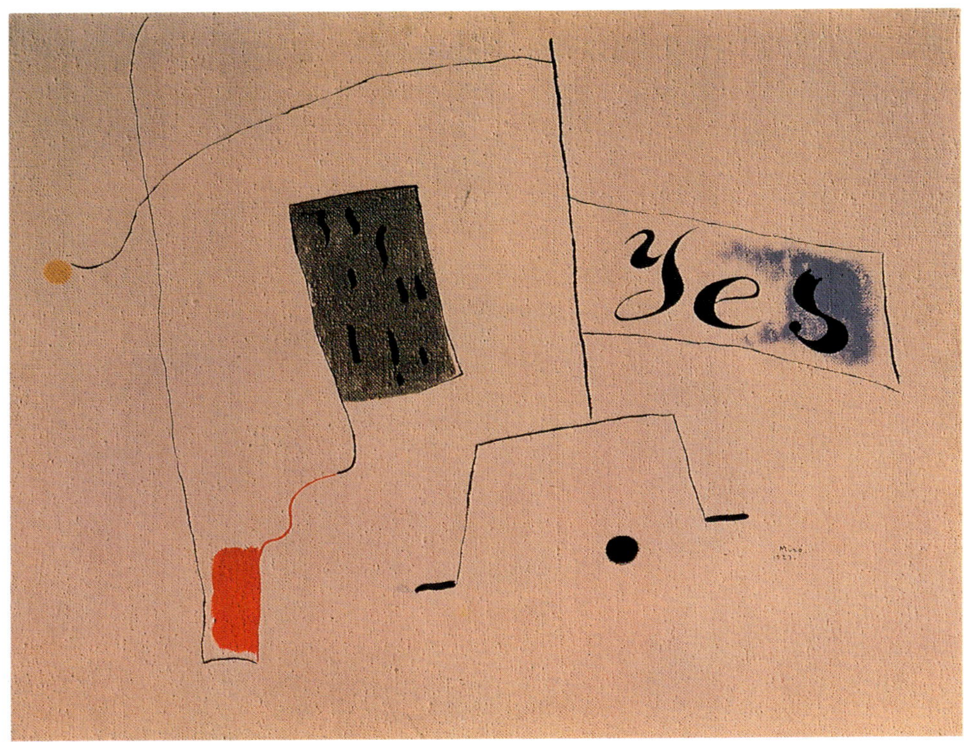

A new grammar

The first decades of the 20th century witnessed such a multiplicity of artistic experiments that it is impossible and pointless to try and list them all. Quite often artists attached themselves successively to several movements and most of the movements splintered into rival chapels. The feature common to them all was rebellion and the search for a new language. Once the rebellion was over, almost as many languages as there were artists came into being.

Miro was interested in Fauvism, then Cubism, then Dadaism, before turning to Surrealism in 1924. But his attachment was of a special type: Miro was never really interested in the theoretical debates which concerned his friends. Gaëtan Picon writes that "Breton reproached him with not having enough intelligence to understand that he did not belong to himself, but was only an instrument in the service of pure imagination, to put it bluntly: with not caring about the Surrealist credo. And in fact Miro [...] kept his distance insofar as he was not in the least concerned with matching what he did with theory: he simply followed his own path."

Miro's work cannot be read by the yardstick of Surrealism alone: at one moment it does express it, then it goes beyond it. Dada wanted to kill art. Surrealism, after setting out to kill it, claimed to turn it into an instrument of esthetic and moral liberation, using the processes of automatic writing (and painting as writing). And it may have been on this point that Miro parted company with Surrealism: firstly because he did not share Breton's sectarian, militant spirit, and secondly because there is nothing automatic about his writing. Miro did not reject reality: he expressed it in a new language, no longer based on representation but on a group of graphic signs which can be assimilated to ideograms. An aspiration to the codification of pictural language of this kind was completely alien to the formal deconstruction brought in by automatic writing.

The same is true of Picabia, who started off as a Post-Impressionist, then like Miro went through Dadaism and Surrealism; but his entire oeuvre is marked by a striving towards extreme formal mastery. Marc Dachy writes: "At the end of his Impressionist phase Picabia's abstraction evolved very freely towards a grammar of abstract forms that belong to him alone, in a 'no man's land' between Cubism and Futurism."

The gap between the leader of Surrealism and these painters was linked to the fact that Breton, despite his revolutionary protestations, went on thinking of painting as "a window" opening onto something. In the final analysis Breton did not question the function of "representation" in painting (even if for him it was dreams that were represented and not reality), whereas it was that very function that artists such as Duchamp and Picabia had come to reject, each in his own way, thus opening up the only really new problematic proposition since the Renaissance, namely that painting should not "represent," but "present."

Miro (Juan) 1893-1983
Composition, 1927
Moscow, Pushkin Museum

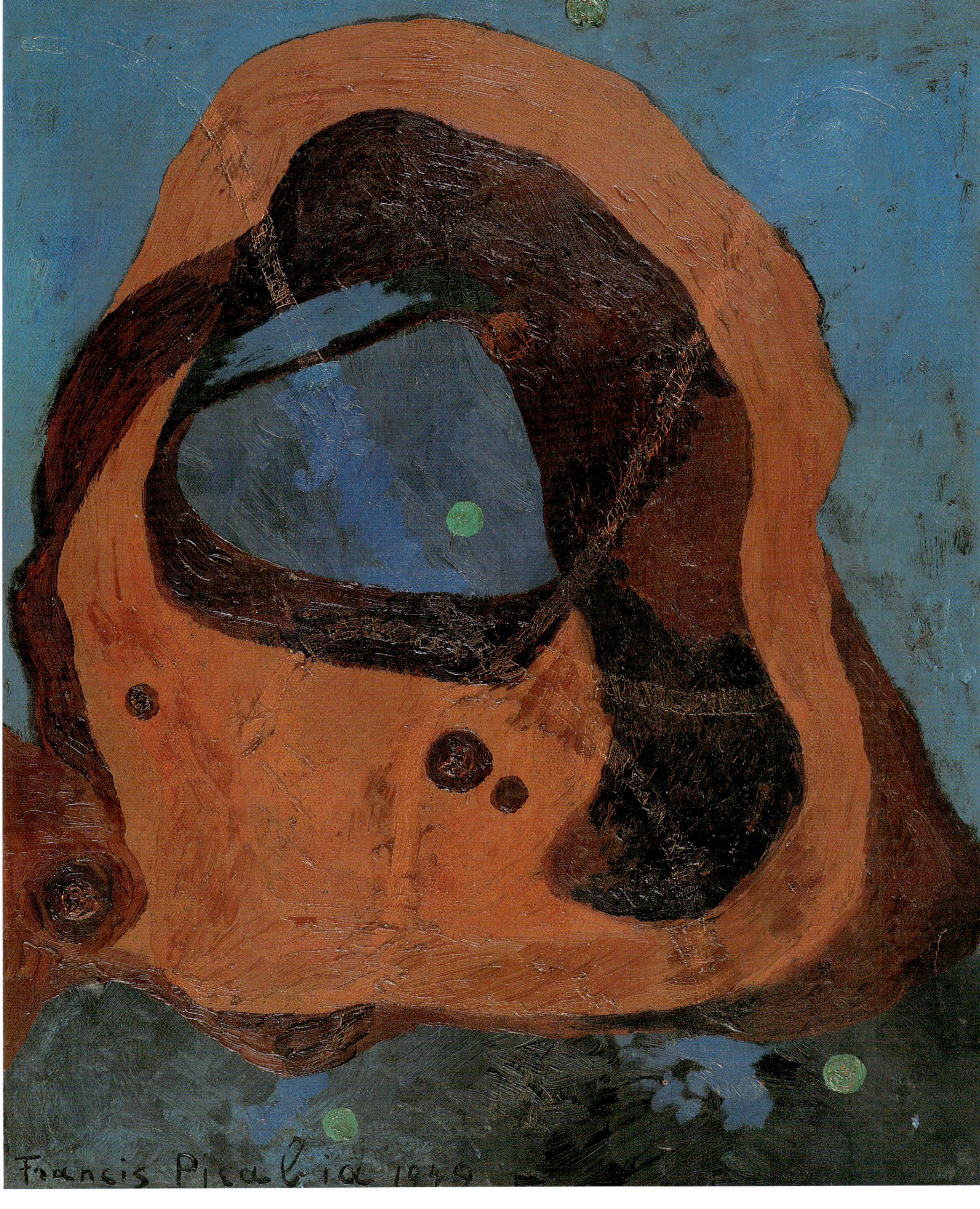

"André Breton makes me think of Lucien Guitry acting in one of Henry Bernstein's plays; he is certainly as good an actor, but more old-fashioned than Guitry."

Francis Picabia
Journal de l'Instantanéisme, 1924

Picabia (Francis) 1879-1953
Knowledge of the future, 1949
Marseilles, Musée Cantini

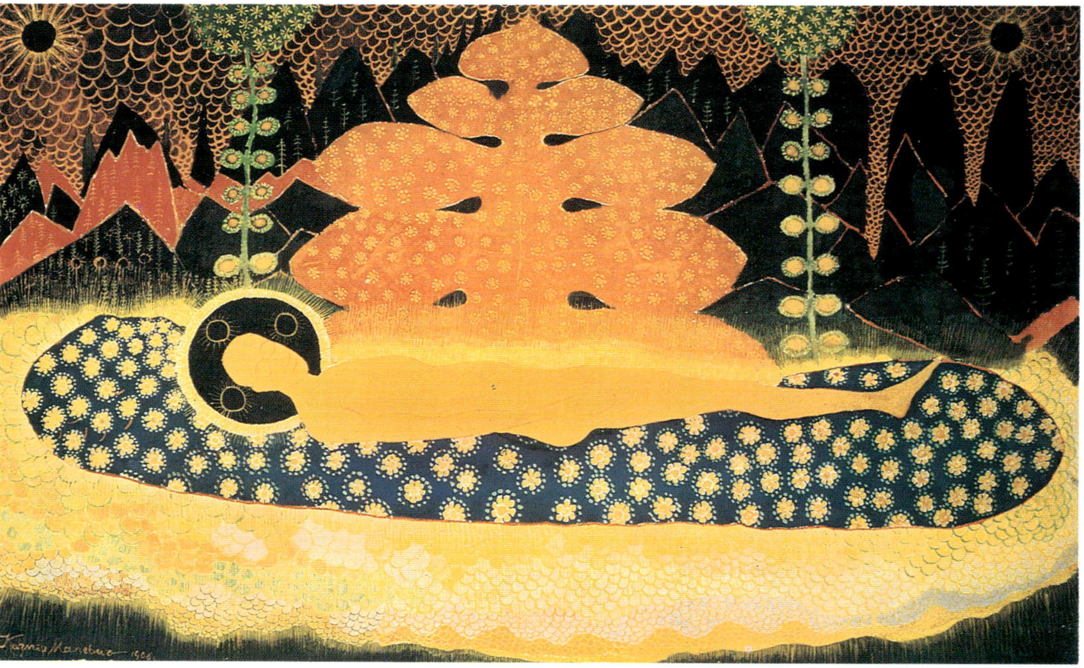

The silence of the real

"Where do these abstract pictures of Malevich's come from?" Dora Vallier mused. "Unexpected as they are they do have roots. But what are they?" Within a few years (from *Black square on a white background* in 1913 to *White square on a white background* in 1918) Malevich took not only Abstraction but painting as a whole to its final conclusion. Dadaism and Surrealism in their search for non-sense went on questioning reality. In subverting it they still stayed within it, or rather beside it, like disgruntled relations beside the death bed of a cousin they had envied and hated. Malevich's pictural nihilism which he called Suprematism was more radical. He painted "a non-objective world," a world without objects: "In the vast space of cosmic repose," he wrote, "I have reached the white world of the absence of objects which is the manifestation of nothingness unveiled."

His *Black square on a white background* is not the representation of a black square on a white background: it is just a black square painted on a white background. The work refers to nothing other than itself. It is not the sign of reality, it is the reality of the picture-as-object. Suprematism is a solipsist art merging the sign with the reality it designates. By turning the given facts completely on their head, Malevich brought in painting in reality instead of reality.

Once this extreme position has been arrived at, is painting of any description still possible? The nihilist attitude of Suprematism is both a zenith and an end, and it is impossible to go on painting that end indefinitely.

In the words of Dora Vallier, Malevich "moved painting out of the external world, reduced reality to silence and in that silence the pure absence of objects was inscribed. [...] But is it really a point of departure? And not an end that is confused with a beginning at the point where the loop closes?" As would be true of Yves Klein at a later stage, Malevich's experiment with the extreme did not open the way to a different kind of painting. It is the final act of the painter, a sort of artist's testament as he immolates his art in the name of the absolute. Behind the "nothingness" of Suprematism there is a tremendous hope that dare hardly admit its own existence. Nihilism leads to mysticism ....

In the catalog of the Tenth State Salon which opened in Moscow in 1918 Malevich wrote: "Now man's path is through space. Suprematism is the semaphore of color in the unlimited. I have pierced through the shade over the limits of color, I have penetrated into white; friends and fellow pilots, come and navigate by my side in this infinite space. The free white sea stretches before you."

Malevich (Kasimir) 1878-1935
Composition , also known as Shroud of Christ, 1908
Moscow, Tretiakov Gallery

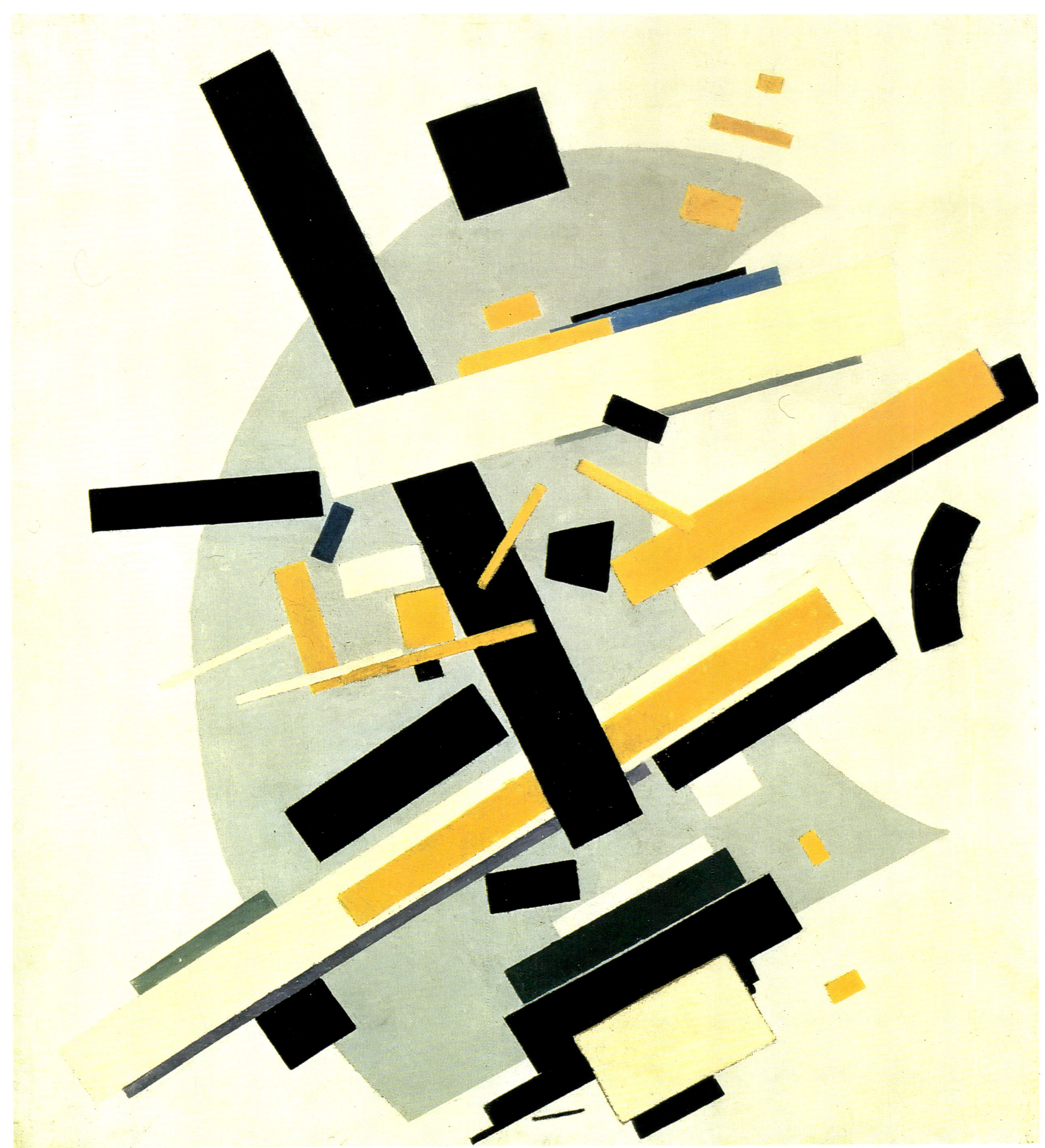

"As well as Kandinsky's fin-de-siècle spiritualism and Mondrian's theosophy there was a third source of abstract art linked to the typically Russian phenomenon of nihilism through the intermediacy of Malevich."

Dora Vallier
L'Art abstrait

Malevich (Kasimir) 1878-1935
Suprematism no. 58 with yellow and black, 1916
St. Petersburg, Russian Museum

Photographic credits: All photographs courtesy of Giraudon Agency, Paris

© SPADEM Paris 1993
Picabia, Francis:
Knowledge of the future
Sérusier, Paul
Woman embroidering
Picasso, Pablo Ruiz:
Large nude with red armchair
Gervex, Henri:
Birth of Venus
Luce, Maximilien:
Factory chimney
Bonnard, Pierre:
Large blue nude
The red check tablecloth
Landscape at Le Cannet

© ADAGP Paris 1993
Picabia, Francis:
Knowledge of the future
Miro, Juan:
Composition
Severini, Gino:
Cannon in action
Dali, Salvador:
Dream caused by the flight of a bee round a pomegranate a second before wakening
Apparition of a face and a fruit dish on a beach
Bonnard, Pierre:
Large blue nude
The red check tablecloth
Landscape at Le Cannet